Selwyn College

A History

Selwyn College
A History

BY

W.R. BROCK AND P.H.M. COOPER

THE PENTLAND PRESS
EDINBURGH – CAMBRIDGE – DURHAM

© Selwyn College, Cambridge, 1994

First published in 1994 by
The Pentland Press Ltd
1 Hutton Close
South Church
Bishop Auckland
Durham

British Library Cataloguing in Publication Data
A Catalogue record for this book is available from the British Library.

ISBN 1-85821-177-8

Typeset by Carnegie Publishing, 18 Maynard St., Preston
Printed and bound in Great Britain by Bookcraft (Bath) Ltd.

Dedicated
to the Selwyn College community
seniors, juniors, and domestic staff
past and present

Contents

Preface   I

Part I – Origins and Early Years

Introduction   5

Chapter 1 The Pure and Heroic Type:
George Augustus Selwyn and the Selwyn Family   9

Chapter 2 Families and Politics:
Gladstones, Lytteltons, and Talbots   19

Chapter 3 The Accommodation of Gladstone:
University Reform and the Origins of
Public Hostels, 1850–71   31

Chapter 4 An Experiment of Doubtful Issue:
the Foundation of Selwyn College, 1878–82   53

Chapter 5 Judicious Rule:
the Mastership of Arthur Temple Lyttelton, 1882–93   81

Chapter 6 A Bold Experiment:
the Mastership of John Richard Selwyn, 1893–8   110

Part II – Floreat Collegium!

Introduction   123

Chapter 7 Standing Firm or Standing Still? 1898–1907   125

Chapter 8 Taking Shape, 1908–14   141

Chapter 9 War, Revival, and Jubilee, 1914–33   156

Chapter 10 Selwyn Men, 1934–39   173

Chapter 11 War and a New Direction, 1939–45   198

Part III – Acceleration

Introduction   209

Chapter 12 An Altered Society, 1946–55   212

Chapter 13 New Perspectives and New Buildings, 1956–69   236

Chapter 14 The Ninth Decade, 1970–80   258

Chapter 15 The Centenary and Beyond, 1981–94   277

Chapter 16 Retrospect and Prospect   304

Appendix A   318

Appendix B   328

Appendix C   349

Index   359

Preface

THIS IS the history of a late Victorian College, founded in memory of a distinguished Churchman, and embodying the ideals of Anglican Liberals at a critical period in the history of English higher education. The aim of its founders was to train young men 'in simple and religious habits according to the principles of the Church of England,' and to do so at a cost that was substantially less than at the older colleges. It was intended that only members of the Church of England would normally be admitted, many of its early undergraduates were the sons of clergy, and even more went on to be ordained; but it was never exclusively clerical. At a time when there were no public awards its lower costs attracted parents who could not otherwise have afforded to send their sons to Cambridge, and many of the graduates went on to careers as varied as those selected in other colleges.

A Royal Charter named Selwyn as a College, but the University refused it collegiate status though permitting its men to take Cambridge degrees. There were early doubts about its survival (two other late Victorian foundations failed), and though difficulties were surmounted poverty remained a grievous handicap. It had no Fellows until 1913 and then seldom more than ten (who had all to be members of the Church of England), it had fewer than a hundred and fifty undergraduates, and its endowments were minuscule when compared with those of the older colleges.

A stranger visiting Selwyn in the last decade of the twentieth century would not recognize it from this description. The old buildings remain as the founders and their immediate successors envisaged, but much else has changed. No one enquires into the religious affiliations of any junior or senior member, and the costs are similar to those in other Colleges (the great majority of students being on public grants). There are over three hundred undergraduates – four out of ten being women – and over a hundred graduate students. There are over forty Fellows holding University or College offices, and at least three more holding endowed research Fellowships. In the early College academic distinction was rare; today its scholarly reputation stands high. It is not numbered among the most affluent colleges but is a good way from being the poorest.

The history of Selwyn is therefore a record of a struggle to implant and preserve a particular view of the relationship between learning and religion, and then, as times and opinions changed, of the abandonment of some early principles but of striking achievement in a period of rapid change. In the past half-century it has presented in microcosm the major developments of university education, and Selwyn's history can be read as a case study in the academic response to the many political, social, and intellectual movements of the age.

This history is a joint endeavour. Peter Cooper is responsible for Part I and William Brock for Parts II and III, but the division of labour has been more even than this might suggest. Part I demanded much research into unpublished sources, but for later years there is the admirable *Selwyn College Calendar* and the individual recollections of past and present members. Their help is acknowledged in the text or notes; but special thanks to E.M. 'Sam' Hall must be recorded, both for his revealing account of undergraduate life in the 1930s and for his frequent reminders, at successive Selwyn Association meetings, that the College lacked a full and up-to-date history. Without his persistence this book would not have been written.

Selwyn College   W.R. Brock
March 1994   P.H.M. Cooper

The Authors

William Brock matriculated at Trinity in 1934 and after graduation was a research student and prize Fellow at that college. In 1947, after war service, he was elected a Fellow of Selwyn and was a Tutor from 1950 to 1967. He was appointed Professor of Modern History at Glasgow in 1967, but having served for twenty years qualified for a life Fellowship at Selwyn. After retirement from his Glasgow post he returned to Cambridge, directed Selwyn's centenary appeal, and edited the *Calendar* from 1990 to 1994. He is the author of several books – of which the majority are on the history of the United States – and is a Fellow of the British Academy.

Peter Cooper was a Selwyn undergraduate from 1958 to 1961, reading history and then qualifying as a teacher. In 1961 he was president of the University Liberal Club. Awarded a Ph.D. by London University for a study of the Church in nineteenth-century London, he taught successively at Emma Willard School, Troy, New York; The College of All Saints, Tottenham; and Middlesex Polytechnic (now Middlesex University). Having served as a Recognized Teacher in the Faculty of Education of London University, he resigned a Principal Lectureship in 1988, to teach part-time for Middlesex University and for the Open University.

Part I

Origins and Early Days

SELWYN COLLEGE was founded in memory of George Augustus Selwyn, a remarkable bishop who personified both the reformed parochial churchmanship of the earlier Victorian age and the finest colonial missionary endeavour of a later time. The story of the College's foundation years, 1878–83, is resonant with some of the enduring preoccupations of Victorian society, as they were refracted through the complex political, religious and moral perspectives of Selwyn's close friend, the great statesman William Ewart Gladstone. These preoccupations, as they bear upon the history of Selwyn College, may be grouped as follows:

(1) the proper limits of central government interference with great corporations, such as the Church of England, universities and colleges, and public schools;

(2) the extensive implications for Church establishment, and for university reform, of a society in which industrialization and nonconformity, the quest for an extended parliamentary franchise, the educational aspirations of the middling classes of society, and secularist assumptions concerning public and private morality were all advancing rapidly; and

(3) what should be, and how should be sustained, the moral nature of a world order for which, in that age, it was not possible to create a League of Nations or a United Nations Organization.

From around mid-century Gladstone devoted enormous intellectual and political energy to all these matters, as – at various times – they arose. That he did so is important to the historian of Selwyn College for two reasons: (1) variously through personal friendship, or political empathy, or marriage, or all three, Gladstone was intimately connected with most of those prominent in the College's early history; (2) in the period 1850–71 Gladstone was the central figure in the parliamentary reform of the ancient universities – reform which the creators of Selwyn had to accommodate, but which caused difficulties for them and for Gladstone, partly because it seemed to testify against such colleges as Selwyn in Cambridge and Keble in Oxford, the creation of which Gladstone himself publicly supported.

In Part I of this history, therefore, attention is devoted to Gladstone and his preoccupations, for they permeated both the controversy in Cambridge surrounding the creation of the College, and the long-term aspirations of most of the creators, notably Charles Abraham, Edmund Hobhouse, Arthur Lyttelton and John Selwyn; without such attention the controversy would seem trivial and self-referring, the aspirations less than wholly comprehensible.

Before long controversy was stilled and the aspirations of the creators were accepted by those who earlier had challenged them, when they had feared (or had pretended to fear) that in some measure the new institution would be a monastery or a seminary. Even so, Selwyn College, with its Christian character — its *peculiarly* Christian character – was very different from other colleges within the University of Cambridge. For generally it welcomed as undergraduates only young men who would admit to being members of the Church of England; of these, provided they were of at least moderate academic ability, it might regard with special favour those who were not well off and so might be disregarded by other colleges, and those desiring ordination, especially if they said they would work in mission-fields, and more especially if those mission-fields would be overseas.

The missionary ideal of Selwyn College, how it was planted and nurtured by the College's founders and its first two Masters, and how it related to the Liberalism of Gladstone, are the principal concerns of Part I.

A note on sources for Part I

The archives of Selwyn College, supplemented by British Library Additional MSS (letters of Arthur Lyttelton to Mary Gladstone and of Charles Abraham to W. E. Gladstone), have been the principal source for Part I; usually, where no other source is intimated, they constitute the authority for what is written. Official government publications, especially *Parliamentary Debates*, have of course been utilized; it is hoped that references to them in the text have been so contrived that, in a work of this kind, precise end-note references to them are unnecessary.

Most of what is said concerning the unpublished letters from and to Oscar Browning is derived from the Browning Archive at King's College, Cambridge, though the rough drafts of Arthur Lyttelton's letters to Browning are held at Selwyn College.

Those already acquainted with the history of Selwyn College, the character of Gladstonian Liberalism, and the career of Oscar Browning, will discern a special indebtedness to the following – to which, generally, end-note references have not been made: Ian Anstruther, *Oscar Browning: a biography*, London, 1983; A.L. Brown, *Selwyn College, Cambridge*, London, 1906; Mrs George Herbert Curteis, *In Memoriam: a sketch of the life of George Augustus Selwyn, late Bishop of Lichfield*, 2nd ed., Newcastle, 1879; George Herbert Curteis, *Bishop Selwyn: a sketch of his life and work*, London, 1889; the *Dictionary of National Biography* (particularly in respect of the Selwyn lineage); J.H. Evans, *Churchman Militant: George Augustus Selwyn, Bishop of New Zealand and Lichfield*, London and Wellington, New Zealand, 1964; F.D. How, *Bishop John Selwyn: a memoir*, London, 1899; Sir Philip Magnus, *Gladstone: a biography*, London, 1954; Lucy Masterman, ed., *Mary Gladstone (Mrs Drew): her diaries and letters*, London, 1930; A.J. Mason, *Life of William Edward Collins, Bishop of Gibraltar*, London, 1912; John Morley, *The Life of William Ewart Gladstone*, 3 vols., London, 1903; Deryck Schreuder, 'Gladstone and the Conscience of the State', in Peter Marsh, ed., *The Conscience of the Victorian State*, Hassocks, Sussex, 1979; Peter Searby, 'A Failure at Cambridge: Cavendish College, 1877–1892', in *Proceedings of the Cambridge Antiquarian Society*, vol.72 (1982—1984, published 1984); Gwendolen, Lady Stephenson, *Edward Stuart Talbot*, London, 1936; Henry William Tucker, *Memoir of the Life and Episcopate of George Augustus Selwyn, Bishop of New Zealand*, 2 vols., London, 1879.

Other works consulted: R.D. Anderson, *Universities and Elites in Britain since 1800*, Basingstoke and London, 1992; Oscar Browning, *Memories of Sixty Years at Eton, Cambridge and Elsewhere*, London, 1910; Christopher Harvie, *The Lights of Liberalism: university liberals and the challenge of democracy 1860–1886*, London, 1976; H.C.G. Matthew, ed., *The Gladstone Diaries*, vol.ix, Oxford, 1986; vol.x, Oxford, 1990; Michael Sanderson, ed., *The Universities in the Nineteenth Century*, London and Boston, 1975; Laetitia Frances Selwyn, *Memorials of Four Brothers*, Richmond, Surrey, 1885 (for the family of William Selwyn III and his wife Laetitia Frances [Kynaston] Selwyn); *Sermons and Addresses of Edmund Hobhouse, with a short memoir by his son,*

Walter Hobhouse, London, 1905; David M. Thompson, ed., *Non-conformity in the Nineteenth Century*, London and Boston, 1972; J.A. Venn, *Alumni Cantabrigienses*, Part II, 4 vols., Cambridge, 1940–1954.

The author gratefully acknowledges the granting by the Provost and Fellows of King's College, Cambridge, of access to the Browning Archive; the permission of Mrs Berta Wortham, custodian of the copyright of all Oscar Browning's unpublished letters, to quote from these letters; and the permission of the Revd Professor Owen Chadwick, OM, KBE, to reproduce an extract from the draft letter concerning the Loyal Toast at Selwyn College.

For their characteristic courtesy and helpfulness the author thanks the staffs of the Cambridge University Library, the British Library Manuscripts Students' Room, the British Library Newspaper Library, the Clywd Record Office at Hawarden Old Rectory, and the National Register of Archives; and Ms Jacqueline Cox, Modern Archivist of King's College, Cambridge.

CHAPTER I

The Pure and Heroic Type: George Augustus Selwyn and the Selwyn Family

WHAT WAS Selwyn College for? Or rather, what was a public hostel *called* 'Selwyn College' for? That, for its critics, had been the question. It was frugal, it was Anglican, it had something to do with widening access to higher education. Yet it seemed disingenuous. Was it frugal that in good conscience it might be Anglican, or Anglican that it might be frugal? If the former, then why should it want to be Anglican? To undermine the intent of a University Tests Bill passed seven years earlier? If the latter, might not frugality be better served if Nonconformists were admitted? Oscar Browning thought so. But if widening access mattered most, then perhaps it should be unequivocally secular? For its founders, though, there were good reasons why a college (or public hostel) in Cambridge should be named after George Augustus Selwyn, and why they should hope that frugality, Anglicanism, and education might be mutually sustaining.

The Selwyns were notable in lineage. Major-General William Selwyn had been Governor of Jamaica in 1703–4. His son was Colonel John Selwyn, aide-de-camp to the great Duke of Marlborough and treasurer of Queen Caroline's Pensions. John's son was George Augustus, rusticated from Oxford for an alleged insult to the Christian religion, but successful as wit, womanizer, Member of Parliament, Clerk of the Irons and Surveyor of the Meltings of the Mint in the reign of George III. He flickers through the footnotes of eighteenth-century histories. Two nephews of John were the brothers Charles and William Selwyn II. Charles was a prominent benefactor of the Church in Jamaica,

and an associate of the renowned General Oglethorpe, philanthropic founder of the colony of Georgia. William was a barrister,
and father of William Selwyn III (1775–1855).

William Selwyn III, also a barrister, was educated at Eton and
at St John's and Trinity Colleges, Cambridge. At the turn of the
century his father desired that he should marry a first cousin,
heiress of a large fortune. The lady proposed was quiet, amiable
and dutiful, but of meagre education and unpleasing appearance.
The younger William thought that on the whole he should not
like her as the mother of his children. And anyway he had seen
and loved another, Laetitia Frances Kynaston, daughter of a very
superior man of Essex, who had trained her in a love of literature,
a reverence for religion, and a careful study of the Holy Scriptures.
William thought she would do very nicely as the mother of his
children. But his father disagreed and when he married her struck
him from his will.

She was an excellent mother of his children, six of whom
reached adulthood. The younger daughter, Frances Elizabeth,
married George Peacock, Fellow of Trinity, a notable mathematician and a future Dean of Ely. The elder, Laetitia Frances,
would become a benefactress of Selwyn College, though a prob-
lematic one. She was practised in frugality, for after the death of
her father – to whom she had ministered – she became principal
of an establishment which was a home for ladies in straitened
circumstances and a training home for young servants. The four
sons were William; George Augustus, born on 5 April 1809;
Thomas Kynaston; and Charles Jasper. William became the Lady
Margaret's Professor of Divinity in the University of Cambridge
and funded the erection of the Divinity Schools in St John's
Street; at his suggestion and largely through his influence was
built the splendid chapel of St John's College. Sir Charles Selwyn
was an MP for the University and became a lord justice of appeal.
Only one, George, became a bishop, but it would not have been
a wonder if more of them had been so. Their mother kept a
manuscript which she called 'Portraits of my dear children'. It
told of feats of nursery scholarship and scriptural erudition.
George when 7, she wrote, knew the Latin accidence perfectly,

read very well, knew much of the Bible, and was very good at geography, writing and cyphering. He wanted very much to be a sailor, but was dissuaded. Of the four, however, Thomas Kynaston was quite the most remarkable, since before the age of 5 he had mastered the cartography of Europe, displayed a reverence for Sunday, and learned a great many hymns, preferring to consume them whole at one go instead of verse by verse as lesser toddlers might. Alas, he was naïve and deficient in comprehension; it was a mercy, they felt, that he died when only 22, before becoming prey to scheming persons.

All the Selwyn brothers went to Eton, where the headmaster was Dr Keate. Keate was amiable and popular but held stoutly to the doctrine that for the moral cleansing of boyish souls the birch rod was the fittest instrument. His regime was meet for one whom a frugal Anglican college in Cambridge would commemorate, for it affirmed the perils of Christian commitment. Once an assistant master sent him a list of boys thought suitable for confirmation, but forgot to head the last to show what it was for. Keate flogged the lot of them.[1]

George Selwyn came to Eton from a preparatory school in Ealing, where the future Cardinal Newman had been a fellow pupil. At Eton he met the future Prime Minister, William Ewart Gladstone, some nine months his junior. They became close friends. The elder boy never quite converted the younger to his own contempt for comfort and luxury, but it was not for want of trying. One Easter, on holiday from Eton, he asked his mother if Gladstone might come to stay. No, no, said Mrs Selwyn, she had not finished her spring cleaning and a guest would be in the way. George rushed upstairs, rushed down again with a mattress and hurled it upon the wet floor boards. 'There now,' he declared, 'where's the difficulty?'

Gladstone idolized Selwyn. Together they edited the *Eton Miscellany*. In later years they shared a sympathy for Tractarianism. John Morley, Gladstone's biographer, believed that it was less by academic pursuits than by the comradeship – scholarly and athletic – of such youths as Selwyn that the mind of the young Gladstone had been 'stimulated, opened and strengthened'. In

1855 Charles Kingsley dedicated *Westward Ho!* jointly to Rajah Sir
James Brooke, KCB, and George Augustus Selwyn, DD, Bishop of
New Zealand. Echoing Kingsley, the elderly Gladstone declared
it Selwyn's particular achievement to have reintroduced into the
ranks of the Anglican clergy 'the pure and heroic type'.

Selwyn became a Scholar at St John's College, Cambridge, in
1827; Gladstone in the following year went to Christ Church,
Oxford. Selwyn rowed at seven in the Cambridge boat in the first
University Boat Race (1829). He graduated in 1831, having been
a low junior optime (a 'third', that is) in the Mathematical Tripos.
He became a Fellow of his College. Then he returned to Eton
College as tutor to the sons of Lord Powis. Upon his appointment
he addressed himself to the dreadful fact that until that time there
had occurred at Eton frequent and fatal accidents on the Thames,
because the College had been lax in allowing boys who could not
swim to go bathing and boating. Selwyn prevailed upon Keate to
institute a 'swimming system', which endured, whereby no boy
would be allowed to boat until he could swim. Selwyn took charge.
Watermen ready to help in case of accidents were stationed in
punts at the weir and the bathing-places. There was a double
bonus, for as accidents were prevented so did the parson in Selwyn
take in hand the watermen, whose characters he 'improved'.[2]

In 1833 he was ordained deacon, becoming curate to the Vicar
of Windsor. He was energetic. He worked in the Sunday schools,
attended to the education of parish children during the week,
created a team of district visitors, consoled the bereaved, instituted
a parish kitchen to relieve the poor (he did some cooking himself),
and accomplished much else besides. In 1839 he married Sarah
Harriet Richardson, daughter of a judge; she was born in 1809
and died in 1907. When he courted her she lived with her family
between Maidenhead and Eton, at Bray, which was distant from
Eton by road but not by ferry. One night he was returning from
Eton after the ferryman had finished his duty. He could easily
have punted himself but he would have left the punt on the wrong
side of the river. His solution prefigured the legendary athleticism
of his New Zealand episcopate: he punted across, undressed,
punted back and plunged in. But Sarah was a match for him, in

intelligence, in Christian endeavour and in physical endurance. Possibly she was the finest episcopal wife of the Victorian colonial era.

In 1841, at the age of 32, he was offered the bishopric of New Zealand, upon the initiative of the Bishop of London. Impulsively he called upon Gladstone, at his London house. Was it practicable and becoming, he asked, that he should accept? Gladstone packed him off immediately across the park to Lambeth Palace, with a letter addressed to the Archbishop's chaplain. The chaplain assured him; Selwyn accepted. On the voyage from Plymouth he mastered the Maori language and used it for preaching as soon as he arrived. A clerical error in his letters patent had included within his diocese the vast oceanic area of Melanesia. But he was not daunted, for upon the outward voyage he had learned also the arts of seamanship and so in the dangerous Melanesian waters was able to captain his own vessel.[3]

He arrived in Auckland, New Zealand, on 30 May 1842, with Sarah, five clergy, four students for Holy Orders, and Rupai, the boy who had taught him the Maori language. One of the clergy was William Cotton, whose magnificent letters from New Zealand to his family in Walthamstow are an important item in the Archives of Selwyn College.

The copious achievements of Selwyn's New Zealand episcopate were the fruits of athleticism (including skilled horsemanship), physical courage and endurance, soldierly self-discipline, and a grand order of pastoral flair and insight. Over the years he accomplished episcopal visitations to the greater part of the country. Often he walked. But once he was with a missionary and they came to a river. The bishop could swim, the missionary could not. So, as he might have dealt with Gladstone, the bishop placed the missionary upon an india-rubber mattress and towed him across, causing Bishop Abraham of Wellington to remark how useful physical powers might be in missionary work.

By sea he visited regularly the scattered islands of Melanesia, until in 1861 Melanesia became a separate diocese. In 1843 he opened what he called the 'key and pivot' of his operations in

New Zealand – St John's College, Waimate (removed to Auckland in 1844), attached to which were two boarding schools, one for Maori boys, the other for Maori girls. The objects of the foundation were to educate all classes of the community, especially the class of young men aspiring to Holy Orders; to accommodate young settlers on their first arrival in New Zealand; and to shelter the sick, the aged and the poor. The theological students of the College were commanded to imitate the asceticism of St Paul. To this end their domestic regimen was modelled upon that of a more frugal Cambridge college. According to Sarah, the fate of the Maori schoolboys was '*very* homely food and some hard industrial work'.

In the 1850s Selwyn effected the subdivision of his diocese into four dioceses, two in North Island, two in South Island. He himself remained primate, as Bishop of Auckland. He obtained also permission for the New Zealand Church to have a general synod (which included laity) to manage its own affairs; his achievement here was consistent with a desire that Gladstone had had as Colonial Secretary in the mid-1840s – namely, to organize the colonial churches upon a lay-representative basis, so that they should have what he called 'a substantive aspect in the face of the State', against a day when a civil and parliamentary power might no longer support them. Selwyn's promotion in New Zealand of diocesan subdivision and synodical government greatly influenced the development of the Anglican Church worldwide. But the Maori wars which commenced in 1860 disrupted much of the Christian order which he had created; he himself incurred unpopularity – from the British because he condemned the contempt with which they had viewed Maori law, and their appropriation of Maori land; from the Maoris because he continued to minister pastorally to the troops of a British queen who seemed to condone the appropriation.

When he visited England in 1854 he did not seem grand or remote; in Owen Chadwick's words he 'profoundly influenced the popular notion of the episcopal office'. He preached four sermons before the University of Cambridge, upon the text 'Christ, the Light of the World'. He appealed for soldiers of

George Augustus Selwyn.

Christ to enlist for missionary service overseas; he inspired Kingsley's dedication. His imagery was appropriate, for it coincided with the appeal for men to fight in the Crimean War. It produced a response in Cambridge: the young Charles Frederick Mackenzie, Fellow of Gonville and Caius, committed his life to the foundation of the Universities' Mission in Central Africa. Probably Selwyn's appeal laid some of the ground for such support in Cambridge as the founders of Selwyn College received onwards from 1878.[4]

In 1867 he came to England again, to attend the first Lambeth Conference, convened to consider the problems presented by the

great expansion of the Church overseas. In England he was offered
and accepted the see of Lichfield. He paid a farewell visit to New
Zealand in 1868, after he had been enthroned at Lichfield. On
the day he finally left the colony, in October, there was a joyous
public holiday in Auckland. It celebrated not his leaving but his
goodness, his creation of a national Church and his contribution
to the building of the nation which it served. Taken as a whole,
therefore, here was one of the redeeming Christian triumphs of
the dark era of British colonialism in Australasia.

His reign in New Zealand impressed Gladstone, other churchmen, and educators. So did his reign in Lichfield, not least when
he created a diocesan synod, the first in England – though he
had to call it a 'conference' because 'synod' was disliked. In 1871
and 1874 he visited the United States. The first English bishop
to do so, he contributed to the renewal of the Episcopal Church.
He was still Bishop of Lichfield when he died, on 11 April 1878.
He was buried in the cathedral close (16 April). Gladstone was
a pallbearer, at Sarah's request.

After the service many of his friends and admirers gathered in
the palace to consider a memorial. The Dean of Lichfield presided.
He said that it had been Selwyn's desire that the three little
mortuary chapels on the south side of the cathedral's lady chapel
might be restored and made fit to receive one or more monuments,
as occasion might require. At Selwyn's request plans for this work
had in part been prepared by the late Sir Giles Gilbert Scott.
Therefore, without presuming to decide anything at that meeting,
would it be worthwhile to consider going ahead with this plan,
and installing an effigy of Selwyn in one of the chapels, as a
preliminary memorial to him? The Dean asked Gladstone to
speak.

Gladstone was diffident and circumspect; he felt he had been
too close to Selwyn to be otherwise in such a matter. But he
thought that any memorial enterprise should be an undertaking
of the diocese of Lichfield, 'in the sense, not that the interest in
it should be confined to the Diocese, but that the motive power,
the directing power, and the choice should come from the
Diocese'. Selwyn – let it ever be remembered – was a 'noble'

man. It was good to be informed of his wishes concerning the chapels. It would not be good, though, to have a 'competition of memorials'. More suggestively, he hoped that 'the meeting would show its love and reverence for the memory of this extraordinary man, by endeavouring to walk in the way that his wishes marked out, in the matter of his memorial'.

After he had spoken Bishop Abraham (then coadjutor bishop in Lichfield) conducted him upon a tour of the cathedral; doubtless they talked about the memorial for Selwyn. A week later (23 April) Gladstone took himself to Oxford, for the opening of the hall and library of Keble College. He was 'greeted with loud, long, and enthusiastic cheering, and waving of hats and caps', said the *Guardian* (1 May 1878), but he stirred up a little controversy by declaring John Henry Newman to be greater 'as an academical name' than either John Keble or Edmund Pusey.

The immediate response to Gladstone's remarks at Lichfield was a suggestion (from Sir Percival Heywood and Lord Selborne) that, beyond the restoration of the chapels, a suitable memorial would be the subdivision of the diocese of Lichfield, which Selwyn himself had wanted. But the suggestion was not pursued.

A memorial committee was appointed, with power to co-opt. It had more than sixty members. They included the Dean of Lichfield, who was chairman; the Lords Lieutenant of Staffordshire and Shropshire; the High Sheriffs of the counties of the diocese – Staffordshire, Shropshire and Derbyshire; three earls (including Powis, who was High Steward of the University of Cambridge); the canons residentiary and non-residentiary of Lichfield; Bishop Hobhouse (formerly of Nelson, New Zealand); the Provost of Eton; the Revd William Selwyn (the Bishop's son); and Sir William Martin, formerly Chief Justice of New Zealand. Bishop Abraham was one of the committee's honorary secretaries, the others being two clergymen of the diocese.

On 26 April the memorial committee unanimously adopted two resolutions. The first simply accepted the suggestion regarding the chapels and the effigy. The second was thus:

That the foundation of a College at Cambridge, to be called the 'SELWYN COLLEGE,' be submitted to the Church at large, as a worthy object by which to perpetuate the noble name and labours of the late Bishop of Lichfield; such College to include provision for the education of the sons of Clergymen and others, to fill posts of Missionary work whether at home or abroad.

The memorial committee appointed a general committee, partly out of itself, of which the chairman was the Dean and the secretary was Abraham. What it achieved is described below, in Chapters 2 and 4.

Notes

1.   Asa Briggs, ed., *Gladstone's Boswell: late Victorian conversations, by Lionel Tollemache, and other documents*, Brighton, Sussex, 1984, p.130.

2.   'An Old Etonian' (*The Times*, 18 April 1878) says that the date was 1832, and the headmaster Keate. Mrs G.H. Curteis (*In Memoriam*, pp.6, 7) says that the date was 1839, and the headmaster Hawtrey. 'An Old Etonian' was probably correct.

3.   On Selwyn's acceptance see Gladstone's letter to *The Times*, 18 April 1878.

4.   Owen Chadwick, *Mackenzie's Grave*, London, 1959, p.22.

CHAPTER 2

Families and Politics:
Gladstones, Lytteltons,
and Talbots

WHAT WAS Selwyn College for? Answer: Chiefly to supply, at moderate expense, men willing to be missionaries, clerical or lay, at home or abroad, but especially abroad, in a world where more than ever they were needed. Selwyn College was largely – by no means *wholly*, of course – an outcrop of British Christian Liberalism in its confrontation with what Gladstone regarded as the immoral imperialism of his Conservative rival Disraeli. Even if 'empire', Gladstone believed, were providential, in a world where as yet there could be no leagues of nations, 'empire' and international relations generally had better be ordered according to Christian imperatives. Therefore planted around the world must be Christian ministers of the stamp of Bishop Selwyn – spiritual, educated, internationalist in outlook, tolerant of ethnic diversity, pastorally accomplished and, not least perhaps, able to row about in boats.

The friends and relations of Gladstone responsible for the founding of Selwyn College did not state the matter quite in this way. But then mostly they were clergymen; none was a politician. Nevertheless they clearly regarded Liberalism – Gladstonian Liberalism, in its domestic and especially in its foreign aspects – as integral to their designs; Liberalism, they strongly felt, was near to godliness. On 9 April 1878, as Bishop Selwyn lay dying, Mrs Gladstone wrote a supportive note to Sarah, who asked Bishop Abraham to reply. He did. His construction of the foreign affairs of his day, and of Gladstone's role in them, was perhaps unorthodox, but in a postscript he wrote as follows:

May I be allowed to say, as the opportunity has unexpectedly offered itself, how deeply I feel the rare grace and blessing God has bestowed on Mr Gladstone, to have permitted one man to have brought about the freedom of two races, the Western people of Italy, and the Slavs of the East?

Moreover the friends of Gladstone and of 'Selwyn College' took for granted that the best of their opponents must be Liberal too — as indeed they were. If this was so, they reasoned in the early months, then there must be a basis for accommodation, since, as Christians must agree, so must Liberals. Early in 1881 Abraham learned that J.W. Clark, Cambridge scientist and antiquary, had told Mrs William Selwyn that many Cambridge men would support a 'Selwyn College' '*if* we would drop the *Church* element'. On 5 March Abraham wrote to the Master-designate of Selwyn:

> I wrote to say that I for one had not the slightest idea of dropping that element, which is to my mind the soul of the body – but I should be glad to meet him and his friends & have a talk about it. If they are Liberals they are abound to let us work out our own ideas freely – and if they cannot work out theirs by themselves, they ought to go with us as far as we work out their views – and support, certainly not thwart, any plan for simple living.

Liberals in Cambridge who were close to Gladstone talked freely of founding a college to restore to Anglicanism its due within the University. They did so; their finest product before the end of the century was William Collins, future Bishop of Gibraltar. But other Liberals, who supposed themselves no less Gladstonian, argued that the principle that all colleges in universities should be open to all men irrespective of religious allegiance must take precedence over any notional refurbishment of Anglicanism, however desirable Anglicanism might be.

There was, then, a fissure in the Liberalism of late Victorian Cambridge; the arguments of one side rushed past those of the other, in opposite directions. Out of the fissure came the controversy over the founding of Selwyn College. Eventually controversy

subsided. But subsidence did not herald comprehension; still in
the twentieth century men of Selwyn did not grasp that it was
not noticeably the Church but a particular kind of Liberalism
that had produced their College. Thus they were dismayed that
whilst the College did much for the Church, the Church, it
seemed, did little for the College. Gradually, of course, the
assumptions of Gladstonian Liberalism faded from society at large.
Thus inevitably the ligaments binding Church and College, nour-
ished by those assumptions, were weakened; the secularism odious
to Gladstone seemed odious no more, at least to those in charge
of Selwyn.

In the spring of 1880 there was a parliamentary election. The
Liberals won. Queen Victoria was furious. She detested Gladstone,
for his attacks upon Disraeli. At first she would not appoint him
Prime Minister. She called his party, the Liberal Party, 'this
shamefully heterogeneous union', and hoped that soon it would
dissolve into its component parts. Her perception was astute; little
did the founders of Selwyn College dream that their venture, as
it unfolded between 1878 and 1883, would bequeath to historians
a cameo of this heterogeneity.

If, however, the Liberal Party was heterogeneous, so in his
own political person was its leader. The political thinking of
Gladstone was the most moral, the most elevated of the nineteenth
century. Yet it was the most ambivalent. Often it bewildered his
contemporaries, though Sarah, Lady Lyttelton, grandmother of
the first Master of Selwyn College, was shrewder than she knew:
'He is so agreeable,' she said, after she had dined with him,
'... though I cannot *quite* enter into his politics, they are so in-
tricate, and I am always forgetting the principle he lays down'.
That was the problem – 'forgetting the principle', or (more likely)
not noticing that 'the principle' was often protean. In a notably
Liberal University the squabbles of 1878–83 regarding Selwyn
College were largely among self-proclaimed Gladstonian Liberals
who wondered why they squabbled, since they were Gladstonian
Liberals. The historian may tell them: they squabbled because,

mistaking a part for the whole, each unknowingly acted upon his own vision of the informing spirit of Gladstone in matters educational, without perceiving that the spirit was discordant because, socially and in religion, the situations it addressed were very fluid.[1]

By the late 1870s, for two reasons Gladstone was highly receptive to notions of extending university education upon Christian principles. First, such extension would contribute, in however limited a way, to the production of educated men fit to exercise the parliamentary franchise which he hoped would be steadily enlarged. Second, in the spring of 1877 Russia went to war with Turkey. In Lichfield Bishop Selwyn fretted about the moral rights and wrongs of the war. Gladstone, though, was against the Turks, for he held that they were infidel, internationally treacherous and oppressive of the Balkan Christians whom they ruled. In July 1878, however, after the conclusion of the war, Disraeli signed a convention with Turkey, whereby Britain received from Turkey the island of Cyprus, and a promise that Turkey would reform her government if Britain guaranteed her future territorial integrity in Asia. Disraeli was acclaimed by the British public but denounced by Gladstone. What business had Britain, asked Gladstone, to temporize with infidelity and international treachery? Britain should aim to create and to sustain a string of soundly Christian nations from the Baltic to the Adriatic – that, he said, would be the way to contain Turkey. Creating Christian nations was difficult business, but it was business which Gladstone addressed during his great Midlothian campaigns of 1879 and 1880, which largely effected the election victory of 1880. In 1878 he had spoken of 'the rising hopes of a true public law for Christendom'; in 1880 he referred to 'the international law of Christendom'. In 1878 Bishop Abraham had told him that 'the great complaint of the Gentry of the Midland and Northern counties is that the *Ministry* of the Church of England is being swamped by "Theologicals" (*non*-university) men'; in 1879, according to Morley, Gladstone was preoccupied with 'the intellectual dignity of the Christian ministry'. Gladstone's utterances were entirely consistent with the desire he had shown in the 1840s for sturdy synodical government in the colonial churches; certainly they should not have been regarded as canting humbug, as they were regarded by some, including some Liberals.

So when in 1878 they proposed 'Selwyn College' their proposal seemed good to Gladstone. For a 'public law of Christendom' required international public Christians. Might not a 'Selwyn College' produce them? Thus in September 1881 the Master-designate of Selwyn could not have been surprised to be told by Bishop Abraham that Gladstone and the Archbishop of Canterbury (Tait) 'dwell much on the *missionary* character of the College'.

But there was irony. In July 1882, only weeks before the matriculation of the first Selwyn undergraduates, Gladstone's administration, acting independently of the other European powers, bombarded Alexandria and put down a nationalist insurrection against the Khedive of Egypt, titular vassal of the Sultan of Turkey. Gladstone's reasons had more to do with the complexities of *realpolitik* than with the protection of Christians in Egypt. One immediate result of the invasion was the resignation from the cabinet on 12 July of the Chancellor of the Duchy of Lancaster, John Bright – 'dear old John Bright', Gladstone called him – veteran Quaker radical, hero of the campaign against church rate and the Corn Laws, and a potent figure in the circumstances which, to Gladstone's supporters, had seemed to render the founding of a 'Selwyn College' so very desirable.

Gladstone's bombardment of Alexandria was a key event in the emergence of the 'new imperialism' – the projection, that is (to adapt a phrase of David Thomson's), 'on to an overseas screen in the form of naked power politics of the interstate frictions and power politics of Europe'. The 'new imperialism' signified necessarily that from the early 1880s to the Great War any prospect that international law and colonial or imperial development might be anchored in gospel Christianity would be progressively forlorn. Nevertheless, amongst Gladstonians the old idealism lingered, even into the war itself. On 9 August 1914, Edward Lyttelton, headmaster of Eton and brother of the first Master of Selwyn, preached a sermon in Norfolk in which he castigated German militarism, asserted the need to believe Britain to be fighting for the rights of Belgium, but – in words with which Bishop Selwyn would have concurred entirely – insisted none the less that the war provided 'a God-given opportunity to prove that the purposes of empire lay beyond commerce and force':

> Travellers and missionaries all tell the same tale of China, India and Japan. Those swarming hordes of coloured people have felt their own old solution – such as it was – of the eternal problems of duty and inclination, hope and despair, joy and cynicism, shattered by the impact of Western life. ... All our outward actions are based on the conviction that naked competition, the outwitting of your neighbour by trickery and force is the secret of progress, happiness and natural strength.

On 26 March 1915, in St Margaret's, Westminster, he preached another sermon, nationally notorious, in which he equated 'the demands of patriotism with the demands of the Christian gospel'. For this he lost his job at Eton.[2]

Nothing, perhaps, signified the passing of the old Gladstonian order more than the dismissal of Edward Lyttelton. For the founders of Selwyn College, therefore, a question was invited which, inevitably, they could not discern. If the aspirations of Gladstonians in respect of the College were so largely stillborn, how, down the years, should the success or otherwise of the College be measured, especially in a situation where the Church was unsupportive? The question remained as late as the 1950s.[3]

But other problems were discerned, and were immediate. In 1854 and 1871, harassed by national nonconformity represented by Bright, Gladstone had been responsible for parliamentary legislation abolishing religious tests in British universities; after 1871 Nonconformist men could graduate and teach in Oxford and Cambridge more or less upon the terms available to Anglicans. This seemed good; certainly it invited the industrial and commercial classes of northern England – politically Liberal but largely Nonconformist – into the mainstream of a university system which ought to serve a modern nation. Questions lingered, though: How 'true' was nonconformity? At what point might nonconformity lurch into godlessness, subverting true Anglicanism as it went? These were the closet fears of high church Gladstonian Liberals.

So for the welfare of Anglicanism Gladstonians thought they would found 'Selwyn College', even if its foundation might contravene the letter and the spirit of the University Tests Act of 1871. To Gladstone they said that their College would be frugal, for frugality might assist in widening the access to university education. To one ever preoccupied with national retrenchment, and who monitored Mrs Gladstone's household expenditure, frugality was exquisite recommendation. In one particular their way was clear, for if, for whatever reason, the University should not allow 'Selwyn College' to be a full college of the University (no matter what it might be called) then probably it could be something resembling an Oxford 'public hall'. The concept of the 'public hall' – something half-way between an undergraduate lodging-house and a full college of the University – had been invented (or rather, reinvented) jointly by Gladstone and the leader of the Whig component of the heterogeneous union, Lord John Russell. Russell had been educated at neither Oxford nor Cambridge, but at the bracing University of Edinburgh, and so held a view less convoluted than Gladstone's of the proper role of universities in nineteenth-century Britain.

Onwards from 1878 Selwyn College was created, and caused a tiresome rumpus. The instrument of its creation was the Gladstone–Lyttelton–Talbot family connection, of all such connections one of the most remarkable of the nineteenth century.

The first Master, installed in 1822, was the Revd and Hon Arthur Temple Lyttelton (1852–1903; Eton, and Trinity, Cambridge), son of the former Mary Glynne, Catherine Gladstone's sister and the fourth Lord Lyttelton's wife; theirs was a double wedding, Mary with Lyttelton and Catherine with Gladstone, in July 1839. Lyttelton's sister next in age to himself, Lavinia, married Edward Stuart Talbot (1844–1934; Charterhouse, and Christ Church, Oxford), grandson of the second Earl Talbot, first Warden of Keble College, Oxford (1870–88), and later Bishop of Rochester,

Southwark, and Winchester successively. His eldest sister, Meriel, married Talbot's elder brother, John. Thus, one may say, Gladstone was uncle both to the first head of house of Keble and to the first head of house of Selwyn. Lyttelton's father was Gladstone's subordinate at the Colonial Office in the 1840s, and his brother Spencer became Gladstone's private secretary. His sister Lucy (born in 1841) married Lord Frederick Cavendish, who was murdered in May 1882 by Fenians in Dublin, soon after Gladstone had appointed him Chief Secretary for Ireland. In the Archives of Selwyn College letters dealing with the foundation of the College dwell also upon this family and public tragedy. Lucy was famed for her work in women's education; her memorial is Lucy Cavendish College (1965).

The relationship between Lyttelton and both Talbot and his wife was notably intimate. First, after Talbot's father had died when he was 8, Talbot's mother formed close friendships with Lady Lyttelton and Mrs Gladstone, so that Talbot, Lyttelton and Gladstone children had been companions together at Hagley and Hawarden, whilst Talbot had been at preparatory school with Gladstone's son Stephen and Lyttelton's brother Alfred. Talbot had regarded Gladstone and Lord Lyttelton as surrogate fathers. Thus it was natural that Lyttelton and Talbot – though Talbot especially – should later be political disciples of Gladstone. Moreover, Lyttelton's sister May was particularly loved by himself and by Lavinia; her death in 1875 enhanced the closeness of Lyttelton's relationship with Talbot.

From 1879 to 1882 Lyttelton was a tutor at Keble, learning from Talbot how best to be Master of Selwyn. Then, during the 1880s, both were among that small group of high churchmen – apart from Lyttelton identified entirely with Oxford – which came in 1889 to publish *Lux Mundi*, an influential volume of essays seeking reverently to cause Anglo-Catholicism to apprehend, in the words of the preface, 'the new social movements of each age'. The *Lux Mundi* group thought themselves the most enlightened yet orthodox of religious progressives, though their religious world seemed remote indeed from the nonconformity of John Bright and commercial England.

Charles John Abraham
Virtual Founder of the College

But for Selwyn College, to the dual liberalism of Lyttelton and Talbot was added the Gladstonianism of one even closer than Gladstone himself to the world of Bishop Selwyn – Charles Abraham (1814–1903), Old Etonian, Fellow of King's College

from 1836 to 1849, sometime Principal of frugal St John's College
in Auckland, subordinate as first Bishop of Wellington to Selwyn
in New Zealand, coadjutor to Selwyn in Lichfield, husband of a
cousin of Sarah Selwyn, and father of another bishop (suffragan
of Derby, 1909–27) who was one of the earliest undergraduates
at Keble College.

Abraham had been Selwyn's most intimate friend since 1838
when he had returned from Cambridge to be a master at Eton,
close to Windsor where Selwyn was curate. After Selwyn's death
he remained in Lichfield. He was not the founder of Selwyn
College (no one person was), but as active secretary of the memorial
committee and of the general committee constituted after Selwyn's
funeral he was by far its most energetic promoter. Moreover he
was a fervent admirer of Gladstone, whom he had known personally for many years. As early as 1850, as high churchmen, they
had consoled each other concerning the Gorham judgement (in
which the Judicial Committee of the Privy Council had appeared
to challenge high church teaching in the matter of baptism). His
desire to sustain the support of a busy Gladstone for the creation
of Selwyn College was unflagging to the point that he suspected
himself of being a nuisance. 'Forgive me if I am more persistent
than I should be,' he wrote to Gladstone (17 October 1878). 'I
have a sort of recollection that Homer compared a hero like Ajax
to a fly because of his persistency – and you may think me more
like the fly than the hero.'

Abraham was the kind of figure needed at its inception by
every voluntary venture of a certain scale; he could think simultaneously and rapidly about very large and very small sums of
money, and about their prudent application, whilst keeping in
view wider moral, intellectual and social considerations. In the
College's new (1964) Senior Combination Room there is a bronze
bust of him.

At his side stood Edmund Hobhouse (1817–1904), notable undergraduate oarsman at Balliol College, Fellow of Merton, Bishop
(under Selwyn) of Nelson in New Zealand, coadjutor with Abraham
in Lichfield, and – in retirement – antiquary of the county of
Somerset. His father, Henry, had been a privy councillor and an

intimate of Sir Robert Peel, having been Keeper of the State
Papers from 1827 until his death in 1854. Thus, might one say,
the younger Hobhouse was (with Gladstone) out of a Peelite
stable. From boyhood, however, his health had been indifferent.
Though in New Zealand he rivalled the physical toughness of
Selwyn and Abraham, performing his visitations on horseback
except when the horse would escape and he would have to chase
it, after Selwyn's death he had not quite the energy of the older
Abraham in the matter of Selwyn College; 'we leave him alone,'
said Abraham, 'and do not ask him to do this or that'. He did
his best, though, busying himself with the design of the College
crockery and with the devising of the College crest, and (in 1880)
exerting himself with Laetitia Selwyn when she was a nuisance
over money. In 1881, when the gabbling at meetings of the College
Council worsened his headaches, he admonished the young
Master-designate that he should be a better chairman, not fearing
to control his elders.[4]

So, there was the Liberalism of Gladstone and Abraham which
was instinctively conservative, the Liberalism of Russell which
was astringently Whig, and the Liberalism of John Bright which
was Nonconformist and which in the early 1880s sometimes rather
fancied that it was Liberalism entire. For Selwyn College, though,
there was a fourth component of the heterogeneous union – the
Liberalism of the egregious and fractious Oscar Browning who,
trumpeting his professed Gladstonianism around Cambridge
(indeed, in October 1878 trumpeting Gladstone in person around
King's College!), contrived nevertheless a comic if momentary
alliance with John Bright's nonconformity, on purpose to embar-
rass the Council of Selwyn College; as he did so he offered a
vision of university education which was professional, dynamic,
consistent with the uncomplicated notions of Lord John Russell
in the 1830s, and therefore inevitably shallow in the eyes of high
churchmen. It was this that caused the rumpus.

Notes

1. Betty Askwith, *The Lytteltons: A Family Chronicle of the Nineteenth Century*, London, 1975, p.86.

2. Andrew Robinson, 'Eton's Great War Scandal', *History Today*, November 1993.

3. See especially, in the Selwyn College Archives, a typewritten paper headed 'Nature and Status of the College', dating from the 1950s and probably drafted by T.G.P. Spear.

4. The present (1994) arms, crest, and badge of the College were officially granted by the Royal College of Arms in 1965, and were based as far as possible on the arms of Bishop George Selwyn. The account of the matter contained in the College *Calendar* for 1965–1966 commences thus:

> The choice of the unauthorised Arms which have hitherto been used by the College must have been an early decision of those responsible for our foundation, since the Arms appear above the main gateway which was built in 1881 and on the Common Seal first used in 1882. The Arms are believed to be those borne by George Augustus Selwyn as Bishop of Lichfield, which were, following the usual custom, the Arms of the See impaling those of the Bishop's family. This was a very natural choice, but the Arms were never officially granted by the College of Arms. The second Bursar, A.P. Humphry, was evidently conscious of this and in 1898 an Armorial Bearings Fund was started with contributions of five pounds from the Combination Room Plate Fund and from Humphry himself. This money was carried forward each year in the books of the College until the mid-thirties, when it was submerged in the general funds.

> In 1963 an old member of the College gave over £300 to revive and augment the Armorial Bearings Fund, thus enabling the College to begin the official process by sending a memorial to the Earl Marshal requesting his warrant to the King of Arms (*Calendar*, 1963–4). It was then discovered that Bishop Selwyn had used incorrectly the arms of another branch of the Selwyn family. This was put right in the arms as approved by the Royal College.

CHAPTER 3

The Accommodation of Gladstone: University Reform and the Origin of Public Hostels 1850–71

IN THE Archives of Selwyn College there is a bad-tempered draft of a letter from Lyttelton to Browning, dated 23 May 1883. It seeks to scotch Browning's notion that an Anglican college for undergraduates should not be founded in Cambridge because the University Tests Act seemed to forbid denominational colleges in Cambridge. It seeks, but is hardly successful, for its eloquence dwells where Lyttelton did not intend – in its scorings-out and incompleteness, as though the Master of Selwyn were an under-graduate of modest ability wrestling with nineteenth-century Liberalism in a History Tripos paper with time running out. 'I had thought', he wrote,

> we had a common ground of Liberalism on which to meet, but your letter shows me that, on this point at least, your Liberalism is not the same as mine. My Liberalism says 'no section of the nation shall be kept out of a public park': yours seems to say 'no one shall have a private park for himself'.

There followed 155 words concerning the College Charter, incor-poration within the University, 'prestige' resulting from the favour of the Crown, public hostels, and the dignity (or otherwise) of Selwyn College. These are scored out. He tried again: 'They are as distinct as polit Libera' – scored out. He managed a coherent paragraph (58 words): 'educat$^{n.}$ to be complete must be religious' – not scored out. Then he had another go at Liberalism, but only one word: 'Liberal' – scored out. Then he capitulated: his lame conclusion – not scored out – supposed that he and Browning wore different coloured spectacles so further argument was useless.

Less than Queen Victoria and much less than his grandmother did Lyttelton grasp the politics of his uncle. Neither did he grasp the complex temper of his age and the significance of the Universities Tests Act. This was inconvenient, for him and for his College.

The University Tests Act of 1871 concerned the Universities of Oxford, Cambridge, and Durham and their colleges and halls. Its object was to detach various university and collegiate emoluments, deriving from endowments, from the condition that their recipients should, in any of a variety of prescribed ways, subscribe to the Anglican faith. It was held that such detachment would render the universities more 'national'. The Act said that persons taking lay academical degrees or holding lay academical or collegiate offices must not be required to subscribe to any formulary of religious faith, excepting persons seeking offices for which Holy Orders had hitherto been required or might in future be required. The word 'office' included every professorship, readership, praelectorship, headship of house (*this* was significant – there had been much debate about this), fellowship, tutorship, scholarship or exhibition, the income of which was paid out of university or college revenues. What was said about 'persons taking lay academical degrees' signified that henceforth at Oxford Nonconformists might become MAs as, since 1856, they had been able to at Cambridge.[1]

Fundamentally at issue in the controversy surrounding the foundation of Selwyn College was whether religious tests could be imposed upon undergraduates in apparent defiance of the Cambridge University Act of 1856, modelled upon the Oxford University Act of 1854. Nevertheless the controversy centred not upon the Cambridge Act, but upon the Tests Act of 1871. This was natural, for enormous symbolism attached to the Tests Act. Religious uncertainty was widespread in the early 1870s; it was not in the mid-1850s. Those who voted for the Tests Bill sat through months of anguished though generally courteous debate; they believed that finally they had ended the constrictive pretensions of Anglicanism in the ancient universities.

Moreover they understood the process of political and civic liberalization to which they were heirs. With Gladstone they knew that the process of university reform which they had brought to an issue in 1871 was a product of the Great Reform Act of 1832. The Oxford and Cambridge Acts of 1854 and 1856 were debated in their day; there was no need to be talking about them in 1870 and 1871. But the Selwyn disputes of 1878–83, and the legal identity of the College as a public hostel subsequently, arose from the same condition of England which had occasioned those Acts and – more remotely – the Great Reform Act. The Great Reform Act invited important questions not only about the future of the Church of England and about Nonconformists and their aspirations, but also about the role of central government in the affairs of public corporations – for example colleges and universities. The social and imperial forces of fifty years shaped the identity of Selwyn College; the College's history, therefore, begins with the Great Reform Act.

The Whigs came to government in 1830, in an industrializing nation. Grievances abounded, especially concerning the character of Parliament and parliamentary elections, and the privileges of a landed aristocracy and the Church of England. Reform came. In 1832, following a widening of civic freedoms for Nonconformists and – thanks to Robert Peel – the emancipation of Roman Catholics, the Great Reform Act redistributed parliamentary seats and extended the franchise. Before mid-century came many other reforms – of factories; the Poor Law; municipal corporations; tithes, procedures for the registration of births, marriages, and deaths; elementary schooling; the county police; banking; the Corn Laws; and public health. All this implied that something should be done about the tranquillities of ancient universities.

Often, though, there was controversy, because the powers of central government seemed dangerously increased to the detriment of individuals, corporations, and local communities. Particularly disliked were the statutory commissions, centrally based in London, whose accountability to Parliament seemed slight. The Tithe Commission (1836) terrorized the farmers for a hundred years; the horrors of the Poor Law Commission (1834) were widely experienced, either directly in the case of the lower orders or vicariously in the case of a reading public apprised of the miseries of Oliver Twist and Betty Higden. 'Centralization' was a pejorative word of the 1850s; it remained so for a generation, its prospect chilling the spirits of many an Oxbridge common room, and occasioning in Gladstone some of his habitual edginess concerning the demands for parliamentary abolition of religious tests in universities.

For churchmen, and – because the redistribution of endowments was so largely involved – especially for those concerned with public schools and universities, four reforms were profoundly significant. The first concerned the Church of Ireland: the Church Temporalities (Ireland) Act (1833), out of regard for the Roman Catholicism of most Irish people, suppressed ten Irish bishoprics and reformed the Church's revenues. John Keble, whom Gladstone and Selwyn admired, condemned it, and so precipitated the Oxford Movement and Tractarianism. The other three (1836, 1838, 1841), inspired largely by Gladstone's mentor Peel, effected realignments of the Church's revenues to satisfy what reformers believed that Anglican pastoral and parochial obligations ought by then to be. Henceforth Anglican Church establishments, guarantors of the liberties of Englishmen, must be public corporations, succouring the poor and needy where appropriate, but mindful particularly that soundness of religious faith and practice would prove contingent upon soundness of financial stewardship.

By happy circumstance these reforms coincided with – indeed to some extent they facilitated – the emergence in city and town and village of a new breed of clergymen: tireless, visionary, sometimes saintly, and exceedingly 'professional'. Some, of course, were high churchmen, wishing with Keble that the Church could reform itself in appropriate ways and not be meddled with by a 'central' Parliament. Among them were friends of George Selwyn. Selwyn in Windsor, nevertheless, was more typical of the new breed taken as a whole; his rapturous reception in Cambridge in 1854 was as much a tribute to the 'new' Church – untainted, for its admirers, by the nastiness of so much of secular 'reform' – as it was to his own missionary episcopate.

But if Selwyns, Gladstones, and Lytteltons could contemplate a Church refurbished and set to grapple with an industrializing age, Nonconformists of a radical or Liberal hue discerned a Church militant teeming with busybody clergymen trampling upon true piety – Nonconformist piety, that is. The hostility of nonconformity was thus recharged. In 1842 Edward Miall (1809– 81), fiery Congregationalist, measured the political feebleness of nonconformity against the political strength of the reformed Anglican establishment, with its Church rate, its ecclesiastical imprisonments, its workhouse chaplains, and its colonial bishops. Nonconformists, he said, 'the *prestige* of their power gone', must take themselves in hand, and concern themselves with a precise objective – 'THE ENTIRE SEPARATION OF CHURCH AND STATE'. In 1844, supported by John Bright, he was instrumental in the creation of the British Anti-State Church Association, later known as the Liberation Society, which, in concert with Oscar Browning, professed Anglican, hoped (in 1883) to bridle the intentions of Bishop Abraham and Arthur Lyttelton.

Soon, then, it seemed that the ancient universities should be reformed. Partly they were Church establishments, because those who endowed them originally had deemed them so and had devised their endowments accordingly. Thus, it could be argued, their endowments were national assets, to be dealt with as Parliament might see fit – as Parliament *had* seen fit in the case of Church endowments. But also they were the nation's foremost cradles of disinterested learning, educating in ways that were appropriate the governing and administrative élites of what Gladstone, in the Oxford University debates of 1854, would call 'the active age in which we live'.

Or were they? That indeed was the point. The Church stood reformed in response to the Industrial Revolution. If the business of ancient universities was not simply religion but also education responsive to the circumstances of industry, commerce, and empire, then should not reform of the ancient universities perhaps be more extensive even than reform of the Church? Universities need not become vocational, of course; but reformers might wish to concede that much of industry and commerce (if not empire) was closely allied to nonconformity, and so was wary of Anglican establishments.

Reform of the ancient universities began in 1850, the year when the plan was published for the founding in Manchester (the 'cottonopolis') of the Owens College, which blazed the trail for provincial university colleges in the great manufacturing cities. In Parliament on 23 April James Heywood – Member of Parliament for North Lancashire, a Unitarian, and a senior optime of Trinity Hall – tabled a motion causing the Whig Prime Minister, Lord John Russell, to set up two royal commissions. One was to enquire into the discipline, the teaching, and the revenues sustaining the teaching of the University of Oxford; the other (of which Selwyn's brother-in-law, Peacock, was a member) into those of Cambridge.

Russell was opposed by Gladstone, who proclaimed that a commission for Oxford was constitutionally odious and probably illegal. He argued that, provided it were combined with university freedom and self-government, the bad teaching of undergraduates would be a lesser evil than anything that Parliament might put upon the University. Though he admitted that the ancient universities had been slothful in the advancement of learning, he said that they had done as much as the country had needed. He contemplated the lawyers, the divines, and the statesmen of England – especially Sir Robert Peel (who had died a fortnight previously) – and demanded to know why Englishmen should be ashamed of the cradles in which they were mainly nurtured. Morley winced; he believed that no worse case was ever more strongly argued. He was relieved that this speech was the last significant manifesto of a personal Toryism from which a wonderful pilgrim was departing for a shining Liberal progress. But Gladstone was supported by Oxford Tories and high churchmen, who set up a fearful clamour. Excitable Bishop Phillpotts declared that the proposal for a commission had 'no parallel since the fatal attempt of King James II to subject the colleges to his unhallowed control'. The commission was nevertheless appointed.

Paradoxically (as it transpired), in the process of university reform extending from mid-century to the early 1880s Gladstone was by far the single most important figure. He more than anyone was responsible for the character of the Oxford University Act of 1854 and for that of the University Tests Act of 1871, and he was significant in the founding of the Colleges of Keble and Selwyn. He changed his mind about university reform in 1853 and again in 1870; but his reasons for doing so were consistent with his changes of mind on other matters of high policy, notably the extension of the parliamentary franchise and Home Rule for Ireland – though hardly, of course, with his developing quest for a Christian world order. Particularly they were consistent with his evolving opinions on the Church–State relationship.

The young Gladstone was a Peelite Tory; the elderly Gladstone was a Liberal prime minister. His odyssey was remarkable in that his political development was an integrant of his religious development. In 1838, fearful that rampant evangelicalism was individualizing the national religion, he published a work entitled *The State in its Relations with the Church*; he argued that the union between Church and State was necessary both so that the Church might imbue the State with religion, and so that the State might attest the distinction between religious error and religious truth as taught by the Church of England. But eventually this moral idealism became moral pragmatism: towards the close of his career he discerned a natural moral harmony between Providential will (God's will) and 'the progress of the age' – that is, *laissez-faire* Liberalism, and the quest for freedom of Western peoples. Most of the nineteenth century, he thought in 1889, had been 'predominantly a history of emancipation – that is enabling man to do his work of emancipation, political, economical, social, moral, intellectual'.

He came to this view gradually. In 1847 Lord John Russell had presented to the see of Hereford Dr R.D. Hampden, whose theology Oxford University had declared to be heretical. On

8 March 1850, in the Gorham case, the Judicial Committee of the Privy Council had determined that Bishop Phillpotts of Exeter could not bar the Revd G.C. Gorham from a Church living because of his irregular opinions concerning baptismal regeneration. Gladstone was shaken: would the Church fulfil the role he had assigned it in 1838? Its evident subservience to the State alarmed him. He pondered its incapacity to stem the rising tide of nonconformity; perhaps moral governance would be better served by a national community of individual Christian consciences. Such a community would have to be contingent upon a Liberal political order, and upon national systems of education kept vigorously Christian through association with a variety of churches – not all of them necessarily Anglican. Yet he did not want denominational pluralism; in 1850 he perceived Russell's proposal for the Oxford commission as a step towards disestablishment of the Church; on 18 July, in Parliament, he opposed it. But in the winter of 1850–1 he was in Italy, mostly in Naples, where he witnessed the awful cruelty to his political opponents of King Ferdinand II of the Two Sicilies; this, he said, was 'the negation of God erected into a system of Government'. His moral idealism wavered again, it seemed inadequate; by the end of February 1851, Dr Hampden, Mr Gorham and King Ferdinand combined had convinced him that the principle of individual Christian freedom might quicken the lives of Church and State alike, provided it were erected upon a tough-minded acceptance of the ordinary man's innate capacity to govern himself.

So before the end of 1853 he was changing tack on the matter of Oxford, and pronouncing that by means of 'halls' an Oxford education might be had by young men whose parents might otherwise be unable to afford it. In February 1859 he met Cavour. In April the war for Italian liberation broke out; his Liberalism was enlarged. Before the end of June he was Chancellor of the Exchequer in a Whig administration; in 1864, in Parliament, he argued for universal male suffrage, to the chagrin of Lord Palmerston, the Prime Minister. Consistently with his pronouncement of 1853 he supported the proposals to found Keble and Selwyn Colleges, in 1866 and 1878. In 1880 he won Midlothian.

In 1885, momentously, he adopted the cause of Home Rule for Ireland; his reasons were ethical, spiritual, and democratic.

Gladstone's Liberalism was adaptable, proving itself in each generation. Lyttelton never quite perceived this, jousting with Oscar Browning. Earlier, an undergraduate was smarter, writing about Selwyn College in *The Cambridge Review* (15 November 1882):

> About ten or twelve years ago the Dissenters ... declared their intention to share the common life of the Colleges. They have done so. Now, if a number of Churchmen, or men of any creed, or of no creed, say they wish to dine and live alone where they can study within the precincts of the University, and actually give up the glory and gold of the old foundations to do so, are they to be driven out or persecuted? Was there ever such a thing heard of as an attempt to enact that young men with the assent of their parents may not choose their society lest they lose their liberality of mind?

Lyttelton, then, could have argued (he did not) that English secularism grew, that the new civic universities were promoting education that seemed morally neutral, and that therefore the founding of Keble and Selwyn Colleges was but a modest redressing of the national balance in favour of religion, the Universities Tests Act notwithstanding.[2]

Russell's commission for Oxford pondered the costive aspects of Oxford's teaching against the boasted efficiency of contemporary German universities, and wondered what might be accomplished for a modernizing society by conscientious lecturers and professors. It recommended abolition of the governance of the University by college heads, and the substitution of an elected governing body.

Its report was published in April 1852. Gladstone found its proposals too many and too complicated, but its evidence less dreadful than he had feared. Gradually he felt that the reform of Oxford would benefit the Church and the nation. It might even attract more undergraduates. So he urged the dons of Oxford to reform their University before Parliament should reform it for them. (They ignored him.) Noticing the shift in his position, a contemporary remarked that Gladstone was Liberalizing the dons instead of their Toryfying him.

Lord John Russell's Whigs had left office in February 1852. The anti-Peelite Tories under Lord Derby had replaced them, but without a majority. In December they fell. In came Lord Aberdeen, with a coalition cabinet of six Whigs, six Peelites, and one Radical. Side by side at the cabinet table sat Peelite Gladstone as Chancellor of the Exchequer and Whig Russell as Foreign Secretary. To Aberdeen's government fell the duty of framing a bill for the University of Oxford. The task devolved upon Gladstone, because Gladstone was one of the University's two MPs. Russell was glad to let him get on with it, for he was busy with another proposal for parliamentary reform, and with the Crimean War. Gladstone welcomed a diversion from the pains inflicted upon his Exchequer by Russell's war.

He set to work with gusto late in 1853. The scheme accepted by the cabinet was essentially his; matters dealt with included University government and endowments, college emoluments, the duties of those receiving them, and professorial teaching. He had consulted most of the colleges, but some college heads imagined a future with themselves as Oliver Twists supplicant before centralized commissions, remote in London and non-accountable. They discounted the prime anxiety both of the commission and of Gladstone that their colleges were not merely independent and non-accountable, but strong in relation to a more or less impotent University. Learning of Gladstone's scheme, the Vice-Chancellor foretold deplorable prospects for the University, the Church, religion, and righteousness. The Dean of Christ Church thought it inexpedient, unjust, and tyrannical.

Russell presented the Bill in March 1854. Gladstone wriggled to reconcile his new-found opinions with the opinions he had held formerly. The opinions he had held formerly were adopted, more or less, by a mischievous Disraeli, who said that nonsense was talked about the erudite professors of Germany being superior to those of Oxford, for the great men of Germany became professors only because they could not become Members of Parliament, Germany not being a parliamentary nation.

To strengthen the central authority of Oxford University and render it more clearly identifiable, the Act of 1854 replaced the old board of college heads (the Hebdomadal Board) with the Hebdomadal Council. A permanent commission was created, with statutory powers to oversee the working of certain parts of the Act. It was this commission which effected the suppression of various fellowships at All Souls, Magdalen, and The Queen's Colleges, in order to endow six new teaching professorships. Section 37 was immensely important. It noted that hitherto colleges so disposed had been individually able to establish 'halls', to make domestic and tutorial provision for young men wishing to become undergraduate members of the University but too poor to become members of a college. It said that colleges were now to be deprived of these powers, which were to be allocated to the University. In addition, section 25 empowered the Vice-Chancellor to license any suitable Master of Arts resident within a mile and a half of Carfax to open his residence as a 'private hall' to serve the same function as a 'hall'.

Morley was pleased with section 37; he said that Gladstone was always for the widest possible diffusion of the good things of life, from education to Cook's tours. The truth, though, was less simple. Gladstone was indeed concerned for the higher education of impecunious youth, hence the provision for 'halls' in his draft Bill; but with Russell and the rest of the cabinet he noted the commission's views that the University was corporately impotent. In introducing the Bill Russell observed that in its early years the University itself had exercised a direct authority over undergraduates in matters academic, tutorial, and disciplinary. There had been no colleges. Instead there were no fewer than three hundred 'halls', in which young men had simply resided to obtain the benefits of the University. Gradually the colleges arrived, the 'halls' disappeared, and the colleges usurped the authority of the University over the undergraduates; but the colleges were far less numerous than the 'halls' had been, so the number of undergraduates was reduced. So, thought Russell, to reinstate the 'hall' in all its frugal splendour would be to supplement the invigoration of the University effected by the creation of the Hebdomadal Council, as well as to widen access to the best of higher education.

But there was a third reason why to Russell the reinstatement of 'halls' seemed desirable. He thought that to young Nonconformists, excluded from the University, 'halls' would afford reasonable but temporary contact with the University until the matter of their matriculation (and perhaps that of their graduation) could be settled by a separate Act of Parliament, which so weighty an issue required. After all, he said, a Master of Arts in charge of a 'hall' could decide for himself whether or not he would admit Nonconformists.

For generations it had been impossible for men to matriculate at Oxford unless they subscribed to the Thirty-nine Articles of the Church of England. By the middle of the nineteenth century it was clearly nonsense to talk of widening access to Oxford if this restriction were to remain. In 1834 Russell, opposed by Peel and Gladstone, had demanded the abolition of university tests. In 1850, though, he had instructed his commission not to consider the matter; but they had done so – and, rather pointedly, they had reported that they had done so – because evidence concerning it had been pressed upon them. Early in 1854 Russell adhered to the view he had held in 1850; in January he told Gladstone that he did not want 'to stir the question in this bill', but that he would support some later Bill which should allow reinstated 'halls' to be the means by which Nonconformists could be admitted to the University on a formal basis. Gladstone at this stage in his religious progress professed to have no settled opinion either way; he believed that the admission of Nonconformists would be 'a great thing', provided it should compromise neither the Anglican character of the University's teaching nor the Anglican character of its governance. But still on the whole he wished that the matter might be left to the University itself.

In Parliament in March Russell and Gladstone looked to their Anglican defences. It was futile. The Nonconformists set an ambush. Miall – now Liberal Member for Rochdale – proclaimed for disestablishment by being passionate for removal of subscription. His leader John Bright achieved a wonderful effect by feigning indifference as to removal, but affirming in a puff of ill-temper, dubious grammar, and misquotation that 'Dissenters are always expected to manifest very much of those inestimable qualities which are spoken of in the Epistle to the Corinthians – "To hope all things, to believe all things, and to endure all things" '.

The upshot was sections 43 and 44 of the Act. Section 43 immediately forbade the University to impose any declaration of religious belief upon those seeking matriculation. Section 44 said that candidates for bachelor's degrees except that of BD need not subscribe, but that henceforth such a degree was not in itself to be regarded as a qualification for the holding of any University office hitherto held only by an Anglican – even if hitherto it had – unless the holder of the degree should subscribe. In other words, because they were not to be MAs, Nonconformists were still excluded from teaching in the University, and from Convocation and the Hebdomadal Council, which were concerned with its governance. Thus were Gladstone's sensibilities accommodated.

For Nonconformists at mid-century Cambridge was a more liberal university than Oxford. Cambridge had never imposed a religious test for matriculation, but in the seventeenth century it had complied with a demand of James I that all seeking its degrees should subscribe to the Thirty-nine Articles and to the Act of Supremacy. In the eighteenth century, upon its own authority, it abandoned this compliance and substituted a requirement that a candidate for the BA degree should simply declare that he was a *bona fide* member of the Church of England. In 1856 Parliament was told that the reason for this liberality was that a medieval pope had granted the University 'a happy immunity' from visitations by the Bishop of Ely; when Archbishop Laud had desired to visit in the seventeenth century he was successfully repulsed because the place was full of Puritans. This wholesome situation had prevailed into the nineteenth century, sustaining the right of Nonconformists to matriculate. Parliament was therefore told that in Cambridge provision of 'halls' would not be so great a boon to the cause of religious liberty as, two years earlier, it had been in Oxford; nevertheless 'halls' in Cambridge, for the same reason as in Oxford, would greatly widen the availability of university education.

The commission for Cambridge had reported less unfavourably than had the commission for Oxford. The 1856 Act for Cambridge was nevertheless modelled closely upon the Act for Oxford. A permanent commission was created; so was the Council of the Senate, to replace the Caput (the old board of college heads). In future no religious subscription would be necessary either for matriculation or for admission to any degree in arts, law, medicine or music; any man holding such a degree, however, might not be a member of the Senate or a candidate for any University office previously held only by an Anglican, even if his degree had hitherto constituted a qualification for that office, unless he should declare himself a *bona fide* member of the Church of England. Gladstone was accommodated.

Section 23 matched section 25 of the Oxford Act; it said that 'any member of the University, of such standing and qualifications as may be provided by any statute hereafter to be made' might obtain a licence from the Vice-Chancellor to open his residence, if within a mile and a half of Great St Mary's church, for the reception of matriculated students. His residence was to be not a 'hall' but a (private) 'hostel', and he himself a 'principal', under the control of specially framed University statutes. But so that young Nonconformists should not be discouraged from applying to his 'hostel' the Act deliberately did not stipulate that he should be a member of the Senate. There was no section in the Cambridge Act corresponding to section 37 of the Oxford Act, since there then existed in Cambridge no 'halls' which might be transferred from college to University control.

In 1862 seventy-four resident Fellows and Tutors at Cambridge started to agitate for the abolition of the religious test for fellowships at Cambridge. This was the agitation that culminated in the University Tests Act of 1871. It worried Gladstone; since undergraduates, Nonconformist or otherwise, were transient, whereas

Fellows and Tutors were usually permanent, would not the advent of Nonconformist Fellows and Tutors signal decisively the secularizing of university education in England?

Although it was apparently Gladstone who had converted Russell to the revival of 'halls' at Oxford, he had been less receptive than Russell to the notion that such a revival might usefully bear upon the aspirations of Nonconformists. His reservation had been in keeping with his wish that the central authority of Parliament should not settle the matter of religious tests. But in a memorandum of 1863 (and also in 1867 – the year after the proposal for the founding of Keble College) he pondered again the matter of 'halls', and wondered what might be conceded to Nonconformists at Oxford to secure their agreement to having no voice in the running of the University or the colleges. He concluded that they might become MAs and also professors (except in divinity), and be 'Heads or Masters' of what he awkwardly referred to as 'Houses or establishments extraneous to the University (?). As 'Heads or Masters' they might 'teach the youth in their fashion', to the end that youth might matriculate and graduate. By way of analogy he invoked the Irish Colleges Act of 1845, an aspect of Peel's policy of conciliation for Catholic Ireland. Peel's Act had created the undenominational Queen's Colleges, out of a desire to extend higher education to the non-Anglicans of Ireland without contaminating the Anglican character of the University of Dublin (Trinity College). Part of the Act had provided for undergraduate boarding houses, under the direction of tutors or masters licensed by the president of the college concerned. Gladstone at the time had supported such provision, but had made it clear that he perceived it as a safeguard for Ireland's Anglicanism, not as an inducement for denominational diversity or religious reductionism. His reasoning in 1863 was therefore subtle, for he might simply have said 'Let us bring section 37 of the 1854 Oxford Act into line with section 23 of the 1856 Cambridge Act, so that a head of "hall" need not be an MA.' But he did not. Whereas Russell was robust, uncomplicated and Liberal, Gladstone was characteristically feline and, by the 1860s, where Anglicanism was concerned, he was thinking almost in terms of quarantine; in the fullness of events it would seem that the idea of the 'hall' had been redesigned by Gladstone from a medieval template, passed on to Russell, decked out pragmatically by Russell with the aspirations of nonconformity, repossessed by Gladstone, filtered by him through the Anglican perspective of Peel, and finally appropriated by high churchmen and Gladstonian Liberals to secure the foundations of the Colleges of Keble and Selwyn as bastions of Anglicanism in a nonconforming and a secularizing age.[3]

The campaign for the abolition of such religious tests as remained after 1856 took wing from 1862, when Edward Pleydell-Bouverie – Liberal Member for Kilmarnock; Trinity Hall, Cambridge – presented to Parliament a petition from the seventy-four resident Fellows and Tutors at Cambridge. In Parliament through the later 1860s the case was pressed. From the early 1860s Nonconformists continuously improved their standing in the Cambridge Mathematical Tripos, yet senior emoluments eluded them. Younger teaching Fellows were very sympathetic. The 'progress of the age' discerned by Gladstone was discerned by others too, in America most notably by Abraham Lincoln and those who listened to him. The American Civil War forged bonds of reformist sympathy between Nonconformist politicians, such as Cobden and Bright, and university liberals morally and professionally embarrassed; by 1870 they were united in legislative aim. In 1868 Mark Pattison, scholarly teacher and Rector of Lincoln College, Oxford, published *Suggestions on Academical Organisation*, controversially demanding a radical expansion of university teaching and research in Oxford, notably for science; the demotion of colleges to the status of halls of residence; and a drastic reduction in the costs of university education. Then came two triumphs for the Liberation Society – the abolition of church rate in England and Wales (1868) and the disestablishment of the Church of Ireland (1869).[4]

In the election campaign of 1868 Liberals clamoured for the abolition of tests. They won the election. Early in 1869 Gladstone allowed Coleridge, the solicitor-general, to introduce a private member's Bill, which publicly he supported. Privately he groaned that it was all worse than odious, and that it vitiated the carefully contrived legislation of 1854 and 1856. He fidgeted about 'secularization'. The Bill was defeated in the Lords. Ten bishops opposed it. Among them was Selwyn, who spoke against the Bill in Convocation and elsewhere. He acknowledged the effect upon himself of the religious life of St John's College, Cambridge, when he had been an undergraduate; he had himself created a religious college in New Zealand; and he believed that at Eton since his day a change for the good had resulted from the more religious tone introduced there.

In 1870 Gladstone was persuaded to change his mind completely, and to make the Bill a government measure. Because he was Gladstone he would brook no opposition from those holding the opinions that he had held formerly. 'Mr. Gladstone', said Morley, 'when once he had adopted a project never loitered'. Mr Gladstone, said a Tory in Parliament, had previously used language against abolition that was more antagonistic, stronger, and more emphatic than any which he himself could use, yet had no difficulty in coming down to the House and declaring that he had altered his mind; would Liberal Members opposite employ an agent to manage their affairs who changed his opinion from day to day? A revised Bill became law on 16 June 1871.

The parliamentary debates of 1870 and 1871 were prolonged, discursive, and anguished, and they exposed the uncertainties of late Victorian faith. There was not the assurance of the mid-1850s. That there was not was significant for Selwyn College; for to some the uncertainties represented a milestone in the progress of Liberalism and good sense: to want to found a 'Selwyn College' in 1878 seemed to them, therefore, perverse and retrograde.

There were two great questions: Where stands religion in contemporary England? And: What were the intentions of ancient benefactors, and how should they be construed in our own day? One question was never asked: Ought we to fashion our university education in regard to the fact that we are an industrial and commercial nation soon to be challenged by other nations in the world economic order?

The great questions emerged as lesser questions. How distant is the day, asks Gladstone, when the Church of England may so lose the allegiance of the people of England that university tests will be even more contentious than they are now? Contrariwise, will the people of England ever consent to divorce religion totally from education? If not, what kind of religion – or what kind of Protestant religion – will they demand? Shall we agree with the Archbishop of York that there are such things as 'the common vital doctrines of Christianity', and that in these alone need university education be grounded? Do the people of England care anyway about universities, and how far are the people of England to be identified with the parents of undergraduates? Tory Lord Salisbury, Chancellor of Oxford University, says that Liberals regard parents as nothing but inconvenient appendages to undergraduates. If Liberals do, are Liberals right? What about the Bishop of Manchester, who thinks that we should welcome Nonconformists, who are thrifty and studious and therefore will improve our universities? How far along the road to toleration of Nonconformists can we go before we reach rationalism, so that universities will be seen as places which carelessly destroy the Christian faith of youths of 18? Shall we exclude heads of houses from our Bill so that Anglican heads of houses may appoint only Anglican Tutors who may do their Anglican duty by youths of 18? May the ungodly be trusted to teach chemistry, logic, geology, and history? Shall we agree with Lord Salisbury that if we abolish the present tests we must have a new one: 'I do solemnly declare that I will not teach anything contrary to the teaching of the divine authority of the Holy Scriptures'? The father of the first Master of Selwyn agreed with Lord Salisbury; he was one of only two Liberal peers who did.

The matter of endowments was sprung from the matter of the people of England. In the Catholic Middle Ages – or during and after the Protestant Reformation, when education was inseparable from religion – did those who endowed esteem the necessities of education above religion, or religion above the necessities of education? And for whom did they endow? Was the nation, in nationalizing the university, simply repossessing its own lost property? Had Parliament in fact from earliest times asserted its absolute right to deal with property held in mortmain? Lord John Manners thought that the university endowments in question belonged to the Church of England rather than to the church belonging to the people of England; what would Liberals think of a Bill which professed that their property was not taken away from them even though everybody else was free to enjoy it?

For the founders of Selwyn College, however, what was said about Keble College in Oxford was immediately significant.

Like Selwyn College, Keble College was facilitated by the debates and the legislation of the 1850s, its status within the University of Oxford being determined by a decree of Convocation of April 1871. John Keble and the Tractarians had welcomed the commission of 1850, but feared that its likely proposals for University reform would encourage liberals to undermine the Church's position in Oxford. So they revived a scheme they had contemplated since the mid-1840s, to create a college of their own which should sustain the Church and educate poor scholars – the original aim of the University of Oxford. Immediately after Keble's funeral in 1866 his friends decided that the College should provide especially for prospective ordinands. Bishop Selwyn agreed; he proposed 'that it is desirable to establish a new College, the aims of which should be to impart a Christian training, encourage industry, and discourage habits of expense'.[6] In 1870 the foundation stone was laid, a royal charter was obtained, and Edward Talbot was appointed Warden at the age of 26. There were rooms for one hundred undergraduates; for the sake of morality they were set in corridors, not upon staircases.

Inevitably questions about Keble College were raised in Parliament during the debates of 1870 and 1871, which coincided precisely with Keble's effective establishment. Was it or was it not the case that Keble would come under the authority of the Act? If it would, then it would not be the 'Keble College' that its founders intended. If it would not, then why not, since it benefited from attachment to a reformed university? And if it would not, then would it be possible down the years to go on founding university colleges upon the Keble pattern? If so, what in principle would be the difference between 'old' colleges affected by the University Tests Act and 'new' colleges not affected? Would it be sensible to insert into the Bill a clause clearly designed to bring such 'new' colleges under the Act? The answer came from Coleridge, on 13 June 1870. After 1870 anyone might found a university college upon a denominational basis, notwithstanding the Bill then proceeding, but he must understand that, upon the principles of future times, a future Parliament might modify the purposes of his endowment. Three weeks later (4 July) Gladstone equivocated:

> Our object is to destroy tests in those institutions which, by their wealth, by their traditions, by their antiquity, by their national privileges, and by the manner in which Parliament had formerly dealt with them, have come into such a position that we are bound in justice to prevent them from being attached to the purposes of any particular denomination or religion. But our desire is to encourage the foundation of colleges, and we will not enquire whether they are to be denominational colleges or not; we claim nothing for them less than absolute freedom.

Parliament was uneasy; it pressed ahead with a College Charter Bill which said that in future any application to the Privy Council for a college or university charter, together with a copy of the proposed charter, must be laid before both Houses of Parliament for a period of not less than thirty days before the Council could contemplate its acceptance or rejection. The Bill became law on 31 July 1871.

When Bishop Selwyn died, the elements of Gladstone's view of a university education were discordant. His quest for a Liberal Britain had persuaded him to promote the abolition of religious tests – in 1854, 1856, and 1871. Along the way he had cultivated an Anglican notion of the 'public hall' at odds with what he had promoted. The notion was consistent with his other quest, for the production of Christian men, university-educated, who would invade the world to effect his 'true public law of Christendom', to complement his Liberal Britain. The founders of Keble College had availed themselves of the notion and, by a hair's breadth, had escaped serious challenge in Parliament. Was Gladstone compromised? In the summer of 1870 he had seemed to say to Parliament that in future a denominational university college might be created and be left in peace as long as it did not cultivate traditions, become too ancient, aspire to national privileges (such as those derived from association with a reformed university?), and acquire wealth which, hitherto (as the debates revealed), men had assumed was a prerequisite of effective scholarship and teaching.

So by 1878 the situation was this: How could you countenance a charter for a 'Selwyn College' to produce George Augustus Selwyns when you had promoted not two but three Acts of Parliament to suggest that you should not, and when your Tractarian friends in Oxford had provoked a College Charter Act which signalled that in future you should have a care what you were about? Here was a problem – for Abraham and Lyttelton, if not for Gladstone.

Notes

1. It is not clear precisely how many such exceptions there were – and would remain, thus to diminish still the desired 'national' character of the universities. In 1870 it was said that at Oxford half the fellowships, numbering at least 130, could be held only by clergymen, and that the corresponding number at Cambridge was thirty (*Parliamentary Debates*, 3rd Series, vol.201, 13 June 1870, c.1968). In February 1871, it was alleged that 'if the bill were to pass in its present shape one-third of the fellowships and three-fourths of the headships at Oxford would be left untouched by its provisions. At Cambridge nearly three-fourths of the headships and the most valuable of the fellowships could only be held by persons in holy orders' (*Parliamentary Debates*, 3rd Series, vol.204, 20 February 1871, c.510).

2. On this point see Owen Chadwick, *The Victorian Church*, part ii, 2nd ed., London, 1972, p.423.

3.   Christopher T. Harvie quotes Gladstone's memorandum in *The Lights of Liberalism: university liberals and the challenge of democracy, 1860–1886*, London, 1982, p.83; T.W. Moody, 'The Irish University Question of the Nineteenth Century', *History*, June 1958.

4.   See Harvie, *op. cit.*, pp.84–96, and (for Pattison) Michael Sanderson, ed., *The Universities in the Nineteenth Century*, London and Boston, 1975, pp.129, 130.

5.   *The Cambridge Review*, 29 October 1879, p.34.

CHAPTER 4

An Experiment of Doubtful Issue: The Foundation of Selwyn College 1878–82

THE FOUNDERS of Selwyn College had a care what they were about. The Charter of incorporation granted by the Queen in Council on 13 September 1882 (see Appendix A) was scrupulously devised so that no one could argue that in some particular it contravened the letter of either the Act of 1856 or that of 1871; for nobody did it prescribe a religious test as then understood. But it sanctioned none the less precisely the kind of institution that majorities in Parliament had seemed to think should not exist.

The sixteen notables who had petitioned for the Charter, together with Arthur Lyttelton whom they had already appointed Master, were constituted a body politic and corporate in law, by name 'The Master and Council of Selwyn College'. The designation 'college' was only a courtesy, implying nothing in respect of the University of Cambridge. But it was very important, since its proclamation on 13 September finally quelled those opponents of the new institution who, throughout the previous summer, had clamoured for another designation – 'Selwyn Hostel'; after all, at the end of the day not even the Senate of the University of Cambridge could gainsay the Queen in Council.

Of the sixteen members of the College Council five were *ex officio*: the Bishop of Ely; the Dean of Lichfield; the Provost of Eton, Charles Goodford, old foe of Oscar Browning; the Regius Professor of Divinity at Cambridge, Brooke Foss Westcott; and his counterpart at Oxford. Amongst the other eleven were Charles Abraham; Edmund Hobhouse; the Earl of Powis, pupil of the young George Selwyn and High Steward of the University of

Cambridge; Joseph Lightfoot, great biblical scholar and, since 1879, Bishop of Durham; and the Revd William Selwyn, son of Bishop George Selwyn.

The Council was to have sole charge of all legal and financial affairs of the College, and of its estate, real and personal. The eleven elected members might continue for life; vacancies in their number were to be filled by co-option. The Master was to be the chairman. His consent, if he were present, was necessary for all acts of the Council except those relating to the appointment or removal of the Master, Vice-Master or members of the Council; clearly, in general, if he should wish to obstruct the desires of the Council he would have to put himself to the trouble of attendance. The Archbishop of Canterbury was to be the College Visitor, with limited discretionary powers concerning the removal of the Master and elected members of the Council. In the case of the illness or absence of the Master the Council might appoint a Vice-Master, with such powers of the Master as might seem expedient.

The Master had always to be a clerk in Holy Orders; thereby the Tests Act was not contested: some might have argued that it was, had he merely had to be an Anglican. Selwyn College thus accommodated the sentiments of those parliamentary Tories who had suggested that, for good Anglican purposes, heads of houses should be excluded from the Act.

The Master was clearly the weightiest member of the Council. Within the College he was indeed a powerful figure, constrained only by a Council which need meet only once a year, and then not necessarily in Cambridge. There were no Fellows of the College. The Master was to have entire charge of the internal and domestic concerns of the College, and entire jurisdiction over all persons within it. The Bursar was to be subordinate to him, though his appointment or removal was vested with the Council. The Council was also formally responsible for the appointment, removal, number, status, powers, and duties of tutors and lecturers; and for the terms of admission for undergraduates – but it was clearly envisaged that its concern with these latter persons would be less than its concern with the Bursar.

The purposes of the College as prescribed by the Charter bore the impress of Gladstone. Those who had met at Lichfield in 1878 had desired Crown protection for a college which, redolent of the character and convictions of Bishop Selwyn, would train young men 'in simple and religious habits according to the principles of the Church of England', whilst making particular provision 'for the education of the sons of clergymen and others to fill posts of missionary work, whether at home or abroad'. What was desired was granted; for good measure the Charter also ordained economical and 'sober living and high culture of the mind'.

On 3 May 1883 Lyttelton put a question to troublesome Oscar Browning: 'Are you quite sure that you are not confusing two very different things, the Charter of Incorporation which we have got, & a Charter of *Incorporation with the University* which we have not got, and did not apply for?' The question was less than honest, for the Charter, by then operative, clearly stated that the College Council should have the sole responsibility 'in obtaining the incorporation of the College with the University of Cambridge'. The aspirations of the founders therefore seemed transparent, not only to Browning but also to a correspondent to *The Times* (12 August 1882), and – very much so – to young Theodore Beck, recently President of the Cambridge Union and later the re-nowned principal of a college on India (*The Cambridge Review*, 8 November 1882); Selwyn's charter, said Beck,

> is not a charter of incorporation with the University, but it greatly facilitates incorporation at a future period ... should a charter of incorporation with the University be demanded, the Crown cannot now say that Selwyn is not a suitable institution to possess a charter ... incorporation with the University is distinctly contemplated in the charter.

The committee of which Abraham was secretary were clearly impressed by the progress of Keble College, and by the financial support it had attracted. An appeal for funds was made accordingly. But there was criticism, from within the community of the Church. To some the scheme seemed too ambitious. Others contemplated the Tractarianism of Keble College and wondered whether it would spread to Selwyn. Some suggested that instead of founding 'Selwyn College' it would be better to attach a hostel for impecunious students to Bishop Selwyn's own college, St John's. The Bishop of Dunedin wanted 'Selwyn College' to be located not in Cambridge but in New Zealand. When it was not he went ahead and himself created a 'Selwyn College' in Dunedin. The Precentor of Lincoln cathedral was notably annoyed. He urged diocesan subdivision and the endowment of Lichfield Theological College, moaning that no sooner was the death of any man of note announced than there was an unseemly rush of *soi-disant* honourers of his name, each eager to be the first to commend his own form of memorial to public patronage, one crying up his church tower, another his reredos, a third his painted window, a fourth his porch, as the one and only proper way of commemorating the departed (*The Times*, 25 April 1878).

Such for the moment were the reservations. Against them, though, stood two of the greatest Christian scholars in Cambridge – Brooke Foss Westcott, Regius Professor of Divinity, and Joseph Barber Lightfoot, then Lady Margaret's Professor of Divinity. Their support was considered by the founders to have been essential to their foundation. Lightfoot, said Abraham, was the 'moral backbone' of the movement; he counselled, he subscribed liberally to College funds, he helped to select the site and to secure its freehold, and he continued to take an active interest even after his departure for Durham in 1879. Another stalwart was Frederick Thatcher, Selwyn's chaplain, who was treasurer of the memorial fund and then of the College.

The response to the appeal was prompt and wide, though in a period of agricultural depression less generous than had been the response to the appeal for Keble College in the more prosperous year of 1868. On 18 July 1878 there was a promotional public meeting at the National Society's headquarters in Westminster. It coincided with the second Lambeth Conference. Tributes were paid to Bishop Selwyn by bishops from England, New Zealand, and the United States. Archbishop Tait of Canterbury urged that the distinguishing feature of the College should be its missionary character. The chairman (Powis) announced that £14,700 had already been promised. Most amounts were relatively small. There were two donations (anonymous) of £1,000 and three of £500 – one from Lightfoot, another from the new Bishop of Lichfield (Maclagan). Large donations came from Abraham, Tait, Lords Salisbury and Powis, and Sybella, Lady Lyttelton (Arthur Lyttelton's step-mother). Gladstone gave £100. In all there were 937 personal donations and 227 collections in churches. At the time of the College's opening Lyttelton revealed that among the gifts were two – one of £1,000, the other of £100 (was it Gladstone's?) – whose donors had stipulated that, after a certain period, they should contribute to the College's training of missionaries (*The Cambridge Review*, 18 October 1882).

On 14 January 1879, Abraham acknowledged a letter from Lyttelton, enclosed in one from Edward Talbot, which had informed him that Lyttelton would agree to be the first Master of Selwyn. Abraham rejoiced. Happiness at Hawarden was crowned; from the diary of Mary (aged 31), Gladstone's daughter:

HAWARDEN, *Sat. 25 Jan.* – Heaps of folk skated, didn't much enjoy it not being up to the mark physically, but the scene was lively enough and the sun shone, lots of children about. Herbert, alas, went off to Oxford at 3. Sunday did morning and afternoon school and church. Miss Bennett's class. Stephy preached. Tea at Cottage. Helen left Monday, a bore. Have enjoyed the unwonted peace of the last days, specially the delicious evenings. Off to Eaton [Duke of Westminster's] with Albert and Mr. Ottley for skating and luncheon. The ice unluckily soft, so it wasn't exciting, though the space was pleasant and the scene bright, it felt so very public ... Enjoyed the drive, it wasn't cold, and ended with M[others'] M[eeting] tea in village. Evensong ... Lucy and F[rederick Cavendish] came and brought the wildly exciting news of Arthur being chosen by Dr. Lightfoot, Westcott and Abraham for HEAD of Selwyn College!! An overwhelming event indeed, bless him; it is not for 2 years, and he will meanwhile fill Mr. Jayne's gap at Keble. May strength and wisdom be his for this great big work ...

HAWARDEN, *Wed. 29 Jan.* – The red-letter day. Happiness over Arthur, enjoyment on the lake with Lucy ...

The following week (7 February), from his curacy in Reading, Lyttelton confided his feelings to Mary:

> ... it is very odd how torpid I feel under all this. I am conscious that I ought to be very much excited or at least anxious, somehow I seem to take it all like pork. The distance of time is partly the cause of this; it is quite impossible that Selwyn should be started under 2 yrs, probably 3, so to me just now Keble is the most engrossing thought. How I shall get on there I can't tell; I feel grossly ignorant, eminently incapable of influencing anyone, especially undergraduates. Meantime it is a real wrench leaving Reading; the work will have all its edges ragged, I don't know who is to pick them up.

On the feast of St Matthias (24 February) he was told that his appointment was confirmed. 'I am now fully & formally Master of Selwyn,' he wrote to Mary (11 March), 'wh: doesn't exist, with £500 a year for 3 years when it does exist. It sounds like great riches to my impecunious ears ...' On 10 March the general committee decided that his title should be 'Master' (rather than 'Warden'). On 19 March Abraham wrote to Gladstone:

> You will have heard that your nephew Mr Arthur Lyttelton has consented to be the first 'Master' of Selwyn College – and has been unanimously elected to the Post. He seems to be a man, for his years, of great judgment as well as energy – and he enters into the idea with courage & hope – yet is wonderfully modest and simpleminded [*sic*] – I look upon it as an earnest of the Divine Blessing to have secured the services of such a man, & such a *name*.

On 10 March the general committee had also modelled a draft constitution upon that of Keble College. Afterwards they turned themselves into a provisional College Council and looked for some land.

Abraham and Lightfoot trudged around Cambridge. They inspected a site at the corner of Lensfield Road, where the Roman

Catholic church now stands, and another beyond Magdalene. They thought them unsuitable. So they ventured into the prairie that was west Cambridge, where cattle roamed, the University Volunteers cavorted, and the Polo Club competed. Here they settled upon the site in Grange Road which, in November, they purchased freehold from the Master and Fellows of Corpus Christi, for £6,111 9s. 7d. Their architect was Arthur Blomfield, son of the Bishop of London who had recommended George Selwyn for New Zealand. A contract was agreed for the erection of the first block of buildings, to accommodate sixty-four under-graduates, together with a temporary hall and chapel and other buildings; the cost would be £18,000.

In the rural west of Cambridge building proceeded discreetly; perhaps no one would notice. But they did. On 29 October 1879, in *The Cambridge Review*, an undergraduate of Trinity, G.W. Johnson, contemplated the prospect of Selwyn College – 'a sister of Keble College, or at least a first cousin ... a strictly sectarian seminary'. It would be contrary to the spirit of all recent university reform, he said, and to the expressed opinion of the age, for it would stipulate that its pupils should learn life separated from the *profanum vulgus*; how could a man's sympathy be widened if he were shut up in a sanctum? Another wag supported him (12 November), writing of 'a deliberate and costly attempt to re-denominationalize the University'. They were harbingers of more criticism from younger members of the University.

Then came affliction, in the shape of Miss Selwyn. In July 1880 Abraham disclosed to Lyttelton the expected bounty of Miss Selwyn, as well as of good sermons:

> ... I suppose I had not told you about our hopes of the £5000 –
> Miss Selwyn (the Bps sister) had promised the Bishop to leave him £5000 for some object as he should approve – We have applied to her to appropriate it to the College, but she had put it rather out of her hands, & left it to William Selwyn her nephew, to devote to some purpose in accordance with his father's mind – She fully believes that the College is the best & most fitting monument of the man – I have got Mrs Selwyn

of Cambridge, & our Mrs Selwyn to bring their influence to bear upon William to give it to the College – Bishop Hobhouse is exerting himself both with Miss Selwyn & William – & we are very hopeful – but that is all as yet – If he agrees to *give* it to the College, then we propose to borrow it at 4 percent to be paid Miss Selwyn for her lifetime. If we get this, I see our way to floating the vessel – Money has been coming in more rapidly of late. I got £35 at S. Mary Magdalene and £100 from a Lady I met after the service at West's house – West will give you an offertory for a sermon next year – I got £12 at Ch. Ch. Albany.

By the beginning of September Sarah Selwyn ('our Mrs Selwyn') had promised a loan of £3,000 at 3 per cent, which loan, Abraham supposed, would become a gift at her death; and Bishop Hobhouse was working upon Miss Selwyn, to secure *her* loan at 4 per cent, and to effect the necessary codicil to her will. (Abraham: 'God be praised! Daylight dawns upon the College'.) A couple of weeks later Miss Selwyn confirmed her sacrifice and recharged their thanksgiving by announcing that her £5,000 would be loaned at 3 nor 4 per cent and that indeed it would become a gift at her death (Abraham: 'I am very thankful to the good God who has put it into the hearts of friends to help us'), even though to raise 3 per cent would involve the buying of an annuity of £150 at an immediate outlay of £1000 from the £5,000.

Alas, as old ladies will, Miss Selwyn changed her mind: she withdrew her promise of the loan and *perhaps* that of the gift eventually — 'without', wailed Abraham, 'giving any reasons & as far as we can judge without having any that she can propound en plein air'. She will not reveal the name of her lawyers; neither her nephew William nor 'Mrs Selwyn of Cambridge' (Professor William Selwyn's widow) can explain it; they are deeply grieved and ashamed; the Master of Trinity (known to fear that Selwyn College will reduce the supply of churchmen to other colleges) is *believed* to be near the bottom of it; what a mercy that £3,000 is on its way from Sarah; pray that Bishop Hobhouse and Mrs Selwyn may make her relent. What chiefly worried Abraham, however, was that the building of the College would be halted and Lyttelton would resign. 'Failing our success in getting the £5000 in a given time, which you might fix,' he told Lyttelton (9 December),

> you ought to be held free to take your own course – I found that your sister Mrs. E. Talbot was very anxious that if you did not go to the College work soon, you should get into some permanent position in London –
>
> I need not say that I contemplate such a step as a grievous blow, but still I see the justice & necessity of it.

But Miss Selwyn relented, before the end of January. She donated £5,000 immediately, in exchange for an annuity, and promised an additional £5,000 at her death. The vessel was floated, Lyttelton stayed. But there had been a great fright; Abraham said they must sign no more contracts without having money to pay.

According to A.J. Brown, the College's first historian, the proposal for 'Selwyn College' which the committee in Lichfield produced originated in the minds of Bishop Selwyn's three closest friends – Abraham, Hobhouse, and Sir William Martin, former Chief Justice of New Zealand. Of these, however, the Liberal Abraham was, as we have seen, undoubtedly the instigator. With its revealing reference to the (Anglican) *gentry*, the account of their desire which Abraham gave in the Selwyn College *Calendar* of 1894 was thoroughly consonant with the complex views of Gladstone as they had emerged by 1871. 'His friends knew', said Abraham,

> how deeply seated was the late Bishop's interest in the professional classes with limited means. He always wished to see their sons admitted to the advantages of a University education, with a simpler mode of living than prevailed generally, and with a more thorough exhibition of Church principles. Moreover, he felt that modern legislation had tended to deprive the poorer members of the gentry of the endowments which were more especially intended for their benefit.

In April 1881, against a background of continuing public concern with university education, an article in the *Church Quarterly*

Review, an organ of the high church party, gave Abraham a fillip, after the affair with Miss Selwyn; it enabled him to sharpen his views as to what had necessitated a 'Selwyn College' in Cambridge. His views thus sharpened in 1881 were a great deal less emollient than his views recollected in 1894.

The article was entitled 'Recent Fortunes of the Church in Oxford'. Its author was H.P. Liddon (1829–90), Dean Ireland's Professor of Exegesis of Holy Scripture at Oxford and the chief standard-bearer of the Oxford Movement after the death of Pusey (1882). Pusey had wanted Liddon to be the first Warden of Keble College; only when he firmly declined was Talbot appointed. He remained, though, a notable supporter of the College as a member of its Council. He was intensely conservative, but he was regarded as a Liberal, not least because he voiced as eloquently as Gladstone himself Gladstone's view of the wickedness of Turkey and what should be done about it. 'Between Russia or England, taken at their worst, and Turkey, the difference is enormous', he said:

> It is the difference which Christianity alone can make. Christianity always carries with it the germs of progressive improvement; whereas Mahomedanism condemns the races which it curses to stagnate in evil ... Russia contains the true secret of improvement, and her advance in Central Asia has been as great a blessing to humanity as our own in India. Each has limited the area of triumphant brutality.

Liberal education policy, however, Liddon regarded as instinctively heathen. Gladstone, though a prophet, was a statesman 'under the strongest temptations to make Church interests give way to the exigencies of politics, and with a fatal power of inventing theories on the spur of the moment, in order to justify these surrenders'. Liddon's view of Gladstone's Liberal following was akin to Queen Victoria's; his 'real misfortune' was that he had had 'a menagerie instead of a Cabinet – herein resembling the assortment of Chaplains at Lambeth'. In the moral world no good ever came of such mixtures.[1]

Liddon's article dealt only with Oxford, which he knew. Oxford, he said, had been passionately religious until 1854, when the

Oxford University Act had dissolved – almost, if not entirely – a union between University and Church which had existed for a thousand years. The Tractarian Movement of John Keble and others had been the day of grace for the Church in Oxford, 'Jerusalem's time of visitation'; it had reinvigorated Oxford society and Oxford's scholarship; it could have redeemed such sloth as Parliament thought it had discerned in the early 1850s. One of its ornaments had been the young Gladstone. But, energetically, the heads of houses had rendered the Tractarian position untenable; they had surrendered to the hostility of Lord John Russell, whose own education owed nothing to Oxford or Cambridge. Russell disliked an intellectual world in which he had had no share; and his attitude to the Church – a mixture of fear and contempt – was typical of the Whig temper. The fruits of his dislike, his fear, and his contempt were an academic revolution embracing the legislation of 1854 and 1871. Gladstone, in 1871, had had to yield to importunity; the stand in Parliament of Lords Salisbury and Lyttelton had shown what was being lost; the contributions of the Archbishop of York and the Bishop of Manchester had been liberal–radical and therefore reprehensible. The Nonconformists admitted to Oxford in 1854 and 1871 were merely the catspaws of the liberal–radicals of London and Oxford. The result was a new type of young Oxford don – a weathercock, turning with every wind of new teaching and apt to mistake intellectual bumptiousness for intellectual strength. Liddon commended the achievements of Keble College and especially those of the young Talbot, hinting at a link between colleges such as Keble, heads of houses such as Talbot, and missionary enterprise.

In utterance generally Liddon made plain a purpose for Selwyn College. In his article he exonerated Gladstone. 'If, as I suppose is the case,' wrote Abraham to Lyttelton (13 May),

> the picture he draws of the effect of the late legislation is applicable to Cambridge, we are not a moment too soon in applying the remedy – Cambridge is not so cynically hostile to Church & Religion – but it may soon become so – at all events it is indifferent on a subject that admits of no such frame of mind ... I think Liddon's article will open people's eyes.

At the time of Liddon's article Lyttelton and the provisional Council began to press the University for recognition upon whatever terms they could obtain. They addressed a circular to the Senate, in which they confidently proclaimed what sort of college they would have. They announced that a site had been purchased; that the foundation stone would be laid on 1 June; and that about £30,000 had already been subscribed, sufficient to pay for the site and to provide accommodation for sixty undergraduates.

They threw down the gauntlet. Most of the circular comprised a statement by Lyttelton advertising the 'two distinctive features' of the College, which would be that 'it should be founded upon the broad but definite basis of the Church of England, neither less nor more', and that 'its aims should be to encourage habits of simple living, and to develop the Christian character in the students'.

In respect of the first, Lyttelton revealed that the founders of Selwyn believed that the Tests Act hindered the older colleges from giving a definite Christian character to their teaching. Selwyn College would not be hindered. It would not impose religious tests, but it would admit 'only members of the Church of England willing to conform to the rules of attendance at Divine Service, etc., which will be enforced upon the whole College'; the words were chosen carefully – at this stage the founders were not willing to proclaim categorically that they would not admit Nonconformists. Tutors, said Lyttelton, need not necessarily be clergymen, but they would have to be loyal Anglicans, so as to guarantee the religious character of their teaching.

Though there was no requirement that Selwyn undergraduates must be prospective ordinands, it was spelled out abundantly that special provision would be made for 'training Missionaries for the work of preaching the Gospel in heathen lands'. Missionaries need not be clergymen; they might be simply 'men of complete education, men of cultivated minds, men of practical ability, men skilled in managing others, in a word men such as an English public school and University are specially fitted to produce'. Selwyn College would produce them. *How* we would produce them – whether by providing missionary scholarships, or special instruction in languages, or ethnology, or sustaining an interest in missionary work by some organized system of reports and visits from missionaries themselves – we should see. But we would produce them, in memory of Bishop Selwyn.

Then Lyttelton addressed simple living and the Christian character. We wished, he said, to combine the advantages of college society and discipline with inexpensive living, so that men of slender means might afford them. Keble College was doing so. We would be at least as economical as Keble: all our meals would be in common; fees would be as low as possible; all necessities would be provided by the College at low prices; and all extravagances in furniture, wine, and other amenities would as far as possible be checked completely. We desired to dispense with the time-honoured need for undergraduates to employ private tutors at their own expense, for we wished to maintain a 'real and living tutorial system', to nurture productive relationships between tutors and undergraduates. We hoped nevertheless to limit the total annual College charge to £80 (in a situation where, though Lyttelton did not say so, some of the 'old' colleges were apparently making a total annual charge of as much as £150).[2]

Finally the circular appealed for subscriptions from Cambridge. A committee of nineteen University personages was formed, to promote the College. It included the Masters of St John's, Clare and Christ's; the Provost and a future Vice-Provost of King's; the Regius Professor of Physic; Westcott; and Fenton Hort, Hulsean Professor of Divinity, with Westcott and Lightfoot one of the great trio of Christian scholars of late Victorian Cambridge. Then as now, however, men were wont more to support their own colleges than to support wider University ventures. The committee was not very successful; such supporters as the College attracted from within the University were famous rather than numerous.

Wednesday, 1 June 1881, was fixed for laying the foundation stone. Bishop Hobhouse sent out what Abraham called 'postcard tickets of invitation' (Lyttelton to Mary Gladstone: 'dowdy little invitation cards'). One was sent to Gladstone. Along with other members of his family, and to the exasperation of Lyttelton, he forgot to reply. Abraham sent him another – wishfully: 'O si!' Still he did not come, though a son and daughter-in-law did.

The day was sunny and brilliant. A distinguished company took luncheon in the hall of King's College, as guests of Selwyn's provisional Council. Afterwards they processed through the Backs to the Selwyn site, where part of the west front was already built. The Church was represented by thirteen bishops; the State by members of both Houses of Parliament; the University by the Vice-Chancellor – Perowne of Corpus Christi, who had sold the land – and by six other heads of houses, and ten professors; the University of Oxford by two heads of houses, one of them Edward Talbot. The wider company included Selwyns and Lytteltons, and the American Minister as a representative of the University of Harvard. A service was conducted by the Bishop of Ely, the singing led by choirboys from King's. On the north side of the main gateway Lord Powis laid the stone, offering up a prayer in Latin composed by Abraham but checked by Lyttelton for compositional accuracy. In English he called his old friend and tutor the 'spiritual argonaut of the southern hemisphere'. Other speeches came from Lightfoot, the Vice-Chancellor, the Bishops of Lincoln and Carlisle, and the American Minister, who on the eve of his departure for Cambridge had been advised by some one that by associating himself with the foundation of Selwyn he was taking part in a conspiracy to defeat the Tests Acts.

On 4 June support for Selwyn came from the *Spectator*, which took the Liberal line of Lyttelton in arguing that the very existence of the denominational colleges of Keble and Selwyn was proof of how genuinely national the Universities of Oxford and Cambridge had otherwise become in the years since the passing of the Tests Act. More original, though, was an article in *The Cambridge Review* of 8 June, by G.H. Rendall, Fellow of Trinity and Principal-designate of the University College of Liverpool, recently founded (1881) with the support of Liverpool merchants. Ignoring the Lent term circular, Rendall noted that the promoters of Selwyn had contrived their scheme outside the University: 'The scheme was devised from without; the needful funds were contributed from without; and such development and definiteness as has been already attained is due entirely to extraneous deliberation.' This was good – 'a university is not the body to make experiments of doubtful issue'. Rendall warned, however, that whilst economy was a very fine thing, institutions such as Selwyn College – and the newly created Cavendish College – could not dodge indefinitely their share of proctorial and examining duties, and of University financial dues, by not accepting a Charter of incorporation within the University. He asked whether such 'collegiate' institutions alone were to plant themselves about the University, claiming equal shares in the advantages of libraries, laboratories, professors and readers, at the expense of the older colleges, which meanwhile they were starving of their natural supply of students. But Rendall supported the Anglicanism of Selwyn College – on Darwinist grounds:

> The true liberal who anticipates progress as the result not of monotonous uniformity, but of free diversity subjected continually to the sure test of natural selection and the safe law of the survival of the fittest, will be glad to see the advocates of the denominational principle evincing the courage and the liberality to put their principles to the test of open competition.

In the early 1880s Cavendish College, to which Rendall referred, attracted hardly less notice than Selwyn, with which it was often compared, to the disadvantage of the latter. Opened in 1877 in Panton Street, in 1882 it removed to buildings which subsequently became the nucleus of Homerton College. Its proprietor was the Revd Joseph Lloyd Brereton, MA of Oxford, who inspired continually (so he said) by the text 'How shall we sing the Lord's song in a strange land?' (Psalm 137, v.4), desired to remove some of what he called 'the "estrangement" between the Gospel and the Land' – 'the Land' representing a constituency indifferent to his desire, namely the middle classes of such rural areas as the distant heathlands of north Norfolk where he had been born and bred. At Rugby he had been a pupil of Thomas Arnold, whose disciple he remained. But he was an educational buccaneer, lurching fecklessly from enterprise to enterprise, founding boys' schools and girls' schools, desiring county colleges for those unable to obtain a full university education, and incurring enormous debts. His incompetence contrasted starkly with the sound financial husbandry and acumen of Abraham in respect of Selwyn College.

Cavendish College was Brereton's grandest venture, named after Lucy Cavendish's father-in-law, the seventh Duke of Devonshire, who was the largest shareholder. Brereton ran his establishment as a licensed lodging-house for non-collegiate students, often admitted at the age of 16. Though the president of its trustees was Chancellor of the University (Devonshire) and it was given improved status in 1882, it lacked the inspirational élan of a name such as Selwyn and attracted inadequate support. Its specially commissioned narrow beds may have served morality as morality was served by corridors in Keble College, it was shortage of money that ordained them and the narrow rooms (cold, austere) into which they were designed to fit. Having matriculated 358 students it closed, bankrupt, in 1892. The story of Ayerst Hall, founded in 1884, was equally short and sad.[3]

During the remainder of 1881 the affairs of Selwyn proceeded mostly unnoticed. Then came mischief.

On Septuagesima Sunday, 5 February 1882, the Revd E.W. Blore, Vice-Master of Trinity and greatly respected in Cambridge, preached a sermon before the University in the shape, mostly, of undergraduates. His text as published was thus: 'I pray not that thou shouldest keep them from the evil: or (Revised Version) from the Evil one' (John 17, v.15). A.L. Brown called the sermon 'the first official expression of disapproval' of Selwyn College – reasonably so; it was, after all, preached from the University pulpit, in Great St Mary's church.[4]

The Revised Standard Version of the Bible had been published in 1881. Prominent among its authors were Lightfoot, Westcott, and Hort. The object of Blore's sermon was twofold: to display Blore's theological mettle as to whether or not evil, for a Christian, should be personified, and – in so doing – to provide theological ballast for a demonstration that by and large Selwyn College had better not be founded. The sermon as a whole comprised 60 per

cent ballast and 40 per cent demonstration, so to persuade im-
pressionable undergraduates that up-to-date Christian scholarship
as represented by Lightfoot and his colleagues favoured the construction of the Tests Act offered by such men as Oscar Browning
rather than that offered by Lightfoot and his colleagues.

The Authorized Version said 'the evil'; the Revised Version
'the Evil one'. Which was more accurate? Would parents reject
the Revised Version because it jarred with the Lord's Prayer
that they taught their children? Did opting for 'the Evil one'
narrow one's perception of the scope of evil? Should a writer
in the *Nineteenth Century* be allowed to depersonify Satan the
better (it seemed) to depersonify the Holy Ghost? Was Lightfoot wrong to prefer 'the Evil one' for the Revised Standard
Version? Blore thought 'no' was the answer to all these questions but took an impressively long time to say so. Eventually
he concluded that 'the evil' and 'the Evil one' were identical,
that Christ enjoined us to be in the world but not of it, and
that to abide in the flesh was as needful for us as for the Philippians
(Philippians 1, v.23), since temptation unconfronted was temptation unresisted.

Which brought him to Selwyn College; to which, he said, he
was not hostile, for he hoped that it would improve the general
tone of the University. But one could not escape the operations
of the Tempter by retreating into the calm of monastic isolation.
Though indeed one might hope that Selwyn College would frus-
trate the designs of 'the Evil one', yet still one might feel that
frustration was best had by churchmen and dissenters consorting
in undenominational colleges, especially in these days of infidelity.
Idleness was the mother of evil; our reformed University was
admirably suited to its prevention without Selwyn colleges. His
conclusion was pointed: 'I have written unto you, ye young men,
because ye are strong, and the word of God abideth in you, and
ye have overcome the Evil one' (I John 1, v.14). Young men
listening to him perhaps concluded that 'the Evil one' was Selwyn
College rather than a world from which Selwyn College invited
isolation.

Through the spring of 1882 the Selwyn controversy rumbled through the columns of *The Cambridge Review*. Would Cambridge become a Babel of the sects, with a Manning College for Roman Catholics and a Spurgeon College for Nonconformists? Would Selwyn really offer an improved tutorial system? Would it really be frugal? What a pity parents themselves had never demanded frugal colleges instead of agreeing with Samuel Butler that Adam was to blame for the costliness of higher education:

> That Adam, with the loss of Paradise,
> Bought knowledge at too desperate a price,
> And ever since that memorable fate
> Learning did never cost an easier rate.

But meanwhile the Selwyn Council was thinking urgently about the College's status within the University, for undergraduates were to arrive in the Michaelmas term. At least for a while it had better not openly aspire to be a University college, since in practice it imposed religious tests even though its foundation ceremony had been but ten years distant from weighty legislation opposing them. The only dignified alternative available was to be a 'private hostel', under section 23 of the Act of 1856; but even that would, constitutionally, place the Master of Selwyn uncomfortably close to poor Brereton trying to turn a penny at the other end of Hills Road, on the wrong side of the railway tracks. Upon such terms the College would be almost a personal fief of Lyttelton, upon whose departure the University might, if it chose, withdraw recognition.

With a view to solving when appropriate the problem occasioned by such institutions as Cavendish and Selwyn, the Council of the Senate produced a unanimous report dated 27 March 1882 which, without naming Cavendish or Selwyn, recommended that such institutions should be considered for a new status, intermediate between that of the 'old' colleges and that of the 'private hostels'. The new designation should be 'public hostel'; to avoid legal and other difficulties a 'public hostel' should never be called a 'college'. The principal of a 'public hostel' must be resident within his 'hostel', and a member of the Senate. The 'public hostel' would be self-governing, and its officers and under-graduates would have the same University privileges as those of other colleges, with some exceptions later made much of by Oscar Browning. On behalf of its members it would pay to the University fees on the same scale as that for other colleges. To be continuously recognized a 'public hostel' must satisfy the University as to its likely permanence and sound government, and the suitability of its buildings.

On 4 May the report was debated in the Arts School, as such reports were customarily debated, at a meeting convened for such members of the Senate as might choose to attend. The fissures in Cambridge Liberalism emerged. Some (including Browning) thought that a 'public hostel' ought never to be called a 'college'; others that Selwyn College would provide a foothold for clericalism. A young Fellow of Trinity spoke of the first flourish of militant clericalism, which would grow into a large blast unless it were promptly stopped. But another, the Revd Coutts Trotter, 'the archetypal university reformer' famous in 1877 for wanting to abolish heads of houses to save money, said that only the appearance of a party of militant anti-clericalism could produce a foothold for clericalism. Three signatories of the unanimous report said that they disliked 'sectarian' institutions.[5]

Support for Selwyn 'College' came from a third Fellow of Trinity, the Revd Vincent Stanton, a member of Selwyn's Council. Stanton did not inform the meeting that on 28 March the Council had submitted to the Privy Council a draft Charter, which had in fact existed since the previous year, and had petitioned for incorporation; and that the draft had come before the Privy Council on 3 May, to be referred to a committee. But then very likely Stanton did not know. For in the College Archive is a printed memorandum, undated but composed at the end of June 1882, subscribed by Arthur Lyttelton and headed 'Private and Confidential For members of Council only SELWYN COLLEGE'. Lyttelton 'informed' (his word) the Council of what he assumed they did not know: namely that a draft Charter had already been submitted to the Privy Council; that 'We have reason to believe that our application will be favourably received'; and that after

acceptance by the Privy Council the Charter must lie on the table
in both Houses of Parliament for thirty days, so that objections
to it might be possible in accordance with the College Charter
Act of 1871. He forbore to add that 'favourable reception' would
probably owe much to William Ford, the College's shrewd Privy
Council agent. Ford to Lyttelton, Gray's Inn, 3 March 1882 (and
again in substance, 23 May 1882):

> ... The interposition of any Minister or ex: Minister would be
> very potential – would it be possible to enlist the sympathies
> of the Prime Minster? He and the Bishop were contemporaries
> at Eton and Mr. Gladstone probably entertains a hearty respect,
> approaching veneration, for Bishop Selwyn. A word from him
> to the Lord President, Earl Spencer [a relative of Lyttelton],
> would make the Charter go through like a shot.

The College was therefore not being frank with the University.
Whilst the University was clearing the way for Selwyn's acceptance
as a 'public hostel', the College, as secretly as circumstances
allowed, was applying for a Charter the wording of which implied
that in the not too distant future Selwyn College should be a full
college of the University.

At the meeting of 4 May the leading opponent of the College
was Oscar Browning, nuisance extraordinary, but very much a
friend of the College in later years – in an odd kind of way almost
an honorary member of the College community, indeed.

Born in 1837, Browning puzzled his contemporaries. He was
full of contradictions and injudiciousness. He became a Fellow
of King's, Cambridge, in 1859. From 1862 to 1875 he was a
housemaster at Eton, loved by boys and respected by parents.
But he was awkward, snobbish, assertive and self-justifying. He
picked quarrels easily and pursued them unsparingly. In 1875, to
the horror of many but the relief of some, he was dismissed from
Eton by Eton's headmaster, undoubtedly on suspicion of spooning
with a pupil, George Nathaniel Curzon. Dr Goodford, the Provost, would not support him; he had quarrelled with Goodford
over the cost of the choir and the chapel organ. Years later, when

Goodford was ill, Browning proffered to Gladstone his advice on the qualities to be looked for when appointing Provosts of Eton. Gladstone enquired after Goodford's health, found it improved, and snubbed Browning. But vanity triumphed; in 1919 Browning solicited a KBE through the same George Nathaniel, now Earl Curzon of Kedleston, but rejoiced to receive only an OBE.[6]

Browning landed upon King's College in September 1866, to resume his active Fellowship. King's was small; its Fellows welcomed him with champagne but wondered how they would cope. He gave outré parties, courted royalty, was indiscreet with chapel choirboys, supported the numerous clubs and societies of undergraduates, corresponded with George Eliot and (later) Oscar Wilde, and rode a hayfork Meteor tricycle. He became the best-known 'character' in Cambridge. His tutorial diligence and inspiration made King's the 'history college' of Cambridge; he claimed he had invented the traditional Cambridge history 'supervision', at which an undergraduate would read aloud his essay to be discussed. He thought he should be Regius Professor. But the books he wrote were popular and unprofessorial, sometimes containing awful mistakes. The University thought he should be no kind of professor and refused him the degree of LittD when he applied. When old he claimed regularly to have attended parties at 10 Downing Street when Gladstone was there. Over the years he corresponded with four of Lord Lyttelton's eight sons (including Arthur), and was a guest at Hagley Hall. In 1886, 1892, and 1895 he was a Liberal parliamentary candidate, supporting Home Rule. He felt that the experience of parliamentary candidature helped him to be a better political historian and history teacher. Few were impressed. Many were relieved when he left Cambridge in 1909.

Yet he was a worthy opponent of Abraham and Lyttelton. He was alert to the improved academic standards characterizing Cambridge in the 1870s. He believed in kindness to young people and in their aesthetic development, and he deplored the glorification of athleticism and team-spirit, the legacy of Thomas Arnold. He corresponded with Selwyn undergraduates, and kept their letters. He lectured and published upon the theory and practice of education, and upon classroom teaching. His lasting achievement was begun early in 1878 – at around the time of Bishop Selwyn's death – when he began to create the Cambridge Teachers' Training Syndicate. In the early 1890s the syndicate became the Cambridge University Day Training College. Browning was its first and inspired principal. The College trained young men to be teachers for secondary schools (a rather novel practice), simultaneously enabling them to obtain Cambridge BA degrees. One of its earliest students was the young L.A. Borradaile, future Fellow of Selwyn, for whom Browning wrote references and testimonials. Later the College became the Cambridge University Department of Education.

The credentials of Oscar Browning for contesting the desirability of a denominational 'Selwyn College' were therefore substantial. His belief that university education should be extended to those hitherto unable to afford it was honourable and unqualified and akin to Lord John Russell's. Yet his touch could be unsure. In May 1883, for example, precisely when he was at loggerheads with Lyttelton over Liberalism and higher education, it was somehow typical of him that he should have been corresponding with Mark Pattison – renowned advocate of university reform, whose views coincided so nearly with his own – not as to the rights and wrongs of Selwyn College, but as to whether or not the poet Milton, in 1644, was an exponent of educational reform.[7]

Browning was Senior Proctor for the academic year 1881–2. On 4 May he declared war on the proposals for 'public hostels'. He scorned Cavendish College; proclaimed that if Selwyn craved frugality it should admit Nonconformists, who were more industrious, thrifty, and moral than anybody else; and asked why – if 'public hostels' should not have to provide vice-chancellors, proctors, university examiners, or professorial fellowships – an 'old' college, liable for such provisions, would not be wise to wind up its affairs and start again as a 'public hostel'. He posed as the truest friend of the Tests Act. Much more would be heard from him.

Some days later eight leading members of the Senate, with preacher Blore at their head, memorialized the Council of the

Senate. They suggested five amendments to the report of 27 March. The first endorsed the stipulations of the Council of the Senate that a 'public hostel' should not be called a 'college'. The next three requested some refinement of the conditions of recognition and of the withdrawal of recognition of 'public hostels', and the scale of fees to be paid by their members. The fifth required that no institution which imposed any religious test should be recognized as a 'public hostel'.

The result was that on 22 May the Council of the Senate produced an amended report which toughened what had previously been said about 'public hostels' not calling themselves 'colleges' ('The word Hostel shall be used with reference to the new institutions and to members thereof in all official documents of the University in which the word "College" would be used with reference to the existing Colleges and the Members thereof'), and furnished the next three refinements which the memorialists had required. On the fifth requirement, however, the Council held firm: nothing was said about religious tests. When on 1 June the amended report came to the full Senate the chief matter of debate was not one directly addressed in the report; it was, namely, whether 'Selwyn College', confined to Anglicans, should be recognized. Notice of *non placet* was given by two MAs – one being Henry Jackson, eminent classicist and University reformer, and as Vice-Master of Trinity in 1916 the most fervent opponent of Bertrand Russell when he was dismissed from his Trinity lectureship. Jackson and his associate, F.M. Balfour (distinguished animal morphologist), argued that the existing provision for 'hostels', deriving from section 23 (1856), was sufficient provision for Cavendish and Selwyn Colleges.

They were opposed by Liberals of another hue. One was Coutts Trotter. The other was Henry Sidgwick (1838–1900), Fellow of Trinity, philosopher, founder of Newnham College, and eponym of an avenue. The support of Sidgwick for the Selwyn venture was notably honourable and, a century on, perhaps the most interesting, for his intellect encompassed the conflicting aspects of the great debate of 1870–1. As a youth he had come up to Trinity intending ordination. But he lost his faith and became a

'scientific' rationalist. Then he discovered that rationalism pointed
to selfishness, since it was not always rational to do one's duty.
But duty was important. He concluded that the duty in which he
believed was contingent upon religion and an after-life, and thus
that the Christianity in which he did not believe was necessary
to the moral government of the world in which he lived. Nevertheless
in 1869 he resigned his Trinity fellowship because it obliged him
to accept the 'dogmatic obligations' of the Apostles' Creed. Thereafter he campaigned energetically for University reform. After it
had come he and Coutts Trotter supported the foundation of
Selwyn College because they believed there would be few
denominational colleges in Cambridge; those which might appear
would yield to Cambridge Liberalism, upon which the stigma of
intolerance must not now be allowed to alight.[8]

The Senate adopted the amended report of its Council by 150
votes to 63, thus virtually conceding University recognition of
Selwyn College. Meanwhile in the Union Society opponents of
Selwyn's foundation were defeated by a slender majority, and
opponents of 'Selwyn College' rather than 'Selwyn Hostel' by a
majority which was larger.

This was pleasing. Nevertheless Selwyn was embarrassed: the
Privy Council was undoubtedly on the way to accepting at least
the draft Charter, which would say that Selwyn was a 'college',
but the Senate of the University had merely paved the way for
University recognition of sorts; as yet it had accorded recognition
to nothing at all.

Meanwhile the College had accepted for October as many
students as it could accommodate, having long since been recruit-
ing. In February Abraham had told Lyttelton that he had adver-
tised in the *Liverpool Courier*, the *Manchester Guardian* and the
Birmingham Post, and recommended they should also go for the
Record (the paper of the Evangelical party), the *Church Times* and
the *Morning Post*. Comicality attached to what appeared in *The
Cambridge Review*, which circulated widely among country clergy.
In the *Supplement* of 8 February 1882, with all the aplomb of a
genteel preparatory school, the College's notice was on the
advertisements page, next to Blore's published admonitions about

'the Evil one' and sandwiched between a notice of the Lent term lectures at Ridley Hall and an advertisement for the Social Purity League, Duppa's Hill, Croydon ('OBJECT. – To bind together workers in the great cause of Social Purity'):

SELWYN COLLEGE, Cambridge. *Master:–* The Rev. the Hon. A.T. LYTTELTON, M.A., Trinity College; Senior in Moral Sciences Tripos, 1873; at present Tutor and Lecturer of Keble College, Oxford. *Bursar:–* Lieut.-Col. H.C. WATSON, late of the Army Pay Department. *Tutor:–* The Rev. G.H. SING, B.A., Fellow and Classical Lecturer of Corpus Christi College; late Scholar of Christ's College, 4th classic, 1879. *Lecturer in Mathematics:–* The Rev. J.T. WARD, M.A., Fellow and late Scholar of St. John's College; Senior Wrangler and 1st. Smith's Prizeman, 1876 ... The College will open in OCTOBER ... to all members of the Church of England ... for particulars ... application should be made as soon as possible to the master ...

The prospect for the Michaelmas term was therefore rather glum. The substance of the second section of Lyttelton's undated memorandum, in preparation for a Selwyn Council meeting on 6 July, was thus:

Under the Senate grace of 1 June an institution desiring to be a 'public hostel' must be proposed to the Senate by the Council of the Senate and accepted by a special grace, of which notice must be given by the Council in the preceding term (in our case the Lent term, 1882, at the latest). We had therefore to hurry; there had been no time to consult the Council of Selwyn College. He had hurried, and given fullest information to a committee appointed by the Council of the Senate to consider Selwyn's application. The committee was favourable, but on 22 June the Council had refused notice of a grace for our recognition because, they said, we had not 'notified the constitution' to them. But as our charter had not yet been granted we could not do so, except provisionally; he had, though, informed the committee that the charter would be settled before the beginning of the Michaelmas term. Thus under the circumstances there could be no recognition of the College as a 'public hostel' until the Lent term, 1883.

What, then, was implied? First, that in the summer of 1882 the urgent process of settling the status of Selwyn College was a lone enterprise. Abraham, Lyttelton's effective 'principal', lived in Lichfield; there were no telephones. Everyone trusted the young Master-designate to go ahead. Second, that even if 'fullest information' *did* signify that Lyttelton had told the committee that an application to the Privy Council had long since been made, it probably did *not* signify that he had told them of the precise contents of the draft Charter, since, had he done so, before dispersing for the summer the opponents of the College might have waited for its tabling in Parliament under the thirty-day rule (which could not occur till 30 June), and then, having seen what was proposed, might have increased their hullabaloo and engaged heaven knows what parliamentary sympathy, particularly concerning the phrase 'in the obtaining the incorporation of the College with the University of Cambridge'.

Lyttelton was crafty – a match for the wily politicos of Cambridge, if not quite for Gladstone, his grandmother, and the Queen. To Lord Powis, 3 July 1882: 'I write to tell you that the charter is laid on the table of both Houses of Parliament. I fancy it is pretty safe now, but still an address may be moved in either House against it, and it is well to put our friends on their guard.' To Mary Gladstone, 3 August 1882: 'Selwyn is getting on only there are any amount of little fusses & things to settle. I am delighted at the Charter having got through the House safely, & very grateful to Uncle W. for giving it a shove. Is he greatly cumbered with Egypt?' More forthrightly to Browning, 23 May 1883, but concerning the events of the previous summer: 'You would not expect us to make a "whip" for our opponents in the natn. at large ... don't blame us for not doing your work.'

Thus, revealed the memorandum, there was a problem as the Michaelmas term approached. The College could postpone its opening for a year – inadvisable on every ground. It could open as a 'private hostel' under section 23 – probably the best course; but the University required that the head of such a hostel should have resided in Cambridge for three terms previous to the opening; this Lyttleton had not done, since he had been completing his apprenticeship at Keble. Or it could open as a licensed lodging-house, as Cavendish had done (Abraham had contemplated this, on 23 June); it should hope, therefore, that during the vacation the Non-collegiate Students Board would agree. The College Council agreed. So, later, did the Board. Selwyn undergraduates were able to matriculate when they arrived in October.

On 7 August there appeared in *The Times* a letter from Cambridge, signed 'S.P.' 'S.P.', so Abraham was assured by his spies in King's, was Oscar Browning – 'Senior Proctor'. The Charter, it seemed, had been sprung upon Cambridge. Nothing had been said of it in the Lent term: the draft had not appeared in Parliament till 30 June, after Cambridge men had departed for the vacation. In respect of permanence and efficiency had the Privy Council sufficiently investigated Selwyn, a pale reflection of the affluent Keble, and too like 'a similar institution at Cambridge', which was making a loss? *Alma mater* had been presented with 'an unwelcome little stranger, truly a weak and puny bantling, in absolute unconsciousness of her approaching deliverance'. The Warden of the 'similar institution', John Cox, protested (laundry and other bills included in fixed charges at Cavendish, not so at Selwyn, etc.); Lyttelton retorted (Council of Senate informed of application at earliest possible date – 20 June, Selwyn about to open with full house, no debts, and in much the same condition as Keble when opened); leading articles appeared in *The Times* (commending frugality) and other London newspapers. Abraham was jubilant. To Lyttelton, 13 August: 'What a godsend that letter of S.P. in the Times was! It had cost us Six Guineas to get an advertisement in the Times – & now we got all that Ventilation for nothing.'

The rest of the summer was peaceful; indeed it was munificent, for some inspired arm-twisting by Abraham produced a gift, from a certain Edward Wheatley-Balme.

Wheatley-Balme ('my good card', as Abraham called him) was a Cambridge graduate, wealthy land-owner and Deputy Lieutenant of Westmorland; probably he knew little if anything about the proposal for 'Selwyn College'. But he had had a friend, Edward Rose, Rector of Weybridge, who had also been a friend of Abraham and Bishop Selwyn, and whose friendship with himself had been discovered by Abraham on Rugby railway station. That was sufficient. Dead friends must have memorials; in the case of Rose, Abraham suggested, to the tune of £1,000. The £3,000 that Wheatley-Balme donated is commemorated by an inscription over the entrance to staircase B – the entrance to 'Rose Building', as Abraham would call it.

Undergraduates arrived in October. At first they came in response to the advertisements. Soon they came with the blessing of Oscar Browning, who was cheerily able to accept the College when once it was established.

Notes

1. E.S. Talbot, 'Some Recollections', in *Henry Liddon ... a centenary memoir*, London, 1929; G.W.E. Russell, *Dr Liddon*, London, 1905, pp.161-5.

2. *The Cambridge Review*, 5 February 1882, p.163.

3. For the recognition of Cavendish as a 'public hostel', see below (pp.70, 75-6). Ayerst Hall was founded in 1884 by the Revd William Ayerst, who was also its Principal. Its primary purpose was to serve theological students who could not afford college fees, but others were invited to apply with the assurance that they would enjoy all the privileges and the status of collegiate students. It did not prosper and accepted no new students after 1896, though in 1899 there were still a few in residence completing their degrees.

4. *Supplement to The Cambridge Review*, 8 February 1882, p.xli.

5. For Coutts Trotter see Christopher N.L. Brooke, *A History of the University of Cambridge*, vol.iv, 1870-1990, Cambridge, 1993, p.70.

6. For Gladstone's reply see Horace Seymour (Downing Street secretary) to Browning, 22 January 1884; Browning Archive, King's College.

7. Mark Pattison to Browning, 25 May 1883; Browning Archive, King's College. (Pattison was the model for Casaubon, in George Eliot's *Middlemarch*.)

8. For Jackson and Sidgwick see Brooke, *op. cit.*, pp.1, 302, 339; for Sidgwick see Robert Skidelsky, *Interests and Obsessions*, London, 1993, pp.3, 4.

CHAPTER 5

Judicious Rule: The Mastership of Arthur Temple Lyttelton 1882–93

TWENTY-EIGHT undergraduates came early in October, to an incomplete college in six acres of ground. The first among them to have his name entered upon the College books, and thus to become the 'first' undergraduate of Selwyn College, would eventually become a clergyman; perhaps it was meet and right that he should have been born on Good Friday (1858), that he would die on Ascension Day (1917), and that his surname should have been Easter.

The quadrangle which they encountered was spectral. Only the west range had been built, upon what in fact was an embankment, created probably by the shifting of soil from the west side of the court to the east to produce a properly horizontal court, which otherwise would have sloped to the east, from Grange Road to the garden. The range comprised two staircases (A and B), each containing thirty-two sets of rooms. In the middle was a gateway, surmounted by a tower. Within the spectral quadrangle, running parallel to that half of the range comprising staircase B, and a few yards distance, was a low white brick shed, shielded by trees on its eastern side, and providing an unpretentious Chapel and an unpretentious Hall. Only the Chapel's sanctuary seemed like a church. The narrow strip of land between the shed and the range was enclosed at each end by iron railings; thus there was a temporary, miniature 'court'. Beyond the shed a straggling kitchen formed the basement of the future Hall. The Master – 'the Mouldy', as undergraduates would apparently call him – had no Lodge; for the first two years he and his family suffered ten adapted sets of rooms in the west range, supplemented by an ugly temporary erection at the south end. He had no kitchen; his meals were prepared in the College kitchen and brought by the College servants scampering up the embankment, sometimes catastrophically. Neither was there a Library. But then there were few books; those available resided for thirteen years in the lecture room above the gateway.

A large quadrangle was of course intended, of 160 square feet. The west and north sides would be residential; the east side would comprise a Chapel, with a Master's Lodge on one side and on the other a Library – which in fact was never put there; and the south side would be reserved for Hall, kitchens, offices, infirmary, and accommodation for servants. The style was to be early seventeenth-century gothic, but very simple, save for the Chapel, the Hall, the Library, and the Master's Lodge.

Beyond the six acres there was not very much. Cranmer Road bisected the prairie, Newnham College was half its later size, and Ridley Hall raced to be completed before Selwyn College – and won.

On Tuesday, 10 October 1882, the Master was installed. Many people came; Church and University joined all the members of the College. At 8 a.m. the Master celebrated Holy Communion. At 11.45 a.m. there was a procession from the 'court' to the Chapel. The choir of St Giles' church sang 'The Church's One Foundation' and led the undergraduates in surplices, officiating clergy, the Master, six bishops including Abraham and Hobhouse, and the Bishop of Ely with his chaplains. The Master was installed by the Bishop of Ely, acting for Archbishop Tait who was dying. Though it was already afternoon the service was Matins, perhaps to sing the joyful canticles of celebration. The Bishop of Ely preached, alluding to the Church's right 'to extend the line of the saints in uniform brightness through every generation', and affirming the Colleges of Keble and Selwyn as suitable means. A hymn for missionaries was sung – 'Thou Whose Almighty Word'; the recessional was 'Soldiers of Christ, Arise'. The powers of darkness and the controversy surrounding the Tests Act seemed trodden down, at least in six acres of west Cambridge.

Bishop Abraham
A.T. Lyttelton   *T.H. Orpen*
First Master   *Tutor and Benefactor*

Then in the Hall there was luncheon for 180, including ladies
(Sarah Selwyn had promised to come), as if to say that the College
would not be a monastery. There were nine speeches. A new
Vice-Chancellor (Porter of Peterhouse) revealed his distaste for
the College, but as a tolerant Liberal promised to assist it to a

proper status within the University. He repudiated 'S.P.', wondering who he was and pretending not to guess. Lord Powis ventured a joke in Latin. The Bishop of Nelson (New Zealand) contemplated the shed and ventured a pun, exhorting the Master to 'do away with the white bricks but to keep the rubrics'.

Selwyn College was launched. The next day the Master petitioned the Council of the Senate for recognition as a 'public hostel'. He submitted a copy of the Charter. On 6 November the Council issued a favourable report, for discussion on 20 November.

'S.P.' was silent. But as 'Oscar Browning' he made his final contribution (8 November) to that part of the Selwyn debate contained in the columns of *The Cambridge Review* (it did not peter out until the end of that term), observing that the virtues of Bishop Selwyn – which the College was established to cultivate – were, in respect of frugality and hard work, as renowned at that time in the Bishop's own college (St John's) as they had been when he was an undergraduate; what secret, then, had the new foundation discovered that made it so cheap? There was no significant rejoinder. On the same page, though, Theodore Beck remarked that if it had been difficult for Cambridge to discuss the Charter on account of the summer vacation (as 'S.P.' had argued in *The Times*), it had been equally so for Members of Parliament, on account of their preoccupation with Gladstone's Egyptian crisis; he would not be so bold as to say what were the motives of those who thus contrived matters.

On 3 February 1883, without much ado, Selwyn College was recognized as a public hostel by grace of the Senate. There was no division.

Sometime during the Mastership of Lyttelton (the date is uncertain) an undergraduate of Selwyn entered the grounds of Newnham College – 'the girls' abode', said a correspondent to a newspaper – and uprooted a tree that Gladstone had planted. Selwyn sent him down. This, said the correspondent, was a disgrace; a 'gating' would have been quite sufficient. In future parents should remember that 'a Lyttelton is head and chief at Selwyn, where any display of humorous Conservatism, which in this instance bent towards Radicalism, is severely repressed'.

The 'head and chief at Selwyn' was, though, a good first Master, as good for Selwyn as Talbot was for Keble. The fourth of Lord Lyttelton's seven sons, his appointment as a page of honour to Queen Victoria had implied that he would become a soldier. But his bent proved literary and philosophical, not military, and so when he came to Trinity, Cambridge, he read Moral Sciences under Henry Sidgwick, the supporter (later) of Selwyn College. He graduated in 1874 and in 1876 was ordained deacon to the parish of St Mary's, Reading. Here he acquired the zeal for pastoral work, and the respect for the uniqueness of individual personalities, that served him well as Master of Selwyn. He was ordained priest in 1877.

Probably from the beginning he felt an affinity with a college destined to be frugal, for his family, though always near the centre of British political and court life, was impecunious in comparison with most other noble families of the time. His apprenticeship at Keble taught him how to set his stamp upon Selwyn, and how to justify its existence in the eyes of the University. 'For both objects', says A.L. Brown,

> Arthur Lyttelton possessed signal qualities of mind and character. The prestige of his name, his intellectual interests and powers, his capacity for work and soundness of judgment – well known already to a wide circle of friends in Cambridge – at once afforded a guarantee of a wise administration, and secured for him a prominent place in the affairs and the society of Cambridge. There were those who did not sympathise with the objects of Selwyn College, but were delighted to have Arthur Lyttelton back in Cambridge, and their regard for the man conduced to a sympathetic toleration for the College, and a ready recognition of the success that attended the Master's judicious rule.

Because the College had no endowments to attract the cleverest schoolboys it did not figure much in the highest divisions of the tripos lists; its reputation amongst undergraduates was determined chiefly by its performance on field and river. The chief part of the teaching burden rested on the Master who was also the Dean and a Tutor. In 1882 there were only two other members of staff: a part-time mathematical lecturer and a Bursar. The part-time mathematical lecturer was the Revd J.T. Ward, Fellow of St John's, whose services were free.

The first Bursar was Lieutenant-Colonel H.C. Watson, a soldier new to university life, who had charge of the College's financial affairs and of its domestic economy. A man of practicalities, he personally superintended the domestic arrangements and taught the servants the art of sweeping rooms. Nevertheless, honourable man though undoubtedly he was, one may suspect that he was trapped between the College's quest for frugality and his own inexperience in the evaluation of prospective domestic staff. He provided a complaints book for undergraduates, pages from which survive. Even when allowance is made for adolescent hauteur and the distance then existing between Selwyn's kitchen and Selwyn's Hall, they afford an affecting glimpse of undergraduate privations during the College's first year. Undergraduates were notably concerned about food and culinary arrangements; in the Easter term they referred to

> the unobtainability of milk; cheese 'too strong for my tongue'; shortage of hot meat at breakfast ('Why is it that there is not enough ... for everybody even when one is down in good time[?]'); meat which arrived cold because the waiters who served it were not 'sufficiently sharp' to ensure it was hot; Yorkshire pudding 'quite uneatable being so underdone as to taste of the flour'; cauliflowers cold and underdone; butter 'in such a state of melted mess' that one had to take it up with a spoon; filthy table cloths and cutlery; mustard pots in need of lids because 'we get as much dust as mustard, under the present arrangement'; and meat of only one kind which was 'in a most uneatable state' in that one could hardly tell whether it was roast or boiled mutton ('Surely when no choice is given at least one should be able to enjoy the only dish'), served with potatoes which were 'almost as bad' and followed by pudding ('such as

it is') which never arrived though sent for: 'is slow starvation the intention of the College to the men, or are they meant to dine elsewhere on these days?' [Bursar's pencilled comment: 'Will the author of this be pleased to sign his name to it. H.C. Watson lt Col *Bursar*'. Another pencilled hand: 'No Notice is taken of Anonymous Contributions'.] One wag requested that the buttery should supply a better brand of cigars, which might prove an antidote to the poisoning likely to result from consuming the cabbage leaves supplied at College meals; 'very good cheroots', he advised, 'can be obtained 5 a shilling'.

Not all complaints had to do with meals. Douglas Ellison, future upholder of a public law for Christendom by way of a job as railway chaplain in the diocese of Grahamstown, South Africa, complained about his dirty windows ('slowly becoming opaque') and the slowness of the College messenger (he should be 'caused to hurry up on all occasions'), and enquired whether 'something more refined than an open doorway [might] be placed to screen the backward parts of the out-door W.C's'. On 13 February he requested

> That some steps be taken to send or give the letters round in Hall, as the atmosphere in the Porter's Lodge, owing to complete absence of ventilation, and the stale fumes of vile tobacco, renders it dangerous to the health of the future Church dignitaries of this Realm to enter into the same.

Lyttelton co-ordinated his staff. Probably from the first term he gathered them in weekly meetings, held on Fridays at midday. All matters concerning the College's internal management were discussed, from the most trivial to the sending-down of undergraduates. As time passed and events occasioned, extraordinary staff meetings were held on other days. During his Mastership Lyttelton was present at all these meetings except one (28 April 1893). His last meeting (7 July 1893) was separated by only nine days from his successor's first (16 July 1893).

Assisting the Master as Tutor was the Revd George Herbert Sing, Fellow of Corpus Christi, who was very energetic. He was Precentor as well as Tutor and in that capacity promptly formed a choir among the undergraduates, and managed such choral services as there were. He became very popular; deservedly so, for, even (he said), 'as one whose zeal for economy is known to you', he represented squarely to the Bursar the complaints of the undergraduates concerning their food (indeed he endorsed them), and he largely created that institution which brought earliest fame to the College within the University – the Selwyn College Boat Club.

On 24 October 1882 Sing presided at a general meeting of the whole College, at which it was agreed that the Boat Club should be formed. It was the earliest of all the College's athletic clubs, and the most successful, for it attained the first division of Cambridge college boats as early as the May races of 1885. Sing agreed to coach the crews, frequently doing so on horseback from the river bank, ably supported by Lyttelton. C.E.G. de Coetlogon and Harry Last were chosen captain and secretary respectively, and the Club's colours were inevitably to be the colours of the College – maroon and old gold, chosen by Mrs Lyttelton since wallflowers were her favourite flower. De Coetlogon, though it was he who complained about the mustard pots, was of the 'pure and heroic' mould, being 6 foot 4 inches tall, weighting over 12 stone, and going to India after he had been ordained. He was the only man amongst the College's first intake to have rowed seriously before arriving, and he contributed enormously to the Club's many successes from the time of his matriculation to his death in 1927.

The story of the Boat Club has been told elsewhere, but the Club's contribution to the furtherance of the Gladstonian 'missionary' ideal may be noted here, for two reasons. First, George Selwyn, his son (the second Master of the College), Bishops Abraham and Hobhouse, and many members of the College down the years have testified to the importance of boats and boating for the nurture of Christian attainments and for learning the management of men. Such testimony, of course, was commonplace in the later Victorian age; but a modern historian endorses it. Contemplating Leslie Stephen and the Trinity Hall Boat Club of the 1850s and 1860s, Noel Annan has discoursed upon the triumph of will over body, the emotion of enduring hardships with one's friends, and the interdependence of individual psychologies and physiques. Even so, there was surely more to the Selwyn College Boat Club than this, for its founders themselves knew full well that they must testify to what boating might achieve in practical Christian terms. In February 1883, the first boat belonging to the Club, launched from Logan's boat-yard, was named after the ship that was meant to take Bishop Selwyn back to New Zealand in 1855 (but could not, since it was in disrepair), and which later did transport him around the waters of Melanesia as the Melanesian Mission ship; it was called *Southern Cross*.[1]

Sing was probably also the senior member of the College most concerned with the formation of the Logarithms, which was founded in his rooms on 11 October 1884, when rules were devised, one of which provided 'That this Society be called (conditionally, until some brighter thought do strike a member) the Logarithms'. To this rule a note was appended in the minute book:

> The Secretary feels that it is but fair to the curiosity of future members to state briefly the origin of the somewhat weird and indefinite title bestowed on the Society. The search for a name had been both long and distracting, when a member, whose brilliant success in the Additional Subjects had put an end all too soon to a mathematical career of no promise, suggested modestly that the Society *might* be called the 'Logarithms' as meeting *after ten* (*vide* Rule 3, 'That this Society do meet on alternate Wednesdays after 10 p.m.'). His mathematical inaccuracy was speedily caught up by the knowing ones, as was also the name which commended itself by its vast inanity.

The Logarithms flourished from the day of its inception, the papers presented at its meetings being as varied and challenging in the 1880s as they were a hundred years later. The memorable Sing left the College in 1886 to become a rector in Dorset; he died in 1901.

Religion in the College was naturally important. For Lyttelton it was central to the College's tone. But he would not impose his high church opinions on others, and he selected his colleagues regardless of their churchmanship and theological complexion. The rule requiring all members of the College to attend Matins every day was lightly enforced, but on Saturday mornings every undergraduate must attend a divinity lecture. Chapel services were usually congregational, without the aid of a trained choir. Holy Communion was celebrated on holy days as well as on Sundays. Compline was every evening at 10 p.m.; once a month it was followed by a service of preparation for Holy Communion, with a devotional address. After Compline all lights were turned out in the court and on the staircases, to encourage the undergraduates to go to bed. But this did not work; '10 p.m. quickly became the starting-point instead of the termination of evening recreations,' says Brown, 'and after a few years the College ceased to be plunged into darkness before midnight'. At ember session special addresses were given for those contemplating ordination, and periodically there were meetings to introduce speakers from the mission-fields, at home and abroad. There were special services for College servants, which College servants did not enjoy. All in all, therefore, from the point of view of the rest of the University there was much novelty in the religious regimen of Selwyn College.

Frugality (or economy in expenditure) was promoted by common meals in Hall, and by sumptuary regulations designed to restrict personal luxury. The College dinner was simpler than in other colleges, and was the same for High Table and undergraduates. On fasting days there was a choice of fish or meat, but no one was allowed both. Private entertaining at luncheon or dinner required tutorial permission. There was a College buttery, but a limit of £5 a term was set for expenditure upon luxuries in the way of food, drink, and tobacco. With the exception of the rule for fasts, these regulations were in force for many years. Lyttelton's aim in making them was not only to facilitate frugality, but also to promote simplicity and self-denial as primary Christian principles.

So by the beginning of the first Easter term (1883) the chief characteristics of the foundation in Grange Road were, as the Master observed them, *esprit de corps* and a determination, alike among senior and junior members, to be as other colleges were. It was all very gratifying.

But then a balloon went up. Upon it was written 'University Tests Act: Selwyn College: Oscar Browning'. This was vexatious – profoundly so, for most of Cambridge had supposed that, with the granting of 'public hostel' status three months earlier, controversy concerning the identity of Selwyn was finally laid to rest.

It was all the fault of the Liberation Society, which was in very fine fettle indeed. Its triennial conference was due that year; there was much to keep it busy, especially concerning the formal relationship between the Church of England and education at all levels – elementary, secondary, college, and university. At Westminster, too, there was the interminable case of Bradlaugh (who represented all that men such as Liddon and Abraham most detested in public and religious life), unsettling Nonconformists and greatly damaging Gladstone's ministry 'by dividing its majority and exhibiting it in postures of impotence'.[2]

Against this background, on 20 April Carvell Williams of the Liberation Society wrote from London to Browning in Cambridge, informing him that at its session on 2 May the conference would discuss a motion 'relative to various branches of the Education question'. A copy of the motion was enclosed. As it referred to the question of denominational colleges, 'in which you are known to be interested', the committee invited him to speak to that '& other topics relating to religious equality at the Universities'. If they sent him a ticket would he come?

Indeed he would. When he arrived at the hall in Cannon Street he found a lively concourse including Liberal and Radical MPs, which that night would hear from 'dear old John Bright' a fiery execration of the iniquities of church establishments, from the support of William of Occam for Louis of Bavaria to the condoning by an Anglican prelate of the recent slaughtering by Sir Garnet Wolsely of thousands of Egyptians at Tel-el-Kebir.

The motion in his pocket desired the amendment of the Forster Education Act (1870), to loosen further the Anglican grip upon elementary education; the creation of unsectarian colleges for student teachers not destined for denominational schools; and unsectarian and more democratic management for endowed schools of the future and for educational charities. Universities were not mentioned, but Browning took Williams at his word. The Liberal *Daily News* (3 May) reported him:

MR. OSCAR BROWNING, of King's College, Cambridge, also supported the motion. He said he stood there as a member of the Church of England, and as one who did not wish to see the Church disestablished, but he was a friend of unsectarian education, and he believed in the absolute necessity of education being independent of all sects or creeds. The removal of the tests had had the effect of greatly increasing the numbers of men of academical distinction who took orders in the Church, and it had also had a beneficial effect on the morality and intelligence of the University. It was with indignation that they heard that with a Liberal Ministry in power a step had been taken of a retrograde character. They had always understood that Keble college was sprung on Oxford. It was proposed that the Selwyn college should be called a hostel, and they were told that if they called it a hostel its promoters would not get a charter. The first knowledge of the intention to get a charter came from one of the officers of this society. He came to London to oppose it, but found that he was quite too late. He trusted that the matter would receive attention, and that the Test Act would be made prospective. (Hear, hear.)
The resolution was then passed and carried unanimously ...

Here was a stirring of a fragrant pot. Liberationists were delighted. They were sorry it was 'hardly given at all in the newspaper reports'. They applied to Browning for a written summary to publish in a pamphlet. Less delighted was Lyttelton when, within hours of publication, a copy of the *Daily News* arrived at the Master's lodging.[3]

The correspondence of May 1883 between Lyttelton and Browning is fun for the historian. First, one man charges another with being 'economical with the truth'. Then, there are three, not two, components – two in the Archives of Selwyn College, one in those of King's. Thus: (1) rough drafts of letters from Lyttelton to Browning, the bad-tempered (and somewhat guilt-ridden?) draft of

23 May, with its scorings-out, revealing what, in the heat of a moment, Lyttelton had had it in mind to say (Selwyn); (2) the letters which Browning actually received, that dated 24 May being the sober version of the draft of the previous day, settled upon after Lyttelton had had a night's sleep (King's); (3) Browning's replies – emollient and self-justifying, yet firm and with the smack (by way of a reference to Cuba) of a good history supervisor (Selwyn). All the embers of the old dispute were raked over. The drift was thus:

3 May: Lyttelton demands to know to whom, in Selwyn, Browning would ascribe 'underhand dealing'. 4 May: Browning prevaricates, and tries to mollify ('... sincere friendship ... which in your case is strengthened by the recollection, of many years, and many dear, tender associations'). 6 May: Lyttelton tries to appear mollified ('I never know whether it is an advantage or a disadvantage of University life that one's contests are always with one's friends'), but ruminates on Liberalism (if Selwyn produces religious *in*equality 'some one must be injured by it. I have read or heard no attempt to show who that someone is'). 20 May: Browning holds firm concerning 'underhand dealing', but renames it *'economy'* (Selwyn College 'by acting as they did, doubtless from an error of judgment ... cannot I think well escape the charge of *economy*'); invokes analogy (the Tests Act has become part of the federal constitution of the University; a new college joining the federation may no longer establish for itself laws of exclusivity, any more than 'a new state Cuba for instance joining the Federation of the American Union would have a right to maintain the "peculiar institution" of slavery'); and refers to the pamphlet ('I will take care that you have a copy'). 24 May: 'My dear Browning ... I still protest most strongly against the charge of underhandedness even though you have changed it to "economy" '.

It all blew over. Term ended. summer came and went. Early in October twenty-three more undergraduates appeared, who did not have to matriculate as non-collegiate students. Some of them read history. To encourage them, and perhaps to please Lyttelton,

Oscar Browning offered a prize. Lyttelton to Browning, 24 October 1883:

> My dear Browning,
>
> I send herewith the essays I mentioned on Sunday. The subject was – The Influence of National History on National Literatures. I hope they are not unbearably bad, but of course the men are only freshmen. Any time this term will do for your award.

> 20 November:
> Dear Browning,
>
> Can you let me have the 4 essays? You did not send them with your note the other day. I think you have given it to the best man.

The arrivals of 1883, and the applications for 1884, had obliged the College Council to address anew the problem of extending the buildings. The Master still lived in ten sets of undergraduate rooms (nearly half of one staircase). Therefore a Master's Lodge was begun in 1883; it was completed in 1884, at a cost of £5,600. In March 1884, for £8,758 (most of it borrowed) work commenced on the north side of the court. New rooms were thus available for the Michaelmas term. Naturally, the building was not complete; for the moment there were no banisters on the staircases, and there were problems from damp. But when they arrived forty more undergraduates were accommodated.

The staff whom they encountered were not identical to those of 1882. Watson, the Bursar, had died during his first year in office. He was succeeded by Alfred Paget Humphry of Trinity College, who stayed for seventeen years. Humphry was astute and devoted to the College. But he did not live in the College; when he came he would 'lord it' over the Tutors – or so said Nalder Williams, one of the earliest Fellows, who heard it from some of them. Ward, the mathematics lecturer, was succeeded in 1883 by the Revd C.A.E. Pollock, Fellow of Corpus Christi, who remained for six years. In 1884 came a second Tutor, the Revd F.C. Searle, and also Henry Joseph Corbett Knight, first as lecturer in theology, then (in succession to Sing) as Tutor. Knight was prominent in the building of the College Chapel, but resigned in 1895 to become Rector of Marnhull, in Kent.

Knight was succeeded as Tutor in 1886 by a former Fellow of Pembroke, the Revd Thomas Herbert Orpen, who belonged to a family of Irish gentry, of which Sir William Orpen, RA was also a member. It was observed of Orpen that his personality lacked animation and that his knowledge of his pupils tended to be vague. Be that as it may, his benefactions to the College were wonderfully generous. In 1887 Searle left Selwyn to teach at Harrow, and was replaced by H.C. Knott, a former scholar of Peterhouse. Thanks to Knott Selwyn produced its first wrangler in 1889, and two in 1890. (Selwyn's first 'first' had been in the Theological Tripos, in 1887.) In 1889 came Algernon Leslie Brown, lately scholar of Trinity, to be a Tutor and classical lecturer until 1906, the year when he published Selwyn's first *History*. From its commencement (1894) Brown was the editor of the College *Calendar*. He was kind to undergraduates, inviting them to his rooms, where he served mulled claret. But they smiled at his nervousness which, they believed, made his voice loud; they said that at early morning service in Chapel against his loudness on one side would sound off antiphonally the little tiny noise arising from a colleague on the other. From 1906 to 1939 he was Vicar of Wonersh, in Surrey.

In 1889 Selwyn College *looked* like a College. The west and north wings, the Master's Lodge, and the kitchen on the south side were all complete; there was a real quadrangular court; and (thanks to Humphry) a garden in the east. The number of student rooms had reached its full complement of 120, the entrance examination had become competitive, in the Michaelmas term forty-seven freshmen were admitted, the staff establishment became three Tutors and three resident lecturers. In the same year the first nomination was made to a Patteson Missionary Studentship, funded between 1882 and 1889 by Bishop Hobhouse and the Revd Charles Warner, Fellow of Worcester college, Oxford, and Vicar of Clun in Shropshire. The Studentship commemorated John Coleridge Patteson, the great martyr-bishop of Melanesia; it defrayed the cost

of the education and the maintenance in Selwyn College of one
or more missionary students. Warner himself was not a missionary,
but from his rural vicarage he took an interest in missionary work,
and was an admirer of Patteson and George Selwyn.

In the summer of 1880 Arthur Lyttelton had married Mary Kathleen Clive of Herefordshire; whilst at Selwyn they produced a
family, two sons and a daughter. Kathleen Lyttelton was scholarly.
In 1886 she published *Nature and the Bible: lectures on the Mosaic
history of creation in its relation to natural science*, her translation of
the fourth edition (1876) of *Bibel und Natur*, a two-volume work
by Franz Heinrich Reusch. Reusch was a German theologian of
the Old Catholic persuasion, which emerged in Germany chiefly
as a protest against the papal dogma of infallibility (1870), and
which enjoyed the sympathy of some high church Anglicans, not
least George Selwyn, who urged inter-communion between Old
Catholics and Anglicans. He was an intimate of Ignaz von Döllinger, the greatest German theologian of his day and a long-standing
critic of papal obscurantism. Döllinger had taught Lord Acton.
Acton was foremost among liberal Roman Catholics in Britain
and in 1895, upon the recommendation of Lord Rosebery's Liberal
administration, he would become Regius Professor of Modern
History at Cambridge. Döllinger was also, distantly, a friend of
Gladstone. Acton and Gladstone thought well of Kathleen's translation of Reusch's work. In 1888, at Gladstone's suggestion, Acton
cautiously suggested to Döllinger that should he require a competent English translation of certain of his own work, then,
through Gladstone, Kathleen might be approached. Kathleen he
identified as the wife of Gladstone's nephew, the Master of Selwyn
College, Cambridge. To contemporaries, therefore, Kathleen as
well as her husband must have defined the Selwyn Master's Lodge
as a Cambridge centre not only of political Liberalism but also
of liberal Catholic scholarship.[4]

There was a lighter side to Kathleen – she was gently feminist.
She wrote a small volume called *Women and their Work* (1901),
which surveyed the position of middle-class women at the turn

of the century, and – in respect of the family, the household, philanthropic and social work, the professions (why should not women be civil servants?), recreation, and friendship – offered improving advice. Kathleen considered especially the role of women as help-meets of men, not least clergymen, who, she advised, must never have cold food on Sundays. Her wider view of woman's duty to man must have gratified a Master of Selwyn: it was that to cause a man to esteem and love her, and to serve him well, a woman must seek not to please *him*, but rather – as the Shorter Catechism had it – 'To glorify God, and to enjoy him for ever.'

A pleasing feature of life in Selwyn College during the Mastership of Lyttelton was the cordiality between the Lytteltons and Oscar Browning, with whom Kathleen got on very well; it was, perhaps, a small token of Selwyn's informal as well as its formal acceptance within the University. Learning that Browning was the collector of moneys for the Cambridge branch of the Society for Psychical Research, which met in his rooms at King's, Kathleen applied to him to join and, it seems, prevailed upon the Master to be interested too. The society had been founded in 1882, with Henry Sidgwick as president and Lewis Carroll as another member. The interest of Sidgwick and the Lytteltons in psychic phenomena was very natural, for Sidgwick sought evidences of the after-life in which otherwise he could not believe; whilst for Kathleen – adherent of high Anglicanism and explorer of the connections between religion and the natural world – such evidences, if they appeared, would have fortified a faith already firm. (Browning's interest in spirits was perhaps less elevated. After his mother died in 1889, says Ian Anstruther, 'he consulted a medium, Mrs Piper, who tried to reach his mother in a trance. The result was not very satisfactory. Mrs Piper closed her eyes and told O.B. that he smoked too much. However, she gave a "strong impression" that Mrs Browning's spirit hovered near.')

Kathleen would invite Browning to social occasions at the Master's Lodge, though since her dating of letters was as carefree as her punctuation it is sometimes hard to determine when. Kathleen to Browning, probably some time between January 1889, and March 1893:

Dear Mr. Browning,

My husband & I both think we should
like it best if Lord Herschell [Lord Chancellor in Gladstone's
third and fourth administrations] dined here Would you come
and meet him, we should be very glad to see you. I suppose
7.15 would be the right hour.

Monday

Dear Mr. Browning,

Will you come to luncheon tomorrow at
1.15 to meet Mr. Gladstone. We have only just ascertained
that he can stay till Wednesday, so could not help the very
short notice [.]

'Monday' was probably 31 January 1887. Fenton Hort to his
third son, Cambridge, Saturday, 5 February 1887:

... On Monday I dined with the Master of Trinity, but in Hall,
not at the Lodge, to meet Mr. Gladstone, who, as I dare say
you saw in the papers, has been paying his nephew, Mr.
Lyttelton, a visit of a couple of days at Selwyn. In Combination
Room the Master proposed his health, and he returned it in a
nice little serious speech. He was very quiet and pleasant, and
I was glad to be able to see him so near, especially his quiet
wonderful eyes. Next morning I sat next to him at breakfast at
Selwyn Lodge, Mr. Lyttleton having been kind enough to ask
me to meet him, with Professor Creighton, Professor Kirkpatrick, and Mr. Stanton. Mrs. Gladstone was also there.[5]

The familial closeness of Gladstone and Lytteltons inevitably
determined that the statesman and his wife were not the only
Gladstones to visit Selwyn during the Mastership of Lyttelton.
From the diary of Mary Gladstone:

CAMBRIDGE, Sat. 4 Nov. [1882] – Great scurry to catch the
train at King's X, having made a mistake about time. Helen
[her sister; Vice-Principal of Newnham College] met me at
Cambridge ... Luncheon at Selwyn. Very exciting getting there,
and so like 10 years ago. Then a troll with Helen at Newnham,
after wh. a run towards the backs. Met the Flying Dutchman

[*Der fliegende Holländer*: Henry Scott Holland, one of the younger Tractarian leaders, contributor to *Lux Mundi*] and walked with him to Selwyn, then some more Newnham, then tea at Selwyn, then Lucy arrived and had a long chat with Mr. Holland in A.'s study. Very delightful. They dined out and Lucy and I were *tête à tête*, read aloud some of Arthur's excellent Carlyle article. Played and talked.

CAMBRIDGE, *Sun. Mar.* 9 [1884] – 8 o'clock, 10 o'clock (with sermon from Mr. Sing on suffering; good but monotonously preached) ... Sat an hour with Prof. [James] Stuart [Jacksonian Professor of Natural Philosophy, notable practical engineer, Liberal MP, favouring votes for women and so very radical], and he came back to luncheon when we tried hard to crack the vivisection and vaccination nuts. Lionised the nice new house and garden and other wing. Talk with Kathleen and picked up Helen at King's, ... and to Trinity where we had tea with Prof. Stuart, meeting Mr. [Henry] George.

'Cheerful and serene and unfussy' hardly described the state of mind of those concerned with the finances of the College during its early years, as they struggled to maintain a prudent balance between frugality, decent domestic standards, and the just remuneration of those whom the College employed. In 1885 an ingenious Bursar contemplated the prospects for vacational feeding:

Maitland House,
Newnham Croft,
Cambridge.   3 March 1885

My dear Master,
                    I have today gone into the question of reducing the daily charge for men staying in College in the Vacation, and I find we can reduce it to 4/– on the following terms;–
                    Breakfast to go on for ¼ hour instead of 1 hour; meat not necessarily given at breakfast, but given according as we have material for it left from dinner. Dinner

not to be required to consist of more than plain joints with vegetables &c., and sweets. Sometimes an entré would be given, as might be found convenient to work in materials. And on Fridays fish as an alternative to meat, as usual.

The shortening of the breakfast time would effect a saving in fuel, and the simplifying of breakfast & dinner a saving in meat, or rather an economy by ensuring the materials of joints being worked in, for the men will eat a certain amount however we manage.

I do not think we can make any management that would enable us to charge less than 4/– without risk of loss.

I think we had better try on these lines this Vac $^{\underline{n}}$ without allowing sizing [i.e., rationing, but allowing undergraduates wanting more to pay extra for it], as we may be able to give meat for breakfast every day or nearly every day, though not quite in so luxurious a manner as in term time. Sizing is contrary to the principle strongly laid down that men who can afford it are not allowed to improve their meals in Hall in contrast to those who cannot.

I do not think that shortening the breakfast hour would be a serious inconvenience with a small number of men in College at a time when they have no fixed morning engagements.

Perhaps a trial of these arrangements may give us some hints for the Long Vacation.

Yours very truly
A.P. Humphry

The following year a more serious concern was the remuneration of the Master and his possible resignation. For during the first two years of his occupancy Lyttelton discovered that he was financing his living in the Lodge largely out of his private income, which had already been reduced and was likely to suffer further reduction. Even though in 1885 his annual salary had been increased from £500 to £540, he determined that in 1887 he would request from the College Council either an increase in salary or an acceptance of his resignation, simply on the ground that he could not meet the necessary expenses of his position. After he had resolved on this he received from the Bishop of Southwell the offer of St Mary's, Nottingham, which, he thought, he should not refuse for the sake of another year at Selwyn. In August (1886), therefore, he put to the Council the request which he had intended to put in the following year. Abraham caused the Council to effect an accommodation with him: his salary was raised again, to £740. He did not resign.

Was there a typical Selwyn undergraduate of the 1880s? Certainly there were two about whom a good deal is known and who, in their very different ways, exemplified the 'Selwyn ideal' (or the 'Gladstone ideal' – or whatever one will call it). For a year they were together at Selwyn; one was William Edward Collins; the other was Charles Edward Fraser Copeman.

Physical and moral courage combined with saintliness and intellectual distinction were the acclaimed hallmarks of William Collins. Born into a large family in 1867, during his early years he was brought up in Cornwall. In 1874 his father became a consulting mining engineer, afterwards spending much time abroad. In 1881 the whole family except the eldest son moved to the Rio Tinto mines in Spain, where William learned the Spanish language. Quite soon he returned to England, to become a lawyer's clerk in London. But the law did not suit him; he desired ordination. He attended the church of All Hallows Barking by the Tower and was befriended by those who recognized his intellectual potential. One of them was Edward Wheatley-Balme. It was perceived that his father, with a large young family and a limited income, could not offer him a university education and that the boy had been insufficiently tutored to obtain a university scholarship. So it was decided that Selwyn College, Cambridge, was just the place for him.

At Selwyn he was not especially happy. He suffered a good deal of ragging, for he wished to be like a Nazarite and so went unshaven. His parents and his older friends entreated him and eventually he shaved. But still he made few friends, except among the dons. He worked very hard, lived severely, and injured his health. He graduated as a junior optime in the Mathematical Tripos.

Stimulated, however, by the teaching of Mandell Creighton, then Dixie Professor of Ecclesiastical History, he had become an omnivorous reader, especially in history as it bore upon religion. In 1889 he received the Lightfoot Scholarship in ecclesiastical history, and in 1890 the Prince Consort Prize for a dissertation on the conversion of Frisia. Lyttelton congratulated him on the former:

> ... I cannot refrain from a line of congratulation, most heartfelt and thorough. It is a real moral triumph over physical difficulties, and one of which you may be far prouder than of the intellectual feat, considerable though it is. I hope you are fond enough of the College to sympathize with my great pleasure over the credit you have won for it.

In 1890 he wrote again: '... It is a very satisfactory sort of prize to get, and I shall look forward to adding the essay to the Library with great pride – the first genuine Selwyn publication.' But Collins was unsatisfied with the essay; he never published it.

In 1890 he was ordained deacon, in 1891 priest. He became a mission preacher at All Hallows Barking. But also in 1891 Lyttelton begged him to return to Selwyn as a lecturer in divinity. When soon after he was also invited to be a lecturer in international law at St John's he determined to return to Cambridge, to occupy both positions simultaneously. Whilst at Cambridge he examined for the history faculty; in the Browning Archive letters from Collins to Browning, neatly written, reveal a shrewd though youthful lecturer well able to withstand the blandishments of the older man in matters affecting undergraduate assessment.

In 1893 he became Professor of Ecclesiastical History at King's College, London, acclaimed as scholar, history teacher and examiner, and intellectual ornament of the Christian ministry. At home and abroad his advice was sought on all kinds of church questions. In 1904, poor health notwithstanding, he was consecrated Bishop of Gibraltar, his diocese comprising all territories bordering the Mediterranean and others besides. One of his chaplains, attending to his concerns in England whilst he was abroad, was Algernon Leslie Brown.

Among Collins' special qualifications for his appointment was his profound understanding of, and sympathy for, the history and the theology of the Orthodox churches. Travelling incessantly and very widely, whenever possible he would cultivate respectful relations with native religious authorities; a Waldensian ordination would attract him, as would the opening of a place of worship for the Reformed Lusitanian Church. He would even attend services in synagogues. To Roman Catholic prelates in whose dioceses he ministered he would show unfailing courtesy, calling upon them and explaining that his work lay solely among English people, and that his own church would not proselytize. Usually the response was friendly. In 1907 he went to Persia and Asiatic Turkey on behalf of the Archbishop of Canterbury's Assyrian Mission. When he returned he published his journal, *Notes of a Journey to Kurdistan*; the events he described constituted undoubtedly one of the most dangerous, fraught yet sanctified episcopal ventures of the twentieth century.

That year he might have become a bishop in England, with prospects surely of an archbishopric later, for Archbishop Davidson recommended him (though not as his first choice) for the diocese of Chichester. But King Edward VII would not accept him because, unreasonably, he believed him too high church. So, to his physical detriment, he stayed in the Mediterranean.

On 28 December 1908 there was an earthquake in Messina. The work of excavation could not be, or was not, organized. Collins was in Malta, where his wife was ill. Hurriedly he left for Messina, where the English colony numbered around 120. With Russian and British sailors, but one night on his own, a frail English bishop scrabbled to retrieve the dying from the ruins of a destroyed city. Eventually he collapsed. He developed a septic throat. Tuberculosis of throat and lung was diagnosed. Early in 1911 he fell ill at the British Embassy in Constantinople, where he had gone to conduct confirmations, and on 22 March, on his way to Smyrna to continue the confirmations, he died at sea, finest exemplar of the missionary faith which his college in Cambridge enshrined, and a rising hope of international Christendom.

The son of an honorary canon of Norwich, Charles Edward Fraser Copeman was three months younger than Collins but came to Selwyn two years later. Having attended King's Choir School, where he had caught the roving eye of Oscar Browning, and Norwich School, he had taken a job in the City. It was dull; in due course Browning agreed he should be rescued from it. Since his father's means were stretched, and since his brother Alfred was about to matriculate at Selwyn (a second brother had entered Corpus in 1879, a third would enter Magdalene in 1884, and a fourth – Alfred, also taken up by Browning – Sidney in 1887), Browning pressed his case with Lyttelton in October 1884, and he matriculated in 1886. He was grateful. Browning was rewarded with the pleasure of financing his Selwyn career with an annual allowance of £100, lending or giving him smaller sums as occasion determined, and being conducted by him and his father around the Norfolk Broads. On 30 May 1886 he wrote to Browning from Norwich: '... *Please* don't expect brilliant or even good prospects for me at Cambridge. A duffer I always was & am likely to remain. I shall be *amply* satisfied with a 3rd Class Hist: Tripos. at [*sic*] present I know absolutely no History ...'.

His judgement was sure: the following July he tried unsuccessfully for a scholarship at Trinity; from time to time at Selwyn he wished that Browning were nearer, to write his history essays; and in 1889 he graduated with a pass degree. Yet he was versatile, enterprising, and very intelligent. Among his chief interests were rowing, football, and the Footlights. He was a member of the College's rugby XV; he rowed in the Lent and May boats and was Boat Club captain in his third year. He also delighted in Selwyn's music, which throve by the mid-1880s and which once at least contributed to 'high culture of the mind' (as required by the Charter) through the singing of the Master's sister-in-law, the Hon. Mrs Robert Lyttelton. His own voice was fine; in 1901 he returned to Selwyn to sing in the May Week concert. Undated

letters from him to Browning offer glimpses of undergraduate
life in a new Cambridge college in 1889:

> ... I am going to stay with a Selwyn chap down in Hampshire
> for a few days when I go down & then go back to Norwich.
> We were going to send a boat to Henley but it has fallen
> through I am sorry to say, as it would have been most enjoyable
> & a very good thing for the College. I collected £70 in ¾ of
> an hour which I call very good for Selwyn.
>
> The Selwyn Concert was a great success & Mrs. Bob
> Lyttelton sang charmingly.

'The Footlights',
Cambridge

My dear Mr. Browning

        I came to see you yesterday, but found
you out. I wanted to thank you personally for so kindly paying
my subscription to the Club again. I don't think I could possibly
have joined this term, if I had been left to my own resources,
as the 'guvnor [*sic*] generously gave me 15/– for the term, which
barely paid railway journey.

        I saw you come up to Selwyn yesterday
to see the Mouldy. I beg pardon I mean the Hon & Rev. I am
going to dine there tonight which I don't much like.

        If you happen to hear of anybody requir-
ing a tutor or Secretary, please remember that I *hope* to have
my degree in June, tho' it is rather doubtful at present.

With many thanks
Believe me
Yours ever
Charles E.F. Copeman

After he had graduated he looked for jobs, temporary and
permanent. He registered with Gabbitas-Thring. During the

summer he got bored in Norwich, except when he could sing, play football, or go rowing. He received money from Browning, sometimes £10 at a time. One letter that he wrote (undated) conveys the frustration of many a youth newly graduated:

> The Prospect Hotel
> Harrogate
> Yorks

My dear Mr Browning

I am rather disappointed not to have heard from you since I came here. I suppose you got the letter I wrote about 10 days ago. I took your advice, inasmuch as I took anything that was offered, but I can assure you that this is far from being the 'beer and skittles' which might be imagined in the post of Secretary to a Q.C.

Mr Griffith is an invalid who does not sleep at nights. I have to write his letters & be with him all day which I find very trying, as I can't play Tennis or go for a strole [sic] in the Evenings or anything of that sort. I get £3 : 3 a week which I suppose is pretty good but it is a terrible way of earning money. You have no idea how dull it is, please let me know if you hear of anything else. I have not had anything from Askin Gabb & Co for such a long time, they really ought to send me some things & so ought Prof: Lewis. Mr Griffith can only walk at snails pace so I get no exercise and have to sit up till past 12 with him dozing on the sofa & I have no books to read. How long are you going to stop at Cambridge? I want particularly to know if you got my last letter as I did not post it but left it at home the day I came away. Splendid weather but this is a very dead alive place, the last place Mr G. [Gladstone?] ought to come to.

If you are in Town I wish you wld. wake Askin & Co up.

> Believe me
> Ever yours
> Charles E.F. Copman

Please don't think me discontented. I am only too glad to go on with this if I cannot get something a little more congenial.

Quite soon, however, Browning found him a job as an assistant master in a school in Bruges kept by his own brother-in-law, a wayward clergyman. Mindful that Browning knew at least thirty-six languages, Copeman composed (or caused to be composed?) a remarkable letter of gratitude, the paragraphs of which were, by turns, in various European languages. For a while he was fulfilled.

Would Bishop Abraham have felt that Copeman justified his place at Selwyn College? Surely yes. He became eventually a solicitor in Wisbech, in the firm of Metcalfe and Copeman. By turns he was also clerk to the Lieutenancy of Cambridgeshire, town clerk of Wisbech, clerk to the county council of the Isle of Ely (for twenty-seven years), clerk of the peace for the Isle of Ely, and a county councillor. On several occasions he was an Under-Sheriff for Cambridgeshire and Huntingdonshire. In 1897 he was commissioned to the Third (Cambridgeshire) Battalion of the Suffolk Regiment. He commanded the battalion in France in 1915, leading it in action at St Eloi and then in the line at Ypres. He was mentioned in dispatches and appointed CMG. He became a full colonel, a Deputy Lieutenant for Cambridgeshire, a justice of the peace for Norfolk and the Isle of Ely, and a holder of the Territorial Decoration. He died in 1949. Browning preserved around 240 of his letters.[6]

Collins and Copeman were two of the 402 young men who entered the College during Lyttelton's Mastership. Of these, twenty-five for various reasons migrated to other colleges and others left Cambridge without degrees. By the end of the Easter term 1893 (when Lyttelton left the College), 285 had graduated, 121 of them with honours. These examination results, modest even when judged against the expectations of a University in which at that time a high proportion of men took only pass degrees, were doubtless explained by the very small number of open and competitive scholarships which the College was able to offer. Nevertheless, five first classes had been won, and twenty-three second classes. J.H. Burrows had won the Tyrrhit Hebrew Scholarship and the Mason Prize. The prizes of Collins have already been noticed.

Burrows as well as Collins became a Selwyn lecturer. Of the other 285, 164 entered Holy Orders, of whom fifteen afterwards worked as overseas missionaries. Three of these fifteen died abroad, as missionaries: William Chambers, a layman and one of the first twenty-eight, died in the service of the Universities' Mission to Central Africa in 1894; his brother, Percival, a clergyman, died working for the same mission, in 1899; and in 1898 Frederick Thonger died in Delhi, after four years' work in the Cambridge Brotherhood. Of the other graduates of the Lyttelton period thirty-nine became schoolmasters, sixteen doctors, nine lawyers, and six officers in the army. Of the schoolmasters probably the most distinguished was Percy Simpson, who came to the College in 1884 (see page 234).

By the spring of 1893 Lyttelton felt that his task at Selwyn had been accomplished: in Cambridge the principle of the denominational university education had been re-established. Desiring to answer a compelling vocation to be a parish clergyman, he accepted from the Lord Chancellor the benefice of Eccles in Lancashire. He had taken a large part in the business of the University; he had been active in many branches of Church work, especially that of the Society for the Propagation of the Gospel; he had publicly supported the saintly Edward King, Bishop of Lincoln, when in 1888–90 he had been prosecuted for alleged ritualistic practices; he had contributed to the journalism of religion; and in 1891 he had been Hulsean lecturer. Above all he had contributed to *Lux Mundi*. When he departed his friends presented to the College a portrait of him, by C.W. Furse.

In 1895 he was appointed an honorary chaplain to the Queen; in 1896 a chaplain-in-ordinary; in 1898 Provost of Lancing College and Bishop Suffragan of Southampton; in 1900, whilst retaining his bishopric, Archdeacon of Winchester. The Council of Selwyn College welcomed him as an elected member in 1901. Higher office called undoubtedly. In 1902, however, his health broke down. He died in February 1903, aged 52. He was buried at Hagley.

Notes

1. For the early history of the Boat Club see A.P. McEldowney, *A Personal History of the Selwyn College Boat Club*, published by the College in 1972; Noel Annan, *Leslie Stephen: the godless Victorian*, Chicago and London, 1986, p.30.

2. Sir Robert Ensor, *England 1870–1914*, Oxford, 1936, p.68. Ensor provides details of the case.

3. Carvell Williams to Browning, 12 May 1883; Browning Archive, King's College.

4. Acton to Döllinger, 22 June 1888, in Ignaz von Döllinger, *Briefwechsel*, vol.3, Munich, 1971, pp.369–70.

5. A.F. Hort, *Life and Letters of F.J.A. Hort*, London, 1896, vol.2, p.361.

6. Some account of Browning's relations with Charles Copeman, and with his younger brother Alfred, appears in Ian Anstruther, *Oscar Browning: a biography*, London, 1983.

CHAPTER 6

A Bold Experiment: The Mastership of John Richardson Selwyn 1893–8

THE second Master of Selwyn College was John Richardson Selwyn, younger son of George Augustus. He was the least scholarly of all Masters of Selwyn, having difficulty with grammar, punctuation, and the use of capital letters, and having no ear for languages. He was nevertheless acutely intelligent, highly articulate, and a fine descriptive writer; his spiritual correspondence bears comparison with that of Bishop Collins. His appointment to Selwyn, thought A.L. Brown, was a bold experiment abundantly justified by its success.

He was born on 20 May 1844 at Waimate in New Zealand, where his father occupied the roomy wooden station building belonging to the Church Missionary Society. There he learned the Maori language along with English. In 1846 St John's College was removed from Waimate to Auckland. The Bishop and his family went too. The young John was taught Latin by the future Bishop Abraham, and was befriended by the Chief Justice, Sir William Martin. In 1854 he came to England for the first time, with his parents. Very soon he went to Eton. His holidays he spent at Ely, in the company of Professor William Selwyn and his sister Mrs Peacock. Upon the river at Ely he cultivated his enthusiasm for boats. At Eton he knew the Lytteltons and excelled at football, rowing, and swimming.

In 1863 he came to Trinity, Cambridge, and rowed twice in the University crew (1864, 1866). Though he read voraciously in history, and had acquired an impressive knowledge of the Bible before he was a teenager, he did not excel academically as an undergraduate, obtaining in 1866 only a 'third' in the Classical Tripos.

In 1867 he departed for New Zealand, to visit his parents. He had decided that on his return to England he would become a lawyer. But in New Zealand two things impressed him and caused him to change his mind. The first was a six-week expedition with his father to the district of the Waikato; the second was the episcopate of Bishop Patteson of Melanesia.

The Waikato was a newly conquered part of New Zealand, offering only hardship to those who visited. In 1896 Selwyn told a Cambridge audience what it had been like:

> Just after I landed my father took me on a six-weeks' tour. I was cook and bed-maker. It was mine to hoist up the little tent, to fill it with fern judiciously arranged, to cut the scanty rasher, and fit it between a clef fern-stick ready for toasting, and, when he came, to do this deftly, so that all the grease might fall on the solitary biscuit which acted as dripping-pan. This was when we camped. Sometimes we slept at settlers' houses, and never did men receive heartier welcome. Sometimes a soldiers' mess welcomed us, and the guard turned out to salute a very travel-stained Bishop, but one who they all knew had gone through hardships and perils for their sakes.

This journey gave him an insight into the essence of muscular Christianity and sowed the seeds of a desire to be a muscular Christian ordained and militant. But then came his awareness of the achievements of Bishop Patteson.

John Coleridge Patteson (1827–71) was a pupil at Eton under his uncle the Revd Edward Coleridge, son-in-law of Dr Keate. Of broadly Tractarian sympathies, he became a don at Oxford and then a clergyman. Bishop Selwyn's visit to England in 1854 determined him to be a missionary, and the following year he accompanied Selwyn when he returned to New Zealand. In 1856 he made his first voyage to Melanesia on behalf of the Melanesian Mission which, during the summer – under the auspices of Bishop Selwyn and with the consent of their parents – brought native boys from the islands for instruction at St John's mission school in Auckland, and then, the next year, returned them to their homes. During Patteson's time the school was removed from Auckland to Norfolk Island, which was warmer, nearer the Melanesian islands, and the home of the Pitcairners who, as descendants of the mutineers of the *Bounty* and their Tahitian wives, seemed specially deserving of missionary attention. Patteson mastered the dialects of the Maori language, treated his boys as though they were Etonians, and taught them well.

Later in 1867 John Selwyn returned with his parents to England. By then he had decided upon ordination. After his father's appointment to Lichfield he went with him to New Zealand for the farewell, and was ordained deacon by him in Lichfield on Trinity Sunday 1869. He served an exemplary curacy in Arlewas, Staffordshire, and early in 1871 became curate-in-charge of St. George's, Wolverhampton. In September he visited America as chaplain to his father.

Meanwhile the clerical error in George Selwyn's letters patent had been amended. In February 1861, in St Paul's church, Auckland, New Zealand, Patteson at the age of 33 was consecrated the first 'missionary bishop among the Western islands of the south Pacific ocean' (bishop, that is, of Melanesia), by Bishops Selwyn, Abraham and Hobhouse; his residence was to be on the island of Mota. He took sole charge of the mission, which was financed partly out of his own income. His episcopate was vigorous; he conducted services, built houses, swam and cooked, tended animals, navigated the *Southern Cross*, translated the gospels of Luke and John into the Mota language, established synodical government, and generally brought civilization where civilization was needed. But often his life was in danger, for in the minds of some of the islanders he was quite improperly associated with a labour traffic in the Pacific which was conducted on behalf of the planters of Fiji and Queensland and which amounted to a traffic for slavery. On 16 September 1871 he was assassinated by natives on the island of Nukapu.

Christian consciences in England were stirred, especially the conscience of John Selwyn. He heard of the death when he returned from America, and felt called to Melanesia as an ordinary priest to resume the work of Patteson. He told his parents, whose approval was given. In January he married Clara Innes, whom he had met at Arlewas. In February 1873 they and their small daughter, Pearlie, sailed for Melanesia via Australia and New Zealand. Laboriously husband and wife learned the Mota language. Because he felt intellectually inferior to his father he had determined, more or less consciously, that his physical prowess, which he had developed at Eton and Cambridge, would be the mainstay of his missionary endeavours. It was humiliating, therefore, that when they arrived in Auckland he had to be carried ashore because of the chronic pain, described as rheumatism, which had struck him during the voyage. He would suffer this progressively, and it would reduce him to an unceasing dependence upon crutches during the later years of his life.

By the beginning of June the Selwyns were lodged in Auckland with Sir William Martin. By the middle of October they were settled upon Norfolk Island, with two other clergymen and their wives. His ministry as priest was modelled upon that of Patteson as bishop; he tended to the inhabitants of Norfolk Island and sailed around the other islands upon the second *Southern Cross* (the first was wrecked in 1860), rejoicing in things nautical and in adventure, and never forgetting that his colonial vocation had been inspired by Patteson's death.

The matter of the bishopric was for long unsettled; not that there was much for a bishop to do, for ordinations were not needed whilst for confirmations the Bishop of Auckland could be summoned. Gradually, though, it seemed evident to everyone that Selwyn should be bishop. On 18 February 1877 after nomination by the mission to the General Synod of New Zealand, he was consecrated at Nelson. At the hour of consecration, 11 p.m. in England, a special service was held in Lichfield cathedral, the elder Bishop Selwyn praying for the younger.

His episcopate was consciously 'muscular', his physical and navigational skills admired by Melanesians. There was, though, unhappiness. Clara died in December 1877, leaving a young son (Stephie) and three young daughters, the youngest of whom died in 1878; and once, courageously and alone in the Solomon Islands, he induced the chiefs of the tribes implicated to surrender for execution the murderers of a British naval lieutenant and his subordinates ('It was ... rather horrid work having to go in for all this murderer hunting, but I am quite sure I was right in doing it, as it saved the whole people from war, and also gave them and all the islands around a very salutary lesson').

On or around 2 July 1878, he learned that his father was dead. As soon as possible he set out for England. When he arrived in Australia he learned of the project for 'Selwyn College'. 'I like the idea of a College as at Keble,' he wrote to his mother, 'but it will take a vast deal of money. However, Bishop Abraham does not seem at all doubtful about it.' In 1885 he came to England again, and married Annie Mort whom earlier he had known in Sidney. In 1888, on Norfolk Island, his health began to fail. He was obliged to return to England, suffering what he called rheumatism, neuritis, and a terrible abscess in his thigh. In the autumn of 1891 he received surgery in London upon his right leg, which had become eight inches shorter than his left. He resigned his bishopric and went to live in Surrey.

In the spring of 1893 Selwyn was staying at Worthing with his daughter Rebie who was ill. A letter came from the Bishop of Peterborough, Mandell Creighton, representing the Council of Selwyn College. It asked him to be Master. Referring no doubt to his invalidity and lack of scholarship, Creighton said that the Council's decision 'was not arrived at without a full consideration of all material facts'. Selwyn took the letter to Rebie's room, threw it upon the bed, and roared with laughter to think that one so unlearned might inhabit a Master's Lodge.

Creighton pressed his case (20 March): (1) Selwyn College must have a Master known outside Cambridge; (2) he must distinctly represent some definite aspect of the work of the Church: Selwyn distinctively did – the aspect of overseas missions; (3) he need not himself teach for University examinations, he would merely be responsible for ensuring that others did; (4) 'Masters of Colleges may be of many kinds. What Lyttelton has done will not be the same as what *any* successor will do. The new Master will follow his own lines.' Selwyn decided he had better accept; his mother especially felt that he should. But he thought it the funniest thing that ever he heard, fancied he must pepper his letters with Latin quotations thenceforth, and said that Annie trembled to think of the bluestockings of Newnham College peeping over the garden wall.

The appointment was popular. The College Council was pleased that a Selwyn would be head of Selwyn College; Edward Talbot (then Vicar of Leeds) rejoiced that out of personal adversity had come a new career for John Selwyn and the prospect of first-rate service for Church and State; and a privy councillor invented a psalm:

Selwyn Boat will be head of the River! New Zealand will be glad. Melanesia will shout for joy. Trinity and Eton will be prouder than ever of their stock. But none will rejoice more heartily than does   Yours most sincerely, G. DENMAN.

On 16 June he was installed by Bishop Abraham. That evening he presided for the first time at High Table, though afterwards he took wine with the undergraduates at the lower tables and announced as a happy omen that Selwyn's first 'first' had been gained, in the Natural Sciences Tripos.

A worldly-wise bishop from the salty Pacific and sometimes quick-tempered, he wondered whether he would hit it off with the dons of Cambridge, who were intellectually superior. But he did. He dedicated himself to the welfare of Selwyn's undergraduates and was concerned with the well-being of the domestic servants, though the magisterial eye which had subdued Melanesian savages and searched the souls of Queen Victoria's sailors flashed still upon the wayward. Some caught it early; after chapel on the Master's first Sunday one of the rowdiest was heard to warn, 'I say, I don't like the look of that chap's eye!' But he hailed them merrily from his study window, invited them into his garden to let off their fireworks on Guy Fawkes' Night, and modified the rule (lightly enforced by Lyttelton) that they should attend morning chapel every day into a requirement of four attendances at week-day services. He probably never knew that sometimes they thought that his sermons and divinity lectures (the latter racy, and too often about Melanesia) were rambling and incoherent, though of course they would laugh at bits of them as might seem polite. The bluestockings of Newnham were hardly a nuisance, but in 1897 some were peeved when he opposed the prospect of degrees for women because study for degrees would harden and spoil them and sully their charm, purity and lovableness.

The chief event of Selwyn's Mastership was the completion of the College Chapel to Blomfield's design. For the new Master the Chapel was important, since on Norfolk Island he had built his pro-cathedral in memory of Bishop Patteson and had believed it beneficial to the tone of his students' lives.

The fund-raising had been inaugurated by Orpen and his wife, who initially offered £3,000 on condition that the remainder should be raised to the amount of £12,000 in sums of not less than £1,000. (In the event they did not need to offer so much, for it was decided that Blomfield's plan would be more modest than at first intended.) The Orpens had been supported by a zealous Henry Knight, by most other members of the College, by the Lyttelton family who contributed £650, and by members of the Council who contributed £750 between them. Lyttelton's last act as Master, in the presence of John Selwyn, had been to officiate at the laying of the foundation stone on 13 June 1893, the day before his successor's installation.

When Selwyn assumed office the funds were still inadequate. To encourage others, he himself, his mother, and his brother together donated £621 to defray the cost of the western screen and the canopies of six of the stalls. By April 1894 the building was sufficiently advanced for *The Cambridge Review* (26 April) to observe that it rivalled in beauty the florid magnificence of its sister at Keble (the rest of the College, it said, was far from beautiful; 'the long northern building must ever remain an unfortunate eyesore'). By the summer of 1895 it was nearly ready for use. In July Charles Gore, canon of Westminster and editor of, and most controversial contributor to, *Lux Mundi*, came to the College to conduct a retreat. But on the 27th he collapsed from the heat. The Master thought he would fare better if he delivered most of his addresses in the new Chapel which, accordingly, he prepared. Gore still could not deliver his first address. So the Master spoke instead – the first words uttered formally within the walls of the new Chapel. Perhaps as a good omen a dove came in, to listen to the *Veni Creator*.

The Chapel was dedicated on 17 October. It was another grand occasion; the many guests included the Archbishop of Canterbury (Benson), twelve other bishops, and over fifty graduates of the College. To supplement the limited accommodation of the College the Master chartered a large part of the *Bull* hotel at his own expense. The festivities embraced two feasts and a crowded luncheon, and there were many speeches. Gladstone sent a felicitous message and was sorry that failing health prevented his presence. The Master solicited a signed portrait of herself from Queen Victoria. When it came, together with a gracious message, it was hung over the dais in the temporary Hall. The Archbishop provided the looked-for Latin witticism, saying that he was not a 'visitor' but a '*visitator*' ('frequentative substantive', he explained), which meant he would be visiting many times in the future. Alas he did not, for he died a year later.

The internal furnishing was completed during the summer. Personal gifts were numerous: in response to an appeal from the Master ninety-three Anglican archbishops and bishops donated the altar; Sarah Selwyn gave the altar cross and a costly set of altar vessels which had belonged to her husband; the Master's brother William with his wife and daughter gave the brass lectern; Fanny Patteson, the bishop's sister, gave his silver pectoral cross, to be inlaid in the centre of the high altar, and an office book which he had upon him when he died; Helen Gladstone and other members of Newnham gave an altar frontal because they were allowed to attend Holy Communion in the temporary Chapel on Sunday mornings; and the Steward and the College servants presented the oak episcopal chair for the sanctuary. Gladstone was persuaded by Lyttelton to donate the louder of the two Chapel bells for, says Owen Chadwick, 'Gladstone evidently thought that undergraduates needed to be well woken if they were to get up betimes in the morning.' [1]

In 1896 the old temporary Chapel was divided into two parts, one to serve as a Library, the other as a lecture room. The new Library was needed, for in the previous year the College had received over 5,000 theological books, chiefly patristic and liturgical, bequeathed by the Revd William Cooke, honorary canon of Chester, whilst in October 1896 came the books of Wheatley-Balme.

Selwyn left his mark upon his office, for what Lyttelton had established he consolidated. If Lyttelton had been preoccupied with the training of individuals, Selwyn cared especially for corporate unity and purpose. He did not increase the number of undergraduates, nor did he inspire great academic success (though he witnessed the creation of the Ratcliffe Exhibition, intended primarily to benefit scholars from King Edward's School in Birmingham). His attributes were moral greatness, muscular piety, and an ability to inspire affection, through which he implanted a Christian vision of spirituality and service which the College's Chapel would sustain in perpetuity.

First of all he reorganized the College staff. Lyttelton had imported into Selwyn College the methods he had learned at Cuddesdon and Keble, which suited his desire to maintain close personal contact with each individual student. But Selwyn, whose knowledge of academic organization was rudimentary and came solely from Eton and Trinity, thought that colleges might be organized rather as were dioceses, with plenty of delegation. He therefore separated the offices of Master and Dean, which Lyttelton had combined; one of the Tutors relinquished his office for the office of Dean, to have charge of routine discipline. Thus did the Master enhance his *magisterium*. He also increased the numbers and the efficiency of the staff. Unlike Lyttelton, he did not aspire to lecture upon anything but divinity. So he appointed a lecturer in history (W.E. Jordan, of King's; he paid his salary from his own); a lecturer in natural sciences (Lancelot Borradaile, a former scholar of the College); and an extra classical lecturer.

The Logarithm Society in 1897.
The Master (J.R. Selwyn) in the centre, to his left a junior member and then
A.L. Brown; in the second row H.G. Knott behind the Master; in the back
row, second from left, L.A. Borradaile.

He tried to treat the lecturers as though they were Fellows; he secured the appointment of one of them to attend meetings of the College Council, with a right to speak though not to vote.

Apart from his work for the Chapel perhaps Selwyn's greatest contributions to the furtherance of College corporatism were his support for the Boat Club and his creation of the annual Festival for the Commemoration of Benefactors.

To the Boat Club he gave impetus. He would encourage young freshmen to row when they thought that they could not. Whenever he was free and well enough he was down on the towing-path on his hand-tricycle, shouting out orders to the Selwyn crew as he kept pace with them in their practice. Once he was helped into the stern of a new Selwyn four, to cox it on its trial spin. To the College he presented the cups which thirty years before he had won in University races.

The festival he established in his first year was designed both to honour his father and to affirm the College's distinctive principles. It was to be kept on or around 17 October – St Etheldreda's Day, the day of his father's consecration. Benefactors were to be commemorated, in an event centred upon the celebration of Holy Communion. Past members of the College were to be reunited; undergraduates were to be invited. The first Commemoration was in 1894.

Possibly at this Commemoration, or around the time of this Commemoration, a custom took hold which was observed ever after. In June 1976 the Queen's private secretary received from the Master of Selwyn a charming explanation and a tentative request. The rough draft was thus:

> ... I have been meaning to write on a most peculiar matter and it may be lèse-majesté. The Fellows of my College (except on rare occasions when there are a lot of people) drink the loyal toast *sitting*; like the Royal Navy, but unlike the Navy in that we have no Bulkheads on which to hit our heads if we stand up. The origin appears to be that we had a Master in 1893–8 who had bad legs, and who could not, or could not easily, stand up; and so the Fellows (at first no doubt only on informal occasions) out of courtesy sat to keep him company. This practice is not motivated by any disrespect for The Queen; for (1) on the whole it has rather the opposite effect; (2) in consequence, partly, we probably drink her health more frequently (though certainly not more Bibulously) than any other College. Now that the 'tradition' has existed for more than ¾ of a century, I wondered whether to ask her if she would be so gracious as to approve our custom in view of its origin (if our historians are right) and circumstances! But it may be that this is the kind of question she prefers not to be asked; or that she would think too unimportant to be troubled with. There is no controversy over the matter, so I am not seeking her in one side of an argument.

Graciously but discreetly Her Majesty intimated that she was fascinated to hear of the custom, that she had no objection to its continuance, but that she felt her formal approval would not be appropriate.[2]

Because he was not academic Bishop Selwyn took little part in University business. But he carried the exhortatory principles of the Selwyn enterprise into the wider community. He continued his interest in missionary work. He succeeded Lyttelton as president of the Cambridge branch of the Society for the Propagation of the Gospel, travelling around on its behalf; he revived the undergraduates' association in aid of the SPG; he became secretary of the Central Board of Mission of the provinces of Canterbury and York; and he largely initiated the 'Foreign Service Order' of clergymen willing to serve abroad for short periods. He accepted the presidency of the Girls' Letter League, which promoted letter-writing between ladies and factory girls. He was involved in mission work in London, especially in the Eton Mission in Hackney Wick. In 1896, in association with Edward Talbot (then Bishop of Rochester) and others, he took a leading part in the transformation of Trinity Court – a lay settlement for social work in Camberwell – into Cambridge House, the task of which was to support and supplement in south London the work of various college missions as, in the East End, they were supported and supplemented by Oxford House.

In Cambridge he became president of, and revitalized, the Barnwell and Chesterton Clergy Fund, which existed to aid the poorer parishes in Cambridge. He visited the Cambridge infirmary regularly, held weekly services in Addenbrooke's Hospital, called upon the sick in the parish of St Giles, and cared for the welfare of little children. Every Whit Monday a hundred or so men from one or other of the clubs managed by Oxford House in Bethnal Green would come to Selwyn College for the day. They had dinner in Hall, the Master presiding.

His health collapsed in the Michaelmas term of 1897. The trouble was said to be bronchial and gastric. On 3 October he preached his last sermon, in St Paul's cathedral. On 20 October he was too ill to receive his guests at Commemoration and the Bishop of Lichfield (Legge) preached for him. Then, for a time, he revived.

On 23 January, worn and ravaged and after six months' absence, he attended Chapel for the last time. He gave the Absolution and the Blessing. On the 25th he left the Lodge to journey by easy to stages to Pau, in southern France. Annie and Pearlie went too, hoping the climate would do him good. They arrived on 2 February. On the 12th he died, murmuring scraps of the collects and the psalms, and recalling the old days on board the *Southern Cross*.

His memorials in Selwyn College were a portrait by Lowes Dickinson, fourteen stall canopies in the Chapel, and (from his relations, and also in the Chapel) a window of coloured glass. A scholarship bearing his name was founded by good Bishop Abraham and perpetuated by Annie. His own bequest to the place to which he had come diffidently was declaratory: an affirmation that humane politics and Christian learning (the bequest of the Lytteltons) were indeed what the College's founders had wished them to be – a sure foundation for missionary endeavour; and that, conversely, missionary endeavour might dignify the academic vocation.

Notes

1.   *Selwyn College 1882–1971: a short history*, Cambridge, 1973, p.5.
2.   Professor Chadwick's draft and the reply by the Queen's private secretary are in the Selwyn College archives.

Part II

Floreat Collegium!
1898–1945

In 1914 the editor of the *Selwyn College Calendar* concluded an article on the recently adopted statutes with this Latin exhortation, but it may well stand as a motto for the whole period covered by Part II of the history. It was a period of consolidation rather than innovation. There was progress, improvement, and growing confidence, but Selwyn remained what its founders had intended it to be.

The links with the Church of England remained strong, with sons of clergy still filling many of the places, a third of the undergraduates in an average year intending to take Holy Orders, and compulsory Chapel attendance continuing long after it had become voluntary in other colleges. It also continued to offer a Cambridge education to men whose parents could not afford the older colleges. With their commitment to physical as well as to spiritual strength, the founders would have been encouraged to learn that the Boat Club had fought its way near to the top of the first division. Above all, they would have rejoiced in the gratitude and affection shown by old members and seldom matched in longer-established colleges.

There was controversy over the establishment of a Fellowship, but the prevailing view was that the men who founded a College intended that in due course it should have Fellows, as in older foundations. A Hall and a Library were built, just as the original promoters had wished. When Selwyn celebrated its fiftieth birthday, the earliest buildings had already the appearance of maturity, but the links with earlier days were carefully nurtured. The men of the 1930s continued to do what the men of 1882 had ordained.

It was not, however, a period of unquestioning optimism. Two long-serving Masters did little to communicate a vision of the future. The status of Selwyn, first as a Public Hostel, then as an Approved Foundation, but not as a College recognized by the University, implied inferiority. There was also the uncomfortable knowledge that Selwyn lacked both money and academic distinction. The period ends therefore on a note of uncertainty: could the College flourish in the future without looking in new directions? The last Master of the period was just the man to give a positive answer to the question, but he had less than five years before the country plunged into war and all plans for the future were postponed.

More space is given in Part II than in Part III to long-serving Fellows. The imbalance is deliberate; the small band of men who led the College in these formative years – wretchedly paid, sometimes discouraged, but giving of their best – deserve this memorial. Notes and comments after each chapter provide more information about Fellows and graduates, together with some anecdotes that amused contemporaries and may inform posterity that life was serious but often fun.

A Note on Money and Values

Amounts are stated in predecimal form: 20 shilling (s) = 1 pound (£); 12 pennies (d) = 1 shilling. As there were 240 old pennies to the pound, 1 new penny = 2.4 old pennies.

In 1900 a middle-class professional or businessman could live comfortably on £800 a year (in a three- or four-bedroom house) with a living-in maid; in 1990 about £25,000 was required to enjoy a similar standard (with no living-in maid, but with a car and a full complement of household equipment). A multiple of 31.25 will therefore convert 1900 values into 1990 values. The equivalent of a gift of £3,000 (pages 127, 128) was £93,750.

By the 1930s about £1,000 was required to maintain the standard outlined above and the multiple to convert values is therefore 25; the 1990 value of a legacy of £10,000 (page 137) is £250,000.

It is possible to obtain indexes based on complex statistical analyses, but for non-technical readers the impression given above may be more revealing.

CHAPTER 7

Standing Firm – or Standing Still?
1898–1907

O N 31 MARCH 1898 the Council announced the election of
the new Master. They believed that they had found exactly
the right man to complement Lyttelton's dedicated energy and
Bishop J.R. Selwyn's sound judgement and human sympathies.
The Revd Professor Alexander Francis Kirkpatrick was a scholar
of the first rank and already well known in University circles. As
an undergraduate at Trinity he had won in succession three prestigious scholarships – Bell, Porson, and Craven – and he was
elected a Fellow of his College immediately after graduation in
1871. As the election was for life he remained a Fellow of Trinity
until his death sixty-eight years later. From classics he turned to
theology and in 1882, at the age of 33, was appointed Regius
Professor of Hebrew (combined at that time with a canonry of
Ely). By the time of his appointment as Master he had written
commentaries on the books of Samuel and on the Psalms, and a
course of his lectures, published as *The Doctrine of the Prophets*,
was in its third edition. During his Mastership he was elected as
Lady Margaret's Professor of Divinity.

His portrait in the Hall makes Kirkpatrick appear an imposing
figure with piercing eyes, high forehead, and flowing black beard.
Here was a man from whom much was expected, and outside
Selwyn there was perhaps some surprise that a man with such
brilliant prospects was willing to accept the Mastership. Inside
Selwyn there were high hopes that he would bring to the College
a reputation for learning, raise the academic performance of its
undergraduates, and advance its interests in the University.

With all his merits, Kirkpatrick lacked some of the qualities
that make for successful leadership – either by getting things done

or by holding out the promise of good things to come – and during his ten years as Masters Selwyn marked time rather than advanced. He may have believed that after a period of growth, time to gather strength was needed, but if so he failed to present consolidation as the prelude to improvement.

Unlike his predecessor Kirkpatrick was never on easy or intimate terms with the teaching staff. To undergraduates he seemed cold, remote, and oddly ineffectual. Years later two who had themselves gone on to successful careers agreed that he was temperamentally unsuited to be the Master of a college. Neither in speech nor appearance did they find him impressive. 'He had no small talk and was not interested in undergraduates and they had no respect for him.' How far these impressions were correct or widely held cannot be known, but there was a notable lack of warmth in later comments on his Mastership.[1]

The difficulty was not merely one of temperament but lay rather in different perceptions of what Selwyn ought to become. According to one view it was fulfilling a useful purpose by training clergy, giving the sons of impecunious clergy the chance of a university education, and offering an education based on the principles of the Church of England to men who intended to pursue lay careers. It was to perform these duties that the Council employed College lecturers whose function was to teach. This seems to have been Selwyn as its new Master perceived it. The alternative view was that the intention of the founders had been to establish a College, and this meant that it must become a place for learning and research as well as education. There was no questioning Selwyn's Anglican character, but in other respects the differences between it and the older colleges must be narrowed, not preserved.

During Bishop Selwyn's illness the Council had appointed T.H. Orpen as Vice-Master, and they may have considered him for the Mastership. It would have been a popular though unexciting choice. His academic attainments did not match Kirkpatrick's, but they were not negligible. After graduating at Trinity College, Dublin, he had come to Cambridge, and he was fourth classic in 1874. In the same year he was elected as a Fellow of Pembroke and served in various College offices until his marriage in 1881. He belonged to a wealthy Anglo-Irish family and had considerable private means from which he had already given generously to Selwyn (notably £3,000 towards the Chapel in 1892). A lesser gift was the Eton fives court in the garden (now sadly derelict) and into middle age he much enjoyed outwitting younger men at the game. In 1898, a vacancy in the Council being created when Bishop Hobhouse's failing health caused his resignation, the Council elected Orpen who thus became the first member of Selwyn's teaching staff to sit on its governing body.

Like many dons of his day, Orpen did not spend time in research and writing, but he had wide cultural interests (including water-colour painting and music) and was a good conversationalist. His *Calendar* obituary spoke of the 'genial zeal' with which he applied himself to College duties, and recalled the gratitude shown by his pupils for hospitality in the house that he had built for himself in Grange Road. He regularly attended Logarithms meetings and later published at his own expense a slim volume of his papers read to the society. There is a good portrait of him in the new Senior Combination Room by C.E. Brock (no relation to the present writer).

The new Master took over a College that was less confident than in its formative years. The Boat Club had had two bad years, losing five places in both Lents and Mays. Rugby and association football, after an auspicious start to the 1890s, had more recently achieved little. Academic performance had also lost momentum. Up to 1890 half or more of those graduating had taken honours, but by 1897 the proportion had dropped – to seven out of twenty-seven in 1897 and to six out of twenty-four in 1898. Even more worrying was the number who failed to get any degree. In the years from 1890 to 1895, 228 had matriculated but by 1898 only 181 of them had graduated. Moreover the situation seemed to be worsening. In the two years 1894 and 1895 seventy-five had matriculated but in 1897 and 1898 only fifty-nine graduated. Nor do the figures include those who were admitted but did not matriculate because they failed to pass the previous examination.

These were matters for internal concern; of more far-reaching importance was the character of the College. It had survived but remained an anomaly on the Cambridge scene: a College but not a College, a teaching staff but no Fellows, a Master with autocratic power but officially inferior to other heads of colleges, and over-riding authority vested in a Council that could meet as well in London as in Cambridge. It had minuscule endowments and was precluded from making a profit by the laudable commitment to keep charges low. The makeshift Hall, Library, and Senior Combination Room were visible reminders that the future was still uncertain.

Money was a crying need and in 1901 the Council resolved to appeal 'to the members of the Church of England generally' for funds 'to complete and endow the College'. The response was mixed. Orpen promised £1,000 but on condition that £9,000 was raised in donations of £1,000 or over (the condition was not met but Orpen gave generously on other occasions). There was one splendid donation of £3,000 from 'an original promoter of the College' (Bishop Edmund Hobhouse). Lord Ashcombe, a member of the Council, gave £250, and by 1902 there were seven other donations over £100. Small gifts were numerous, but the total fell far short of what was needed and there was no collective effort by leaders of the Church to endow the College.[2]

The wording of the appeal is revealing. It claimed that:

> the College is doing an important service in the Church by enabling both candidates for Holy Orders and those who are looking forward to other callings to obtain a university education economically but also under conditions especially favourable to the development of a religious and manly character.

Conspicuous by its absence was any reference to learning, research, or the advancement of knowledge.

This was a strategy of doubtful wisdom. A greater emphasis on the need to provide university places for young men from families with limited means might have roused more interest, but an avowed aim to create a centre of Christian learning might have caught the imagination. In an age when much private philanthropy was directed toward the endowment of libraries and museums (and in the United States to the establishment of universities) this was a missed opportunity. As it was, the wording of the appeal emphasized a fundamental difference between Selwyn and other colleges. The older foundations had grown up around endowments to support a community of learned men, but Selwyn had been founded, in the words of the Charter, with 'the especial object and intent' of providing a College for 'persons desirous of academical education and willing to live economically'. In other colleges past history and present customs made the support of Fellows their first priority, but in Selwyn there were no Fellows to support.[3]

The Charter directed the Council to take steps to obtain 'the incorporation of the College within the University of Cambridge', from which it might follow that as circumstances allowed the differences between Selwyn and the traditional college pattern should be narrowed. An obvious starting point would be the establishment of a Fellowship, and in March 1902 the College meeting formally requested the Council to make new statutes to provide for the election of twelve Fellows.

The prime movers were T.H. Orpen and L.A. Borradaile. Borradaile drew up draft statutes, and Orpen presented the case in a printed paper circulated in 1904. He argued that the creation of a Fellowship would remove 'an unnecessary distinction' between Selwyn and the older colleges. Objections to the proposal 'gathered force from the idea that Selwyn was not a College in the strict sense of the term' – but the Charter made it a College without qualification and the establishment of a Fellowship would be a step towards the completion of the founders' work.[4]

The way in which Kirkpatrick handled the proposal is puzzling. It would have been open to him to say, at an early stage, that the move was premature and could not have his support. This would have been unwelcome, but at least people would have known where they stood. Instead he allowed Borradaile to go ahead with the draft statutes, and it was not until 1904 that he made known his implacable opposition in a reply to Orpen circulated to the Council. In Cambridge, he said, the title of Fellow had always meant membership of a self-governing body with absolute control over college property; at Selwyn it would therefore 'mean something quite different from the title of Fellow at any other College'. If he had stopped there, his case would have been difficult to answer; but he went on to speculate on the qualities of men who might be elected as Fellows in terms that were certain to give offence. A lecturer once appointed would expect election in due course to a Fellowship, and 'in the main the staff of the College must be drawn from the class of men who have not been and are not likely to be elected elsewhere'. A Fellowship at Selwyn would therefore 'come to be regarded as a rather cheap and inferior distinction'.

Orpen replied with a list of those who had served as lecturers since 1882, of whom the majority had either gone on to Fellowships in other colleges or were, by any normal academic standards, eligible for that distinction. The Master replied that this proved his point: those who were of Fellowship calibre had not remained at Selwyn and it was 'from those who fail to get Fellowships elsewhere that the staff of this College must be recruited'. The logic was faulty because it relied on past evidence to predict what would happen in changed circumstances, and the needless offence given to long-serving lecturers can well be imagined.

It was true that Selwyn with its tiny endowments might not attract the ablest men, but not true that those who accepted election would necessarily be inferior to the average run of Cambridge Fellows. Most High Tables were small, the competition for Fellowships was stiff, and the outcome was often influenced by personal considerations that had nothing to do with academic merit. If the Selwyn lecturers holding office in 1904 had become Fellows they would have included a man with a first in classics who had been fourth in order of merit (Orpen), a first in both parts of the Natural Sciences Tripos (Borradaile), a Wrangler (Knott), a first in theology (A.L. Brown), and a Lightfoot Prize-winner with firsts in both classics and theology to his credit (Jordan).

The Council was divided. Sir Richard Jebb (Regius Professor of Greek) and the Bishop of Bristol (G.F. Browne) supported Orpen. V.H. Stanton (Ely Professor of Divinity) and W. Ince

(Regius Professor of Divinity at Oxford) agreed with the Master. The harshest rebuttal came from Sir Francis Powell, Bart., MP: 'The so-called Fellows ... would regard it as a grievance that they had no powers and the distinction between their position and that of Fellows of other Colleges would require explanation to those outside'. In other words, the 'so-called Fellows' would soon ask for more and outsiders would not understand why they lacked the power to obtain it.

The views of other members of the Council are unknown, but as no act was valid without the consent of the Master when present, it was pointless to persist against his strongly expressed opposition. His resolution was reinforced by a private assurance from the Warden of Keble that no such proposal had been made in his College and would be resisted if brought forward.

There was more to this than a dispute over the ripeness of time or the right to dispose of property. At stake was the authority of the Master, who had unlimited power to appoint lecturers, admit undergraduates, and make rules for internal management or discipline. A claim by Orpen that there was no intention to diminish the Master's power was disingenuous. His plan gave the Council responsibility for the election of Fellows, but limited its choice to persons nominated by the Master *and* Fellows. The Council could refuse to elect but no one could compel the Fellows to nominate; the Master might refuse to nominate but could not force the election of a candidate whom he preferred. In other but less clearly defined ways the authority of the Master would be diluted, for whatever his formal powers he would have to work with men who had been nominated by their colleagues, were elected by the Council not appointed by him, and could be dismissed only for gross misconduct or dereliction of duty. He would have to listen even if there was no obligation to consult.

The resentment caused by the suppression of the Fellowship scheme can be judged by an extract from a memorandum addressed by Borradaile to the then Master (Murray) in 1910.

> I think anybody who has held a Fellowship elsewhere and taken it more or less as a matter of course must find it hard to realize

how bitterly the withholding of this simple title can be felt by men who have borne the burden of College work (and done it as well, perhaps, as the Fellows of most Colleges) for years ... Our humiliation is the humiliation of the College, which we are trying to make an institution worthy of flying the flag of the Church of England in Cambridge.

This was the first but not the last test of the Charter's ambiguous wording. If Selwyn was to be a College, as the term was generally understood, then it must eventually adopt the collegiate pattern; but if the word 'College' meant something else, then another form of organization must be sought – without precedents to follow or models to imitate.

This is an appropriate point at which to notice the men who carried the principal burden of teaching and administration, and would have become Fellows under the Orpen plan. Orpen himself has already been introduced. He left the College in 1904 to become vicar of Great Shelford, but he continued as a member of the Council with a very active interest in the College. W. Nalder Williams, who succeeded Orpen in 1905, was the youngest of the group, but frequent references in the following pages to his reminiscences entitle him to first consideration.

Williams came to Selwyn from Trinity with firsts in classics and a post-graduate qualification in law. He helped to edit the revision of a standard work on Roman law but closed his career as a scholar in 1921 when he became secretary of the Local Examinations Syndicate. He laboured for more than twenty years to shed the 'local' image and establish bridgeheads in every part of the British Empire as it then was. The work put him in touch with many who were prominent in university affairs and gave him a wider view of educational problems than more inbred members of the society. His keen interest in music and art also brought to the society something that his older colleagues lacked. Increasing responsibilities forced him to give up teaching in 1930, but he remained active in College business and, as far as possible, kept up pleasantly informal contacts with undergraduates. After his retirement in 1945 he continued to visit Cambridge on syndicate business and delighted younger dons as a lively septua-genarian interested in everything that was new. His recollections of earlier years are lively, candid, and occasionally harsh in judge-ment, but running through them is a deep affection for the College.[5]

H.C. Knott was born in 1861, graduated at Peterhouse as 12th Wrangler in 1883, and was appointed a lecturer in mathematics at Selwyn in 1887. He became a Tutor in 1897 and Bursar in 1900 – combining the two offices until 1920, when he gave up the Tutorship, and continuing as Bursar until his retirement in 1928. Like many dons of his day, he devoted himself to College affairs and had no thought of research or even of keeping pace with advances in mathematical science. He was a keen sportsman, played tennis and fives into late middle age, and was a first-class billiards player. In an obituary tribute the then Vice-Chancellor described him as a man of 'conspicuous candour, downright in speech, and impatient of pretence ... combining a genuine modesty and an eager desire to give of his best in service to the community'. Nalder Williams, who knew him both as a colleague in Selwyn and as an active member of the Local Examinations Syndicate, remembered him as 'one of the simplest and most straightforward men I have ever known', but added that 'his mind could not readily give acceptance to new ideas'. As Bursar he had oversight of notable developments – the building of the Hall and later of the Library – but it is probable that in his later years the College would have been better served by a younger man. His successor as Bursar (G.B. Perrett) found that he had kept few records and handled the accounts in a way that only he understood. There is a good portrait of Knott by J.K. Green in which he appears, with high collar and drooping moustache, as the epitome of an Edwardian don.[6]

L.A. Borradaile has a unique place in Selwyn annals. He was one of the earliest Selwyn graduates and the first to be placed in Class I (in both parts of the Natural Sciences Tripos). He was appointed a College lecturer in 1895 (possibly as the result of a recommendation by Oscar Browning) and served continuously until his retirement in 1938 (with a further spell during the Second

Top left: L.A. Borradaile.
Top right: W.E. Jordan.

Left: W.N. Williams.

World War). For much of his life he lived in College and when he moved out he was no farther away than 31 Grange Road.

Borradaile was physically small, always in a hurry, always busy, often excitable, but invariably punctilious in everything that he undertook. His most memorable physical feature was a moustache with carefully waxed and upward reaching ends. He was easy to caricature but impossible not to respect. Twenty years after his death Nalder Williams described him as 'the Selwyn man who saw, sooner than anyone else, possibilities ahead of the College as a developing institution ... and it was to him more than to any other person living or dead that the College owes its present prestige in the University'. S.C. Carpenter thought that he had three overmastering interests – Selwyn College, zoology, and correct use of the English language – in that order. To this should be added devotion to the Church of England.[7]

A passage from Borradaile's obituary in the *Calendar* is worth quoting in full, both for its appreciation of the man and for its portrayal of the obligations felt by an old-style don toward his College and its men.

> He was deeply interested in improving the College buildings and adding to its furniture; he was even more interested in the progress of his pupils in their studies and in the maintenance of a healthy corporate life in the College ... He was glad when his pupils did well in examinations, but he would never let them forget that learning is not everything, and that he wished them to take their full share in all departments of College life. He set them a good example. He was most regular (though seldom punctual) in his attendance at College Chapel; he rarely missed a meeting of the Science Club or of the Logarithms; he appeared at College concerts, though he had no real liking for music; he made a point of being seen on the towpath at the Races, and upon the playing field at important College matches, though he had little interest in games as such, and was apt to sneak away unobtrusively once he was satisfied that his presence had been noticed by the right people.

He made numerous benefactions to Selwyn, none very large but cumulatively important, and he was the first Fellow of the College to win scholarly recognition (and an ScD) for his work.

His reputation as a scientist rested upon numerous papers in professional journals, on his *Manual of Zoology* (published in 1912 with eleven revised editions to follow), and on lectures that were revised every year but still managed to impart the freshness of

The Master, Lecturers, and Scholars in 1910.
Front row: Jordan (with his hat on), Murray between two scholars, Srawley,
Knott, Williams. Borradaile, at the left end of the second row.

discovery. According to C.F.A. Pantin, a major figure in the history of Cambridge zoology, 'there can have been few men who influenced the career of so many students'. He demanded much from the audience but 'to those that followed him he gave ... an intense appreciation of the beauty and variety of things to be seen in the natural world'.

Despite his abiding devotion to Selwyn, Borradaile was not an easy colleague to work with. Nalder Williams said that he was not 'an attractive personality and much resented opposition in any form from those he expected to support him'. Others who knew him well made similar judgements. He was absurdly sensitive to imagined affronts, resented criticism, and relapsed into long periods of brooding silence when things did not turn out as he wished. Gratitude for what he did was often voiced, but seldom affection; and from those who knew him only in his later years less gratitude came than was his due.

W.E. Jordan was in many ways – appearance, manner, and attitude to life – the antithesis of Borradaile. A large, portly, ponderous man, and regarded by undergraduates as something of a snob, he dominated any company in which he was found. Nalder Williams thought that he had a 'great facility ... for mastering a subject without too much burdensome study', but for a clever man he was curiously lacking in intellectual ambition. He was a successful lecturer and attracted men from many colleges to his courses on ancient history and the medieval English constitution, but he wrote nothing, conducted no original research, and in his later years intelligent undergraduates detected that he had read little of the recent literature. In College business he was quite content to leave the hard work to Knott and Borradaile, but might then oppose them on grounds that were unpredictable.

Jordan had private means, supplemented by good earnings from lecture fees, and owned a house in Suffolk to which he withdrew during the vacations. It was said, not perhaps with complete accuracy, that he came up to Cambridge on the first day of full term and left on the last, and that he kept no tutorial files, but relied on memory and brief notes scribbled on the blank pages of his University diary. In all he was a gifted man who did less with his talents than might have been expected, but he gave to the High Table a style and urbanity that would otherwise have been lacking. S.C. Carpenter thought that behind a cynical façade was a profound devotion to the Church and to the College. No benefactions were recorded during his lifetime and to many undergraduates he seemed to be a country squire with little interest in the College; but when he died in 1935 Selwyn became the richer by a legacy of £10,000 (over a quarter of a million in end-of-the-century terms).

The Revd A.L. Brown left Selwyn in 1907 and has already been noticed as the first historian of the College. He was a good classical scholar with wide cultural interests and a more than amateur knowledge of music. His manner was often abrupt and Williams did not 'find him an easy colleague in ... classical teaching'. His devotion to Selwyn was apparent in his *History*, but he probably disliked the constraints of College life and was delighted to accept the College living at Wonersh in Surrey, where he enjoyed many fruitful years as a parish priest. When he died he left a legacy and some furniture to Selwyn.[8]

In 1905 there were eight members of the High Table. Six were bachelors and dined together every night in full term, and the two married men dined frequently. They did not form a very happy society. Nalder Williams was 'horrified at our absence of decent social manners when discussing the problems which necessarily faced a new foundation ... [and] some of us definitely felt uncomfortable when anything in the nature of scene followed a piece of deliberate provocation from one or other member of the society'. Borradaile was touchy and easily offended; Jordan was sarcastic, mischievous, and liked to bait Borradaile. He also liked to shock Williams (whom he judged to be a little prim) with mildly salacious anecdotes. A.L. Brown had 'certain faults of temper' that could be embarrassing. Knott was genial but his combination of two offices – Bursar and Tutor – was resented and his argument that this concentration of power was the best way to combat magisterial autocracy was not appreciated by the others. This social tension was a symptom of frustration. The College officers could talk but only the Master and Council could decide.

In 1907 Kirkpatrick was appointed Dean of Ely and resigned the Mastership after a regime that had been strong but negative. Nalder Williams recorded a verdict that is difficult to challenge.

> He undoubtedly did impart to the College over which he presided a certain dignity exceeding that of any other holder of the office ... [but] it is not easy to see what he did to help forward the development of Selwyn. He was a slave of duty and did what he considered right but I never thought that he had a full appreciation of the potentials of a new College in the University; he regarded it more as some of his Trinity contemporaries had done – as a religious seminary.

To say that Kirkpatrick regarded Selwyn as a religious seminary overstates the case but contains a visible grain of truth.

There might be a more generous assessment. External observers knew nothing of internal disappointment. For them the most obvious conclusion was that thirty years after the plan for Selwyn College was first formed it had become a stable element in the chemistry of university education. As Selwyn continued to attract students there was *prima-facie* evidence that it satisfied a need and justified its existence. As a Public Hostel it had harmed no one and benefited many whom it had enabled to graduate with Cambridge degrees. The less complacent members of the University may have seen its existence and survival as a good precedent for opening more widely the Cambridge doors. Seen in this light the fact that it had been headed by a distinguished scholar – now become a dignitary of the Church – was an asset, not a liability.

Notes and Comments

1. *Kirkpatrick as Master*: The two old members were Colonel F.A. Woods and Prebendary S.J. Hughes. Professor Chadwick kept notes on a conversation with them in 1957. Kirkpatrick's obituary in *The Calendar* (1940–1) said that as Master 'he was careful and punctilious in all affairs of the College and solicitous that it should maintain a high standard of academic performance' but said nothing about him as a personality. *The Times'* obituary gave bare mention to the fact that he had been Master of Selwyn.

2. *Bishop Hobhouse's gift of £3,000*: Orpen's offer prompted him to give at that time rather than by legacy. He was not named publicly as the donor until after his death in 1904.

3. *The Church and learning*: Writing to Kirkpatrick (28 May 1898) Bishop Abraham repeated a remark made to him by Bishop J.R. Selwyn when the plans for founding the College were being prepared. 'If you can, don't let it be said that the Church of England will be content with a lower standard of intellectual distinction, than what is demanded of men in other Colleges of the University.' This was advice that might have been given more serious attention.

4. *The Fellowship plan, 1902–4*: Papers relating to the proposal and its suppression are in the Selwyn College Archives. Sir Richard Jebb was the most distinguished member of the Council (a leading Greek scholar, Member of Parliament for the University, and holder of the Order of Merit).

5. *Reminisencies by Nalder Williams.* He dictated a 'Social History of Selwyn College' late in life and there is a typed transcript in the Selwyn Archives. Dr P.J. Durrant, who came to Selwyn as a Fellow in 1923 and knew many of the people mentioned, thought that judgements in the 'History' were sometimes sharp but generally fair.

6. *H.G. Knott*: He was much respected by the undergraduates, and was often remembered in later years for his sound commonsense and helpful advice. As Bursar, at least in the 1920s, he had less respect from his colleagues. In a conversation with Owen Chadwick in 1961, Perrett said that Knott 'muddled everything, and yet insisted on his own way'. Perrett found that trust funds were being used for general purposes – as a result of errors in accounting, not attempts to deceive.

7. *S.C. Carpenter*: This and later references to his opinions and observations come from an unpublished autobiography. A typewritten copy is in the Selwyn Archives.

8. *Selwyn livings*: The advowson of Wonersh was given to Selwyn by Lord Ashcombe, a member of the Council, in 1905. The other Selwyn living, Old Cleeve in Somerset, was given by the rector and patron, the Revd W.W. Herringham, in 1900, but subject to arrangements already made for the next vacancy.

CHAPTER 8

Taking Shape
1908–1914

THE COUNCIL chose as Kirkpatrick's successor another, but a very different, former Fellow of Trinity. The Revd Richard Appleton had no previous connection with Selwyn but was the kind of man whom the College had been founded to help. The son of a country clergyman with a large family, he was educated at Christ's Hospital (where parents paid very low fees), won a minor scholarship at Trinity, was elected a Fellow after graduation, and served for many years as a Tutor. At a time when specialization was not demanded he successfully supervised in mathematics, theology, and Hebrew. He was also superintendent of the Jesus Lane Sunday School, then a thriving institution serving children from the poorer Cambridge parishes. He left Trinity to occupy the College living of St George's, Camberwell, but after some years moved to quieter pastures at Ware. He had been examining chaplain for Bishop Lightfoot of Durham and continued under his two successors.

Appleton was a modest, likeable man. Nalder Williams wished particularly to record that 'we found it natural to receive, as we did at times, letters from him signed "yours affectionately" '. Everyone who knew Appleton at Selwyn spoke of him with enthusiasm, but he was an improver rather than an innovator. In the words of Professor V.H. Stanton, a life-long friend, 'he continued that which had been well done before, enlarging it and introducing improvements in plan and method; he left the tasks for those who should follow easier'. His Mastership was tragically short, but he was remembered with gratitude for promoting a more congenial social climate and for getting the Hall built.

Some years before Orpen had launched a plan to raise money for a Hall and Senior Combination Room, donated £500 (the equivalent of about £20,000 in the 1990s) and promised more. The project then hung fire until Appleton put new life into it by appealing personally to possible donors and by setting up a fund-raising committee that included junior as well as senior residents. His first estimate was £7,100, but allowed only £560 for architect's fees and heating and even at that time this was too low. A year later the estimate recorded in the Calendar was £9,600.[1]

By October 1909 members of the Council, the College staff, and graduates had contributed £4,695. Resident undergraduates and BAs raised £265, and well-wishers (the majority being resident members of other colleges) contributed £926. A further £1,000 had been promised by Orpen and the Council squeezed £1,000 out of reserves. Although this still left a gap, Appleton persuaded the Council to go ahead, commission an architect, and engage a contractor.

In addition to Orpen, other large donors were Appleton himself, Mrs Annie Selwyn, Prebendary William Selwyn and Professor Stanton. News that the Hall was certain to be built brought more support, and £1,800 was raised in the next twelve months. Mrs Selwyn contributed a further £1,200 for the Senior Combination Room and Prebendary Selwyn another £300 for the screen at the east end of the Hall.

So the Hall was built – and very well built. Appleton is remembered by his initials on the front of the staircase. The initials of the lecturers of the day are modestly inscribed on the external cornice. The arms on the inside of the screen are those of Mrs Selwyn and T.R. Orpen. The style was explained by E.A.L. Oulds, the chief architect, on historical principles. The early Tudor of the oldest buildings and the late Gothic of the Chapel was followed by a Jacobean Hall, just as it might have been in any group of buildings erected piecemeal between the fifteenth and seventeenth centuries.

The original plan included a storey above the Senior Combination Room and a three-storey wing extending almost to A staircase, but it was decided to dispense with these features for the time being. In the event the rooms over the Senior Combination Room were never added and it was not until the 1960s that the

The Chapel and the Hall.
The pictures show both buildings as they are in the late twentieth century. In
1914 the court was about three feet lower with steep banks up to the path.
The temporary library and a large tree would have been seeni n the left fore-
ground. The panelling in the Hall had been recently installed. At the east end
the copy of Richmond's portrait of G.A. Selwyn (the original being then in St
John's College) was in pla;ce, and possibly the posthumous portrait of Appleton.
Murray (at the extreme right) would wait for several years to be painted. The
High Table would normally have been laid for six or seven. In other respects
the Hall has remained as it was planned and built.

west wing was built, on a more extended plan than had originally been proposed. What Selwyn got, without these additions, was a dignified Hall, more spacious than in many larger colleges, and a pleasant panelled Senior Combination Room. What was not realized at the time was that the Hall had excellent acoustics for chamber music.

It was intended to hand over the completed building to the College on 1 March, but instead came the shock of Appleton's tragic death from a virulent form of influenza. Modern medicine would probably have ensured his quick recovery, but in 1910 it was all over in less than a week. By a cruel coincidence E.A.L. Ould also died before the building was complete.

Although the Hall was ready for use in October 1913 the panels planned for the interior were not yet in place, but this delay proved to be fortunate. Since the late seventeenth century there had been an English church in Rotterdam, reputedly designed by Sir Christopher Wren. The British government had subscribed £2,000 for its restoration in 1815 but by 1913 it no longer served a congregation and in spite of appeals for its preservation demolition was ordered. The controversy attracted the attention of A.C. Benson of Magdalene, who bought as much of the woodwork as could be rescued, gave the pulpit to Lincoln cathedral, the altar rails to St Giles' in Cambridge, and the altar-piece with additional panelling to Selwyn in memory of his father, Archbishop Edward Benson.[2]

Pursuing the historical sequence suggested by the original architect, it was appropriate to place in a Jacobean building the kind of embellishment that an eighteenth-century benefactor would have chosen. When first received the panels were covered by many coats of varnish; cleaning brought out their enduring quality and the details were picked out in gilt. Later they were listed as Selwyn's only ancient monument.

Appleton's successor was J.O.F. Murray, also a Trinity man, then Fellow and Dean of Emmanuel, and at the time of his appointment Warden of St Augustine's College at Canterbury. He had visited

Selwyn several times as patron of the lay readers who held (and still hold) their annual meeting in the College. Murray was scholarly, kindly, and well liked by the undergraduates, but not a forceful personality. Nalder Williams thought that he wasted opportunities at a time when Selwyn was ready to move forward. To be just, it must be noted that four of his nineteen years as Master were taken up by war and that the College was in good heart when he retired in 1928; but Williams was correct in saying that he imparted no vision of future growth and had little interest in wider academic issues. In his annual report to the Council the foremost and most detailed item was always an assurance to members that the rules for Chapel attendance and the compulsory divinity lectures were being observed, and everything else was dealt with briefly and as formal items.[3]

Nalder Williams also observed that during his long period as Master, Murray 'was not prominent at any stage in University affairs'. At a time when Selwyn needed to cultivate a more positive presence on the Cambridge scene it did not help to have an invisible Master. In many ways Mrs Murray, a good musician and talented artist who took an active interest in the material and moral welfare of undergraduates, made a deeper impression than her husband.

Although Murray initiated little, he did not oppose revival of the Fellowship plan. The resignation of Kirkpatrick had opened the way, Appleton had been sympathetic, and in 1910 the Council set up a committee, drawn from its own members and the College officers, to consider revision of the statues. Its recommendations, accepted by the Council, were to create a Fellowship of not fewer than six or more than ten, and to constitute the Master and Fellows as an administrative body with responsibility for academic and domestic management of the College.

In announcing its decision the Council took pains to refute the arguments advanced by Kirkpatrick six years earlier: 'There is now no doubt that men of the same type as in other Colleges are available to fill College offices in Selwyn.' Perhaps Orpen, still a member of the Council, suggested the wording. In the *Calendar* Borradaile explained that the new Fellows would enjoy the same rights and exercise the same responsibilities as the Fellows of other Colleges save for ownership of the College property. This one exception had been recognized as insufficient ground for denying them the title of Fellow.

The first Fellows, installed in 1913, were – in order of seniority – H.C. Knott, W.E. Jordan, L.A. Borradaile, the Revd S.C. Carpenter and W.N. Williams. Four have already been introduced. Carpenter would later be Dean of Exeter and the author of well-written books that made theological learning available to a wide public. He resigned his Fellowship during the war when Selwyn was unable to pay stipends to its Fellows, returned in 1919, and then became vicar of Bolton in Lancashire before being appointed at Exeter. Unlike his Conservative colleagues, he was an early supporter of the Labour party and took a lively interest in social questions. Two chapters of his unpublished autobiography contain much interesting information about Selwyn during the time that he knew it.

The new statutes required Fellows, Scholars and Exhibitioners to be members of the Church of England. It had been the invariable practice to confine College appointments to Anglicans, and the Charter had committed Selwyn to providing academic education combined with 'Christian training, based upon the principles of the Church of England'; but apart from the requirement that the Master should always be a Clerk in Holy Orders, no denominational tests had been prescribed. In restricting the Fellowship to members of the Church of England, or of a church in communion with it, the new statutes imposed a legal requirement that had not previously existed, and the move that brought Selwyn closer to the traditional format of a Cambridge college also erected a new barrier to recognition by the University.

The amenities of College life were old fashioned even by the standards of the day. There was gas lighting in the Fellows' rooms but undergraduates had oil lamps. There was no running water in rooms and no toilets on the staircases; hip baths and chamber pots were the rule. All the service was provided by gyps who often slept in bare comfort in the gyp-rooms. Except for a few cleaning women the College had an all-male domestic staff. Apprentice boys occupied dim attics on C and D staircases (and later on F). All servants living in College had to attend the service of Compline at 10 p.m.

Cheap labour made life pleasant for the dons and undergraduates. The gyps carried up the coal, lighted the fires on winter mornings, brought up a jug of hot water for the morning wash and pailfuls for an evening bath, made the beds and cleaned the shoes. All meals were included in the terminal fee, with a large breakfast, a bread and cheese lunch (a hot dish for one shilling extra), and a plain but plentiful dinner. The dons always had breakfast and lunch sent to their rooms. Undergraduates could ask permission to have lunch sent from the kitchen if they were entertaining guests.

The ethos of the College was formed in the body of the Hall rather than at High Table. The majority of undergraduates were there because Selwyn had accepted them when their parents could not afford any other Cambridge college, and their gratitude was real and lasting. The sense of being different from the rest of the University generated a determination to show that they were as good if not better than anyone else; but geographical isolation meant that much energy and enthusiasm was expended in the College rather than flowing out into wider University channels. With fewer than 130 undergraduates in residence, everyone knew everyone else by sight and usually by reputation, and there was an expectation that every individual would pull his weight in some way. Support for Selwyn boats, teams, and other activities was treated almost as a moral obligation. All this made for a lively and happy community, but also for inbreeding and limited privacy.

Admissions in 1908 and 909 give a good impression of the Selwyn 'constituency'. In these two years sixty-four men were admitted, of whom twenty-four were from public boarding schools, three from public day schools, twenty-eight from grammar schools or the equivalent, two were from overseas, and five cannot be identified. Of twenty-nine admitted in a single year (1913) seven were from public boarding schools, four from public day schools, sixteen from grammar schools, and one is not identified.

One might suppose that Selwyn was in advance of its time by admitting so high a proportion from non-élite schools, but it is more correct to say that it adhered to a pattern that had been normal in earlier times. In his history of the University of Cambridge Christopher Brooke notes that in the 1880s 23.2 per cent of the undergraduates at Caius came from grammar schools or the equivalent, but that by 1907–11 their share had fallen to 10.3. This was evidence of a change in educational fashion not social composition. In the middle of the nineteenth century it was normal for professional men and the lesser country gentlemen to send their sons to the local grammar school. Then public boarding schools came into vogue and more were established to meet the demand. However, there were still many families with high social status but low incomes – the parish clergy were typical – who could not afford boarding school fees and it was from this stratum that Selwyn drew most of its grammar school applicants.

A glance at parental occupations proves the point. In 1912 the fathers of freshmen included eleven clergymen, three schoolmasters, two doctors, two civil servants (probably in the Colonial Service), one lawyer, one naval officer, one architect, and one superintendent of a reform school. Only three were in business (two stockbrokers and one vaguely described as a merchant). Four were identified only as 'Esq.', but at a time when this designation still meant something they would certainly have described themselves as gentlemen. Only three parents – a copper warehouse man, a builder, and an iron moulder – were from a lower social class. A note by the name of the iron moulder's son, saying that fees would be paid by St Augustine's, Canterbury (a training school for non-graduate clergy), shows that a boy from a humble family might still climb the clerical ladder, just as so many eminent churchmen had done in the past.[4]

Ordinands were always numerous. In his 1906 *History* A.L. Brown recorded that from the foundation to 1903, 440 men had taken degrees (223 obtaining honours) and that 309 of them had taken Holy Orders. In the early twentieth century the proportion of clergy among graduates was lower and falling gradually, but they remained the largest single body among old Selwyn men. Although the news of old members published in the *Calendar* inflated the number of clergy (because their appointments and preferments were reported in the national press), their predominance over laymen was significant. For instance, in 1914 clergymen accounted for sixty out of seventy-three whose activities were reported.

Apart from the large number of clergymen, there was nothing unusual about the careers chosen by Selwyn men. In 1914 the old members noted in the *Calendar* included six schoolmasters, one Oxford don (Percy Simpson, University lecturer in English), two colonial civil servants, one doctor, one inspector of schools in India, and one director of a mining company. This selection of middle-class professions was typical of the careers sought by Cambridge undergraduates at the time. Most colleges had more academic high-flyers than Selwyn; these would be thinking of the Home or Indian Civil Service, the Inns of Court, academic careers, or posts at the more prestigious public schools. They would also have had more who expected to inherit wealth and took life easily. Apart from these exceptions the chosen careers of Selwyn men were similar to their contemporaries in other colleges. A few Cambridge graduates might enter family financial, commercial, or manufacturing businesses, but not for another forty years would a significant number look in these directions.

There was no absolute bar to the admission as commoners of men who were not members of the Church of England, but the prospectus invited applications only from members of that Church, so few non-Anglicans were likely to apply or to be accepted if they did. The rare exceptions were men from Christian but non-Anglican schools overseas where there had been no alternative Christian institution. However, it had been known for a point to be stretched when an applicant was a very promising oarsman.

There was no room for discretion when Scholarships and Exhibitions were awarded. Applicants had to prove membership of the Church of England, or of a church in communion with it, before entering for the examination. This restriction was written into the new statutes against the advice of the Visitor, Archbishop Randall Davidson, who believed that to require a declaration from a young man when so much was at stake invited insincerity, and that it would be better to ask of them no more than their willingness to accept instruction according to the principles of the Church of England. He may also have hoped that young Nonconformists in an Anglican society might be drawn towards the Church of England.[5]

Men who did not win awards might face financial difficulties. Although the costs at Selwyn were low, some parents with modest incomes and large families could not afford to meet them. In other cases circumstances might change on the death or incapacity of an undergraduate's father, and there were no College funds available to help undergraduates in need. There were often some men who could not afford to take up places that had been offered and others who faced the prospect of having to leave Cambridge. Probably help was sometimes given by individuals, but as might be expected no publicity was given to such gifts. Bishop J.R. Selwyn's widow, Annie Selwyn, realized that there were often genuine cases of hardship and offered help to deserving men if the circumstances were made known to her, though she hoped that recipients of her generosity would be sons of gentlemen.[6]

The number of men who encountered such difficulties was not great, but most Selwyn men came from families with limited means and knew that if they wanted to succeed they must rely on their own talents. They also knew that in most occupations that indefinable element called 'character' would count for more than academic performance. A degree was proof that three years had been spent in the University and that the time had not been wasted, but except for schoolmasters the subject mattered little and the level attained mattered less. Indeed future employers tended to look with suspicion on applicants who were too clever. They wanted well-rounded personalities and a good sporting record counted for more than examination results.

This explained though did not wholly justify the enormous amount of energy and interest concentrated on sport. It should also be added that with the scale of values as they were, the College gained more from its reputation on river, field, and track than from a handful of firsts, and some striking successes made

Selwyn's name more widely known. On the river Selwyn was in the first division along with the largest colleges. Other sports made a respectable showing with a particularly good record in association football.

The importance attached to sport can be measured by the space taken up by reports from the College clubs in the *Calendar*. In addition to general accounts, individual achievements or failings were recorded after the manner of school reports. The Boat Club report for 1912–13 conveys some impression of the spirit of the times. One 'conscientious worker ... did much towards promoting good fellowship' but 'should try to think more of minor points of style'. Another 'confirmed his previous reputation as a rough oar but a hard worker; if he could have overcome general clumsiness and a tendency to lose his head he would have proved a really good oar'. The captain-elect for the coming year was not spared: he had been 'rather a disappointment as he failed to combine body and leg-work, consequently his blade was seldom in the water for more than half the stroke'. The cox of the first boat had 'improved vastly in steering, but should bear in mind that it is also his duty to assist his crew by a judicious use of his voice'. The Rugby Football Club noted 'a useful and heavy forward ... he should learn to keep in the back row [but] as a forward had improved immensely'. This was F.S. Marsh, a future Fellow and Professor of Divinity. More than faint praise went to a member of the hockey team who 'considering his fairly complete ignorance of the game made quite a good show at back'.

Intellectual life in the College was represented by the Music Society, the Science Society, the Debating Society, the Logarithms, and the Controversialists. There was also a crop of short-lived societies that must have provided entertainment or even food for thought while they lasted, and 1911 was a bumper year with the Differential Calculus (probably a rival to the Logarithms rather than a mathematical society), the Discussionaries (to consider drama and distinguished from the Controversialists who dealt with English poetry), the Hittites (said to be social and literary but with no indication of which had priority), and the Monks (a debating society that included members from Newnham and Girton).[7]

Compared with the bright sporting prospects, academic performance was dim but must be set in the wider University context.
In his *History* Christopher Brooke records that in Caius from
1907 to 1911 an annual average of 31.2 per cent went out with
pass degrees and 15.9 per cent left with no degree (a total of 47.1
per cent without honours). Selwyn had proportionately more pass
degree men than Caius, but few left without degrees. Outright
failures were few and Selwyn had no wealthy, sporting or dilettante
young men who were not interested in getting a degree.

In 1908, a typical year, exactly half of the thirty-two freshmen
had still to pass the previous examination before they could matriculate, and required intensive coaching by College lecturers
before they could proceed. Most modern dons would resent the
call for so much elementary teaching, but the collective experience
did something to create a shared sense of corporate identity.
Nalder Williams remained 'convinced that the friendships thus
formed played some part in creating a deep sense of loyalty to
the institution'. The standard required was not high, few failed
completely, and there was usually a dispensation for undergraduates
who missed out on one paper and wanted to try again.

Once through the previous examination, or exempt from it by
examinations passed at school, a majority set their sights on an
ordinary degree. In 1906 (a typical year) thirty-three freshmen
were admitted but only thirteen read for honours. Three years
later the harvest reaped by this thirteen included one Wrangler
(19th in order of merit), four in the upper division of Class II,
two in the lower division, three in Class III, and three who failed
honours but were allowed the ordinary degree. One was successful
in the Mus Bac. Of the men reading for the ordinary degree
eighteen completed the course in three years and one in four.
Thus, with the inclusion of the three honours candidates allowed
the ordinary degree, exactly two-thirds of those who matriculated
in 1906 went out with pass degrees.

In 1914 there was joy at the top with a Wrangler in mathematics
and two firsts in natural sciences, but the honours tail was long
and weak with one in the upper division of the second class, seven
in an undivided second class, seven in the lower division, thirteen

in Class III, and one allowed the ordinary degree. In the two years 1913 and 1914, only five ordinands read for honours in theology (three seconds and two thirds) and thirty took special examinations in theology for the ordinary degree, with twenty-two in Class III. Of the sixteen candidates taking an examination in history for the ordinary degree eleven were in Class III. Fellows made no public complaints and consoled themselves with the knowledge that many with modest results in past years had gone to be admirable parish priests or lead useful lives in other spheres; but privately they must have hoped for better things.[8]

Despite the meagre academic record there was optimism in the air in June 1914. Things were going well and would go even better. There was euphoria on the river and the *Calendar* report declared that 'if it were allowable to talk of a red letter *year* we should say that the Boat Club had just passed through one'. In the Lents the first boat went up three places and the second two; in the Mays the second boat did not get on, but the first went up three places to tenth. It had only once been higher. At Henley they reached the semi-final of the Thames Cup and lost by only a length to the eventual winners. On the combined performance in Mays and at Henley members of the first boat won their oars.

Nor was this all. 'The season has been an excellent one', reported the Cricket Club. Association football 'looked back on the year's performance with extreme gratification' The hockey team had 'enjoyed a most successful season'. Rugby football, tennis, and athletics were more restrained but held out hope for the future. Nor were things of the mind neglected. The Debating Society had 'passed through a very successful year', and enthusiastic reports came from the Logarithms, the Science Society, and the Controversialists.

For their part, the Fellows were content with the new statutes and confident that the society would soon be enlarged as new members were elected. They were proud of their new Senior Combination Room, and it was noticeable that much of the asperity noted by Nalder Williams in earlier years had worn away. When the College was full there was a surplus of about £1,000 a year to put into reserve or to pay into the recently established Master and Fellows Endowment Fund, and with an unprecedented number of applications for admission the future was secure.[9]

The affection for Selwyn shown by so many old members was proof that past labours had not been in vain. The College's growing reputation in schools promised much for the future. It seemed that Selwyn stood on the threshold of greater achievement, and justified a confident exhortation by the editor of the *Calendar* – Floreat Collegium!

Then on a fine day in August hopes were abruptly dashed. In October few than half of those who had been expected to fill the College came into residence, and many absent friends were already in uniform.

Notes and Comments

1. *Building the Hall*: There is much material, including architect's drawings, in the College Archives. Fund raising is recorded in the *Calendar*, but Appleton's unexpected death meant that celebration when the Hall was opened was subdued.

2. *The Hall panelling*: Its provenance, history, and reception is fully covered in the Selwyn Archives.

3. *Murray as Master*: Williams was not alone in denigrating him. Many years later F.H. Woodward referred to his "nineteen sterile years" in the Lodge (in an obituary of Bishop Chase). In spite of his benign appearance, some people found him cold and unsociable. After dinner in the Senior Combination Room (according to C.W. Phillips) he read the newspaper and never talked to anyone. Rightly or wrongly, most people assumed that during his Mastership Borradaile, Knott, and Jordan ran the College.

4. *Parental occupations*: Murray kept an admissions book in which the parental occupations were recorded; unfortunately the record for his own years is incomplete and there is no consolidated record for other periods.

5. *Archbishop Randall Davidson and religious tests*: His views are set out in a paper preserved in the Selwyn Archives, but there is no record of how it was discussed or why it was rejected.

6. *Undergraduates in need*: Mrs Selwyn wrote to Murray offering financial aid to 'the right kind of young man' offered a place at Selwyn but unable to accept it. 'If you have *good* men and *Gentlemen* for choice & to whom it will be a real help ... let me know ... Only I would confess I prefer that it should be given to Gentlemen's sons as a rule.' There were later examples of private generosity.In the 1930s John Breay was in difficulties because of unforeseen changes in his family circumstances. Through the good offices of the Bursar (G.B. Perrett) he received help each term from a lady who remained anonymous. To this day he does not know the name of his benefactress, but as she was known to Perrett she had probably helped others.

7. *Clubs and societies*: P.M. Morrow used the *Calendar* and *The Sell* (an undergraduate magazine) to compile a list of clubs and their ties. Some of the latter are framed in the College bar, and the results of his enquiries were published in the *Calendar* for 1990–1. The list is admittedly incomplete but gives a good impression of the varied activities and interests in Selwyn before and after the First World War.

8. *The Wrangler in 1914*: He was L.J. Sutton. After graduation he joined the Egyptian Meteorological Service (at Knott's suggestion), serving both before and after the country's independence, and acquired an international reputation for his studies of climate. After retirement he embarked on a second career as a mathematics master at Dudley Grammar School, and after his second retirement was for several years active in local affairs. When he died in 1990 at the age of 97 he was the oldest Selwyn man. He left to the College a very handsome legacy.

9. *Finances in 1914*: The information comes from a memorandum prepared for the Council by Knott in 1919, reviewing the prospects for recovery after the war.

CHAPTER 9

War, Revival, and Jubilee
1914–1933

THE OUTBREAK of war closed an era, opened an age of anxiety, and swept away familiar landmarks of civilized life. This was the effect on the nation, but for Selwyn it was less dramatic. The class most affected by change was the old social élite, with which Selwyn had but tenuous links. The Fellows were too old for military service and no one was drawn into civil administration. The trauma of mounting casualties and wasted lives inflicted emotional damage that could never be repaired, but even among junior members there were enough survivors to pick up the threads that had been broken. For the College the first World War was not so clear a break with the past as the second was to be.

There were 483 past and present members of the College who served in the army or navy, including eighty-six chaplains with the forces. Other Selwyn men had served with the YMCA or Church Army in theatres of war. Of those on active service, seventy were killed, seventy-three wounded, and seven made prisoners of war. In addition eight who would have matriculated in 1914 had been killed. Seventeen College servants served in the forces and two were killed. To honour all who had given their lives an appeal was launched to record their names in the Chapel and build a memorial library.

The greater part of the College was requisitioned for service use (including rooms for a number of army nurses – a female invasion that the Fellows hastened to obliterate from memory). Visually the most obvious effect of war was grass growing high in the court and a wilderness in the garden save where vegetable plots had been dug. Unseen was the serious damage done to the precarious College finances. The loss of income from fees had left Selwyn with a debt of £2,000 and capital reserves had vanished. As a desperate measure the Council stopped the payment of all salaries, except to the Master and Bursar. Fellows with private means or other paid work in Cambridge stayed; S.C. Carpenter, who had neither, left during the war to work with a mission in Bermondsey for £200 a year.

Once the war was over Selwyn had to start again along the difficult road to financial security, but things were not quite so bad as pessimists had feared. The *Calendar* for 1919–20 claimed that 'the College has stood the strain of war astonishingly well – far better than we should have ventured to anticipate'. Applications for places soared, the debt would soon be paid off, and an anonymous gift of £5,000 to the Master and Fellows Fund was 'a very important step ... to meeting what is probably our most important need – the provision of adequate emoluments for the teaching and administrative staff of the College'.[1]

There were no government grants for men whose education had been deferred or interrupted by war service; but officers were given a small gratuity on release, some chose to use it to pay for a university education, and the demand for places was brisker than before the war. A happy consequence for Selwyn was that the ban on accommodating men in lodgings was lifted and thirty were allowed as a temporary measure (made permanent in 1926). In the Lent term of 1919 there were ten new admissions, seventeen more at Easter, fifty-five in October and a further fifteen were expected as soon as they were released. There were also twenty naval officers on short courses.

In addition to newcomers there were men who had matriculated in earlier years and returned to complete their degrees. To them, wrote the editor of the *Calendar*, Selwyn owed 'an immense debt ... Boating, cricket, and tennis started again under their charge, and it is owing to them that in difficult circumstances we have kept our good place on the river. Their presence has saved the traditions of the College.' S.C. Carpenter singled out two men for special praise: A.C. Telfer, whose brother would become Master in 1947; and D.J. Wardley, who would later occupy the ancient office of deputy master and worker of the Royal Mint.[2]

Everyone wanted to do their best by the men who returned from the war, but things were not easy for them or their teachers. S.C. Carpenter wrote that they were 'a good lot but found it hard to become students'. Some had been wounded or gassed, many had endured long periods in the trenches, and most of them found study difficult. 'They would sit with books in front of them but could not concentrate.' In some cases the release from tension resulted in irresponsible behaviour, rowdyism, and excessive consumption of alcohol, but the presence of so many ordinands saved Selwyn from the worst of these excesses.

S.C. Carpenter had resigned his Fellowship in 1915, and though he returned after the war he did not intend to remain for long. The Revd S.C. Phillips had been elected as a Fellow in theology but made known his wish to move to a parish as soon as possible. Fortunately in January 1920 the Revd F.S. Marsh, a Selwyn graduate, was persuaded to return to the College. He brought to it dedication and distinction for the next thirty years.

Marsh had come from a poor farming family, won a scholarship to Selwyn, and obtained first classes in the Theology Tripos. After ordination he served as a curate in London and then as a chaplain in the army. He had then been appointed as a lecturer at King's College, London, but gave up this better paid post to return to Selwyn. As an undergraduate he had been an enthusiastic games player, trying his hand at almost everything, but an attack of poison gas on the Western Front condemned him to a less active life and chronic respiratory complaints.

During the 1920s and early 1930s Marsh was a Tutor and greatly enjoyed the work, but he also built up a wide reputation as an Old Testament scholar. His lectures left a lasting impression on generations of ordinands, and many boxes of notes in the College Archives bear witness to his assiduous scholarship. He was a very early riser and much of his work was done while others still slept. In 1935 he was elected Lady Margaret's Professor of Divinity (he was the first Selwyn graduate and Fellow to occupy a Cambridge chair), and though he was required to give up his Tutorship he continued to take a keen interest in Selwyn men, particularly those who entered the Church or excelled in sport. Some dignitaries in the Church might well have been embarrassed to know how accurately he recalled their academic performance.[3]

To the regret of his friends, Marsh published nothing except, in early life, an edition of one rare text. Outside the lecture room he could seldom be persuaded to talk about his work, observing (and expecting others to observe) the convention against talking shop in the Senior Combination Room. He was also conscious that what he said might shock people who believed in a literal interpretation of the Bible but knew nothing of its social context or original language. He sometimes recalled that as a curate he had been rebuked by his bishop for trying to put the fruit of scholarship into his sermons.

Another Fellow elected in 1920 left a lasting impression on undergraduates, and enriched oral tradition with a stock of anecdotes. G.B. Perrett was a popular lecturer in history but made the greatest impact in his supervisions, in which shrewd comments and cutting criticisms were interspersed with talk about shooting, fishing, country life, and sporting friends. Doubtless some of the irrelevance was calculated. Not everyone appreciated the style but many (including some of the best) remembered him with respect. He contributed to a collection of essays on eighteenth-century France, but published nothing further and lectured on Tudor and Stuart England. He supervised for every paper in the Historical Tripos (except ancient history) but, whatever the subject, the Tudors were likely to come into the picture. In 1933 he became Bursar but continued to carry a heavy burden of teaching until his retirement in 1946.

There were innumerable tales of Perrett's idiosyncrasies but none told without affection. It is worthy of note that Professor Herbert Butterfield, Master of Peterhouse and an influential historian, thought highly of him. Before coming to Selwyn Perrett supervised for Peterhouse and Butterfield recalled both the title of his first essay – 'Art is history made organic' – and Perrett's prediction that the young freshman would be a Fellow of Peterhouse.[4]

In 1923 P.J. Durrant was elected as the first Fellow in chemistry, and in 1928 the Revd A.C. Blyth as a Fellow in theology. Their services to the College will be described in a later chapter. Knott retired in 1928 and his place as Fellow in mathematics was taken by F.H. Woodward, a Selwyn graduate, who was also an economist. In addition to his teaching duties, Woodward was appointed Assistant Bursar in 1930 with special responsibility for finance. There was not much room for manoeuvre in financial matters but he handled investments boldly and in doing so learned much about the ways of the City. In 1944 he decided to leave Cambridge for merchant banking and made a great deal of money. He continued to advise Selwyn on financial matters and was also a generous benefactor. In 1983 the Fellows showed their appreciation by electing him to an Honorary Fellowship.

By 1921 the great majority of freshmen came once more direct from school. A higher proportion than in pre-war years came from grammar schools but social composition remained much the same as in pre-war years. During the war many serving officers and the widows of those who were killed could not afford boarding school fees, so more of their sons went to grammar schools.

Among the newcomers in 1921 was E.L. McEldowney (the one and only 'Mac' to generations of Selwyn rowing men). In later life he recalled a College that was 'bubbling and throbbing with such energy and enthusiasm that one felt that it would take off at any time'. Even the primitive amenities were seen through a golden haze – the mellow light of the oil lamps, the hip baths in front of a blazing fire, and those 'most excellent men', the gyps. 'These were halcyon days and we can only hope that the present-day undergraduates are as happy as we were.' He was surprised when Mrs Murray, the Master's wife, visited all the freshmen in their rooms to warn them against 'certain women of the town', but though unexpected and perhaps unnecessary this evidence of concern for undergraduate well-being was appreciated.

'Mac' devoted most of his energy to rowing and it was largely due to his leadership that these were years of extraordinary success. Two of his oars, won as stroke in the Selwyn first boat, now hang in the College bar. After he had gone down he came back every year to coach the boat, exhort the crews, and detect any sign that they had got their priorities wrong – first things should come first, and that meant the Boat Club. He was such an engaging character that no one minded this single-minded devotion to a cause.

He had, perhaps unexpectedly, a gift for expressing himself on paper. The quotations given above come from his evocative pictures of undergraduate life in those days. He also wrote a history of the Boat Club, and left an unpublished account of his experiences as an army medical officer during the retreat to Dunkirk that is now deposited in the Imperial War Museum.

The prominence of the Boat Club in College life can be gauged by the length of its reports in the *Calendar*. In 1926 it filled no fewer than fifteen pages – nearly half of the whole issue apart from the official record and the directory of members – but in this, the *annus mirabilis* of the Selwyn Boat Club, exuberance was justified. The first boat made five bumps and the second boat four in the Lents, in the Mays both made four, and the Club was awarded the Mitchell Cup for the most consistent success. The first boat went on to win the Thames Cup at Henley with a time in the semi-final equalling the fastest on record. *The Times'* report on the Mays considered that the Selwyn first boat was the fastest on the river with 'poise and balance forward ... rarely if ever seen equalled even among first class Australian crews'. McEldowney was not in the boat at Henley (he was busy qualifying as a doctor), but a Selwyn man on the umpire's launch recorded that 'though not in the boat, it was his spirit that animated the crew'.

Men who did not row, and whose principal interests were intellectual or cultural, may have found less to be happy about. For some the predominant mood in Selwyn was not so much anti-intellectual as inactivity in things of the mind. Societies were revived, but the Science Club was the only one dedicated to an academic discipline and the pre-war enthusiasm for the formation of small literary societies and discussion groups seems to have waned. There was not, however, a great gulf between the oarsmen and the men of books. E.E. Rich, the future Master of St Catharine's, was in the triumphant first May boat in 1926, and in the second May boat A.P. Rossiter, a future Fellow of Jesus, had just completed the papers that won him first-class honours in English.

These were events that interested undergraduates (and most of their seniors), but there were duller topics with lasting significance. The investigations and recommendations of a Royal Commission led to the Universities Act of 1926. Among its reforms were important changes in the organization of teaching. Hitherto professors had been paid fixed salaries by the University, but decided for themselves how many lectures they would give and when. All other lecturers, whether appointed by the University or a college, were paid out of fees collected from those who attended. To appear on the official list a college lecturer had to be recognized by his subject board, but there had been nothing to prevent a college lecturer not on the list from making private arrangements with other colleges to send their men to him. In either case a lecturer was responsible for collecting names and sending his claims for payment to the colleges. A popular lecturer on a widely studied subject earned a substantial income; but another, in a subject that attracted few students, might get very little. Under the new arrangement the University appointed lecturers, paid them all a fixed salary, and charged undergraduates a composition fee.

Fellows who had been giving lectures approved by their subject board had the option of joining the new scheme at salaries fixed according to their seniority and previous earnings. Jordan and Borradaile came in at the top of the scale at £400 a year, Perrett at £300, and Marsh at £200 plus £25 for additional work. For the time being this made little difference to College finances, but in later years the responsibility assumed by the University for lecturers' salaries would have striking consequences.

The new Act prohibited the admission of students who had not passed or obtained exemption from the previous examination. This caused alarm as it was predicted that Cambridge rowing and other sports would be ruined, but strangely the clubs survived without an appreciable fall in standards. What the new rule did mean was that a number of young men who had been admitted conditionally had to work hard to pass the required papers at the then equivalent of GCSE in June or the previous examination in September. Sixty years on their successors would be in a similar position but struggling for the highest grades at A-level.

For Selwyn the most important gain from the Universities Act was recognition by Act of parliament as an Approved Foundation. The status of Public Hostel, often interpreted outside the University to mean an institution that housed but did not educate students, had long been resented. 'College' (in the full sense of the term) would have been preferred, but 'Approved Foundation' had undeniable merits. 'Approved' set a seal on what had been done since 1882, and 'Foundation' carried with it an implication of permanence. The Act also recognized the Master and Fellows as the administrative body responsible for the internal management of the College. What had been done by College statute in 1913 was now the law of the land.

To have asked for more might have revived controversies best laid to rest. As it was, those who still objected to denominational tests for College membership were satisfied by certain restraints that applied to an Approved Foundation, and members of the College were satisfied because they meant very little. The Master could not be Vice-Chancellor, but in former times all members of the Senate had been eligible for election to this office, so the precedent was there if the University wanted a future Master of Selwyn as its Vice-Chancellor. Selwyn could not nominate Proctors, but this right, once highly valued, was regarded as an inconvenience in several colleges and might soon be abandoned voluntarily. There was nothing to prevent a Fellow of Selwyn accepting nomination as a Proctor from his own former college. An article in the *Calendar* on the changes concluded with the assurance that 'with the lapse of time, our nominal standing will matter less and less'.

Murray reached the age of retirement in 1928, and though the Fellows complained privately that he had not done enough, the state of the College at the end of his time was ground for congratulation. Successes on the river had continued; the first boat was fifth in the Lents and eighth in the Mays and there were two blues (N.M. Aldous and A.L. Sulley – the latter also coxed the Olympic VIII). The rugby football 1st XV had lost only one match in the season and produced a blue (McIlwaine). The association football XI had won every match in the third division. G.C. Weightman-Smith had won a blue for athletics and had run for South Africa in the Olympic Games.

Academic performance had edged upwards. In 1928 there were eight first and twenty-four second classes in tripos examinations. The tail of thirds and pass degrees was still long but shorter than in earlier years. The College was full and its growing reputation was shown by the fact that in November 1928 there were already more applicants for admission in October 1929 than places to fill.

Despite poverty some material improvements had been made by 1928. Electricity replaced gas and oil, with ceiling and reading lights in all undergraduate sitting rooms – though two-way switches prevented both from being used simultaneously – and although staircase lights were few and dim they were an improvement on flickering gas. The hip baths in rooms had given way to modern baths behind the Hall ('better and more numerous than in some colleges and more conveniently placed than in many of them', reported *Varsity Weekly*). Three improvements had been made possible by gifts from Borradaile: the low wall on the Grange Road boundary; the iron railings of admirable design in place of the wooden fence, overgrown with ivy, between the Chapel and F staircase; and the wall with a niche filling the gap between the Lodge and the Chapel.

Without exaggeration the new Master, George Ernest Newsom, declared that it was his 'happy lot to have been made Head of the College at a moment when it has reached the height of its achievement'. On their part, members of the Council believed that they had chosen the right man to build on these foundations. He had had a distinguished undergraduate career at Oxford, spent nineteen years at King's College, London (thirteen of them as Professor of Liturgical and Pastoral Theology), and was then for twelve years vicar of Newcastle upon Tyne. There was a hint that work in a very large city parish with many ancillary duties had brought him to the verge of physical exhaustion, but much was expected from a man with many friends, no enemies, great energy, and a reputation for efficiency. His work in organizing the first residential hostel for King's College, London, and raising the funds to place it on a secure financial footing, must have impressed the Council. Selwyn was in dire need of similar treatment.

'From the first day of office he was a popular and efficient Master', declared a passage in his *Times* obituary, probably contributed by Borradaile. Not all were unstinted in their praise. C.W. Phillips, a Selwyn graduate who became Librarian in 1929 and a Fellow in 1933, found him 'kindly but vague' and thought that in middle age his 'vigour and businesslike qualities had declined'. A passage from his obituary in *The Guardian* reconciles the two assessments: 'His most evident characteristic was a certain mellow geniality ... It was plain that he wanted all his friends to be as happy as he himself was.' To a young Fellow, hoping for change and dissatisfied with the College's academic performance, Newsom might seem too anxious to avoid giving offence to the older men and too ready to accept things as they were, but *The Guardian* obituarist sensed that behind the accommodating manner was 'a shrewd and powerful mind'.[5]

Newsom's greatest handicap was that Cambridge treated him as an outsider. In later years the appointment of an Oxford man to head a Cambridge college would cause little surprise; in the 1920s it was unusual and to many unwelcome. In his six years as Master he was not appointed to any University boards or committees, and despite his years as a professor was not welcomed by the Faculty of Divinity. Perhaps this neglect was not wholly the fault of the University authorities. Nalder Williams thought that Newsom was always reluctant to cross the Cam, and he certainly preferred to spend his free afternoons watching University and College teams rather than sitting on dull committees; but it did not help Selwyn to have its Master ignored by the academic establishment.[6]

Newsom was Master for only five and a half years. He tried but failed to rescue the College from crippling poverty, but three achievements stand to his credit. He got the Library built, organized the Jubilee celebrations, and initiated moves that led to the foundation of the Selwyn Association.

In his first report to the Council he emphasized the financial difficulties that faced Selwyn. In Cambridge the average emolument for a Fellow from his college was from £200 to £250 a year; at Selwyn it was £65. A University lecturer who was not a Fellow received an additional payment greater than £65, so that he would lose money by accepting a Selwyn Fellowship. Those who were already Fellows had shown remarkable devotion to the College by working so hard for such small stipends, but one could not rely on such devotion in the future. There were a number of endowed scholarships but few produced enough income and most had to be made up from ordinary revenue (in effect parents who paid full fees subsidized those who did not). Even with supplementation Selwyn could offer its top Scholars only £60 a year when other colleges had major scholarships of £100. He recommended an appeal for £60,000 to meet both of these urgent needs.

The approach of Selwyn's fiftieth birthday or Jubilee was a fitting occasion for an approach to old members and possible well-wishers, but before doing so Newsom revised some estimates and identified other needs; looking to the future, £15,000 was required to endow scholarships, £50,000 to raise the stipends of Fellows, and at least £10,000 to form an essential capital reserve; but £2,000 was also required immediately to replace shabby furniture in undergraduate rooms, and the annual cost of maintaining 50-year-old buildings could not be less than £1,000. When these needs had been met others should be taken in hand: the stalls in the Chapel awaited completion, a better playing field was needed and a much better Junior Combination Room. Looking further ahead, a new residential block would soon be required and 'a smaller and more convenient Master's Lodge'.

To keep old members in touch with the College, Newsom promoted a scheme to elect or appoint secretaries for each year, and in 1934 this led, in altered form, to the foundation of the

The Chancellor and the Master at the Jubilee.

Selwyn Association. The primary purpose was not to raise money, but men who were frequently reminded of their College days were likely to give help when it was needed. For the time being, however, the response to the appeal was meagre. There was no lack of goodwill among old members but the majority of Selwyn graduates were in low-paid professions. Clergymen and school-masters gave generously but the total edged up very slowly and far from the figure that was required.

Newsom scored one notable success. The War Memorial Fund had paid for the large tablet in the Chapel, but its second aim was a new Library that would cost at least £6,000 and by 1928 there was only £3,000 in the fund. Nevertheless, Newsom per-suaded the Council to go ahead. T.H. Lyon (who had designed the new railings) was appointed as architect, some money was donated by old members approached privately by the Master, the rest was borrowed, and the new Library was built. After fifty years the last of the temporary buildings in the court was demol-ished and traces of them were obliterated by smooth lawns. This and the other improvements already described were notable achievements in a College where every penny had to be counted.[7]

The celebration of Selwyn's fiftieth birthday was fixed for mid-summer day 1933. By noon over four hundred past and present members of the College were assembled in the Hall and ladies crowded the gallery. The Right Hon. Stanley Baldwin, Chancellor of the University, received the Vice-Chancellor, seven heads of houses, and other distinguished members of the University in the Senior Combination Room, and then took his place on the dais.

Baldwin's reputation has been dimmed by time, but in 1933 he was at the height of his powers and the most important man on the political scene. Though he was no great orator, his phrasing was felicitous, his delivery inspired confidence, and no one could have wished for a better or more generous tribute. His brief had been prepared by Newsom but he improved upon it.

Baldwin gave special praise to the senior and junior members in Selwyn's earliest years:

> These were the men on whom everything depended as to whether the College would pass out or whether grasping firmly the ideals which had led to its foundation ... would be a living thing at first, might grow and grow until it became what, thank God, it has become.

Every college, he said, had a distinct character built around 'something very private and peculiar'. At Selwyn this inner strength was 'a determination to work for a common end without caring who got the credit'. This had carried the College far and would carry it further; but even the stoutest body must have sinews to sustain it and Baldwin closed his address with the hope that 'as a result of the interest that may be taken by the outside world in this Jubilee, someone might be moved to make some substantial contribution to an endowment, which is badly needed and more than worthily deserved'.[8]

As the euphoria of the Jubilee faded, those who guided Selwyn's destiny had to ask themselves what kind of college it should be. There was no thought of radical change, but hope that it would win a secure place in higher education, set apart by its special character but respected for being what it was.

Poverty was the greatest handicap, not only to future development but also to present reputation. Most of those who denigrated Selwyn did so not because it was denominational but because it was poor. Had the College been richly endowed, all kinds of points might have been stretched. Had its Fellowship dividends been on a par with those of richer colleges and its High Table as affluently served, there would have been no shortage of Fellows competing for election. As it was, there were few endowments, the College depended on fees paid by students (a precarious source after the economic crisis of 1931), and even if applications rose the University restriction on numbers allowed in lodgings meant that the College could not take full advantage of growing popularity.

Sober calculation did not cheer. Improvement in academic performance must be slow. The name of Selwyn had not been written large on the map of learning. The College had a well-deserved reputation on the river, but an institution could not live by oars alone. No large donor had appeared to set the College on a firm economic base. Pride in achievement had to be tempered by the knowledge that Selwyn was and must remain a poor relation in the Cambridge family.

Notes and Comments

1. *The anonymous gift in 1919*: The donor was the Revd Stephen John
    Selwyn, a grandson of Bishop G.A. Selwyn. He wrote to Knott that
    he had unexpectedly inherited a very large sum from a cousin, and
    had decided to give Selwyn £5,000. He insisted that his name should
    not be revealed, even to members of the Council. He said that he
    feared a deluge of begging letters if his good fortune became known.
    So far as can be ascertained, anonymity was preserved and the name
    of the donor was never made public. After correspondence with Knott
    he asked that the money should go to the Master and Fellows Fund
    but to be used exclusively for the benefit of the Fellows.

2. *Two Selwyn graduates of the 1920s*: Malcolm Muggeridge became in
    later years Selwyn's best-known alumnus, but no one predicted a
    career of distinction when he was in residence from 1920 to 1923.
    C.W. Phillips, a contemporary, described him as a very difficult un-
    dergraduate, rebellious and unpopular. The fact that his father had
    been a Labour Member of Parliament probably did not commend
    him at a time when undergraduate conservatism ruled. Academically
    he did no more than get an allowance toward the ordinary degree
    after failing to obtain honours in natural sciences and completed his
    BA with an ordinary examination in English. A period as a journalist
    in Moscow began a pilgrimage that ended late in life to conversion
    to Roman Catholicism. He was an amateur but perceptive historian
    of his times; editor of *Punch*; and in later years a frequent contributor
    to the press, a broadcaster, and a champion of moral values in the
    permissive society. He was elected Rector of Edinburgh University
    but resigned when asked to back the student demand for freely available
    contraceptives.

    At Selwyn Muggeridge got to know Alec Vidler, who remained a
    life-long friend and to whom he attributed his recovery of faith in
    later life. Like so many Selwyn men of his day, Vidler was ordained
    after graduation, but unlike most of them he went on to an exceptional
    career. As Owen Chadwick wrote in his obituary in *The Independent*:

    > Without ever writing a profound work of theology, he was a
    > most unusual stimulus to other minds ... By nature he was an
    > Anglo Catholic Liberal: that is, he liked High Church forms of
    > prayer, was deeply read in the historic traditions of the Church
    > of England, and felt freer in doubt than was then usual with
    > Anglo-Catholics.

    Vidler prided himself on having been banned by one bishop because
    he was too high church and by another because he was too heretical.
    He was for some years a canon of Windsor, and moved from there

to become Dean of King's College, Cambridge. This was a position for which he was particularly well suited, meeting the radical dons of the College at their own intellectual level and enjoying worship in one of England's most splendid chapels. He retired to Rye, his home town, and was mayor there from 1972 to 1974 – the office was held by his father, grandfather, and great-grandfather before him.

3. *F.S. Marsh and the new translation of the English Bible*: In the 1950s poor health prevented him from accepting regular membership of the commission charged with this task; but the members valued his help so highly that they spent two full days in Selwyn to obtain his opinion on difficult points.

4. *G.B. Perrett*: Always remembered were the appalling cigarettes that he rolled for himself. He usually dressed like a farmer down on his luck and when he came from work in his garden or allotment looked very rough. There was a perennial story about mistaken identity when a freshmen encountered him on one of his weekly visits to collect swill from the kitchen for his pigs.

He had an endearing habit of blending fiction with fact. No one really believed his fishing stories, but everyone encouraged him to tell them, and the fish grew weightier every year. He claimed to know Welsh and from this to understand spoken Breton, but Welsh speakers said that his knowledge was limited to a few conventional phrases. At the end of the 1930s some of the younger Fellows would conspire to turn the conversation to some country of which they were certain he knew nothing; but sure enough, once he had caught the drift of the conversation, he would come in with 'When I was last in ...' This was recorded by Professor L.W. Forster but recalled by others who knew him.

5. *C.W. Phillips*: For an account of this remarkable personality see page 188. In this and the next chapter there are several other references to his unpublished autobiography and to letters about his Selwyn days. *The Guardian* was not the present publication of that name, but a church newspaper.

6. *Admissions procedure – 1930 style*: An anecdote illustrates Newsom's style. An old member recalled his interview with him when he applied for admission. He had already had two interviews on the same day. He was rejected at Caius. At Downing he was accepted but thought the atmosphere cold and formal. He arrived at the Master's Lodge at Selwyn in mid-afternoon and Newsom said that he was just in time for a game of solitaire. After playing until tea-time (and a very good tea), Newsom said, 'Do you play games?'

'Yes, soccer.'

'What position?'

'Left back.'

'We are badly in need of a left back next October. You must come here.'

He did.

7. *The new Library*: Lyon's original design was for a much larger building of neo-classical design, between the Chapel and F staircase and set well back but raised to court level on what is now the garden's principal lawn.

8. *Jubilee proceedings*: There is a full account and the text of Baldwin;'s speech in the *Calendar*. A draft of what must have been Newsom's 'brief' for the Chancellor is in the College Archives. There is also a photograph of the whole company assembled on that day.

CHAPTER 10

Selwyn Men 1934–39

IN FEBRUARY 1934 Selwyn was stunned by the sudden death of Newsom. A chill, aggravated by watching football on a cold winter's day, developed into pneumonia that proved to be fatal. He had imparted new energy into the College and earned sincerely uttered tributes, but his successor had assets that he had been denied. The Revd George Armitage Chase was the son of a former President of Queens' and Bishop of Ely, a Tutor of Trinity Hall, and a long-serving elected member of the Council of the Senate. No one was nearer to the heart of the Cambridge academic establishment, and it is reasonable to infer that he regarded Selwyn in a different light from that seen by his predecessors. For them it had been a Church of England college that happened to be in Cambridge; for him it was to be a Cambridge college that happened to have a special relationship with the Church.[1]

The character of the Approved Foundation that the new Master took over must be seen in its national context. In the whole United Kingdom there were no more than fifty thousand university students and a quarter of them were in Scotland. The vast majority of English adolescents left school at 14 and had no further education. A minority went on to secondary education and of those a tiny fraction might go to a university.

Independent schools charging high fees provided the majority of applicants for admission as commoners, but by no means all their pupils followed this path. A university degree was essential for certain professions but the sons of many well-to-do parents went straight into business or joined one of the armed services. Some upper-class parents sent their sons to a university as a social rather than an academic experience, but their number was limited. There was, therefore, no great pressure on admissions, and the annual problem for the less fashionable colleges was not to select but to wonder whether all places would be filled. Any applicant for admission as a commoner who passed or was exempted from the previous examination would normally be accepted.

Things were very different for those who could not come to the university unless they won a scholarship or exhibition. Competition was intense, and for the sons of parents who could not afford full fees a few marks, one way or the other, made the difference between looking for work in an office or climbing the professional ladder. To stand any chance a good secondary education was essential, and though the able and lucky son of a shopkeeper, small farmer, or skilled worker might win a scholarship, the odds against the son of an unskilled factory worker or agricultural labourer were astronomical. In addition to college awards there were a limited number of city or county scholarships, but here again the principal beneficiaries were the sons of middle-class parents of modest means. The opportunities for girls were even fewer than for their brothers.

The maximum number of Selwyn undergraduates was 176. In 1932 the total was only 164, but the College was again full in 1933. The figure for graduate students was more flexible but there were not many of them (nine in 1931, thirteen in 1932, and nine in 1933) and most were on a teacher training course. There were a few students from overseas (fourteen in 1933 but the seven of 1934 was nearer the average) who came mainly from Christian colleges in India or Africa. There were occasional affiliated students with a degree from another university who were reading for a Cambridge tripos.

In 1933 twenty-five freshmen were from public schools and twenty from grammar schools. In 1934 the public school element was larger (thirty-one to eighteen), but it was smaller in 1935 (eighteen to twenty-eight). The proportion from grammar schools was probably higher than in most other colleges, but the social composition was much the same. A public school education was invariably an indicator of social class but not necessarily of parental income. In addition to offering scholarships that met a substantial part of the fees, most public schools had assisted places – endowed by memorial funds – for the children of former pupils killed in the war, and some public schools accepted day boys at modest fees. But a public school would probably reject a boy whose parents spoke with the wrong accent (unless they were very wealthy) and would not accept as a day boy the son of a local tradesman, however affluent.

Conversely, education at a grammar school was an indicator of parental income but not necessarily of social class. There were many fathers who classed themselves as gentlemen but could not afford boarding school fees, and it was from this class that the majority of Selwyn's grammar school applicants were drawn. Selwyn's social composition was therefore much the same as other colleges but without a top slice of men from socially élite or wealthy families.

Why did they come to Selwyn? Some parents were attracted by its Anglican character, especially if the father was ordained. Other parents might not be strong churchmen but liked the sound of a college where moral standards were high. However, religion had not collapsed in Cambridge, and many sound Anglicans would think first of their own former colleges.

Many parents were attracted by lower costs. The Selwyn prospectus claimed that £170 a year with 'exercise of economy' would cover University fees, Colleges tuition, rooms, breakfast, and dinner. This compared favourably with the £230 a year that local grant-giving authorities reckoned as the average for arts students at older colleges (it was a little more for scientists). A saving of £60 for a family living on £600 a year or less was significant. It was also important that Selwyn charged a single fee to cover all meals and once this was paid a parent was assured that there would be no hidden extras. These savings were offset by the fact that the local authority figure was comprehensive and might be supplemented if the parents could not support their son in vacation. Selwyn's £170 covered only term-time expenditure and did not include travel and some non-recurrent University fees. Selwyn's lower charges were therefore an important consideration, but the saving might not be great enough to attract a parent whose son had a good prospect of cutting costs by winning a scholarship elsewhere.

ADMISSIONS AND COSTS

The following extracts are from the Calendar for 1935.

They were unchanged throughout the decade.

ADMISSION.

The College is open to members of the Church of England or of any Church in Communion therewith, whatever career they intend to follow.

A candidate for admission must either (*a*) present a Certificate or Certificates exempting him from the Previous Examination or (*b*) pass Parts I, II and III of the Previous Examination.

The Previous Examination (Parts I, II and III) is held four times a year, in March, June, October, and December. The University Registration Fee (£3 and the Examination Fee (£1 for each part) must be paid before the date of the Examination. Anyone accepted as a candidate for admission to the College can be entered for this Examination. The passing of the Examination does not bind the College to accept him.

Candidates for admission who intend to read for the Degree of Bachelor of Medicine will be required to pass or gain exemption from Parts I and II of the First M.B. Examination before coming into residence.

All applications for admission are made to the Master.

Entries must be made on a form obtainable from the Master. Testimonials of character from the Schoolmaster, Tutor, or Tutors of the candidate for the last two years at least, and a certificate or other evidence of Baptism must be sent to the Master with the entry form, together with a Registration Fee of £1.

COLLEGE FEES AND CHARGES.

Terminal Fees.

The College Charge for Undergraduates residing in College is £40 a term. This includes Tuition, rent of furnished rooms, with attendance and fuel and all ordinary expenses of board during Full Term. It does not include University Fees, Lecture and Laboratory Fees, College Fees for Degrees, or residence outside the limits of Full Term. Undergraduates residing out of College also make a payment of £40, £30 of this sum defraying the cost of Tuition, establishment charges and dinner and plain luncheon in Hall, the remainder is applied towards the payment of the lodging-house keeper's bill, and any further sum necessary for this purpose is charged on the Student's College Account. For students who have graduated from the College residing in College the charge is £36 a term; for Research Students residing in College the charge is £38 a term. Graduates and Research Students residing out of College make similar payments, and the excess over £19 for Graduates and £21 for Research Students is applied towards the lodging-house keeper's bill as in the case of Undergraduates.

B.A.'s residing in Lodgings for the purpose of Study or Research in their 5th or any later year of residence pay a Terminal Fee of £5. This fee defrays only establishment charges and the payment for 2 dinners per week.

The College charge for residence during seven weeks of the Long Vacation is £15, exclusive of Fees for Instruction.

The College Terminal Fee is paid at the beginning of each Term and no Caution money is required, but students whose parents or guardians are not domiciled in the United Kingdom pay a deposit of £50, which will be returned when they cease to reside.

All current College, University, and personal expenses in Cambridge, with the exception of Lecture and Laboratory Fees may by the exercise of economy be kept within an average sum of £170 per annum, during the three years' residence required by the University for the Degree of B.A. This estimate should be regarded as a minimum and does not include expenditure on clothes and travelling. Lecture and Laboratory Fees vary with the subject of study but will usually be not less than £15 or more than £50 per annum.

The University Fees, payable by all members of the University alike, at intervals during their three years' course, amount to between £33. 15s. and £40. 15s. according to the Examinations taken, and the B.A. Degree taken at the end of the ninth term. These fees consist of the Matriculation Fee (£5), the Capitation Tax (£5. 5s. per annum), the Examination Fees, the B.A. Degree Fee (£3 at the end of the ninth term 35 at other times), and the Fee for Registration as a Parliamentary Elector (10s.). The College Capitation Tax amounts to £1. 2s. 6d. a year, and the College Fee for the B.A. Degree is £1 at times of General Admission, £1. 10s. at other times.

Often a significant factor was not the saving in fees but the lack of social pressure to live extravagantly. In this Selwyn was helped by the picture of Cambridge life conveyed in the popular press and in so many works of fiction. Idleness and indulgence seemed to be the way of life for undergraduates, and although this was a travesty – save for a tiny minority of the idle rich – it was enough to make 'sober living' sound like a salutary curb.

In many instances parental choice was a minor factor and a schoolmaster's advice decisive. Selwyn had a substantial number of schoolmasters among its graduates, and though they might not send their most gifted pupils they could be relied upon to see that their old College was well served. Nor did it need an old Selwyn man to tell a promising oarsman that it was a good rowing College or a prospective ordinand that he would find favour there.

Although Selwyn offered few scholarships and none of more than £60, any award opened the door to a Cambridge education and there was no shortage of candidates. The examination was held jointly with St Catharine's in March and, as all other colleges examined in December or January, Selwyn hoped to pick up promising young pupils put in for a 'trial run' but was more likely to get older candidates for whom the March examination was the last chance. They were not necessarily inferior to successful candidates at other colleges. Apart from the very small number of outstanding performers whom no one could miss, it is never easy to spot promise among a mixed bag of young candidates and some good men slipped through the net. The scholarship examination did not result in ready-made firsts for Selwyn but it did bring many sound and intelligent men who exceeded expectations.

Selwyn had few graduate students. Not many research students migrated to Selwyn from other universities and few Selwyn graduates attained the standard required, but at that time the small number was no reproach. All colleges were undergraduate orientated; graduates from other universities were regarded as anomalies and no proper provision was made for them. They often had to find their own lodgings, but were obliged to pay their college for services that were hard to define and for dinners that they did not want. Science students had their laboratories as social and intellectual centres, but arts students might lead lonely lives. Selwyn was a little in advance of some others in providing them with a combination room (the present Lyttleton room) in which they could take coffee after dinner, but it was used for other purposes during the day.

If there were more applicants than places, few colleges were guided exclusively by academic considerations. Many favoured the sons of old members, few would turn down a potential 'blue', and most would welcome the son of a titled father. Selwyn did not get aristocratic applicants, but favoured the sons of old members and hoped that potential blues would manage to pass the previous examination. No one questioned the right of a college to give a traditional preference to men destined for certain professions (the law at Trinity Hall and Downing, Medicine at Caius), and at Selwyn young men who intended to take Holy Orders were preferred. The Church needed parochial clergy, and there was no reason to apologize for accepting an ordinand rather than a man without a vocation who might do a little better in examinations.

In this Selwyn continued its established tradition. In 1931 almost exactly half the old members on the College books were clergymen (seventy-six MAs and twenty-five BAs were in Holy Orders, eighty-one MAs and twenty BAs were laymen), and almost half of the most recent graduates were awaiting ordination. By the end of the decade the proportion was down to about one-third, but this was still high enough to spread the belief to many outside the University (and some in it) that Selwyn was primarily a College for intending parsons or even that it was a theological college whose students were allowed to take University examinations.

The *Calendar* reports indicate the careers chosen by Selwyn laymen. In 1934–5 there was news of thirteen schoolmasters, three in higher education, three working as scientists for private companies, five practising as physicians or surgeons, and ten in the Colonial Civil Service or holding public appointments in British protected states. This was a typical distribution. A Selwyn man in the administrative grade of the Home Civil Service was a rarity. The decade produced one talented musicologist (Percy M. Young), but no novelists, poets, or artists are recorded. It was exceptional for a Selwyn graduate to go into banking, commerce, or industry, and there were no Members of Parliament.

In many aspects of undergraduate life Selwyn was guided by the customs that prevailed in other colleges. In the 1930s and even as late as 1970 paternalism was the rule. The Fellows were *in loco parentis* and a college was an enlarged family. An undergraduate might not regard his Tutor as a father figure, but a Tutor liked to think of himself in that light. And as a symbol of the relationship between seniors and juniors all came together at the end of the day, just as younger members of a family would join their parents for the evening meal.[2]

As substitute parents the seniors were responsible for the moral welfare of their juniors, and University regulations were designed to shield the young against temptations of the flesh. The college gates closed at 10 p.m. and residents could enter but not leave after that hour. At midnight all guests had to be out, the gates were locked, and until 6 a.m. the college was a closed community. If undergraduates lived outside the college they could do so only in premises licensed by the University, and lodging-house keepers had to keep the same hours and report infractions. Late leave was given sparingly by Tutors, and hardly ever for entertainments in town or parties in other colleges.

After dark undergraduates away from their colleges were required to wear cap and gown, and the University Proctors patrolled the streets in full academic dress to see that they did so. If an offender tried to escape, the Proctor's attendants – two top-hatted 'bull dogs' selected for their physical stamina – gave chase, but there was a humane convention that once a delinquent got through the gates of his own college he was immune from arrest.[3]

The Proctors would also be summoned to any disturbance in which members of the University were involved. They would take names, order offenders back to their colleges, and either hand out punishment the following day or request the college to take appropriate action. They were particularly concerned to see that undergraduates did not consort with women of ill repute, and if they saw one in bad company would order him back to his college.

They also made regular visits to certain public houses where barmaids were suspected of serving more than beer. For obvious reasons the names of pubs on the black list were never published, so an undergraduate might not know that he had erred until he was found on the premises and reported to his Tutor. Normally no penalty followed but this evidence of possible depravity might be remembered.

For deliberate but minor breaches of University regulations the normal fine imposed by the Proctor would be 6s. 8d. (a third of £1, the medieval mark). In college an undergraduate breaking rules or reported by the Proctors would normally be 'gated' for one or two weeks. This meant that he had to be in by 7 p.m. and report to the Porters' Lodge at hourly intervals. A persistent or serious offender might be 'rusticated' (sent away for a stated period) and if this meant that he could not spend the statutory sixty nights in college during term he would have to return for an additional term before qualifying for a degree. The ultimate punishment was to end a man's University career by sending him down, but a penalty with such serious implications (including loss of income for the college) was not hastily imposed. The one compelling reason for doing so was a fear that others might be corrupted by the influence or example of the offender.

People accustomed to the more relaxed regime of later years will be surprised to learn that these rules caused little resentment. For men educated in British boarding schools life in the University was a welcome change from constant surveillance, and many from day schools found it less demanding than the tight parental discipline to which they were accustomed. Nor should it be forgotten that people are often happier when sheltered by familiar restraints than when constantly required to make moral decisions for themselves.

Acceptance of regulations as a part of life did not mean their scrupulous observance. Breaking the rules and getting away with it provided interest, occasional excitement, and endless anecdote. A considerable folklore developed around climbing into college after midnight, and the exploits of night climbers were even celebrated in a handsomely illustrated book. Selwyn men had limited opportunities for practising this skill, but the roof of the chapel was a challenge for ambitious climbers.

There were well-known routes into Selwyn after midnight, and little hesitation about using them. E.M. Hall, an undergraduate in the 1930s, recalled helping a future bishop whose foot was caught between bars of the railings. One can be sure that if the climber felt remorse it was caused by his physical ineptness, not by stirrings of conscience.[4]

Dons played the game in the same spirit: rules must be maintained and penalties exacted, but good relations between Tutor and pupils were undisturbed unless the offender thought the verdict unfair or the penalty unduly harsh. No one in authority thought any the worse of a man who committed minor offences, though tolerance might be strained beyond breaking point if he became a nuisance. Different standards were applied if the offence had a moral dimension. Alcoholic high spirits after a Boat Club dinner could be ignored, but persistent drunkenness would probably incur rustication. Climbing in after midnight might be a joke, but a young man found with a girl in his room after midnight could expect no clemency.

In addition to University regulations, Selwyn imposed some rules of its own. Undergraduates had to attend three weekday services and one on Sunday (relaxing an earlier rule that had required attendance daily and twice on Sunday). In 1930 a petition against compulsory Chapel was signed by a large majority of undergraduates but summarily rejected. Another rule, unique to Selwyn, was that first-year men were required to attend divinity lectures given by the Master and be examined on them. These were on Saturday mornings, but a man with a University lecture or practical was excused attendance and most scientists gained exemption. For those who did attend, the course was neither demanding nor appreciated.[5]

Apart from these two rules, the most obvious difference between Selwyn and the older colleges was its geographical isolation. The new University Library, opened in 1934, was a portent that the academic centre of gravity would shift to the west, but in the 1930s there was no Churchill, no Clare Hall, no Robinson, and no residential buildings for Trinity, Corpus, or St Catharine's along Grange Road. The Cavendish Laboratory was still in Free School Lane, there was no Veterinary School on the Madingley Road, gardens and a playing field occupied the present Sidgwick Avenue site, and all the West Road and Grange Road houses were still in private occupation.

Most people made the best or even a virtue out of Selwyn's separation from the rest of the University, but isolation was not greatly appreciated when men had a long walk or bicycle ride to lectures rooms, laboratories or other colleges. It also made Selwyn seem remote to other members of the University. On a winter afternoon hundreds might tramp up West Road to the University football ground, but still not know the way to Selwyn. The psychological effect of this isolation was intangible but none the less real.

The freshman coming to Selwyn could hardly fail to notice evidence of poverty. E.M. Hall, who matriculated in 1935, remembers that 'straightened circumstances ... were manifested in a general air of austerity and some drabness and gloom, both in the passageways, lit by low watt bulbs, and in the sparsely furnished rooms, many of them distempered in a depressing shade of green'. Amenities throughout the University fell far short of what would now be regarded as normal, but Selwyn suffered by comparison with colleges where rooms were larger, decorations brighter, and furniture more attractive. Selwyn might make a virtue of plain living but it was shortage of money, not high thinking, that lay behind its austerity.

Freshmen soon learned to make more than the best of things. They were all housed in College – a much better arrangement than being placed in lodgings, as was the custom in most other colleges – and were quickly made aware that they belonged to a lively community. Food was plain but plentiful, and compared favourably with that in colleges where the menu was pretentious but the portions small. Undergraduate life was sometimes boisterous but cheerful and friendly. It is a tribute to the spirit of those times that many who came to Selwyn conceived a lasting affection for the place, became anchormen in the Selwyn Association, and subscribed generously to appeals in the 1960s and 1980s.

Morale was boosted by the continuing success of the Boat Club. The decade started auspiciously with the first Lent and Mays boats both rising to third place. Ups and downs followed, but in 1938 the three boats on the river made a total of fourteen bumps in Lents and Mays, and the first boat rose from twelfth to fifth place in the Putney Head of the Tideway race. In the Mays the second boat won promotion to the first division, but penury cast a shadow even over this success because the College could not afford the lightship that would have enabled the crew to compete successfully in this high position. Of Selwyn oarsmen during these years the most famous in rowing annals was W.G.R.M. Laurie who stroked the 'Varsity boat twice to victory and crowned his achievements with an Olympic gold medal in 1948.

Rowing attracted more attention nationwide than it does today, perhaps because there were fewer sports to compete for media attention. The University Boat Race was on a par with test matches and cup finals as a major sporting event, many people learned of Selwyn as a rowing college who would otherwise have been ignorant of its existence, and success on the river raised the standing of the College in other fields.

Foreign visitors were often puzzled to find that in a university renowned for learning, so much respect was given to people who played games well. A 'first' received congratulations, but a 'blue' adulation. To many old-style dons this was neither wrong nor irrational. It was the function of the University to train men for public life, and good athletes – endowed with energy, determination, and an instinct for success – were probably destined for positions of greater responsibility than men of books. And they would carry those responsibilities more effectively after spending three years practising their sport in an environment where importance was also attached to clear thinking. In Britain's great tropical empire it was said that blacks were governed by blues.

The best aspect of exaggerated attention to sport was that almost everyone played something. Blues were acclaimed but the humble member of a college second boat or team got a lot of satisfaction from healthy exercise and good company. Because everyone participated, everyone's morale was raised when the College did well.

Plenty of enthusiasm and energy was displayed on the river and playing fields, but people with other interests sometimes wondered whether their fellow undergraduates had anything else to talk about. A certain amount of envy went into these complaints, but Selwyn was probably short on intellection stimulation, and there was no proliferation of small literary or political societies, as in some other colleges or in Selwyn before 1914.

The long-established Logarithms society continued to gather dons and selected undergraduates at fortnightly intervals to hear and read papers. Curiosity is aroused by a paper on 'Profane reliques of a Jubilee' by Dr Durrant. There may have been other less formal and more ephemeral literary societies, but if so they left no record of their activities. Though unemployment, slums, the Spanish Civil War, and the rise of Fascism kept many young people arguing far into the night, there is no record of political controversy at Selwyn. In 1936 the Debating Society met only once, and then to elect officers of the Junior Combination Room. Theological controversy was also in the air, but if the budding theologians argued with each other they did so behind closed doors.

A classical society was started in the 1930s, but the principal exception to low-key intellectual life was the lively Science Society that usually met in Dr Borradaile's rooms. Undergraduate members were encouraged to give papers and frequent visiting speakers took them towards the frontiers of knowledge. The intellectual curiosity thus aroused does much to explain why scientists performed better in examinations than their colleagues in arts. A long-remembered meeting was held in 1938 when a larger than normal audience gathered in the Tower room to see television demonstrated by a representative from Pye. This required the temporary erection of a fearsome array of aerials, and was probably the first occasion on which those present viewed the new marvel. Pye showed the prototype of a model they intended to produce in large numbers and market for £50. The war put an end to that but the event is a reminder that Britain was once a world leader in the electronic revolution.

There were talented individuals in the Music Society but performances were normally limited to two smoking concerts a year and a May week concert. There was no hint of later developments that would give Selwyn music a high reputation. Without a Fellow in music the organ scholar carried a heavy burden, being expected to play at all services, train the Chapel choir, and organize all other musical activities. The new Master did something to raise the level of musical appreciation, and anyone who wanted to listen to his large collection of records was welcome in the Lodge on Sunday evenings.

Even at a time when all colleges had many who rose no higher than Class III honours or who took the ordinary degree, Selwyn's record was undistinguished. There were exceptionally good results in 1933 and 1934 with twenty in each year in Classes I and II.1, but thereafter the trend was downwards. In 1938 there were only eleven in these two classes. In 1939 an increase in the number of upper seconds raised the total to eighteen, but there was no knowing whether this marked the beginning of a revival. Even in good years there was a weak tail. From 1932 to 1938 206 of the 545 men entered for honours were either in the third class or allowed special examinations counting toward an ordinary degree.

Almost half graduated with ordinary degrees. Their results are difficult to disentangle because candidates who failed could retake papers, and candidates for honours allowed specials had normally to take one or more examinations to complete their degree. A distinction could be drawn between general degrees (demanding five subjects selected at random) and vocational courses (for example military studies and estate management) with a fixed syllabus. The ordinary degree in theology (taken by a majority of the ordinands) was also a structured course, specifically designed to train parish priests. What is clear is that in all these ordinary degree examinations the majority rose no higher than Class III and therefore graduated with the lowest possible qualifications.

College Fellowships were much smaller than they are today. Selwyn – with two theologians, two historians, two natural scientists, one classicist, and one economist who also supervised mathematics – was not far below the average for small colleges. In all colleges teaching requirements were the primary consideration when making elections, but most also used a portion of their

SELWYN RESULTS IN TRIPOS EXAMINATIONS
1932-9

This table lists results for second, third, or higher years. It does not include preliminary examinations taken in the second year or examinations for the MB.

Year	I	II.1	II	II.2	III	Special
1932	4	9	9	20	23	6
1933	10	10	8	16	46	3
1934	9	11	9	11	26	
1935	6	14	3	13	31	
1936	4	10	11	15	20	4
1937	7	9	6	15	22	
1938	5	6	4	19	18	7
1939	5	13	8	16	23	2

A note on Part I of the Modern Languages Tripos
Two languages were examined separately (normally one in the first and one in the second year). The first-year results are not included in the table. Second-year results constituted only half of Part I but no account is taken of this in the table.

Total taking honours
1932 – 71, 1933 – 93, 1934 – 66, 1935 – 67, 1936 – 64, 1937 – 59, 1938 – 59, 1939 – 67. The numbers entered for honours and placed in Class III in 1933 were exceptional. They included several ordinands who would normally have taken an ordinary degree examination in theology.

endowments to support a limited number of Research Fellows and mature scholars who did little or no teaching. Selwyn had no endowments for this purpose and only on rare occasions could it find the money to support one of its own graduates as a Research Fellow. The emphasis on teaching and pastoral care meant that all colleges relied a great deal on Fellows who had put research behind them, devoted all their time to teaching and college business, and sought no reward save respect from their colleagues and gratitude from those whom they sent on their way to the wider world. In this category Selwyn was well served.

The small band of Selwyn Fellows formed a compact body, held together by conventions that were not statutory but treated as moral obligations. Sunday evensong was attended by a majority of the Fellows and there were always some at Sunday communion and weekday services. Fellows living in College dined in Hall every night in term, and married Fellows three or four times a week. If one was not seen for several days his colleagues feared that he must be ill. Most of the time they dined together because they thought it a good custom though doubtless not unmindful of the fact that the food was free.

Before 1935 Fellowship elections were rare. In 1933 two Selwyn graduates, K.A.C. Elliot in biochemistry and C.W. Phillips in history, were elected. Elliot did not stay long but went on to a distinguished academic career in Canada. Phillips, an unusual and gifted man, had already been the librarian and a lecturer in history for five years, and his teaching was much appreciated. One Selwyn man (later a Professor of Economic History) remembers with gratitude the help he gave to a bewildered freshman. By the time of his election his main interest had shifted to archaeology, in which he rapidly built up a wide reputation. In 1938 he was put in charge of the most important British excavation of this century, the Sutton Hoo ship burial. He had a keen sense of humour with a gift for expressing the unexpected and Fellows enjoyed the weekly 'Phillipiads' – as they called his mock lugubrious comments on current events.[6]

For Fellows the pleasantest time in the day was the hour or half-hour spent 'combining' after dinner. Port or old oloroso sherry was served when there were guests to entertain or something to celebrate. On 14 March 1928 they drank the health of Selwyn's first two rowing blues, N.M. Aldous and A.L. Sulley, and a few days later they celebrated a Cambridge victory (by a good ten lengths). In March 1930 they celebrated another rowing blue (A.S. Reeve, later to be Bishop of Lichfield and an Honorary Fellow). Academic successes were rare but in 1934 six firsts in the Natural Sciences Tripos justified a bottle. In the same year they drank 'a bottle on the occasion of the first appearance of the College waiters in raiment bright'. A good deal of amusement was generated by fining each other for minor breaches of propriety, improper dress, or unfortunate remarks. The fine was always a bottle to be consumed by those present. Borradaile (then the only one with a doctorate) was sometimes caught out for wearing a black gown on scarlet days, but on one occasion he fined himself, as senior Fellow, 'for putting up with the impudence of his juniors'.

Fellows occasionally placed bets and the loser paid for a bottle. Nalder Williams bet that over three hundred volumes had been published in the Loeb Library and lost to Phillips. He lost again when he maintained that the Hobson of 'Hobson's choice' was not Milton's Hobson, but won when Borradaile insisted that the Chapel bell rung on 'white nights' (when surplices were worn) was higher in tone than that rung for weekday services. A jury of Fellows with musical knowledge found that the ordinary bell was an augmented fifth higher than the white night bell. A wine book kept in the Senior Combination Room recorded all the bets and fines.

It was, on the whole, a friendly society but it was not without minor irritations. The other Fellows sometimes thought that Borradaile took too much upon himself, and he reacted by treating opposition as a personal affront. Nalder Williams liked to display his cultural interests, but Perrett prided himself on not being an intellectual. Marsh, with all his learning, hated to hear anyone 'talking shop' and turned to College sport or clerical gossip if conversation strayed too far into cultural fields. Sometimes discussion of books circulating in the Book Club introduced more varied themes. One survivor from those days recalled no occasion on which wider educational issues were discussed, but for another the society was best remembered for its friendliness and good humour.

The strength and weakness of a small academic society are illustrated by one small incident learned from an authentic source. A man from another college with an excellent academic record was being considered for election to the Fellowship. The junior Fellow present observed that he had known him at school and had not liked him, and, much to his surprise, the man was immediately dropped from the list of 'possibles'. The preservation of harmony in the society was more important than adding to the Fellowship a man of academic promise.[7]

The relationship between senior and junior members was good though usually formal. Selwyn could not afford entertainment allowances and social contacts between senior and junior members were limited. Some Fellows made a habit of being 'at home' in their rooms on one evening a week for anyone who cared to drop in, and married Fellows sometimes invited undergraduates to tea. Nalder Williams and his wife were exceptional in being 'at home' to both Selwyn men and Newnham girls. No one had yet thought of matriculation and graduation dinners or of entertainments for Scholars and graduate students.

A Tutor had overall responsibility for the men 'on his side' but for most undergraduates this meant no more than routine visits at the beginning and end of term, occasional requests for exeats or late leaves, and an unwelcome summons if they fell foul of University or College regulations. If anything was wrong the Tutor was there to advise or to reprimand, but the majority of undergraduates took emotional problems in their stride and did enough work to avoid censure. There were no counsellors, help-lines, or psychotherapists, but being unaware of these later additions to university life undergraduates did not complain of their absence. They often formed closer associations with their supervisors, whom they saw every week and often in all three years, than with their Tutors. Not all subjects could be supervised in the College, but several members of other colleges had long-standing arrangements to look after Selwyn men. Coaches (now an extinct species) earned their living by getting indolent, inattentive, or slow-witted men through their examinations, but Selwyn men seldom sought their services – partly because of the expense but also because their own dons were willing to do a great deal of hard work with slow pupils.

Twenty years later, when congratulating W.O. Chadwick on his election as Master, Chase wrote that he would find the post exciting, 'for Selwyn is still young and making its traditions'. It was with expectations of change that Chase himself took office and this made a marked impact on the younger Fellows. C.W. Phillips believed 'that the strong conservatism of some of the Selwyn Fellows would [not] be allowed to stand in the way of beneficial change', and that the ultimate aim would be 'new Statutes and full recognition by the University'. He described Chase as 'the second founder of the College'.

We do not know how this experienced College Tutor and University administrator arranged his priorities, but some guesses can be made. He had no intention of relaxing Selwyn's link with the Church of England but believed that in the future it might be interpreted in a different way. The government of the College must be changed with the eventual aim of placing control in the hands of the Master and Fellows. The academic level of the College must be raised, and the amenities for both senior and junior members improved. Somehow the financial position must be strengthened, and though this might take many years a start could be made by getting rid of the restriction on the number of men that Selwyn could place in lodgings. A larger college would mean higher income and a more cost-effective use of facilities. In general, the differences between Selwyn and the older colleges should be narrowed to the point to which there could no longer be valid objections to full recognition.[8]

It was premature to talk of doing away with the Council, but as the eleven elected places fell vacant they could be filled by Fellows. The process had already begun when Chase became Master, and when he resigned in 1947, on appointment as Bishop of Ripon, there were Fellows in nine of the elected places. As two *ex-officio* members, the Provost of Eton and the Dean of

George Armitage Chase, 1934.

Lichfield, never attended and the Bishop of Ely rarely, the Fellows – with a majority of one in the full Council – had normally a working majority of five. The *ex-officio* members who attended regularly came to regard their function as advisory rather than executive, and though the Charter gave the Master a veto on Council decisions, he was unlikely to go against a majority of the Fellows.

Chase also aimed to raise Selwyn's academic standing. In 1934 only three Fellows held University posts and one of them (Borradaile) would soon retire. Apart from Borradaile's publications, Marsh's reputation, and recognition of Phillips as a gifted archaeologist, the scholarly record was thin. Fellows were then less often judged by what they put into print than they are today, but in the long run a society of scholars could only be judged by its contributions to scholarship. By this standard Selwyn fell short of other colleges.

In the fifteen years from 1920 to 1934 there had been only six elections, two of which replaced retired Fellows; during the eleven years of Chase's Mastership (including the six years of war) there were nine. Some of them will be noted in later pages of this volume, but one, elected in 1935, deserves mention at this stage. W.J. Sartain, a Christ's graduate and Fellow in classics, quickly made an impression on College life. He was a glutton for work and a shrewd judge of men and issues, but also a likeable personality and very good company. As Dean he introduced a new combination of firmness and understanding into relations between seniors and juniors. With F.H. Woodward, then managing College finance, he quickly formed an alliance to work for bolder decisions on future development. When he decided to move into University administration (rising eventually to the top of the tree as Secretary General of the Faculties) Selwyn lost something, but also profited from his widening knowledge of University affairs and his continued attention to College business. In future years a proposal supported by Sartain was seldom rejected and one that he opposed was seldom approved.[9]

Chase's political skill was demonstrated soon after he became Master when the Council of the Senate was persuaded to lift the irksome restriction on the numbers allowed in lodgings. Newsom had tried and failed, but before Chase pleaded for relaxation of the rule he had probably had some quiet words with those who were likely to influence the outcome. The Vice-Chancellor of the day is reputed to have said, 'Surely Selwyn is old enough to be allowed to manage its own affairs' – and so it was done, with consequences that were symbolic at the time but later of great moment.

Chase proposed to remove two further differences between Selwyn and other colleges: the course in divinity for freshmen and compulsory Chapel attendance. The first had few defenders but the second was controversial. Compulsory chapel was unpopular with undergraduates. Even regular churchgoers disliked compulsion, and the truly pious were often pained by the perfunctory manner in which others observed the rule. For the older Fellows neither the example of other colleges nor undergraduate opinion was a sufficient reason for what they regarded as an abandonment of the principles on which Selwyn had been founded. Whether by coincidence or collusion, the former Master, J.O.F. Murray, preaching the Commemoration sermon in 1936, stressed Selwyn's special responsibility for religious education, and Borradaile, then editor of the *Calendar*, printed his words in full. They could be read as a rallying call to old members to defend the status quo. Controversy was stilled by war, but when things returned to normal in 1946 compulsory chapel and the divinity lectures had gone.

Others matters also led to disagreement between the Master and Borradaile, who reached the age of retirement in 1937. He may have expected to remain a member of the administrative body and certainly to retain his place on the Council. What was said in private cannot be known, but Chase probably put it to him that government of the College ought to be in the hands of those who held teaching and administrative posts. Borradaile acquiesced but took it hardly. Since his time many have enjoyed their status as Fellows in Class E (Emeritus) that gives them privileges without burdensome duties, but Borradaile (as his *Calendar* obituary observed) 'did not find it easy to be a spectator on the field where he had played so strenuously and so long'. He continued to dine in Hall but would never do so on nights when the administrative body met.

Borradaile's spirits were revived during the war when age limits were relaxed and he returned to duty in the University as a lecturer and in Selwyn as Director of Studies, but when his second retirement came in 1945 he could not bear the prospect of watching from the sidelines and decided to leave Cambridge. The move was barely complete when he had to enter hospital, and died after an operation that had not been regarded as serious. It was a sad close to the life of a man to whom much honour was due.[10]

In 1939 as in 1914 there was a feeling that change was in the air and that Selwyn was on the threshold of a new era. The form that it would take was not yet clear and the dark cloud of poverty still hung over the College. The small Fellowship and Scholarship endowments limited the possibilities of attracting good men at either level. The denial of full collegiate status was an irritant rather than a serious handicap, but because Selwyn now performed exactly the same functions in the same way as other colleges the irritation was increased. As the College was virtually self-governing and its future no longer in doubt, non-recognition was more distinctly a censure on Selwyn for sticking to the principles on which it had been founded and maintained for more than half a century.

These uncertainties did not dim the mood of optimism, but the international situation did. In the academic year 1938–9 there was first elation in the belief that the Munich agreement had dispelled the threat of war, then disillusion, and finally fatalism as it became clear that neither agreements nor threats would halt Hitler's planned expansion to the east and south-east. Hope lingered that rational calculation of what was at stake would succeed where appeasement had failed, but in September the German invasion of Poland brought speculation to an end.

One result of the agonizing months preceding the outbreak of war was that the nation was much better prepared than it had been in 1914. Contingency plans had already been made and affected every aspect of national life. No transition could be smooth, but in the autumn of 1939 things were not chaotic. The

Fellows of Selwyn were forewarned that some would go and some would stay, that much of the College would be requisitioned for service use, and that those in residence would have to learn quickly how to cope with danger from the air.

Notes and Comments

1. *The choice of Chase as Master*: It seems that though his name was considered, Chase was not first on the Council's list. Some years later he told Owen Chadwick that he was approached privately and asked whether he would accept nomination; he said that he would give it serious consideration but heard nothing more until Canon B.K. Cunningham called to seek his advice on whether to accept the Mastership of Selwyn.

2. *Regulations and conventions*: Though this account of undergraduate life is placed in the 1930s, much of it would apply equally to any period before 1970. The only change of substance was that Chapel attendance ceased to be compulsory after 1939.

3. *Cap and gown*: The cap was a mortar board. The board was often broken in three or four places, and the headpiece crushed, so that the whole headgear could be lodged in a pocket. It would be pulled out and perched on the head when a Proctor was sighted. A porter on the college gate would report to the Tutor if an undergraduate came in after dark without a gown, but in Selwyn the occupants of ground-floor rooms often obliged by leaving their outward-facing windows open. They were barred but a gown could be left on the sill for the use of any ungowned man returning to College. It was understood that once safely inside, the borrower must immediately return the gown for the use of others in need.

4. *Sam Hall's recollections*: E.M. ('Sam') Hall recorded his memories in an account now deposited in the Selwyn College Archives. There are further references to this account in the following pages. As noted in the preface, it was largely his persistence in raising the question at Selwyn Association meetings that caused this history to be written.

5. *Compulsory chapel*: Information about the petition came from Professor S.G. Lythe, who was an undergraduate at the time. There is no record of it in the College Archives. Lythe did not himself sign the petition; he did not like compulsion, but having accepted an obligation thought that he ought to stick to it. Many years later an old member told Owen Chadwick that the Head Porter could be bribed to mark absentees as present and that there was a well-understood tariff: 1s. 6d. on

weekdays, 2s. 6d. on Sundays. One man who never went to Chapel was reported to Marsh, who was his Tutor. The absentee explained that he was not a Christian but a sun-worshipper. Marsh said that he understood and gave orders that the Night Porter must wake the man at dawn every morning so that he could perform his devotions.

6. *C.W. Phillips as supervisor*: Professor Lythe was particularly grateful for the help that Phillips gave him as a freshman – a class he gave on constitutional documents was a model of its kind.

7. *The junior Fellow's veto*: The junior Fellow was Professor L.W. Forster. He was most surprised by the reaction to his remark, but W.J. Sartain told him later that it was essential that people who had to work together in a small College liked each other.

8. *Chase as a benefactor*: He had considerable private means and used them generously. He forewent a part of his salary, paid for a new chapel organ, and made a large contribution to the cost of a new playing field. He also advanced money after the war for the purchase of houses in Grange Road. It was his special wish to be buried in the College garden and he now lies just outside the east end of the Chapel.

9. *One bold decision*: Woodward promoted. Borradaile opposed, and Chase backed the purchase of the freehold of the land between the College and West Road. In the 1950s it was decided, wisely as it proved, to purchase the houses on this land rather than wait for their leases to expire; but it was the decision of the 1930s that made possible the contemplation of a new North court for the twenty-first century.

10. *Borradaile, Chase and 31 Grange Road*: Borradaile owned no. 31 Grange Road, but had declared his intention of leaving it to Selwyn when he died. Nevertheless, when he decided to leave Cambridge he placed it on the market. Rightly or wrongly, it was thought that he did so to show his displeasure with the way in which Chase was leading the College. As will be seen in the next chapter, Selwyn decided to buy the house and it is believed that Chase gave or lent the money that made this possible. When Borradaile died unexpectedly it was found that he had not altered his will and Selwyn would have inherited the house had it remained part of Borradaile's estate.

CHAPTER 11

War and a New Direction
1939–45

WAR PRESENTED numerous and unusual problems but made long-term planning irrelevant. The hope for the future was that the College would be able to resume normal working when peace returned, the present task was to deal with immediate needs as they arose. Yet the war was a turning point in Selwyn's history. This chapter will deal briefly with war-time experience, then consider some of its general consequences, but a fuller consideration of post-war conditions and the response to them will be postponed to the next chapter.

The following account is drawn mainly from an unsigned article in the *Calendar* for 1946–7 describing the experience of Selwyn at war. Inasmuch as it made no mention of the Revd A.C. Blyth, who carried heavy administrative burdens, it is probable that he was the author. It has also drawn upon the memories of some who were in residence during the war or returned shortly after it.

As soon as the war began everything from food to fuel was rationed, but the Bursar had had the foresight to accumulate stocks of coal and the most visible evidence of war was a huge black mountain in the garden. Nevertheless, throughout two exceptionally cold winters the allowance for rooms was no more than half a bucket a day.

Buildings were requisitioned and service personnel had to be housed and fed, but there were still some undergraduates in residence to be provided for. Selwyn's precarious finances suffered from a sharp drop in the income from fees, and what remained was barely enough to pay a depleted domestic staff. All but the most urgent maintenance tasks were postponed indefinitely, the slender capital reserves were dissipated, and nothing was put by for the future. The government paid for the requisitioned build-ings and services provided by the College staff, but the office staff had to keep track of what was used and submit claims that might then be questioned. When payments were made they barely covered costs and were often months in arrears.

When the war began it was already known that the Air Ministry would take over A, C, and E staircases and some other rooms, and in October 1939 two flights of an initial training wing moved in. In October 1943 they were replaced by flights of an RAF signal wing that remained until March 1945. Nearby, in Cranmer Road, was the headquarters of a Polish armoured train, and in the summer of 1943 Selwyn became the headquarters for a British liaison unit with the Polish army.

All the RAF, Polish, and British liaison officers were made welcome in the Senior Combination Room and given dining rights. This hospitality was particularly appreciated by the Polish exiles, who expressed their gratitude by giving the College a plaque embossed with their regimental badge. Selwyn was also the temporary home for many members of the American and British dominion forces attending courses arranged for them by the University. Other visitors included members of the forces from Norway, Czechoslovakia, and China. Sometimes old members of the College on leave visited Selwyn, bringing news and anec-dotes from all parts of the world at war. In this way new and old friends brought variety, interest, and much pleasure during the grim and anxious years.

Each term a new intake of RAF cadets arrived, some for initial training and some for special courses. In later years some who survived returned to complete degrees at Selwyn. The Junior Combination Room (now the television room) became a canteen, and the Porters' Lodge was used as a guard room. The kitchen staff had to provide two sets of meals – one for undergraduates and one for the Royal Air Force – and the normal slack time during vacations was no more; but no one complained when contributions to the war effort were demanded.

As in the 1914–18 war, female voices were heard around the College because members of the Women's Auxiliary Air Force occupied some rooms. The author of the *Calendar* article remarked that 'if any of the celibate dons were alarmed, or pretended to be alarmed, by their presence, fears proved groundless', but it would be more than thirty years before women again lived in Selwyn.

Air-raid precautions were demanding. Selwyn had to provide air-raid wardens to patrol or be on call twenty-four hours a day, every day of the year. Their principal duties were to see that blackout regulations were strictly observed, to direct people to shelters when an alert was sounded, and to give whatever assistance was necessary if bombs fell. Most readers of these pages will have little idea of what blackout meant. In the streets there were no lights; the court was dark; every window had to have blinds, and if the faintest chink of light shone through a warden would be at the door demanding instant action to conceal it. Persistent offenders were prosecuted. If a door was opened to let someone in, it had to be closed immediately, with no gossiping at the threshold. The problem of blacking out so large a building as the Hall can well be imagined. The Chapel was not blacked out and services were normally held in daylight, but if it had to be used after dark a couple of candles were permitted.

In September 1939 an air-raid warning siren was installed on the tower and until it was linked with the town air-raid command post in the spring of 1940 the College was responsible for manning it. Fellows took it in turn to sleep in the Porters' Lodge to sound the siren if an alert was called. The tower was also an official look-out post during air-raid alerts, and during the dark hours of 1940 and 1941 lurid lights in the southern sky carried the message that London was having another awful night. There was no mass attack on Cambridge but several raids by single enemy planes caused considerable damage. The only University building hit was the Union Society.

F.H. Woodward took charge of air-raid precautions and managed them most efficiently. Senior and junior members were asked to sign on for voluntary warden duties, and it was noted that the Master's initials (G.A.C.) appeared with great frequency. During vacations, when undergraduates were not available, some old members of the College helped with these necessary but usually boring duties. As a precaution against failure of the main water supply, a large static water tank was placed between the Library and Grange Road, and in the attics the long-discarded hip baths, filled with water, kept silent watch against fire by night.

Throughout the war years a few undergraduates were in residence. There were 130 in the Michaelmas term of 1939, and as many rooms had been requisitioned most of them had to share. The age for conscription was at first 21 but was later lowered to 18 and thereafter the only men who came into residence were either unfit or studying subjects deemed to be of national importance. There were medics, a few engineers, and some scientists, all due for call-up, but sent instead to Cambridge to take accelerated two-year courses. There were also some candidates for commissions in technical branches of the services sent on six-month courses, and others on crash courses in foreign languages (especially Russian). These additions kept the number in residence above seventy, but by the Michaelmas term of 1943 only fifteen were enrolled for normal degree courses.

The men in residence were lucky not to be in combat zones, but did not lead easy lives. Shortened war-time courses meant that three years' normal study was crammed into two. Men who were medically fit had to train with the University Naval Division, the Army Training Corps, the Air Squadron, or the National Fire Service. Fit or unfit, they had to take their share in College air-raid precautions involving night patrols and training sessions for action to be taken in emergencies.

Despite these demands on undergraduate time, normal recreation continued and somehow the College clubs kept going. Blues were not awarded during the war but Selwyn produced two presidents of the University Boat Club and four members of the Cambridge crew. In some instances the shortage of experienced oarsmen revealed unexpected talent, and for one undergraduate there was an unlikely sequel to a health warning. Having been told to drop rugby football on medical grounds, he sought gentle relaxation on the river (never having rowed before), and soon found himself rowing in the boat that came sixth in the May races. In addition to the oarsmen, other Selwyn men joined teams that opposed

Oxford: one in rugby football, two in association, one in hockey, six in cross-country running, and no fewer than twelve in athletics.[1]

In 1943 eight undergraduates, determined perhaps to prove their fitness for commando training, succeeded in rigging a cable from the housing of the clock on the Hall to the Chapel and giving it sufficient tension to carry the weight of several chamber pots. Three were caught, severely reprimanded, and fined by the Senior Tutor; but as they left the room Blyth called after them, 'Next time don't get caught'. Sir Edwin Nixon, forty years later an Honorary Fellow of the College, pleads guilty to both charges – perpetrating the deed and getting caught.

The younger Fellows quickly disappeared. L.W. Forster was the first to go (to the Admiralty Intelligence Service). J.C. Walker followed, to the Ministry of Aircraft Production; C.W. Phillips, to RAF Intelligence; and J.K.S. St Joseph to Operational Research at the Ministry of Aircraft Production. One older don, P.J. Durrant, joined the Civil Service and after a spell in the Ministry of Home Defence was posted to the Bristol area as regional civil defence director.

This left normal College administration in the hands of the Master, Bursar, and Senior Tutor. One piece of doggerel recorded the many hats worn by the Revd A.C. Blyth:

> The Chaplain, Vice-Master, and Dean,
> As Fellow and Tutor is seen;
> The Bursar and Chef
> Are all that is left,
> But on neither of these is he keen.[2]

There were numerous domestic problems, and finance was an exasperating puzzle. The Bursar had to keep track of all payments due from the government, expedite their settlement, find money for repairs that could not be delayed, and bring to the notice of officers in charge damage done by their men. Food rationing made catering difficult and loaded the office with paperwork.

After two years of war-time exigencies, G.B. Perrett had had enough and resigned as Bursar. Fortunately an admirable replacement was found in Sir Hubert Sams, an energetic septuagenarian, former colonial civil servant, and more recently Bursar of Peterhouse. Sams was efficient, cheerful, and much liked. One of his innovations, not strictly in the line of bursarial duty, was to organize open-air dances in the court in aid of Toc H in two successive summers.

Another veteran recalled to duty was Dr Borradaile, who resumed his familiar role as a Director of Studies in natural sciences and took over as Garden Steward with the practical but heartbreaking responsibility for converting lawns and flower beds into vegetable plots. Just enough petrol was found to mow the lawn in what was then the sunken court and Professor Marsh revealed unexpected skill with a scythe – learned many years before as a boy on the farm – to keep the banks more or less trim.

Twenty College servants joined the armed services and five were directed to other forms of national service. In Selwyn as elsewhere women filled the gaps. This innovation survived the coming of peace and in later years one often wondered how the pre-war College had managed without the ladies who have made such indispensable and cheerful contributions to College life. Services that had been normal in better days were drastically cut, some never to be restored. Never again would dons have breakfast sent to their rooms or undergraduates have their shoes cleaned before they stirred from their beds. Meals with rationed food were small by pre-war standards but, in common with most of the civilian population, residents discovered that survival – even rude health – was possible without a daily intake of three large meals, coffee at mid-morning, and cakes for tea.

An incomplete list of Selwyn men on service contained over six hundred names. The casualty rate was lower than in the four years of the first World War, but the second lasted longer and there were almost as many names (fifty-nine against seventy-three) to be added to the war memorial. Happily all the College servants in the forces survived.

The *Calendar* account concluded with an evocative paragraph:

Perhaps the pleasantest memory … is the picture of a party of undergraduates on a very hot summer afternoon in May 1945 demolishing with shovels, barrows and sledge hammers the sand bag wall with concrete base which had protected the windows of the Porter's Lodge (the Wardens' Post), and, incidentally, shut out all the light and most of the air. Their energy was only equalled by that of the Master with some of the Fellows and College servants who erected the structure on an equally hot morning and afternoon in September 1939. Its demolition marked in more senses than one the end of many dark days.

It meant also the beginning of a new era, and in popular speech 'before the war' became another time, removed from the present by more than a mere six years.

There was a social revolution in the making with wide-ranging implications for the University and colleges. In 1914 it was assumed that there was an 'officer class' and promotion from the ranks was exceptional, but from 1939 onwards everyone went through the ranks. Selection for officer training depended on performance, and a very large number not drawn from the traditional officer class won commissions and commanded troops with distinction. The young pilots of the Royal Air Force came from a particularly wide social spectrum, and it was remarked that if Waterloo was won on the playing fields of Eton, the Battle of Britain was won in the class-rooms of grammar schools.

As a leveller, war weakened the hold of the social élite on national life and rammed home the message that great reserves of talent had been untapped in former years. In higher education, where the door had been closed to so many unable to afford it and opened to so many who profited little from it, the effect was profound.

Generous grants were available to enable discharged servicemen of all ranks to complete their higher education or for others, including many who had not contemplated it before the war, to begin. For the first and so far the only time the colleges were full of mature students and late developers. There were also far more applicants than in any normal pre-war year, and in justice to those who had done the fighting most colleges increased their intake. By October 1947 the undergraduate population of the University was almost twice what it had been in 1939.

The newcomers were a different breed from the freshmen of the inter-war years, and in many ways different from those who had returned in 1919. A war of movement on the ground and battles in the air, much of it in distant parts of the world, produced men with a wider outlook than those who had lived through the prolonged agony of the Western Front. Some in Signals or Intelligence had worked with apparatus of much greater complexity than any handled by their predecessors. Officers on staffs or in the service units had solved logistic problems that demanded a high level of intelligent innovation. Intellectually the first World War had often arrested development; the second accelerated it.

For Selwyn especially the second World War was a distinct break with the past. As the College filled in 1946 and 1947 there was no large body of third- and second-year men to pass on the customs of the College. Tradition faltered, and to many students the past history of Selwyn had little significance. They had not chosen Selwyn because it was Anglican, cheap, or a rowing college, but because they wanted to come to Cambridge and Selwyn offered a place. They were asked for proof of Christian baptism but this did not signify anything exceptional about the College and for them the distinction between 'College' and 'Approved Foundation' was meaningless.

The number of school-leavers seeking admission was limited because conscription was still in force and the majority did their compulsory two years' national service before coming to the University. However, there were clear indications that the post-war demand for places would not prove to be a temporary bulge. The Education Act of 1944 projected a great expansion in the secondary schools, and from this it would be a short step to an increase in the number entering higher education. To meet the increased demand local authorities were given more money for discretionary grants (on a scale related to parental income) to qualified students offered a university place. Such grants would become mandatory in the 1960s. Thus the rescue operation of 1946 and 1947 became the prelude to a new era in which there would be many more applicants qualified to read for honours degrees, selection would be wider in social class, grants would be made to students on a standard formula, parental ability to pay would be irrelevant, and academic merit would be the principal if not the only qualification for admission.[3]

For Selwyn the consequences were dramatic. As everyone accepted for admission was assured of financial support at a standard rate, one aim of the founders became obsolete. The rising demand for university places meant that the Fellows would never again wait anxiously until September to know whether all places for October had been filled. Selection would become rigorous and former preferences – whether for ordinands or athletes – would be called in question unless those concerned could equal the academic standards of other applicants. There were also financial implications. More students would mean more income, and there would be no incentive to reduce fees if a year's working showed a surplus.

Consequences for the Fellowship were indirect but important. More students implied more Fellows, but here another factor was brought into play. The Act of 1926 had made the University financially responsible for all its teaching officers but not for those who had only college appointments. In the 1930s the part of a teaching officer's salary paid by the University amounted to less than half of what a man of that status expected to earn. His college would find the rest out of supervision fees collected from students, payments for administrative duties, and an annual dividend (being the individual's share of the surplus – often barely visible at Selwyn).

This system continued after the war, but as the salaries of University teaching officers were tied to a rising national scale while college payments increased very little, the University's share of a lecturer's earnings rose proportionately. There was a deduction from the University salary if a lecturer held a Fellowship, but this was small and a college had to contribute very little to compensate him for loss of income. It was therefore becoming cheap for a college to elect a Fellow with a University lectureship; but expensive to elect one without, as the college would have to match from its own resources the salaries paid in University employment. As a consequence a college without large endowments could afford a Fellow without University office only if he worked full-time as Bursar or a Tutor, or supervised in a subject attracting a large number of students. If a college took a gamble on a young man of promise, it would probably elect him for a limited period and make renewal conditional upon his obtaining a University appointment.

With every college in the same situation, the competition for men with University posts or good prospects of obtaining one was stiff, especially in popular subjects with many people to be taught. The richer colleges might be ready to take a chance, but Selwyn had to move cautiously and not run the risk of carrying complete financial responsibility for a Fellow for many years to come.

In this competition Selwyn had other handicaps. It could elect only members of the Church of England, or of a church in communion with it. Its academic reputation was weak. It had inherited the traditions of an institution founded to teach, not to support learning and research. A symbol of this difference was a limitation in the provision of High Table meals; in older colleges they were available throughout the year, but in Selwyn the privileges of a Fellow were curtailed when there were no undergraduates in residence.

Selwyn owed a great debt to the Fellows of earlier years who had been prepared to accept very low remuneration for their services, but after 1945 the idea that Fellows of Selwyn must make sacrifices faded from consciousness. Instead it was assumed that Selwyn must strive to make the privileges and amenities for its Fellows equal to those enjoyed in other colleges. It was understood that with little money to spare progress must be slow, but generally agreed that this was the course to steer.

In these ways the Second World War was a turning point in Selwyn history. Still clinging to old traditions, it became not a new College but a much changed College. Other colleges faced similar problems but solved them within the framework of conventions and ideas erected over centuries; for Selwyn it meant a change of direction. Looming ahead, though dimly perceived, was the need to reconsider the aims of the College; the principles on which it was founded; the part that it ought to play in higher education; and how best to hold the balance between religion, education, and research.

Notes and Comments

1. *Unexpected success on the river*: The undergraduate who had never rowed before and was warned off violent exercise, but rowed in the first boat, went on to a distinguished career in aeronautical engineering – he was D. Rowley, DSc (Eng) (Hon), FEng, FRAeS.

2. *The Revd A.C. Blyth*: The doggerel rhyme about his many duties was recalled by the Right Revd David Cartwright. Some notes on Selwyn during and immediately after the war were also contributed by Mr J. Hallowell and Professor J.K.S. St.Joseph.

3. *Universities after the war*: As so often happens, there was little guidance from the government about the possible consequences of new policies for higher education. In 1945 an enquiry about academic prospects (in another college and from Fellows who were expected to be well informed) elicited the opinion that contraction would follow the post-war bulge and that academic posts would be few. No one seemed the foresee the great expansion that would take place during the next decade and after.

Part III

Acceleration

In Part II the theme was consolidation within the framework set up by the men who founded the College; the theme of Part III is growth and radical change. In many instances the driving forces lay outside Selwyn – in government policy, in changes that transformed higher education, and in social attitudes that discarded past assumptions – but this does not diminish the respect due to those who charted a course in unfamiliar seas. Toward the end of the period, heightened academic reputation and strengthened finances opened a new era in which the driving force would be internal rather than external.

The Fellowship grew more than fivefold. Student participation in College government was first accepted and then made statutory. The old framework of rules governing student life collapsed. The admission of women marked a decisive change in the character of the College. A striking increase in the number of graduate students went far to creating a community within the community.

The Fellows have been so numerous that all cannot be noted. Those who have held substantive college office as Vice-Master, Bursar, or Senior Tutor are mentioned in the text, together with some others who have had a marked influence upon College policy or whose election symbolized a new stage in College history. Some others are mentioned in the Notes and Comments, but the majority must be content with the inclusion of their names in the list given in Appendix C. In these crowded years it has been possible to give even less space to individual undergraduates and graduates. The broad sweep is of more lasting importance than personal achievement, and in this period the sweep has been broad indeed.

A historian of this period encounters problems in nomenclature. When it began it was still customary to use surnames alone as the normal mode of address; nicknames were sometimes used, but Christian names only between close friends and relations. All this has changed. An unadorned surname is regarded as derogatory and the use of Christian names, even between casual acquaintances, has become almost obligatory. Not only personal address but also general descriptions create difficulty. The use of 'don' may be on the way out, and 'student' has certainly come in. In former times there were 'undergraduates', the collective noun was 'men', and 'students' were people who went to less prestigious universities. Now 'student' is preferred as being gender neutral and non-élitist. The principle followed in this history has been to describe people in the way that their contemporaries understood. As time moves on 'undergraduate' gives way to 'student' and Christian or first names are more freely used.

A Note on Money and Values

In this period the country experienced inflation on an unprecedented scale. Academic salaries illustrate what happened. In 1946 the gross salary of a professor (before deduction of tax) was £1,200, by 1970 the average was £4,500, and by 1990 it was over £30,000. To calculate the value in 1990 of 1946 figures multiply by 25; and for the value of 1970 figures by 6.66. However, when considering the cost of house purchases in 1947–50 and the cost of building Cripps (1966–9), larger multiples based on house prices are required. A house that sold for £3,000 in 1946 fetched £15,000 in 1970, £150,000 in 1980, and £220,000 in 1990 (a slight fall from a peak in 1988); the multiples are therefore 66.7 for 1946 to 1990, 13.3 for 1970 to 1990, and 1.5 for 1980 to 1990.

As in the preceding period there are more accurate statistical analyses available, but these rough and impressionistic calculations will impress upon the non-technical reader the reality of inflation.

CHAPTER 12

An Altered Society 1946–55

T HE DECADE following the end of the war was critical in the
history of Selwyn. It began with a momentous increase in
numbers, closed with a radical departure from tradition and after
seventy-four years of active life Selwyn was accepted as a College
by the University. Some general trends and influences have already
been outlined, and this chapter will examine in more detail their
impact upon Selwyn and the decisions that ensued.

During the academic year 1945–6 seventy-five men who had
completed one or two years' study before being called up were
released to complete their degrees. There were also forty-two new
admissions, and another 110 in October. Including research students,
men on teacher training courses, and colonial probationers the
number in residence rose to 240 – sixty more than the pre-war
peak – and in the following year it topped three hundred.

As early as June 1945 two external members of the Council,
Professor C.E. Raven and W.G. Corfield, stressed the need to
plan for a permanent rather than a temporary increase, and the
Master must have congratulated himself on having persuaded the
University to end the restriction on numbers. It would probably
have been lifted to meet the post-war pressure, but there was no
need for negotiation or delay and the newly appointed Bursar,
T.G.P. Spear, applied himself immediately to the administrative
problems that would arise from expansion.

The majority of colleges faced difficulties in accommodation
at a time when many pre-war lodging-house keepers did not wish
to continue. To find rooms for the new intake, Fellows and their
wives canvassed vigorously from door to door in different parts
of the town, and the fact that most potential lodgers were returned
warriors may have helped to soften the hearts of householders
with a room to spare. Somehow everyone was housed, and though

some lodgings were inconveniently far from the College, laboratories or lecture rooms, and of a standard that would have been unacceptable before the war, the men could come to Cambridge – and that was what mattered.

Future plans were much discussed. Temporary buildings were suggested, but older Fellows remembered that the last of the wooden buildings erected in 1882 remained in the court until 1929, and the prospect of unsightly huts disfiguring the garden until the end of the century did not appeal. Luck and a bold decision prompted a better policy; the luck lay in the appearance of neighbouring houses on the market, the boldness in taking a financial gamble to buy them.

It had already been agreed to purchase 31 Grange Road from Dr Borradaile for £4,000; this was to provide three flat for Fellows (an urgent need as housing was very short). Then 2 Cranmer Road and 43 Grange Road (known as Saxon Barns) were offered at £3,000 and £3,800 respectively. With an alacrity rare in academic deliberations it was agreed to purchase with mortgages on the three houses to a limit of £15,000. After abortive negotiations with a building society, Barclay's Bank lent the money with no strings attached.

Thus a policy was inaugurated – followed when other neighbouring houses came on the market – that reaped many rewards for Selwyn and its undergraduates. In earlier days the Council might have shied away from incurring so large a debt; but the day of deficit financing had dawned, and the certainty that undergraduates would get public grants dispelled doubt about dependence on room rents to meet interest charges. By November 1946 twenty-one undergraduates were accommodated in the newly acquired houses.

Despite financial improvisation, poverty remained a grievous handicap. In 1946–7 Selwyn had an income from external sources (investments and property) of £1,949 and only £486 from endowments. There was a very wide gap between this and the next poorest colleges (Magdalene with £7,935 and £3844, and Trinity Hall with £9,962 and £5,916). Income from fees increased in the following years, making it possible to budget for a small surplus after the interest on mortgages had been paid, but capital reserves mounted very slowly and as in early years no large donors appeared. Fortunately the new Bursar, pressed by Sartain and Durrant, realized that debt need not be shunned if the loan acquired an asset. Interest on a first mortgage could be paid from room rents; a second mortgage could be used to buy another house for conversion – and so on. It was not easy, but it worked.

Fellows returned from the war, others were elected, and if a visitor to the Selwyn High Table in October 1947 had been endowed with supernatural foresight he would have seen promise of distinction that could match any older college of comparable size. J.K.S. St Joseph, a Selwyn graduate, was about to leave geology to pioneer the use of aerial photography in academic study. He would close his career many years later having been awarded the CBE, a LittD, and a Fellowship of the British Academy. In the College he would serve for many years as a Tutor and then as Vice-Master. G.D.H. Bell, who had come to Selwyn as a graduate student in 1928 and was elected a Fellow in 1944, was at the start of a career as Director of the Plant Breeding Institute that would bring him international recognition. In 1954, when the Institute was taken over by the Ministry of Agriculture and the Agricultural Research Council and severed its link with the University, he resigned his Fellowship but in 1965 he returned to the Selwyn family as an Honorary Fellow. In later years he was awarded many honours, including the CBE, Fellowship of the Royal Society, and an honorary ScD from the University of Cambridge.

H.B. Cott, a Selwyn graduate appointed in Borradaile's place as a Fellow in zoology, had already won recognition with a path-breaking book, *Adaptive Coloration in Animals*. In appearance and manner of speaking he could well be mistaken for an army officer with conventional opinions, but behind the façade was an acute and sensitive mind. He followed his work on animal camouflage with an investigation into the palatability of birds' eggs, and on one memorable occasion the High Table were served with scrambled rheas' eggs as an hors d'oeuvre. In his later work his

interest shifted to larger and larger animals and when he was
well into his 70s he conducted safaris in the African Highlands.
He was also a talented artist and a posthumous exhibition of
his black and white prints attracted much favourable attention
and those on sale found their way into many Cambridge homes.
He made over to Selwyn a substantial sum of money to enable
junior members to undertake the kind of scientific expeditions
to distant parts of the world that had laid the foundations of his
own career.

Two other Fellows were soon appointed to professorships in
other universities: W.E. Burcham, a physicist and later a Fellow
of the Royal Society, at Birmingham; and L.W. Forster, elected
in 1938 as the first Fellow in modern languages, at University
College, London. In 1961 Leonard Forster returned to Cambridge
as Professor of German and became once more a Fellow of Selwyn.
He became a Fellow of the British Academy and received many
honorary awards. There are several references in the following
pages to his account of Selwyn during his first period as a Fellow.
Modesty might forbid but accuracy demands the mention of the
present writer, who became a Fellow in 1947 (the last to be sought
out and nominated by Chase).

This record of individual achievement has been given to
underscore a significant message. All these young Fellows were
intellectually ambitious, and though they were no less assiduous
than their predecessors in developing the talents of the men whom
they taught, their hopes were fastened on reputations to be won
in the world of learning. It was probable that most future Fellows
would have the same priorities – especially if they were elected
because they held, or had a good prospect of holding, a University
teaching post for which scholarly potential was the principal
criterion. In electing a University lecturer the College entered
into an unwritten contract to support his research as well as asking
him to teach, and to give this obligation statutory form, they
were forbidden to do more than a stated number of hours' college
teaching. The rule was not strictly observed but it was a safeguard
against a man's scholarly light being extinguished by an overload
of college duties.

Nevertheless good administration demanded the election of some Fellows who could spend their whole time on College business. Perrett had been for fifteen years both Bursar and a University lecturer, but since then it has been recognized that conflict between the claims of the College and the University must be avoided. It is difficult to lay down any rule for other college offices, but a college normally runs better if it has two or three Fellows who give their whole time to its affairs. Selwyn was fortunate in having two Fellows of high calibre who did so.

The Revd A.C. Blyth's interests were pastoral rather than academic. He wrote nothing (though many of his lucid and thoughtful sermons deserved publication), but he was an exacting supervisor and a Tutor who knew everything about the men under his charge. His comments could be devastating when pretentiousness, sloppy thinking, or idleness were detected; but behind the outward austerity there was a generous and kindly disposition. Once men got to know him they gave him great respect and genuine affection.

Blyth had been badly wounded during the 1914–18 war and was often in pain (though never allowing anyone to perceive it). He was interested in everything that the College did, but as an old rowing man his strongest commitment was to the Boat Club and he endeared himself to generations of Selwyn oarsmen. In College business he was usually found on the conservative side of an argument but was never intolerant of innovation. One looked to him for cautious wisdom with absolute confidence that once a decision had been made it would be implemented conscientiously, whatever his private opinion. He played no part in University administration but was widely respected as a man who embodied the best qualities of the old-style college don. The College owns a very good line and wash portrait of him by H.A. Freeth. Mrs Lorna Blyth was almost as much a part of the College as he, acting as hostess at tutorial tea parties and in the post-war years helping the bewildered young wives of married undergraduates and graduate students. She outlived her husband by many years, dying in her late 90s, blind and housebound but with her mental faculties unimpaired.

P.J. Durrant had been disappointed in the 1920s when he was not appointed (unjustly as many thought) to a University lectureship in chemistry; but this was Selwyn's gain (because he devoted himself wholeheartedly to the College), and a blessing for generations of sixth-formers who learned their chemistry from his outstandingly successful *General and Inorganic Chemistry*, published in 1939, and his *Organic Chemistry*, which followed in 1950. In preparing these books his constant aid and severest critic was his wife Beryl, also a top-class scientist, and together they were joint authors of the *Introduction to Advanced Inorganic Chemistry*, published in 1962 and intended for older students. Durrant's reputation in schools brought many gifted young scientists to Selwyn, and having got them there he saw that they were taught well. During the many years that he directed studies there were usually at least two firsts and several upper seconds in both parts of the Natural Sciences Tripos.

Durrant was a very useful man to have on a committee and Selwyn owes much to his wise advice given behind closed doors. Finance, building, and the improvement of amenities were his particular interests. G.D.H. Bell was responsible for restoring the College grounds after their war-time conversion to food production; but after he resigned his Fellowship Durrant took over and was Garden Steward for the next fifteen years. He was also keenly interested in music and gave much help to the Music Society. Royalties from his books made him a wealthier man than most academics, and nothing gave him greater satisfaction than giving money to Selwyn to carry out much needed improvements. There is a line and wash portrait of him by H.A. Freeth that some prefer to the oil painting in the new Senior Combination Room.

T.G.P. Spear was appointed as a full-time Bursar, but this was not a complete departure from previous practice as he also supervised in history and continued with academic work. He had graduated from St Catharine's before the war, joined the Indian Civil Service, and formed a close relationship with St Stephen's College in Delhi. He had no previous experience of college administration, but proved to be a very good Bursar. Always proceeding with a due proportion of caution and imagination, he steered Selwyn successfully through difficult years of adjustment, improvisation, and constructive innovation. But when his work on Indian history brought him belated appointment as a University lecturer, he took the view that a man cannot serve two masters and resigned as Bursar.

Recalling the difficulties encountered with the men who came from the services to Cambridge in 1919, some older dons looked forward to 1946 with apprehension. Would the returning warriors be unruly? Would they be intellectually stultified? They need have had no fears. For reasons already discussed in the previous chapter, the mood was very different from that of 1919. The undergraduates of 1946 and 1947 were serious, eager to learn, and certainly not dull.

Leonard Forster, who had worked on secret intelligence during the war, was enthusiastic about the quality of the men whom he encountered on his return to Selwyn:

> They knew why they had come to the university – to prepare themselves for civilian life – and they knew that there was more than one way of doing this. They were persons of experience and maturity, who had seen a great deal of the world (more than most of the Fellows) and many of them had been intellectually starved for many years. They were eager for something they could get their teeth into ... They had a sense of liberation ... They were a pleasure to teach.

The intellectual level was also unusually high because all the war-time Scholars who had been unable to take their places came up in 1946.[1]

Men who had commanded troops in the field accepted with good-humoured tolerance rules designed to give moral protection to boys just out of school. This was a small price for the privilege of being in Cambridge. As Peter Collister (who came up to Selwyn in 1946 and was later followed by two sons) wrote: 'I never crossed King's bridge without giving thanks that the Granta in '46 was not the Irrawaddy in '42 and this overriding sense of gratitude pervaded our attitude to University and College.'[2]

There was no upward surge in the number of firsts, but there were more seconds and fewer thirds. Except for some special courses (such as the Certificate in Christian Knowledge) few entered for the ordinary degree or were relegated to it. Whether the innate ability of the post-war generation was superior to that of their predecessors is open to question; but their academic motivation was stronger. Nor was it all work and no play. Selwyn sport was soon back in full gear, and thanks to enthusiastic help by former rowing men (especially the ebullient and ever-youthful McEldowney), the Boat Club was full of vigour and rewarded by modest success.

Equally striking were cultural activities that brought new vitality to College life. Drama had not had a noticeable presence in Selwyn before the war, but it sprang to life with a memorable performance of *The Rivals* in 1949. Prompted by Dr Spear, a History Society was formed with lively and well-attended meetings. Above all, music flourished in the new era. F.W. Rimmer, later to be professor of music at the University of Glasgow and an Honorary Fellow of Selwyn, arrived in 1946 as the Organ Scholar (affiliated from Durham where he had taken his first degree). He raised the Chapel choir to a level not hitherto attained, organized other musical activities in the College, and started the Sunday evening concerts that have continued since his day. Equally impressive was the record of his successor, D.J. Lumsden (later to be Sir David Lumsden, Principal of the Royal Academy of Music, and also an Honorary Fellow of the College). In 1954 another outstanding Organ Scholar was G.R. Hendrie, later professor of music at the Open University. In those days young professional musicians were often ready to accept a Sunday engagement for a nominal fee and Selwyn was privileged to hear many performers who later filled the largest concert halls in the country.

When there were more applicants than places, all colleges faced problems of selection. The majority of applicants depended on government grants, and though there was nothing to prevent a college from admitting an applicant from a socially élite family whose father was prepared to pay the full cost, a better qualified candidate from a poorer home would probably be preferred. Promising athletes with weak scholastic records presented a more difficult problem. If admitted, they would raise college morale, and everyone could remember blues who had struggled to get a pass degree but had gone on to useful and distinguished careers. Should promise of this kind place them above men with better academic potential? Human nature being what it is, some college Tutors continued to give preference to possible blues, but it was a dying custom and incurred reproach when too openly practised. Curiously enough, there was no catastrophic drop in sporting standards – though some athletes of international class may have been turned away.

In most colleges the likelihood that an applicant would obtain second-class honours was becoming the normal justification for admission, and this raised a special difficulty in Selwyn where it had been customary to admit ordinands for whom a third class or an ordinary degree was the probable ceiling. Many past Selwyn men had achieved nothing higher but had gone on to serve as admirable parish priests, and there were arguments for continuing this service to the Church. It was not normally a choice between a pass man and a possible first, but between a man with a vocation and one without who might get a low second. Continuing discrimination in favour of ordinands was strengthened by a government decision to recognize the Certificate of Christian Knowledge (with the status of an ordinary degree) as a course that grant-giving authorities should support, and each year eight or nine candidates for it were admitted. Not all the Fellows were happy, and some began to ask whether ordinands deserved a place when men who might be equally useful in other walks of life were rejected. This argument carried more weight when new universities came on stream in the 1960s and the rejection of an ordinand at Selwyn did not mean that he was deprived of the chance to obtain a degree.

Scholars and Exhibitioners were still obliged by statute to be members of the Church of England. The majority of commoners belonged to the Church and on admission they had to sign an undertaking to join in corporate worship, but the exclusion of non-Anglicans was less rigid than it had been. Agnostics, if they were known, were barred, as were members of non-Christian faiths, but many of the ex-service men were asked only for proof of Christian baptism. Chapel attendance remained good, but a considerable number of undergraduates seldom set foot inside the building. Selwyn was a long way from being a non-denominational or secular institution, but junior members were less conscious than their predecessors of the nature of the relationship between the College and the Church.

A new Master had to guide the College in these difficult times. G.A. Chase was appointed Bishop of Ripon and his successor was the Revd W. Telfer, for many years a Tutor at Clare and recently appointed Ely Professor of Divinity (a post he had to resign as it required residence at Ely for the greater part of the year). He already knew a great deal about Selwyn from his brother, who had come to the College as an undergraduate in 1912. Telfer had been trained as a mathematician, but turned to theology and became an authority on the early history of Christian doctrine. During the First World War he had won the MC, but never talked about his war experiences. He had keen intelligence, and a diffident manner concealed a strong will. He quickly won the confidence of the Fellows, and in addition to his other qualities proved to be a very good man of business, with a quick eye for essentials and a firm grasp of financial problems. He was un-married and his sister acted as hostess in the Lodge.

Telfer was a strong churchman and may have accepted the Mastership with the express purpose of preserving Selwyn as an Anglican bridgehead in the University. In time this led to funda-mental disagreement with a majority of the Fellows, but the test did not come until near the end of his Mastership. In the meantime he was as determined as his predecessor to reduce the differences between Selwyn and other colleges.

It was Telfer who first proposed that Selwyn ought to have an annual feast to which the College should invite official guests. This departure from austere traditions was envisaged as a graceful way of thanking people who had helped, winning the goodwill

William Telfer, 1956.

of those who might do so in the future, and honouring Selwyn men who had achieved distinction in academic or public life. It has since retained this character.

Another new departure was the first May Ball, requested by undergraduates and, after much earnest thought, permitted by the Fellows provided that the cost was kept low (it was initially fixed at £3 for a double ticket). A local band was engaged, all the entertainment was home-made, and everyone enjoyed it. The Master showed his goodwill by putting in an early appearance and then, to everyone's surprise and delight, re-emerging at 6 a.m. for the survivors' photograph. Telfer also encouraged the Music Society by holding very pleasant 'at homes' – with madeira or soft drinks – after the Sunday evening concerts. His frequent appearance on the touchline when Selwyn had an important match or on the tow-path was also noted with pleasure.[3]

The undergraduate request for a May Ball was a symptom of changing attitudes toward the College and its traditions. 'Selwyn was to be a college like any other', wrote Leonard Forster, 'because it did not occur to these people that there was any difference.' Other changes were in the wind. Fellows were given an allowance to enable them to entertain undergraduates, and what mattered was not so much the money (most overspent their allowance) but recognition that closer social relationships between seniors and juniors were worth paying for. Undergraduate parties in College were on a scale that would have been regarded as undesirably extravagant in the 1930s, and it was not long before someone thought of starting a Wine Society. Selwyn men also played more part in University activities than their predecessors, and in 1951 the College had its first president of the Union (A.H. Sampson).

The Fellowship expanded slowly. Though it cost little to elect University lecturers, few were available in subjects requiring most supervision. A geographer (A.A.L. Caesar) was elected in 1949 but was soon recaptured by his own old College (St Catharine's) with the offer of a Tutorship. Robert Auty, a distinguished scholar in East European languages and later a professor at Oxford, came in 1950 as the first Fellow in modern languages. In 1952 James Winny, a Selwyn man with an outstanding undergraduate record, was elected as the first Fellow in English. In 1955 there was another new departure with the decision to look for a Fellow in engineering. Donald Welbourn was elected and within a short time made a subject that had attracted few students before the war one of the strongest in the College. A note at the end of this chapter also records the election in 1951 of Percy Simpson, an early and distinguished graduate, as an Honorary Fellow.[4]

The growing strength and increasing number of the Fellows highlighted their relationship to the College. Carried over from the far-off days when the lecturers had been people employed by the Council to teach, a distinction had remained between the College and the Fellows. This was partly explained by the fact that no Fellow had had experience in another college; but without formal resolutions, the former assumption that the College and the Fellows had different, and perhaps conflicting, interests was being replaced. The Fellows were not apart from the College; they *were* the College. It was symbolic that the period during which Fellows had a right to a stated number of free meals each week was being extended. Financial constraints made progress slow but step by step it was recognized that a Fellow's work did not end when the undergraduates went down. Research and writing were full-time occupations.

When Chase had become Master the relations between the Fellows and the Council had been very poor. The Fellows who were on the Council assumed superiority over the rest, regarding themselves not as representatives of the Fellows but as agents of the Council to see that Fellows toed the line. The situation improved as Fellows filled vacancies on the Council when they occurred, but the Charter fixed the number of elected places and as the number of Fellows grew more of them would be excluded from policy-making. This raised further questions. What was the Council for? Did the College need an 'upper house' with overriding authority? Why could not all power be vested in the Master and Fellows as in other colleges? If these questions were to be answered constructively, a full revision of the Charter and statutes would be necessary; and once this was undertaken, a larger issue would arise. What was needed to win for Selwyn recognition as a College rather than an Approved Foundation?

There were three related issues and each touched upon the relationship with the Church of England: the Council with its *ex-officio* members, the requirement that the Master must always be a Clerk in Holy Orders, and the Church of England test for Fellows and Scholars. If one assumed that recognition as a College was the paramount aim, the Council and the denominational tests must go. And though the University had never made the requirement that the Master must be a Clerk in Holy Orders a ground for non-recognition, this Charter provision could hardly escape scrutiny. If one began with the conviction that the paramount aim was to keep Selwyn as an Anglican College, then *ex-officio* membership of the Council might be defended, the Master must be a clergyman, and the Fellows and Scholars must be members of the Church of England or of a church in communion with it. The positions were irreconcilable and one or the other must prevail, though perhaps with concessions that would be symbolic rather than real.[5]

Ironically the easiest position to defend – the retention of the Council – was the first to be abandoned. It would have been possible to enlarge the Council to include all or nearly all the Fellows and to reduce to two or three the *ex-officio* members. Whether this would have satisfied the University cannot be known, but the effect would have been to put government in the hands of the Master and Fellows but, following business practice, with the addition of two or three non-executive directors. This would have been a workable and possibly useful arrangement but was not seriously considered and the decision to abolish the Council and to constitute the Master and Fellows as a governing body was quickly reached.

The crucial issue was the test for Fellows and Scholars. Discreet enquiries made by Chase in 1944 revealed that this was still the principal – and for many members of the University an insuperable – obstacle to recognition as a College. Even if the Council of the Senate thought otherwise, there would be fierce opposition in the Regent House, probably an adverse vote, perhaps debate in Parliament, and certainly much unwelcome publicity.

An appeal to the Charter led, as in the Fellowship debate of 1902–4, to no certain conclusion. The founders had intended to establish a College but this had proved to be incompatible with their determination to make it an Anglican College. Lawyers are familiar with the many problems that arise from the conflict of laws, and the Fellows had now to consider a conflict of purpose in the knowledge that circumstances had changed. What the founders had not wanted, it could be argued, was a weak College, and retention of the tests kept Selwyn weak.

Apart from satisfying the University, it was argued that academic prospects would be improved by dropping the tests. Selwyn was handicapped in the search for Fellows and not only because it excluded men who did not belong to the Church of England. There were many Anglicans who thought that denominational tests were an encroachment upon academic freedom and would not accept election. There were also Fellows who had no theoretical objection to denominational tests but thought that insistence on religious conformity damaged the College without serving the Church.

The case for allowing the election of a layman as Master rested wholly on practical considerations. The field was too narrow. Clergymen with the right personal qualities to head the College might lack academic distinction. The number of ordained academics had shrunk since 1882, and those who remained were much in demand to fill deaneries and bishoprics. The restriction also made it very unlikely that a scientist would ever become Master of Selwyn.

Dr Telfer was convinced that Selwyn must remain an Anglican College. Most Fellows took it for granted that whatever the outcome of the debate commoners of any faith would be admitted, but this was not the Master's view. He was not disposed to demand strict conformity, provided that applicants continued to sign a declaration that they agreed to take part in corporate worship (even though many might never attend Chapel once they were in residence), but he thought that the line must be drawn somewhere and when he learned that two undergraduates had become Roman Catholics decided to draw it.

The two men were not expelled but the Master told them firmly that they were morally obliged to end their membership of a Church of England College. On admission they had signed the declaration that they would take part in College worship and they now belonged to a church that forbade them from doing so. It was irrelevant to argue that many who had signed were never seen in Chapel because there was a clear distinction between laxity and doctrinal prohibition. He made arrangements for them to transfer to Fitzwilliam, then a non-collegiate institution, but it is not clear what would have been his next step if they had refused to move. They did so under protest and the leaders of the Roman Catholic community in Cambridge decided not to make an issue of their treatment. Had they done so, Selwyn would have attracted much unwelcome publicity. As it was, the majority of Fellows did not like the way that the matter had been handled and hardened their opposition to all denominational discrimination.

Dr Telfer believed that if the price for sticking to the principles on which Selwyn had been founded was non-recognition, then paid it must be. It should be added that for him the Church was very broad, demanded no dogmatic test of faith, had room for Christian humanists as well as fundamentalists, and displayed an intellectual vigour that challenged the notion of sterility. This was the foundation on which a strong Christian culture could be built, and if Selwyn followed this path it would win recognition of another kind. Searching for historical examples, he drew attention to the great Franciscan house that had once stood on the site occupied by Sidney Sussex; though never a college of the University it had been one of the most distinguished centres of learning in late medieval England.

This argument might have won more support had there been a strong call from leaders of the Church to stand firm. Archbishop Geoffrey Fisher was invited to make an official visitation to the College and gave helpful advice, but, in the opinion of most Fellows, he carefully refrained from urging the Fellows to keep the religious tests. This was something that they must decide for themselves. The two Regius Professors of Divinity on the Council, both from colleges of great distinction, showed no enthusiasm for the retention of a weak Anglican bridgehead in a University that did not want it.

Dr Telfer often assumed that if logic led him to a certain conclusion others must be travelling the same road. Clearly he expected a majority of the Fellows to adopt his plan to strengthen Selwyn without modifying its Anglican character and at a most unhappy meeting he asked each Fellow in turn, starting with the most junior, to declare his views. His mounting distress was apparent as one after another (in the final count, all but two) declared in favour of abolishing the test for Fellows and Scholars.

The next contentious issue was the Mastership. Some who had voted for the abolition of tests for Fellows were content to keep the requirement that the Master must be in Holy Orders, but the majority were impressed by the argument that there should be an escape clause to permit the election of a layman. Some favoured an appointed rather than an elected Master. C.P. Snow's *The Masters*, published shortly before, described the bitter internal conflicts surrounding the election of a Master in a small college, and Professor Burnaby, the Regius Professor of Divinity and a Fellow of Trinity, thought it a great blessing for his College that the Crown appointed its Master (and had never made an unworthy choice). But who would appoint a Master of Selwyn? The Crown was unlikely to accept the responsibility, and there was little support for the idea that it should be given to the Visitor. The thought that a future archbishop might see fit to appoint an Archdeacon Grantly or a Mr Slope was enough to kill the suggestion.

The outcome was a somewhat uneasy compromise. The Fellows would elect the Master, with a majority of two-thirds required for the successful candidate, but were bound in the first instance to look for a Clerk in Holy Orders. If they then decided by a majority of two-thirds that they could find no clergyman whom they considered suitable they could proceed to elect a layman, provided that he was a member of the Church of England. Difficulties could be foreseen if a majority short of two-thirds wished to elect a clergyman and the minority held out for the election of a layman. It would also create an unpleasant situation if a well-qualified clerical Fellow were a candidate but the majority decided that no suitable Clerk in Holy Orders could be found.

It should not be assumed that the majority of the Fellows were swayed by a simplistic argument against denominational tests. All were communicant members of the Church of England, attended Chapel regularly, and had willingly accepted Fellowships from which other denominations were excluded. As a theoretical proposition all would have defended the right of a corporate body to decide on its own membership. Tests had been rightly condemned when they were imposed by all colleges, but now that non-Anglicans had plenty of choice among colleges, there was no logical case against their exclusion from one. On these lines a Fellow of Selwyn might have justified his own previous decision to accept election, but with one important qualification. He had not come to Selwyn to serve the Church but to follow his chosen path as a scholar. It was as an academic that he hoped to win acclaim, not as an Anglican missionary in a secular society. He fully recognized his obligation to the College and wished to see it prosper, but saw no reason why its prospects should be sacrificed on a denominational altar.

Once a majority arrived at this conclusion, the principle that a corporate body had a right to decide its own membership could be invoked in another sense; no longer to defend self-determination against uniformity, but to maintain the right of the present not to be bound by the past. Circumstances changed and opinions must be allowed to change with them. It was recognized that an ordained clergyman of the Church of England might take a different view, but when agreement was impossible the majority must prevail.

The Master could have used his veto, but wisely decided not to do so. The issue had been long debated, the conclusions first reached individually and then collectively would not be abandoned, and the society would be dangerously divided if he did so. The Master may also have had it in mind that his own tenure was drawing to a close, and that no successor could be elected who did not undertake to accept the decision of the majority. With reluctance, but with better judgement than he had displayed in the case of the Catholic undergraduates, he accepted the decisions that had been made, worked hard with a select committee to get the new statutes drafted, and contributed a graceful note to the *Calendar* explaining the changes.

With the most contentious issues settled in principle, the legal problems proved easier to solve than had been anticipated. Advice was sought from a law Fellow of Keble College, Oxford, where similar changes had been made slightly ahead of Selwyn. Somewhat to the surprise of the Selwyn Fellows, he said that a simple preamble would be sufficient. It should state that 'the Charter of 1882 remains in force except as amended by the following statutes'; the Council could then be abolished despite the precise definition of its composition and powers in the Charter, and a layman could become Master despite the categorical assertion that he must always be a Clerk in Holy Orders. The tests for Fellows and Scholars were not in the Charter, and the final acts of the Council could be to change the statutes in any way that was desired. The approval of the Privy Council would be necessary but its only concern would be to ensure that there was no conflict with the law as laid down by Parliament. An appeal to the founders' intention would be treated as irrelevant.

The old College Council met for the last time on 22 February 1957 and approved the new statutes. On 14 October 1957 a report by the Council of the Senate of the University noted that the three principal differences between Selwyn and the older colleges had been government by an external council, the requirement that all Fellows should be members of the Church of England, and a similar requirement for Scholars and Exhibitioners. As the revised statutes removed these differences there was 'now no reason why Selwyn College should continue to be classed as an Approved Foundation rather than as a College in the full statutory sense of the term'. The grace embodying this recommendation was unopposed and Selwyn became a College, in the 'full statutory sense of the term', with much goodwill from other members of the University community.

On 14 March 1958 the Queen in Council approved the following amendments to the University statutes:

STATUTE H

Chapter I

APPROVED FOUNDATIONS

By repealing Section 6

STATUTE K

By inserting in Section 3(a) after the words 'Downing College' the words 'Selwyn College'.

SCHEDULE C

By adding the following item:

Selwyn ... 2

Only by reference to the bulky volume of the statutes and ordinances of the University of Cambridge could one discover that these laconic statements formally ended Selwyn's status as an Approved Foundation, recognized it as a College, allowed its Master to be Vice-Chancellor, permitted it to appoint Proctors when its turn came round, recorded that it must make a contribution to the University Chest, and required it to elect as Fellows two professors of the University. Henceforth Selwyn was equal in status, rights, and duties with all other colleges, and it did not have to wait long before its Master served as Vice-Chancellor.

The passing of the old Council should not be recorded without an appreciation of its services. In the early years the College could not have survived without the active support and guidance of men who served without financial remuneration or enhanced reputation. There had been many occasions on which miscalculation or misdirection could have killed the infant, and in later years the College had benefited much from oversight by men whose experience of academic and public life was much greater than that of any Fellow. Two elected members who continued to serve after the war deserve special mention: Albert Mansbridge, CH, was a pioneer of the Workers Educational Association, and was thus familiar with the wider issues raised by new educational policies; W.G. Corfield was a Selwyn graduate and businessman who gave

much valued advice on financial management at a time when no
Fellow had knowledge in this field. The two Regius Professors
of Divinity attended regularly and their advice was much valued.
Charles Raven was forceful and far-sighted. Michael Ramsay, later
Bishop of Durham and then Archbishop of Canterbury, was an
impressive but usually silent member. The last two Regius Pro-
fessors before the abolition of the Council, John Burnaby and
Leonard Hodgson from Oxford, were of great help during revision
of the statutes and the concurrent business of electing a new
Master, and it was fitting that one of the first acts of the newly
constituted Governing Body was to elect them both as Honorary
Fellows.

There are three postscripts to the adoption of the new statutes.
One presents a puzzle, one notes an omission, and the third
records a fortunate occurrence. The puzzle is found in the Master's
article in the *Calendar* explaining what had been done, in which
he said that the Fellows were bound to consult the Visitor (the
Archbishop of Canterbury) before proceeding to consider a layman
as Master. This was a proviso that had been discussed but there
is no trace of it in the statutes as finally approved by the Privy
Council. Dr Telfer was not a man to err on a matter of fact so
there must have been some misunderstanding or an omission in
the final draft, but no one admitted error or claimed credit. It is
doubtful whether Fellows would have agreed to a procedure that
would allow the Archbishop to veto an election, but they may
have agreed to consult him without being bound by any advice
that might be given.[6]

The omission was that the power to make or amend statutes
was not transferred from the old Council to the new Governing
Body. Consequently all later changes in the statutes between 1957
and 1985, including the admission of women in 1976, were made
ultra vires and would have been declared void if challenged in the
courts. A private Act of Parliament was required to remedy the
omission and give retrospective legality to all changes since the
abolition of the old Council.

The fortunate occurrence concerned the election of a successor to Dr Telfer. His term expired before the new statutes were in force and consequently the next Master was elected by the old Council and had to be in Holy Orders. One of the first to be mentioned was the Revd W.O. Chadwick, then an Assistant Tutor at Trinity Hall, but he was put aside as being too young at 40. After a long search through *Crockford's Clerical Directory*, many personal enquiries, and two offers declined, his was the only remaining name on the clerical short list. Had it then been possible to look for a layman, the hesitation over age might have prevailed. As it was they proceeded to elect the man who would serve for twenty-seven years, confer great benefits upon the College, and earn all the rewards and honours that the world of learning can confer.

A founder of the College, returning in spirit to watch over these events, might have been dismayed by the outcome, but a glance into the Chapel would have brought consolation. Sir Arthur Blomfield had planned forty-six canopies over the stalls, but at the time only the two for the Master and Vice-Master were erected. In 1901 fourteen were added as a memorial to Bishop John Selwyn, but there were no more until after 1945 when seven on either side were erected and dedicated by donors to the memory of individuals. Subsequently two more were added by personal gift, but there still remained fourteen to complete the original design. In 1950 Dr Durrant set about the task of raising money by private approaches to old members, and was so successful that all were completed and dedicated on 10 April 1953.[7]

A memorial fund launched in 1946 raised enough money to pay for a tablet, dedicated in April 1951, recording the names of Selwyn men killed in the war and also to pay for improvements to the east end of the Chapel. The existing arrangement of the sanctuary, with the altar raised high and reached by unattractive wooden steps, had given the east end a cramped appearance. A new plan was adopted under which the altar was lowered and the whole east end paved with stone slabs.

A tapestry had formerly hung between the altar and the east window, but could not fill the wall that was now exposed. The original plan had not included a reredos and, after taking much professional advice, a young sculptor, Karen Jonzen, was commissioned to present a design in which the ascending Christ would be the central figure. Her design, with balance achieved by an attendant angel on either side, was approved.

The work, completed in 1957, won felicitous praise from J.W. Goodison, then assistant director and later director of the Fitzwilliam Museum:

> The boldness of the three separate figures gives the composition the dominance of pattern essential to its commanding position, and the upward lines of the design, naturally appropriate to the subject, unite the features of the East Wall of the Chapel into a harmonious whole.

He described the figure of the risen Christ as 'strikingly effective by the quality of its sculptural design, embodying a conception which lends to it a character at once explicit and mysterious'.

So, sixty-four years after the laying of its foundation stone, the Chapel was complete. There remained some windows without stained glass, but since that time the prevailing view has been that the Chapel, with soft light from the plain windows illuminating what might otherwise be a sombre interior, is better without more stained glass. The work is noble and a fitting link between past ideals, present practice, and enduring faith.

Notes and Comments

1. *The post-war undergraduates*: This tribute is taken from an account of these years given by Professor Forster and deposited in the College Archives. It represents a widely held view.

2. *Some Selwyn men of these years*: The comment by Peter Collister comes from an account of Selwyn in these years deposited in the College Archives. He went on to a varied career as a schoolmaster at home and overseas, one of Her Majesty's Inspectors of Schools, an adviser on educational problems in Asian and African countries, author, and historian, and he was to write an account of the Kingdom of Bhutan that proved him to be one of the few people in England who know anything about that remote country. Two sons followed him at Selwyn.

Among others of this generation (and their future positions) were Arthur Portere (Vice-Chancellor of the University of Sierra Leone), J.R. (Jimmy) Jones (Professor of History at the University of East Anglia), Peter Kidson (an authority on medieval art and professor at the Courtauld Institute), and Marc Van Hasselt (Headmaster of Cranleigh). For Edwin Nixon and Derek Rayner (now Honorary Fellows), see page 287.

3. *The first May Ball*: The principal promoter and organizer of the event was H.E. Hall, brother of E.M. ('Sam') Hall, whose recollections of Selwyn in the 1930s were quoted in Chapter 8.

4. *Percy Simpson, DLitt, LittD (Hon)*: The election of Dr Simpson as an Honorary Fellow in 1951 forged a notable link. He was born and brought up in Lichfield in Bishop Selwyn's time. As a boy he attracted the attention of Bishop Abraham, who was impressed by his intelligence and arranged (and perhaps found the money) to send him to Denstone School, from where he won a Scholarship to Selwyn and matriculated in 1884. He was already deeply interested in English literature, but there being then no English Tripos, he read classics and obtained a II.2. For the next twenty-five years he was a schoolmaster (twenty of them at St Olave's Grammar School), but won a reputation as an authority on Elizabethan and Jacobean literature. In 1913 he was appointed as a university lecturer at Oxford (elected a Fellow of Oriel in 1921), and embarked upon a second career of great distinction. His major work was a multi-volume edition of the works of Ben Jonson, but his books and articles covered a wide field. He was awarded a LittD by Oxford, given an honorary doctorate by Glasgow, and in 1951 – at the age of 85 – an honorary LittD by Cambridge. He dined in Selwyn after receiving the degree but as it had been a long day for a man of his age the time of dinner was advanced to 6.30 p.m. Three and a half hours later the company finally dispersed with Percy Simpson still leading the conversation on a vast range of topics. He published his last book, on Elizabethan drama, in 1955. When he died in 1962 aged 97 he was the last and most unusual survivor of Selwyn's first generation.

5. *Making the new statutes*: The account in the text relies mainly on personal recollections. Surprisingly little documentary evidence has survived apart from the formal record. Although only the Council could make a statute, all the crucial discussions took place in the governing body so that Fellows not then on the Council could have their say.

6. *The new statutes*: Dr Telfer's article on the new statutes was fair but had a slightly apologetic tone. He seemed to be addressing and seeking

to reassure old members who would deplore what had been done. There may have been some who felt that way, but if so they kept their thoughts to themselves. Pleasure that Selwyn had won equality with the older colleges outweighed any doubts about the steps that had been necessary to achieve it.

7. *Some curious initials*: The part of the wall where the new stalls were erected had been covered by a curtain. When it was removed the initials 'V.B.' were discovered on one of the bricks. Knowing that services to the College had been commemorated in this way (*vide* the Hall), a search was made, without success, for a benefactor with these initials. However, one of the craftsmen working on the stalls solved the problem – 'V.B.' denoted 'Ventilating Brick'.

CHAPTER 13

New Perspectives : New Buildings 1956–69

For junior members of the College the adoption of the new statutes made no perceptible difference to their way of life, and for a majority of the senior members it was the expected outcome of trends that had set in around 1934 and accelerated since 1945. Nevertheless, the change was fundamental. All safeguards that the Charter and former statutes had contained for Selwyn's Anglican character were gone: the Council with *ex-officio* membership, the requirement that the Master must be in Holy Orders and the autocratic power bestowed upon him, and the tests for Fellows and Scholars. The College prospectus no longer implied that only members of the Church of England need apply. The unwritten obligation to favour applications from ordinands was under threat.

Though weakened in recent years, commitment to the Church of England had provided the assumptions around which the ethos of the College formed. These assumptions were no longer shared. The way was open for newly elected Fellows to be of any faith or none, and for undergraduates to form a heterogeneous body of all religions and several races. Yet Selwyn would have obligations to all Fellows elected and undergraduates admitted – and to all the same obligations. All that could be asked, but could not be enforced, was a decent respect for the religious traditions of Selwyn.

Reformulation of purpose had to be made at a time when the place of higher education in the nation was under radical scrutiny. In spite of the post-war expansion there were still too few university places, the educational ladder was still too steep and narrow for the children of working-class parents, and in all classes the opportunities for girls were too limited. Of students who did win university places too few were mathematicians, scientists, or engineers.

There were some who held tenaciously to the belief that the function of a university was to train an élite which must by definition be small. There was also a widely held view that though a university education was necessary for some professions, business and industry was better served by people who joined young and learned on the job. Many employers were actually prejudiced against the employment of graduates, who were thought to know too much about the wrong things, too much about theory, and too little about practice. Against this were the widely publicized facts that in other advanced nations a greater proportion of young people went into higher education and that British management was not matching the skill or flexibility of competitors. Opportunities lost and bad labour relations told a sad story, and there was growing support for the view that more and better higher education could be one remedy.

In 1962 the celebrated Robbins report came down firmly against élitism and for the admission to higher education of all who could benefit from it. The government accepted the principal recommendations, made grants mandatory for all qualified students, and undertook to finance the creation of new and the expansion of old universities. At the same time the policies initiated by the Act of 1944 were raising the number of school-leavers qualified under the new policy and demand threatened to overtake the increased capacity. The majority of university teachers welcomed the challenge, but a minority tried to stem the flood by fighting a rearguard action under a banner inscribed with the slogan 'More means worse'.

In the event, more did not mean worse. Nationwide the increase in the number of first classes was slow but not negligible. Of greater significance was the big increase in the number of second classes and the withering away of pass degrees in English universities. Although the amount to be learned in all subjects grew, performance improved, and it was not long before those who had cried 'More means worse' were complaining that there were too many upper seconds.

What more did mean was that as pressure on places increased, it became harder to justify selection on any criteria save academic performance and promise – the first judged by examination results and the second assessed in interviews. Boys from even the most prestigious public schools had to compete on equal terms with the rest. Indeed a candidate from a poor background and a weak school might be preferred if he did as well as someone with all the advantages of upbringing and education. Old members had to be told, regretfully but firmly, that their sons would get no special preference. Promising athletes had got to produce the required number of high grades at A-levels. For Selwyn the most difficult decision was to refuse places to ordinands who could not match the qualifications of other applicants.

With applications running at three to four for each place, selection had to be rigorous; limited accommodation made it impossible to raise the undergraduate total, and many men who would have been welcome were turned away. With a few out-standing exceptions Selwyn did not get the academic high-flyers, but did attract a growing number of strongly motivated men who were capable of getting sound second-class honours. There was also a subtle change in the relationship between the College and its undergraduates. All were delighted to be accepted, but also conscious of having earned success by doing well in examinations and selling themselves at interviews. There might be occasions when the thought might occur to an undergraduate that Selwyn was lucky to have got him.

There was no dramatic change in the social composition of the College. Many of the beneficiaries of the new policies came from the middle-class families with modest incomes from whom Selwyn had formerly drawn the bulk of its undergraduates. How-ever, there was some shift from middle middle to lower middle class: from the sons of clergy and schoolmasters to the sons of shopkeepers and managers of small businesses. A small but significant number of sons of skilled workers climbed the educational ladder provided by the direct grant schools (mainly old grammar schools that received government grants on condition that they offered a stated number of free places). It is probable that this change in social composition, small though it was, brought to Selwyn a larger number of boys who knew little or nothing of the Church of England.

THE OCCUPATIONS OF SELWYN GRADUATES
As recorded in 1969 and 1970

	Matriculated before 1945		Matriculated since 1945		
	No.	Percentage	No.	Percentage	
Clergy	47	32.4	46	12.2	(−20.2)
Schools	18	12.4	64	16.9	(+ 4.5)
Colleges etc.	22	15.2	61	16.1	(+ 0.9)
Lawyers	4	2.8	12	3.2	(+ 0.4)
Doctors	6	4.1	19	5.0	(+ 0.9)
Business	16	11.0	59	15.6	(+ 4.6)
Industry	9	6.2	53	14.0	(+ 7.8)
Applied science	0	–	10	2.6	(+ 2.6)
Public service	11	7.6	32	8.5	(+ 0.9)
Others	12	8.3	22	5.8	(− 2.5)
Total	145		378		

Notes

Colleges etc.: all forms of post-secondary education. After 1945 a higher proportion in degree-giving institutions.

Applied science: all scientists working in industry or government employment.

Public service: civil servants, local govrement officers, employees of Commonwealth and foreign governments (other than teachers).

Others: before 1945 most of these are persons whose occupations cannot be identified; after 1945 they are a mixed bag of musicians, authors, journalists, and others employed in the arts or the media – all rare before the war.

The reasons why men sought a university education were also changing. This change is illustrated by the occupations of old members reported in the *Calendars* for 1969–70 and 1970–1. The sample was small (523) and the result impressionistic, but the trend is clear. The table separates those matriculating before and after 1945, and as the College was smaller in the earlier period percentages tell more than gross numbers.

Too much should not be read into the figures. There was still a higher proportion seeking ordination than in other colleges, the Anglican atmosphere was still unmistakable, and many who went on to other careers had a more than nominal attachment to the Church. However, fewer men came to Selwyn because it was Anglican and none because it was cheap, and a good many came because a place at any Cambridge college opened the door to careers in which they might expect to make a great deal of money. This did not necessarily imply vocational training, because the more far-sighted corporate managers wanted trained minds as well as specialists, and a graduate in classics had as good a chance as any to land a post as a management trainee.[1]

There was a touch of irony in that after all the agonizing over changes in the statutes, the new Master, with the task of redefining Selwyn's character, was exactly the kind of man whom the founders would have chosen. The Revd W.O. Chadwick was an ordained clergyman and a former rugger blue with an outstanding academic record. At 40 he had already established himself as a scholar, and it was confidently predicted that he would come to occupy a high position in the Church. In his person he therefore drew together concepts that hitherto existed in uneasy partnership: the College performing a service to the Church, the College with a duty to teach and form character, and the College as a place of learning.

It was not his way to make policy statements, but his three basic aims were that Selwyn must become an excellent teaching institution, support a body of scholars advancing knowledge in their subjects, and preserve its character as a Christian community. There was no question of priority and the three must be pursued concurrently.[2]

William Owen Chadwick, 1957.

The first two aims were unambiguous but the third was more difficult to define. Less would be heard about the principles of the Church of England, more of the Chapel as the focal point in College life welcoming all its members. For those of other faiths or none the objective could not be to convert but to win respect and foster understanding. There was a way in which civilized people, from whatever background, understood one another and behaved together. At a time when everyone was being told to count the cost of everything, it was essential that education should pass on the value of something; but this could not be done didactically.

The idea of a community was that people learned from each other in many informal ways, and in a college relaxed social relations were of the first importance. There should be more generous entertainment allowances, more occasions on which members of the College enjoyed each other's company, and a deliberate enhancement of Selwyn's reputation as a friendly College. All should enjoy their time at Cambridge but behind the fun was a serious purpose.

For a community to be real it was important that all its members should live close together and be in touch with each other every day. To this end there must be more residential accommodation in the precincts: it was not irrelevant to think about bricks and mortar when the first priority was to think about people.

To be successful a community must also have something to be proud of. There were all kinds of activities which people should be encouraged to do well: a widening choice of sports (with such hitherto unrecognized games as basketball and table tennis winning recognition), music, drama, and participation in University political societies. Around the Chapel clustered a number of worthwhile programmes, from Bible reading to work with delinquent boys. But in an academic environment the only thing that brought lasting satisfaction was academic excellence. One might fill a college with good chaps but bad scholars and life would be enjoyable; but then at the end of the road Selwyn would have to come to terms with being second-rate. This was a fate to be avoided.[3]

Community and the pursuit of excellence were closely linked with the size of Fellowship, but not always in ways that were easily made compatible. The government of the College was going to be easier and more harmonious if the number of Fellows were kept within bounds, but teaching needs might demand expansion.

NEW PERSPECTIVES : NEW BUILDINGS

In addition there was growing pressure upon colleges to elect from among the growing number of University teaching officers who had no Fellowships and resented their exclusion from college life. To consider this question the University set up a committee under the chairmanship of Lord Bridges (formerly head of the Treasury) on which two Selwyn Fellows served: Donald Welbourn as a member and Paul Melville as secretary. The majority favoured a quota system by which colleges would be bound to elect University lecturers in the same way that they were already committed to elect professors. This solution proved to be unacceptable to most colleges, but the issue had been raised and there was pressure to act voluntarily to avoid compulsion.

The Master put the case against expansion of the Fellowship in the *Calendar* for 1961-2:

> For the society to flourish, the Fellows need to know one another, as friends as well as colleagues. A certain atmosphere of the family has been, and we may hope will continue to be, a proper background for the administration of the college, and all the more proper when the foundation of the college is religious.

He thought that an optimum number for a college the size of Selwyn was twenty-three or twenty-four, but he also warned that it might be impossible to resist the pressure for expansion.

Some Fellows agreed in principle with the need to curb expansion but nevertheless thought that thirty would be nearer the mark if teaching needs were to be met. The Fellowship was bound to include two professors and a Bursar. Experience had shown that it was best to give the Chaplain a Fellowship. So with twenty-four Fellows there would only be twenty available for teaching, and if Research Fellows were included – and perhaps at least one distinguished scholar who did little supervision – the number available for a full teaching load would be further reduced. Some popular subjects already felt the need for additional help, and some were not represented at all. In 1961 there was no Fellow in mathematics, geography, physics, or biochemistry. Even though a college could not expect to do everything, these were large gaps.

Supervision could usually be found outside the College, but performance was significantly better when a substantial part of the supervision was done by a Fellow of the College.

One consequence of enquiries by the Bridges committee was to stimulate interest in the foundation of new colleges. The Master became chairman of the development committee of University (later Wolfson) College and of the Trustees of Robinson College. Other new ventures were Darwin College, Clare Hall, and Leckhampton House for Corpus graduate students. These moves alleviated but did not cure the ills identified by the Bridges committee. There was not only dissatisfaction among lecturers in subjects such as engineering and veterinary medicine, where few members of the Faculty held Fellowships; but also among those in subjects that attracted few students, such as archaeology, Chinese, Egyptology, music, oriental studies, and Slavonic languages.

Whatever arguments were advanced behind closed doors, expansion took place. From 1957 to 1970 retiring Fellows in theology, English (two vacancies during the period), classics, and history were replaced. Additional Fellows were elected in chemical engineering, physics, medicine, engineering (second and third Fellows), French, history (second Fellow), mineralogy, linguistics, mathematics, music, economics, oriental languages, Slavonic languages, and law (first and second Fellows). Research Fellows with limited tenure were elected in history, physics, mathematical physics, metallurgy, chemistry, economics, engineering, medicine, French, and mathematics.[4]

Donald Welbourn (a strong advocate of expansion) was active in seeking funds from industry to support research, and the fortunate outcome was the Mullard Research Fellowship in physics or mathematical physics. In the ten years from 1959 to 1969 this endowment enabled Selwyn to give a start in academic life to six outstanding young scientists. All went on to other universities but with gratitude to the College that had given them support at a critical period in their careers. By the 1990s they included two professors, one Fellow of the Royal Society, and others in senior posts in British, Australian, and American universities. Donald

Welbourn also raised some of the money for a third Fellow in engineering.

Endowment for one of the Fellowships in law was found by R.G. Lloyd QC, mainly out of his own pocket, and this is therefore an appropriate point at which to give some account of this distinguished old Selwyn man and generous benefactor. Gerran Lloyd matriculated in 1925 and read natural sciences, but after graduation he read for the bar. His combination of scientific and legal knowledge, together with court-room skill, brought him very high earnings as a patent lawyer. He greatly admired Dr Durrant, his former supervisor, and called him on several occasions as an expert witness. Donald Welbourn and David Harrison also acted for him in a similar capacity. He was active in Liberal politics, being chosen as president of the Welsh Liberal Party (1971–4) and of the United Kingdom Liberal Party (1973–4). In 1973 he was made a life peer, taking Lloyd of Kilgerran as his title, and quickly established a reputation as a 'working peer', especially on committees dealing with scientific and technological questions.

Lord Lloyd was elected as an Honorary Fellow in 1967 and much enjoyed the opportunities that this provided for frequent visits to Selwyn. He seldom missed a guest night and never a Commemoration or College feast. Among his services to Selwyn was the endowment by the Tallow Chandlers Company, of which he was a past Master, of the Imber-Lloyd Prize, awarded annually to the Selwyn undergraduate who had made the greatest all-round contribution to College life. Until shortly before his death in 1991, aged 84, he retained all the energy and intellectual vigour of a much younger man. Among his many memorials is an annual prize, awarded nationally by the Foundation for Science and Technology – of which he was the first president – to the person who had made the most notable 'application of science and technology for the benefit of society'.

By 1970 there were thirty-four Fellows (excluding Fellows in Class E – retired Fellows who had become emeritus) and twenty-eight of them were available for College teaching duties; but this was not the end of the story. From 1945 to 1960 the Fellowship more than doubled in size; from 1960 to 1990 it almost doubled again. Selwyn had become a different College.

Academically it was also a stronger College, but at a price. Meetings of the Governing Body became unwieldy, though usually controlled by skilled chairmanship. The fellowship was less cohesive than in former days. Many took lunch but fewer dined. Some Fellows were seldom seen in College and met their colleagues only to transact formal business. . Expansion was not the only cause. A majority of married Fellows, deterred by the price of houses in Cambridge, moved to villages scattered over the county. They came in to work a 9 to 5 day (though in practice it was often nearer 7 than 5) and then hurried back to join their families. There was an academic pressure to research and publish; reputation and promotion were determined by little else. Except on very special occasions, few could be persuaded to stay on for a society meeting or social event. There were fewer resident bachelors, and the old-style don who dined every night and attended evensong on most was no more seen.

The number of graduate students also grew and by October 1969 there were eighty-three, of whom forty-two were registered for research, twenty-six were on postgraduate courses, and fifteen were affiliated and reading for a Cambridge Tripos. One College hostel was reserved for them but until the last year of the decade the majority of graduate students lived in lodgings, and there was no adequate Middle Combination Room to provide a social focus.

Every new Fellow and every additional graduate student meant more pressure on accommodation, and it was becoming more difficult every year to find lodgings for undergraduates. Four plans for new buildings were given serious consideration, of which one proved to be impractical, one yielded a new SCR and JCR, one failed to get planning permission, and the fourth led to the building of Cripps Court.

The first plan was prepared by James Stirling, who won international acclaim as one of the most prominent and innovative British architects of the century but is known in Cambridge principally for his controversial History Faculty building. The firm of Stirling and Gowan was commissioned in 1961 to draw up a development plan that would include a residential block for immediate construction. They envisaged a new court with one range parallel to Grange Road, another parallel to West Road, and an open east side. From both the old and new courts the eye would be drawn to a new residential block of striking design running north and south at the east end of the garden. The underlying principle of the plan, as explained by Dr Durrant in the *Calendar* for 1969–70, was 'the generation of an architectural bond between the present court and the new north court by giving them a common focus on the glittering glass front of the new building'. To open a vista from the main gate to the new building the railings between the Chapel and F staircase would be removed and replaced by a broad patio on to which would open a new Junior Combination Room built as a separate two-storey pavilion beyond F staircase.

Selwyn owned the freehold of the land between the College and West Road, but most of it was occupied by houses in private occupancy with leases that would not run out until the end of the century. The new north court could be only a distant dream, but work could start on the new residential block in the garden, the Junior Combination Room, and the patio as soon as agreement was reached and the money found.

The new block was to be four storeys high and raised to the level of the old court. The west front was on a zigzag pattern with each room facing south west and catching the afternoon and evening sun through a great expanse of glass. Visually, from the court on a sunny afternoon, 'the glittering glass front' would hold the eye.

The plan divided the Fellows into enthusiasts, a few determined opponents, and several doubters. Among the doubters some deplored the loss of the garden and others wondered whether they would not live to regret so sharp an architectural contrast between old and new. There was also criticism of the proposed patio, which looked so lively in the architect's drawing, with groups of students foregathering in the sunlight, but might be cold and featureless on a winter's day.

However, the most potent objection came from the University syndicate responsible for developing the Sidgwick site as an arts and social science complex. Work had not begun on the economics building, beyond the east wall of the Selwyn garden, but its plan had been approved. Parallel to it and less than 50 yards away would be the back wall and service areas of Selwyn's new building. The chairman of the syndicate expressed dismay in a private letter to the Master, and it seemed certain the University would object if Selwyn asked for planning permission.

An alternative site was difficult to contemplate without abandoning the development plan and altering the architecture of the building. If it extended east from the C to F range it would face south and the zigzag pattern would be pointless. Moreover, a building of startling new design might be attractive standing on its own but as an extension of a nineteenth-century Tudor range would be incongruous. In effect, the architect would have had to start again from scratch, and this he was not prepared to do.

No building could be contemplated without money, and estimates for the Stirling building exceeded by a wide margin the limits set in the brief. An appeal to old members was projected, but its success must be in doubt when opinion was divided and opposition by the University certain. Even if a majority of the Fellows voted to go ahead, was there any real prospect of getting the building built? With the question put in this way, rejection was inevitable. The Fellows of Selwyn are still blamed by some architectural writers for timidity or aesthetic obscurantism, but disgruntled users of the History Faculty building congratulate them on a happy deliverance.

It was a new Bursar who faced the continuing problem of accommodation and plans to relieve it. In 1963 the University gave belated recognition to Indian history and appointed Percy Spear as the first lecturer in the subject. After his years of bursarial toil during the difficult period of recovery and transition, he was glad to devote his whole time to writing and teaching in the field in which he had already achieved distinction. By good fortune a Selwyn graduate and a former Fellow, C.M.P. Johnson, was ready to give up his career as a physicist and accept appointment as

Bursar. For the next six years he tackled with remarkable success the perennial problem of making both ends meet, and handled two ambitious building projects with measured efficiency. The reputation thus gained put him at the head of the list when St John's sought a new senior Bursar, and though he left Selwyn with regret the invitation to manage the property and finances of a large rich college could not be refused. He remained the anchorman of the Selwyn College Association and had the satisfaction in later years of seeing St John's give most generous help to his old College. In 1990 Selwyn made him an Honorary Fellow.

The quest for more residential accommodation continued to exercise the minds of Fellows, but in the meantime thoughts were directed to their own amenities. The Fellowship was growing too large for the Senior Combination Room. It was congested when all were present and the Governing Body had to meet in the uncongenial Tower room. At the same time there were serious doubts about the propriety of spending money saved from the fees of juniors on the comfort of seniors. Endowment by private donors would be preferable and by good fortune Selwyn had among its Fellows a man to take the initiative and among its old members two with goodwill and money.

Lord Lloyd of Kilgerran later explained how it happened:

> Dr Durrant rang me up one day to say he would like to present a new building to the College and would I assist. As I was so indebted for all that Selwyn had done for me, I agreed to contribute up to one third of the cost, a suggestion he leapt at, if in some astonishment.

Dr Durrant himself contributed a third and L.B. Barr, an old Selwyn man who was also the College solicitor, put in a similar sum. It has been said that there was a fourth intended donor who died before the project matured, but neither the written record nor oral tradition has preserved his name. A plaque opposite the main entrance of what is, by general agreement, the best modern Senior Combination Room in Cambridge records the gratitude of the College to the three donors who made it possible.

The plan was to fill the gap between the old SCR and A staircase with a three-storey building, the new SCR occupying the whole of the first floor. Completion of the ground and second storeys would require some extra money from the College, but this was found. The architect chosen was Stirrat Johnson-Marshall and his proposal won immediate approval.

The new room had to be furnished, and Owen Chadwick later described 'the most comic meeting of the Fellowship we ever had'. John and Beryl Durrant obtained four very large Persian carpets for inspection. 'The Fellows took off their coats and manhandled carpets all evening, surveying them from various angles.' Dr Durrant finally 'persuaded them that one was necessary for the beauty of the room and though by far the most expensive, history would see it as an economical buy. Which some people thought of as a plausible argument but history proved it to be true.' There was less harmony over other furnishings, and some old hands recall a fierce dispute over the hanging lights and regret, though now with good humour, the outcome.

It was decided to use the space above the new room for a Fellow's set and a senior guest room of ample proportions. On the ground floor the first intention was to house the College offices but this proved to be impractical and instead the space was put to better use as a new and much needed Junior Combination Room. To complete this work £25,000 was borrowed. The new Junior Combination Room was of the same fine proportions as the Senior Combination Room overhead but unfortunately later generations have seen fit to furnish it like an amusement arcade.

The undergraduates quickly realized that there was now room for a College bar, and asked the Governing Body to follow the example of other colleges and allow one to open. After much anxious deliberation permission was given. In its first location and later, in what used to be part of the kitchens, the bar has been a notable social success. It gets crowded and noisy, but there is general agreement that it is better for students to be gregarious in their own bar than roaming the city pubs. Though intended primarily for students it is a College bar, used frequently by College servants and not infrequently by Fellows. A long-term benefit, not appreciated at the time, was that a well-appointed bar is an asset when seeking to attract conferences and thus helps to boost College finances.

The problem of residential accommodation remained and became more acute each year. After rejection of the Stirling plan attention shifted to the corner of Grange Road and Cranmer Road where three houses had been purchased by Selwyn and used as hostels. The freehold was owned by Jesus College, but purchase by Selwyn, at a very reasonable rate, was agreed with the proviso that building for College use must begin within five years.

An appeal directed principally to members of the Selwyn Association was launched to raise money for the project. Johnson-Marshall was commissioned to prepare a development plan and his principal proposal was a nine-storey tower block set in the middle of the site. Had it ever been built one can imagine the demand for upper rooms among football enthusiasts – they would have commanded a fine view of the University ground – but there was local opposition to so high a building in a residential district, and the objectors persuaded the city planning committee to refuse permission. Johnson-Marshall then began work on a more conventional building with about thirty undergraduate sets.

At this stage a powerful new actor appeared on the stage in the person of Humphrey Cripps, who was chairman of the Cripps Foundation endowed by his father. The elder Mr Cripps, like other twentieth-century benefactors of higher education, was a self-made man with no schooling beyond the age of 12. He had made a fortune in metal manufacturing, and used a substantial part of it to set up an educational foundation that had already built halls of residence at Nottingham and the new court of St John's College (where Humphrey Cripps had been an undergraduate).

In 1964 the Master wrote to Humphrey Cripps (who had been his contemporary at St John's) outlining Selwyn's needs and plans. He said that the appeal was going well but most Selwyn graduates were men of limited means. Many contributions were also given as seven-year covenants, and even if the total exceeded expectation there would not be enough cash in hand to meet the stipulation that building must start within five years.

To find out more about the College he was being asked to help, Humphrey Cripps acquired a copy of the first history of Selwyn College, by A.L. Brown, and (as he said in a speech in 1969) found it 'both fascinating and spiritually uplifting'. He praised 'the selfless dedication of many men of this University who worked for a mere pittance, but none the less gave all their energies and indeed their lives and possessions, so that poor students could come to Cambridge', and added that it was:

> the record of those men who built up this college, who really shamed me into exploring the ways and means by which we could help and show that this generation too, could exhibit its responsibilities and have faith in the future of higher education, in this College, this University and this country.

This link between past ideals and later generosity deserves to be remembered by those who know Selwyn only in more prosperous days when early memories are less tenaciously held.[5]

The initial commitment by the Cripps Foundation was to pay for one residential block, leaving the College and the appeal to handle whatever else was necessary. A planning committee was set up with Humphrey Cripps as a member. The pressure of other work persuaded Johnson-Marshall to resign his commission and Gordon Woollatt took his place. Draft plans were prepared, and presented for approval. With memory of controversy over the Stirling plan still fresh, opposition in the Governing Body was anticipated, but with unusual rapidity for an academic body it was agreed to go ahead. This, said Humphrey Cripps, 'encouraged the Cripps Foundation to offer more' and at a meeting of the committee, long remembered by those who were present, he observed that though the response from old members had been gratifying the total was going to fall far short of what was required. The Foundation therefore proposed to pay for all residential accommodation. It took members of the committee some moments to realize that this statement, made without earlier intimation or detailed elaboration, promised Selwyn over half a million pounds.[6]

The new building was designed to house 130 undergraduates, thirty-two graduates, and eleven Fellows, together with two guest rooms and a graduate common room. The detached 'Diamond', paid for by the appeal, was designed for multi-purpose use as a meeting or party room, cinema, and cafeteria serving breakfast, light meals, and refreshments when required.

The architecture attracted criticism but will stand the test of time. It is also fair to the architect to recall that its least satisfactory feature – the cluttered roof line – was not what he first intended. His original plan included a pitched roof with large dormer windows, but this, like the tower block, was refused planning permission. Private enquiry elicited the information that refusal had been prompted by advice from the Royal Fine Arts Commission and that the principal objection was to the pitched roof. Gordon Woollatt then redesigned the building with a flat roof, some minor adjustments to introduce greater variety into the external aspect, but otherwise unchanged. In this form planning permission was given, The consequences of the earlier rejection were unfortunate. The pitched roof would have been in keeping with the older College buildings and with the neighbouring houses. The large dormer windows would have been aesthetically more pleasing than the oblong boxes containing the fourth-floor rooms in the approved version. The unsuitability of flat roofs for a northern climate were not then understood and in common with many other owners of flat-roofed buildings, Selwyn had later to spend a great deal of money to put right the damage caused by leaking seams.

The interior of the building was meticulously planned. The committee had a mock-up of an undergraduate room constructed in the old bicycle shed (near the later Library extension) and much thought went into choosing the dimensions, lighting, plumbing, and cupboards, and the location of furniture. The architect was co-operative throughout and altered the detail in room and staircase plans until the best solutions were found. The rooms were ready for occupation in October 1968 but it was not until the following May that the building, appropriately named Cripps Court, was formally opened.

The contribution of Cripps Court to College life has been incalculable. Together with the hostels on Grange Road and West

Cripps Court.

Road it made possible the accommodation of all undergraduates and nearly all graduate students in the precincts. There would be no more desperate searches for lodgings, and no more frantic bicycling from distant parts of the city. Of greater importance was the strength given to the idea of the College as a community.

One happy result was an improvement in graduate accommodation. For some time it had been the aim to bring advanced students into College, but with facilities separate from those of undergraduates. In the Cripps building they were allocated two staircases and their own combination room. Some continued to live at 29 Grange Road, but the Cripps building provided a focal point for their social activities and emphasized their position as a community within a community.

Two additional items are worth noting. The first records a vagary of planning and the second questions the doctrine of 'demolish and start again' that dominated urban development in that decade. Planning permission was given on the strict condition that an ancient and very large walnut tree was preserved, but when the city planning department later decided that the whole building must be set further back from Grange Road the tree was sentenced to instant execution without a thought of preservation. The second note concerns the fate of Saxon Barns (43 Grange Road), demolished to make way for the new court. It was a dignified house, with some architectural distinction, built around the turn of the century for Joshua Taylor who owned the well-known Cambridge store. Had the plan been projected in 1990, when architecture of this period stood in higher regard, someone among the dons or planners would surely have insisted on the preservation of the house and its incorporation into the new scheme. This would have meant an entirely different kind of development but posterity has no means of judging what might have been.

An old member of Selwyn, revisiting the College in 1970 after long absence, would have been astonished by the changes that had occurred. He would see the shining new Cripps Court, the fine new Senior Combination Room, the new Junior Combination Room, and the much used bar. He would learn there that all undergraduates lived within a hundred yards of the Hall and Chapel. Enquiry would reveal that the Fellowship had grown almost threefold in twenty years, and that the handful of graduate students had grown to over eighty.[7]

If the visitor had a keen eye for painting he would have been delighted to observe that St John's College had given Richmond's portrait of Bishop Selwyn to replace the copy that had hung in the Hall. If he had walked as far as the playing field on Barton Road he would also have seen an improvement not yet recorded in these notes – a fine new sports pavilion, paid for mainly by King's, but shared by Selwyn.

However, when old members attended Commemoration or Association meetings little attention was given to these changes and improvements. What invariably attracted comment, much of it unfavourable, was that the former sunken court was now a level lawn. In 1961 it was learned that the contractor for the new Caius building on West Road would have a large amount of soil to sell and transport very cheaply. Architects and landscape designers quickly consulted were unanimous that the buildings would appear to much greater advantage if the court were levelled up. Generations had accepted the sunken court as part of the unalterable scheme of things, but it had made the Chapel look top-heavy, affected adversely the proportions of the other buildings, and by optical illusion foreshortened the vista from the main gate.

The ground slopes to the east (the garden is about four feet lower than the main gate). Some soil must therefore have been moved in the College's early days, raising the east side and leaving an embankment in front of A and B staircases. It is thought that Sir Arthur Blomfield hoped to level the court when the Chapel was built, but the temporary Hall and Library still occupied the court. When they were finally removed there was no money to spare. The court remained sunken, with steps leading down to four gravelled paths meeting at right angles in the centre, and came to be regarded as a distinctive feature of the College rather than as evidence of poverty.

The deed of levelling was done – not quite as quickly as had been hoped, because the largest carriers could not get into the court, but before anyone could raise objections, organize petitions, or demand reconsideration. It did everything that its advocates had predicted and gave Selwyn the most attractive modern court in Cambridge; but old members with long memories found it difficult to forgive the Fellows for what they regarded as an act of desecration. In its way the levelled court was a symbol of more profound departures from tradition as Selwyn moved towards its ninetieth birthday.

Notes and Comments

1. *Two notable ordinands*: R.D. Harries graduated in 1961. He is now (1994) Bishop of Oxford. P.A. Crowe followed in 1962 and is Principal of Salisbury Training College. Both are widely known for their frequent contributions to 'Thought for the Day' on Radio 4.

2. *Aims and community*: This paragraph is based on a letter written in 1964 by Professor Chadwick to the author (copy in Selwyn Archives). He went on to state emphatically the need for additional residential

accommodation in the College precincts. The reflections on the meaning of a Christian community that follow are the author's own, but were read in manuscript by Professor Chadwick.

3. *Selwyn men and University politics*: Selwyn men were more active in the University than heretofore. In 1961 J.S. Gummer (the later cabinet minister) was chairman of the University Conservative Association, P.H.M. Cooper (author of Part I of this history) was president of the Liberal Club, and N.A. Egerton (now a merchant banker) was runner up for chair of the Labour Club. John Gummer was president of the Union in 1962

4. *The Fellows*: The first Fellow in law was P.B. Fairest, since 1974 Professor of Law at Hull. The new Fellow in Engineering was R.B. Jackson (in 1994 the second most senior Fellow still active in teaching). One of his special interests has been in the development of mechanical aids for disabled people.

5. *Sir Humphrey Cripps and the Cripps Building*: He gave this explanation of how his interest was aroused in his speech at the opening of the court named after him. Since then he has continued to display an active interest in the affairs of the College and in 1971 he was elected as an Honorary Fellow. Among other benefactions he endowed the annual College feast now known as the Cripps Feast. There is a portrait of him in the new Senior Combination Room wearing his official uniform as Deputy Lord Lieutenant of the County of Northampton.

6. *Planning Cripps Court*: The description of this meeting draws upon the recollections of Dr Johnson and Mr Welbourn.

7. *Two Honorary Fellows in 1965*: In this year Selwyn honoured G.D.H. Bell (see p.213) and Robert Kweku-Alta Gardiner. Robert Gardiner is a Ghanaian who graduated at Selwyn in 1941. After the war he had a distinguished career as an official of the United Nations, being for over fifteen years a member of the UN Economic Commission for Africa (and its executive secretary 1963–75). He attracted worldwide attention in 1961 when he was the UN Special Envoy to the Congo (Zaire) at a time of unhappy and violent internal conflict. In 1965 he was the Reith Lecturer for the BBC. He holds honorary doctorates at Bristol, Aderdan, Makere and Strathclyde Universities.

CHAPTER 14

The Ninth Decade 1970–80

IN THE Michaelmas term 1969 old and present members welcomed the installation of the Master of Selwyn as Vice-Chancellor. Apart from recognizing Professor Chadwick's personal standing in Cambridge, this was a decisive moment in Selwyn history. Only twelve years after formal recognition as a college its Master took his place as head of the academic community, and Selwyn would act as host on many official occasions, honouring visitors of international distinction.

The Master's duties as Vice-Chancellor inevitably took up much time that would otherwise have been devoted to College business, but he left matters in safe hands. As Vice-Master Wilfred Sartain had an unrivalled knowledge of University business and a long record of service on College committees. David Harrison, appointed as Senior Tutor in October 1967, was an elected member of the Council of the Senate and secretary of the tutorial Representatives, and was winning a reputation that would lead to his appointment as Vice-Chancellor of Keele and then of Exeter, before returning to Selwyn as Master in 1994.

In the previous chapter the sensations of an old member re-visiting Selwyn after many years were imagined. Then he would have been most impressed by changes in the material environment, but returning again after ten years the way that students lived would make the greatest impact. About a third of them would be women, and both sexes would normally be dressed in a way that hardly merited the adjective 'informal' – the old member might think 'sloppy' more appropriate. Gowns would be less frequently worn, and it would even be rumoured that some Tutors told their pupils not to bother to wear them when they came on official business and also that they preferred to be addressed by their Christian names. He would have been disturbed to learn that the framework of rules that once regulated collegiate life had broken down, with the gates open until 2 a.m., keys available at the Porters' Lodge for anyone who wished to come in later, and no one asking or seeming to mind where or with whom the night had been spent. He would be heartened though puzzled to learn that despite the apparent lack of discipline there had been a marked improvement in academic performance. If the visitor talked to students he would also sense that the social spectrum from which they were drawn had widened since his day. Finally, he would be surprised to learn that student representatives attended Governing Body meetings and that consultation had become the rule.

If the visitor reflected upon what he had seen he would realize that the outward signs of changing times, in life-style, dress, and behaviour, were symbols of more profound alterations in the way that students regarded the College and the College viewed its responsibility to them. Paternalism was out, participation was in. The College as a family was a fading vision, to be replaced by the College as a community in which seniors and juniors worked towards common ends.

In this as in other decades national currents had carried Selwyn further away from the institution that the founders had envisaged. The past was respected but could not rule. The challenge was not to stand firm but to decide when, in what manner, and how fast to move. Unanimity could not be expected, but it is a tribute to all concerned, and particularly to those who influenced events, that the Selwyn Fellowship ended the ninth decade without falling apart in factions or dividing sharply between conservatives and reformers.

Nationally and internationally the late 1960s and early 1970s saw much student discontent and protest. Cambridge was less affected than some universities and Selwyn hardly affected at all, but it was impossible to ignore demands for a different relationship between educators and educated. The lowering of the voting age to 18 made it difficult to argue that men and women judged fit for national responsibility, and selected because of their high intellectual capacity, should be denied the right to be heard before decisions affecting them were made.

The first move toward student participation in College government at Selwyn was the launch of a consultative committee with joint senior and junior membership in May 1969. It met regularly, reported to the Governing Body, and its student members had the right to attend when its recommendations were discussed and to speak though not to vote.

This was a half-way house and at an open Junior Combination Room meeting on 21 January 1971 the students resolved that their representatives should attend all Governing Body meetings, though recognizing that some questions should be reserved for separate action by the Fellows. With surprising alacrity (probably explained by support from the Master and the Senior Tutor) the Governing Body agreed on 9 February that the President and Secretary of the Junior Combination Room and the President of the Middle Combination Room should attend all meetings as observers except when reserved items were considered. What should be reserved was not defined but would certainly include the election of Fellows and Scholars, the appointment and duties of College officers, and disciplinary questions. The student representatives still lacked the right to vote and it would probably have been illegal to give them this privilege without changing the statutes, but they could ask for their views to be minuted and the Fellows were unlikely to proceed without further consultation if all three were opposed. It was also becoming common practice to add student members to committees considering domestic issues. This kind of influence can be more effective than a formal right to vote, but in the nature of things it looked like half a cake, and pressure for full voting rights continued until met in the 1980s when the revised statutes made three student representatives *ex-officio* members of the Governing Body and of the newly created Council.

As students acquired new responsibilities the old status of the Fellows *in loco parentis* was called in question. For better or worse, rules designed to preserve the notion of a family, discourage extravagance, and shield immature youths from temptation became obsolete and were soon forgotten. Dining ceased to be compulsory, the College gates were no longer closed at 10 p.m., and guests – even of the opposite sex – were no longer required to leave by midnight. As for extravagance, it was now the students who asked for better cooking facilities on the staircases so that they could prepare their own meals and save money.

Greater student influence coincided with growing national concern over discrimination against women, and in the Easter term of 1969 a Selwyn JCR open meeting voted to ascertain the views of junior members and examine the consequences of co-residence. A paper and questionnaire were prepared and circulated to all junior members. Of the 159 who replied, 93 per cent said that there should be more places for women at Cambridge, 85 per cent were in favour of some men's colleges becoming co-residential, and 79 per cent thought that Selwyn should be one of them. There were 84 per cent who said that had there been a mixed college they would have made it their first preference. These figures illustrate the enormous shift in opinion that had occurred since 1921, when an unofficial poll of undergraduates recorded 2,339 to 884 against making women members of the University.[1]

Student opinion was almost equally divided between those who thought that men and women should live on separate staircases and those who favoured random distribution; a small minority thought that men and women should be housed in separate courts, and a large majority thought that, however accommodated, there should be no restriction on internal visiting – though there was some support for a 'privacy rule' after 10.30 or 11.30 p.m. On the number of women to be admitted, 29 per cent favoured a fixed ratio of women to men, but 71 per cent thought that admission should be on merit without regard to sex.

The JCR meeting then instructed its members on the consultative committee 'to urge the Governing Body to introduce co-residence as soon as possible'. A paper was prepared for presentation to the Governing Body giving reasons for the recommendation and anticipating all the arguments over which their seniors would agonize for the next five years. It was also, in the strict sense of the word, disinterested. Even if the Governing Body acted with all possible speed the youngest of the signatories would have gone down before the first woman undergraduate crossed the Selwyn threshold.

The JCR paper declared that 'the task of a university is education and not specifically training for a career, and thus everybody suitably qualified should have an equal opportunity of university education'. Teaching was already co-educational, but teaching was only a part of education, and co-residence 'should relieve much of the tension in Cambridge, resulting in a more natural environment, intellectually, culturally and socially'. At a majority of universities women were admitted as a matter of course: many students chose them because there was no discrimination between sexes, mixed halls of residence had been successful, and 'no disciplinary problems had proved to be insoluble'. The paper concluded that 'if the university wishes to retain its reputation in a world of changing educational patterns, it too must change ... It must examine the subject of co-residence in depth, and as soon as possible.'

Now that the question has long been settled it may be difficult to understand the tenacity with which many Cambridge men resisted the idea of sexual equality in the University and succeeded in making Cambridge the last British university to give women equal status with men. In the year that Selwyn was founded women were for the first time allowed to take honours examinations and to have their classes published (though listed separately from the men), but they received no degree. In 1921 a move to make women full members of the University was heavily defeated, but they were grudgingly allowed the 'title' to the degree (saying, in effect, that they would have been awarded a degree if they had been men). The Royal Commission of 1926 recommended full status for women (this was ignored) but stated specifically that no all-male college should admit them.

Not until 1948 were women allowed to take degrees (back-dated to the year in which they acquired the 'title'), even though they had for sixty years attended the same lectures and taken the same examinations as the men. Without the BA a woman could not become an MA and a member of the Senate, and thus join the governing body of the University. As the powers of the Senate had been whittled away, the important thing for a woman resident was that because she held no degree she could not be a member of the Regent House, the General Board, or the Council of the Senate. Women who were University lecturers were given the title of MA – and appeared as MA in official lists – but not being members of the Regent House had no public voice in University affairs.

Official discrimination was reflected in the colleges by social discrimination. It was out of the question to invite a woman to formal dinner either at High Table or in Hall. It went without saying that no woman, whatever her age or distinction, could sleep for a night in college. In a small concession to changing times after the Second World War, several colleges introduced an annual ladies' night, when Fellows could invite their wives or fiancées to dine in Hall. Selwyn had its first ladies' night in 1953, but that was the limit and in some colleges (though not in Selwyn) older bachelor Fellows thought that a dangerous precedent had been set and were conspicuously absent on these occasions.[2]

The argument over the status of women was bound up with the question of how many of them ought to be in the University. In 1926 they had been restricted to 500; by 1968 this had been raised to 900 (but with the increase in student population the sex ratio was no better). This was too low, as even those opposing the admission of women to hitherto all-male colleges admitted; but what was the remedy? It was unthinkable that any men's college would change sex and become exclusively female. It might be right to have new colleges for women, but where was the money coming from to endow eight or nine? The logical conclusion was that if more places for women were to be found they must be in the existing colleges.

There was no University policy, and collegiate autonomy meant that the debate was always focused on what one college should do, and from 1969 to 1985 there was never a year when, in one college or another, the same debate did not go on with much the same arguments deployed on either side. Opponents of the move to admit women might have drawn upon evidence that some

young people are happier and perform better in single-sex institutions, but this would have meant admitting evidence that for
other students the reverse was true. Theoretically both needs
could be met if some colleges became co-residential and others
stayed as they were; but who was to decide? In every college
some Fellows (ultimately a majority) wanted to get the women
in, and others wanted to keep them out; neither relished the idea
of giving way to serve some supposed common good.

The arguments against women were normally based on traditional
usage, the intentions of past benefactors, the lack of evidence that
any change would be for the better, and practical difficulties such
as the provision of separate toilet facilities. Underlying these often
specious arguments was a serious concern over the moral consequences of co-residence. Supporters argued that in the real
world outside males and females lived and worked side by side
in the same community; but in which communities, the opponents might ask, did upright parents allow cohabitation under
their own roofs?

Supporters stressed the need for more places for women, the
more 'natural' environment that would follow, the experience of
other universities, and – increasingly as time went on – evidence
that good candidates were making mixed colleges their first preference. On the moral question few were prepared to give outright
endorsement to free-wheeling permissiveness, but could argue
that all the restraints imposed in the past had not prevented
promiscuity outside the College or checked homosexuality inside it. The most persuasive argument on these lines was that
young people must learn to choose for themselves and that
they could learn to make moral decisions better in a mixed than
in a segregated society.

Having received the JCR paper, the Governing Body agreed
by a majority in April 1970 to set up a committee under the
chairmanship of Mr Welbourn, with two Fellows (the Revd R.M.
Hardy and Dr E. Royle) and three undergraduates as members.
Almost a year later they presented a report that recommended,
strongly and unanimously, the admission of women in the Michaelmas
term 1974 or as soon after that as possible.

The committee's recommendation was backed by thorough investigations of the principle involved, opinion in the College, and possible administrative difficulties. A poll of undergraduates secured a large response (223 out of 329 in residence) and 91 per cent said that they would still have applied to Selwyn had it been co-residential, 81 per cent thought that it would be in Selwyn's interest to admit women, and 78 per cent were personally in favour of doing so. Taking into account the necessarily speculative evidence about the number of qualified women likely to apply, the committee suggested an initial (but variable) target intake of twenty-seven women and eighty-three men. They favoured, at least to begin with, separate staircases for the two sexes.

In June 1971 the Governing Body agreed, again by a majority, to hold a special meeting in October to consider revising the statutes to admit women, and the prospect seemed bright. Even if the proposal failed to obtain the two-thirds vote required to amend a statute, a majority in favour would ensure that the question remained alive. However, the reformers suffered a severe set-back. The motion to amend the statutes, moved by Mr Welbourn, failed to win support from a majority, let alone two-thirds. It was then agreed to adjourn the discussion *sine die*, with the implication that the majority wished to hear no more for the time being. It would seem that some Fellows who had been with the majority in the earlier votes, and favoured the equality of sexes as an abstract proposition, were swayed by the argument that the consequences of admitting women were too uncertain, by warnings that the necessary modification of toilet facilities would be costly, and perhaps by moral doubts. There was also a suggestion that federation with Newnham should first be explored, though there is no evidence that this idea was ever seriously considered and a strong possibility that it would have been rejected out-of-hand by Newnham.

A small door was left open by setting up a standing committee to watch developments in other colleges and report from time to time. Dr Harrison, as chairman of this committee, was personally in favour of admitting women, but judged it inopportune to press for early reconsideration of the question. For the next two years his committee collected a great deal of evidence, and finally presented a long and detailed report that included data both on the general situation of women in Cambridge and on experience in three colleges that had already admitted them. King's had a reputation for radicalism, Churchill was new and in conservative eyes too much swayed by fashion, but Clare was old and 'sound', and its Master was the highly respected Sir Eric Ashby (later Lord Ashby). In the light of all the evidence, the committee concluded with a recommendation that 'it would be in the long-term interests of the College to become co-residential'.

At the conclusion of a long and tense Governing Body meeting on 4 December 1973, seventeen out of twenty-five Fellows present voted to accept the recommendation. This was not decisive as a majority of two-thirds (twenty-one) of the whole body of the Master and Fellows (thirty-two) was necessary to change the statute. An abstention would be as damaging as a vote against. The crucial meeting was held on 14 May 1974 with the Master and twenty-nine Fellows present (two being on leave). After a long discussion, with strong emotions voiced on both sides of the question, the motion to revise the statutes was approved by twenty-two, with four voting against and three abstaining.

Dr Harrison counted twenty-three in favour rather than twenty-two and his arithmetic seems to have been correct, but as the recorded vote was sufficient he did not ask for the Minute to be changed. The Master, in the chair, was one of the non-voters and had not declared his opinion. Had the vote in favour been one short of the required two-thirds it is thought that he would have voted in favour. A situation in which a minority that included non-voters thwarted the long-matured wish of a decided majority would have been unfortunate, particularly as it would have ranged youth against age with all but one of the Fellows under 40 in favour. The final and formal motion to amend the statutes was passed with twenty-one in favour, one against, and five (including the Master in the chair) not voting.

The first women matriculated in October 1976: thirty-two as undergraduates, two as affiliated students, two for the postgraduate Certificate of Education, and one for the LLB. The *Calendar* for

1977–8 recorded that their arrival 'took place with a smoothness which surprised us all'. The women were accommodated on the upper floors of D and the whole of H staircases (this partial segregation was later abandoned). None of the fearsome problems that had been predicted materialized. Old rowing men were reconciled when they learned that the girls had got a boat on the river – but what, they might ask, was the feminine of 'oarsman'?

The academic consequences of admitting women are hard to evaluate. In 1979 women obtained five firsts out of a total of thirty-two; this was a lower proportion than their numbers warranted but if upper second classes were included the ratio was exactly what it should have been. It had been confidently stated that many good male applicants would not choose a single-sex college; there is no way of verifying this prediction, but firsts and upper seconds in 1978 and 1979 were more numerous than in any earlier year.

It had been expected the women would have a tonic effect on the Chapel choir and the Music Society, but wholly unexpected were the additions that they made to Selwyn's tally of blues and half-blues. In 1977–8 twelve men and six women achieved this distinction; in the following year there were again twelve men and no fewer than eleven women. The women included Fiona Morrison, who had never rowed before coming to Selwyn but won a blue in two successive years and was then elected president of the Cambridge University Women's Boat Club. There were three other rowing blues for women, two for lacrosse, and two for athletics. In 1979–80 the captains of the ladies' swimming team and the ladies' athletics team were also from Selwyn.

A number of other colleges admitted women at the same time and Selwyn was therefore in the second wave. Some colleges held out for over ten years more, but by 1990 every former all-male college admitted women, one former women's college admitted men, and only Newnham and New Hall remained exclusively for women. Lucy Cavendish, a new all-female college, catered for mature students and graduates.

On reflection, and given that sooner or later women were going to be admitted, one cannot but regret the rejection of the first attempt to do so. In 1971 the new departure would have attracted much publicity (and, as everyone knows, even unfavourable publicity is better than no publicity at all), and for two or three years the College would have had a flood of very good women applicants. This would have eased when other colleges opened their doors, but the reputation won might have endured.

The College had grown in stature during the 1960s but its academic performance had still caused concern. Although the decade had started well, with twenty firsts (including four in prelims) in 1960, the subsequent years were disappointing. The following figures give the number of firsts in all University examinations (including preliminaries and first-year triposes):

1961: 13	1962: 11	1963: 11
1964: 10	1965: 14	1966: 14
1967: 14	1968: 12	

Then in 1969 there was an upward leap to 20 and this proved to be the beginning of a trend, not a freak year:

1970: 20	1971: 21	1972: 24
1973: 30	1974: 24	1975: 22
1976: 16	1977: 25	1978: 32
1979: 32		

It will be observed that even the weakest of these years (1976) improved upon the best of the preceding decade. From 1961 to 1968 under 4 per cent of the students in residence were in Class I but just under 9 per cent from 1970 to 1979, and in the two latest years the figure was over 10 per cent. There was also a marked rise in the number of upper seconds.

Performance was improving in most colleges for several reasons. The popularity of Cambridge meant that they could be highly selective. Applications were encouraged from a wider social spectrum than before, and new talent was discovered. More maintained schools mastered the difficulty of shifting from selective to comprehensive entry. The admission of women to hitherto all-male colleges also brought more top-class girls to Cambridge.

Several other colleges had always had a higher proportion of firsts than Selwyn, but in the 1970s Selwyn had the fastest rate of increase. The two principal reasons for this improved perform-ance were a vigorous campaign to attract good applicants from schools that had seldom thought of sending pupils to Cambridge and a decision to give conditional pre-A-level offers of admis-sion. The two policies worked together because schools that had hitherto thought that even their brightest pupils stood little chance at Cambridge were persuaded that they had nothing to lose by sending them for an early interview, and that if they subsequently failed to obtain the necessary A-level grades they could still get a university place elsewhere. The pre-A-level conditional offer has since become standard practice, but Selwyn was a pioneer.

In the 1960s a high proportion of accepted candidates had come from about twenty schools (mainly independent) with an-other ten appearing quite frequently. There was nothing improper in a close relationship between a college and a school, but it was suspected that several of the schools that sent boys regularly to Selwyn treated the College as a good bet for their less promising pupils. In the 1970s Selwyn did not turn its back on schools from which it had taken so many in the past, but sent them a tactful but clear signal that the competition was going to be tougher while passing on to less prestigious schools the message that their people had as good a chance of acceptance as anyone else. Examination results were evidence that this policy paid dividends. In 1978 and 1979, with thirty-two firsts in each year, twenty-two and twenty-five were from state maintained grammar schools, comprehensives, sixth-form colleges, and (in one case) a college of further education, and the majority had come to Selwyn as a result of pre-A-level conditional offers.

There was, however, no ground for complacency. In the light of the high A-level results required for admission, there were still too many who failed to get the upper second that had been predicted and too many in the third class. Although the academic strength of the College had improved out of all recognition since the 1930s, it was still normally near the bottom of the annual 'league table' compiled from final-year results. By 1980 the Fellows were congratulating themselves on what had been achieved, but in the next decade they would look more critically at future prospects.

The sporting record of the College prompts further reflection. Old members sometimes lament that the pursuit of academic excellence means ruination to College sport, but it did very well in this decade of improving academic performance. In 1979–80 Selwyn enjoyed the unusual distinction of providing the presidents for both the men's and the ladies' University Boat Clubs. There would probably have been two more male rowing blues, had illness not prevented them from rowing against Oxford. One of them – Hugh Laurie, heir to a name famous in rowing circles – was stricken with food poisoning on the day of the race, but had better luck and a blue in the following year (which was an unusual apprenticeship for a man who went on to win a national reputation as a comic actor). In addition to blues awarded, Selwyn's boats and teams did well. In 1976 and 1977 Selwyn won the athletics cuppers and in 1979 narrowly missed repeating this success. In 1979 the first men's boat rose from sixth to fourth (the highest position since 1931) in the Mays, the third and fourth boats won their oars, and – not to be outdone – the ladies' first boat maintained an already proud tradition of never conceding a bump and went up two places. In the same year the 1st XV had a successful season. In the decade Selwyn also provided captains for the Sailing Club (Mark Strucket), the Ladies' Sailing Club (Elizabeth Jory) and for two sports that had never previously appeared in Selwyn annals: clay pigeon shooting (Francis Nation-Dixon) and angling (Trevor Perrior, who was also second in the national universities' competition).

The Fellowship continued to grow. From 1970 to 1979 forty-four Fellows were elected, of whom sixteen were Research Fellows on limited tenure or others who left after a short stay, one was a professorial Fellow, one a Bursar, two were Chaplains, and fourteen replaced long-serving Fellows who had retired or moved away. There was a net addition of six to the permanent staff.[3]

In 1970 Selwyn received an unexpected gift of £60,000 from the Henry and Anna Keasbey Memorial Foundation to endow a Research Fellowship in American studies. At the time this was the only research post in the country specifically assigned to this field. It is not known why the Keasbey Foundation chose Selwyn for this honour, but over the years it has brought to the College a succession of promising young scholars, both British and American, of whom several have gone on to hold key posts in American studies in British universities.

It was becoming common for Cambridge colleges to look to officers recently retired from the services when they sought a new Bursar, and in 1970 Selwyn appointed Commander David Burge, RN. Although a sailor, he had had considerable experience of business and financial management, having been in banking before joining the navy, and in the service he was a paymaster responsible for supply to ship and shore establishments. His last post before retirement from the navy had been as Headquarters Commandant for NATO in Malta.

Selwyn was still the poorest college, save for the recently founded New Hall, but the gap was narrowing between it and some of the older colleges. Magdalene and Downing were in the same range, and five others not far above it. The improvement was due to good housekeeping, sound investment, and an increasing number of conferences housed during the vacations. In 1975–6 the gross income was £303,345. Endowments amounted to £296,117 but most of this sum was in named funds and not available for general College purposes. The free income from endowments had risen to £3,200 by 1975, but this was a tiny sum when compared with the old and richer colleges. The lack of capital reserves had compelled Selwyn in earlier years to borrow in order to provide student accommodation, and the interest plus capital repayment amounted to £8,000 a year.

Selwyn benefited from the Colleges Fund, to which the richer colleges contributed and from which the poorer colleges received grants. The amount paid in or drawn out was determined by what was called the assessable income (what remained after deduction of all standing charges). Selwyn's assessable income rose from £11,853 in 1969–70 to £33,040 in 1973–4, but this was partly the result of exceptional inflation during these years and the money allocated from the Colleges Fund rose to £30,000 in 1976 and £40,000 in 1977.

In a formal letter to the Registry in 1975 the Master described the principal restraints that tight finance imposed on the College. He wrote that although most colleges needed Fellows for teaching and administration who did not hold University posts, it was very expensive to support them. Selwyn already had six in this category, could not afford more, and was thus unable to cover some subjects adequately. The College had occasionally been able to elect Research Fellows, and would like more. The library could not keep abreast of student needs because it was short of money. Selwyn had strained its slender resources to provide teaching and promote research, but there was still far to go.

Even if education and learning were adequately covered, much would still be required to bring the amenities of the College up to an acceptable standard. The kitchens were old and in many ways unsuited to meet the demands placed upon them. The Junior Combination Room was comparatively new, but should be larger now that almost all students lived in College or close by. There was an urgent need for an additional lecture room with more space and better furnishings than the Tower room.[4]

As the centenary year approached it was to be expected that thoughts would turn to an appeal for financial help addressed to old members, business, industry, charitable foundations, and others who might be prepared to help. Discussion began in 1977, and probed some fundamental problems. Fund raising to celebrate the Jubilee had produced disappointing results; would a centenary appeal do better? This would depend upon convincing possible large donors that Selwyn had claims upon their generosity. How could this be done? Behind these questions there was another yet to be answered. How could one explain to outsiders – or indeed to insiders – that Selwyn had a special character? This had been easy enough when Selwyn was still firmly Anglican, but what now?

Selwyn had indeed a character of its own, but not one that could be explained in a few sentences (as the Council had done when appealing for funds in 1901). For many years past the emphasis had been upon eliminating the differences between Selwyn and other colleges, and with this achieved it became more difficult to describe where Selwyn was distinctive. It could no longer claim a right to do what others did but must prove that it could do it better. To this end teaching must be of the best; and amenities, facilities, and arrangements for communal life must create an environment in which individuals could develop their talents to the utmost.

Did Selwyn accept a special responsibility for helping students from schools that had never before sent pupils to Oxford or Cambridge? To a mild degree there might be some discrimination when making conditional offers in favour of applicants from comprehensive schools without gifted teachers and from families with little idea of what advanced education meant; but all colleges were committed to seek out hitherto hidden talent, and at Selwyn half or a little more of those accepted still came from independent schools. This requires some explanation.

In the 1960s many professional families sent their children to good direct grant grammar schools, and the smaller public boarding schools felt the strain as fewer pupils came their way. Then the direct grant schools were forced to choose between going independent and becoming comprehensive (and non-selective), and many chose the former. There were no more free places and therefore no pupils from poor families, but otherwise their social composition was unchanged. Where there was only a comprehensive school available, many middle-income parents scraped or borrowed to send their children to public boarding schools. Less well-known boarding schools that had been near collapse in the 1960s now found themselves with full waiting lists and cash to improve their facilities. Independent schools were successful in the competition for University places because they could afford better equipment and employed good teachers.

Some new comprehensive schools (mainly in suburban districts) were able to compete, but for the majority it would take time and inspired leadership. As far as the College was concerned, and with all the goodwill in the world, it did no one any good to accept an applicant who was poorly prepared and would soon be defeated. The pursuit of excellence would be slowed down if resources had to be employed in teaching for the lower reaches of the pass degree.

Did Selwyn hold out some special advantages to students? In earlier days, when the majority of Cambridge places depended upon parental ability to pay, Selwyn men, being grateful to the College for giving them a Cambridge education at a cost that their fathers could afford, did not complain when living conditions were more austere than in older colleges. All this had changed. The students now in Selwyn were there because the College wanted them. This impression was reinforced by open days to attract applicants and visits by Fellows to schools. This was no bad thing – it was better to be wanted than to be taken on sufferance because there was a place to fill – but it meant that the College must live up to expectations. The students were paying the same as their friends in other colleges, and expected the same or better value for money. Student representation ensured that these demands were fully aired and that answers must be given.

What Selwyn did claim was to manage this new relationship well. There were, of course, moments when exchanges were heated, and no Junior Combination Room can (or perhaps should) function for long without passing resolutions that blame the College authorities for something. But the sores did not fester. Student representation did a great deal to take the heat out of complaints that might have become serious without an opportunity to voice them. Once given the right to be heard, the student representatives were usually constructive and certainly possessed the capacity to exert influence.

In exploring this new relationship a powerful binder for potentially divisive issues was the idea of a Christian community, difficult though it might be to define. Although many, perhaps a majority, of students were not members of the Church of England and some never set foot inside the Chapel, the pastoral tradition was strong. This was not paternalism revived, but a relationship in which those who were spiritually strong ministered to the weak. Selwyn was fortunate in a succession of Chaplains who ensured that religion was an active force in College life and saw to it that those outside the Anglican fold were not excluded from their care. Respect for individual personality rooted in the Christian tradition was at the heart of the friendly reputation that Selwyn cultivated.[5]

Notes and Comments

1. *The controversy over the admission of women*: The account that follows is taken from a file kept by Mr Welbourn, supplemented by notes made by the Master, now in the College Archives, and by conversations with Dr Harrison.

2. *Social conventions and the all-male era*: There were a few occasions (such as the May Week concert) when ladies were entertained in College, but a firm line was drawn between these events and formal dining. When Newnham was recognized as a full College (before Selwyn had that status), the Fellows of Selwyn agreed to show goodwill by entertaining the Fellows of Newnham. It was a black-tie occasion, but the Master (Telfer) sent the invitation for 'an evening meal' out of term in the belief that the ladies would understand that, this being an informal occasion, gowns would not be worn. Nevertheless, the Newnham Fellows arrived in gowns and when one moved to disrobe, the redoubtable Mistress, Dame Myra Curtis, signalled her to desist. So the ladies dined in Hall in academic dress while their male hosts remained, with some embarrassment, ungowned. On another occasion Dr Spear (who had nonconformist views on the question) nominated the Indian Ambassador for invitation to the College Feast. This was duly approved until it was revealed that the Ambassador was an Ambassadress. The invitation was hastily cancelled (fortunately before it had been despatched).

3. *The Fellowship in the 1970s*: One election deserves special notice. In 1977 Jean Chotia was elected as the first woman Fellow. In 1978 Lionel Lionel Charles Knights was elected as an Honorary Fellow. He was a Selwyn graduate, Professor of English first at Bristol and then at Cambridge, and a leading Shakespearean scholar.

4. *College facilities and College earnings*: Improved facilities would help to attract conferences and boost the College income, but as Selwyn competed with other colleges in the conference trade this point could not be made in a presentation to the University.

5. *The Chaplains 1965–84*: Robert Hardy (1965–72), later Bishop of Lincoln and an Honorary Fellow, had deep convictions, warm human sympathies, and massive commonsense. These qualities were invaluable at a time when all kinds of disturbing winds were blowing. David Garnett (1972–7) was a large, cheerful personality who got on very well with the undergraduates; he developed links between the Chapel and Newnham (and married a Newnham girl), helping greatly when the first Selwyn women arrived in 1976. Richard Hunt (1977–84) radiated energy and sincerity, built up the Chapel congregation, and persuaded the most unlikely people to join him on walking tours in remote parts of Britain or to work with children in the red-light district of Birmingham. He had spent some time in Jamaica before coming to Selwyn and maintained his contacts with that country.

CHAPTER 15

The Centenary and Beyond
1981–94

O NCE MORE the observations of an imaginary old member visiting Selwyn can be invoked. It is now 1994 and some fifteen years since he was last in Cambridge. At first sight the College looks much the same, for the most important physical changes are inconspicuous though important. Behind the Hall is a large new kitchen block, and where cooks once toiled under the Hall is a spacious bar and a large room for meetings and lectures. On the other side of the court, behind the C to F range, is an extension to the Library and lawns and shrubs have replaced the bicycle sheds and handyman's workshop that had survived from Selwyn's earliest days. On the corner of Grange Road and Sidgwick Avenue the College offices now occupy the house called Selwyn Close, and up the staircase to the east of the Hall, once the Bursar's domain, are the Archives, rare books, and music practice rooms. In the Chapel a new organ, or rather an old one of superlative quality restored, has been installed. Under the court the tentacles of a computer network reach out to various parts of the College.[1]

The visitor would learn some surprising facts about the Fellowship. It had seemed large enough in 1978 with forty Fellows, including eight in Class E (emeritus), but in 1994 there were sixty (twelve in Class E) and one more prelected to take office during the year. The changes were even greater than the figures suggested. Four former Fellows in Class E had died, so the increase to twelve meant that eight had moved to this class on retirement and had been replaced. Two Fellows moving to posts elsewhere had been replaced; and seven more had been elected to cover new fields or reinforce old ones. There were three endowed

The Old Court in 1990.

Research Fellowships and their holders had come and then moved on at the end of their tenure or when appointed to posts elsewhere. Until 1991 (when this practice was discontinued) there had also been a number of pre-doctoral, non-stipendiary Research Fellows who held the title for less than a year. There was a new category of Bye-Fellows, who were often visiting scholars or school teachers given this status for a single term. There were also some lectors in foreign languages.

Changes at High Table were frequent and numerous. Newcomers arrived each year; some stayed on as holders of University or College posts, but others remained only for an allotted time and were then replaced. There was, however, a stable nucleus of Fellows who had served ten years or more and might expect to continue until retirement or promotion. The Fellowship included three professors, four readers, and a number of younger people making distinguished contributions to their subjects. Numerous publications, conference appearances, and invitations from other universities demonstrated that in academic reputation Selwyn could match any college of comparable size and outdistance several of them.

One contrast between 1978 and 1994 was in the number of advanced students. Then there had been twenty-eight registered for post-graduate degrees including one for the MPhil; in 1992–3 there were seventy-three, almost a third of them (following a trend in the University as a whole) being candidates for the MPhil, MEng, or MBA. There were more staying for three years after graduation to complete an MB or Veterinary MB, and more newcomers taking one-year professional courses. With affiliated students, the total number of advanced students was 107 (almost a quarter of the students in residence). A very lively Middle Combination Room had become the focal point for what was almost a graduate college within the College.

New statutes had been framed and finally approved by the Privy Council in 1989. Executive authority had been transferred from the large Governing Body to the smaller Council, of which the Master, Vice-Master, Bursar, Senior Tutor, and three students were *ex-officio* members, together with eight elected Fellows. The

Governing Body (consisting of all Fellows and three students) remained responsible for the general direction of policy and approving changes in the statutes, but under the new dispensation it seldom met more than once a term. Its normal business was to approve (or disapprove) what the Council had done rather than to initiate policy. In both bodies there were items reserved for Fellows only, but on general problems of College management the three student members of the Council knew more and could have more influence upon policy than a majority of the Fellows. This was a far remove from earlier ideas of the proper relationship between senior and junior members.

The language of the new statutes made it clear that women could occupy any post, including headship of the College. A future Master or Mistress was no longer required to be a member of the Church of England, but was required to respect the Anglican tradition of the College. Thus the one statutory link with the Church, retained in the 1955 statutes, was removed. Another change in headship of the house (a phrase adopted to avoid constant repetition of 'Master or Mistress') was to lower the retiring age from 70 to 67.

The academic record had maintained the momentum of the 1970s. The results in 1986 had been disappointing, with just sixteen firsts, but in no other year had there been fewer than twenty-five; in 1992 there were thirty-six and in 1993 a record-breaking forty-two. A better measure of overall performance was that in 1993 over 60 per cent of the candidates for honours were in Classes I and II.1. In the 1970s Selwyn had normally been near the bottom of the unofficial but influential 'league' table, but by 1990 it was normally somewhere among several colleges in the broad middle band. More important than placing in the league table was satisfaction, expressed by most students, with the attention and encouragement that they had received.

The pursuit of academic excellence had not impoverished sport. In 1985 Selwyn scored its first cup-tie success in a major sport with a win in the finals by the Association Football Club. The Men's Boat Club had varying fortunes and was low in the first division in the early 1990s, but in 1992 the ladies' first boat won its oars in the Lents, bumped its way into the first division in the Mays, and lost in the second round at Henley only to the eventual winners. In the same year the rugby football team had a good season, association football and cricket made the best of not very good jobs, but both men's and ladies' hockey were in good heart. In tennis the Selwyn men were third in the first division and the ladies made it to the cupper quarter-finals. Selwyn rose to fourth place in netball. Athletics had a mediocre season after a run of good ones, but cross-country sometimes fielded more runners than all the other colleges put together and four members of the club ran against Oxford. Both athletics and cross-country were open to both sexes, and in 1991 the captain of the former was a lady. Altogether there was a mixed bag of successes and disappointment during the decade, but plenty of evidence of wide participation and much enjoyment.

The chosen careers of Selwyn graduates continued the trends noted in earlier years. In the 1991–2 *Calendar* an unusually large number of old members reported appointments or promotions. With some additional information about members not listed it was possible to make up a sample of 326, or about 5 per cent of the total membership. The clergy still formed the largest single group, but business, banking, industry, engineering, and scientific employment in industry claimed a larger share than ever before (over a quarter of all recorded). There were more in medicine and in law than in earlier periods. Accountancy, formerly claiming few Cambridge graduates, now attracted some of the brightest. The large number in university posts or serving their academic apprenticeship as research students indicated Selwyn's higher standing in the world of learning.

The career aspirations of undergraduates followed the same pattern, except that fewer thought of ordination, more studied law and considerably more veterinary medicine. Merchant banking, accountancy, and financial management had run very strongly among ambitious undergraduates in the late 1908s, but slackened with the recession of the early 1990s.

THE CAREERS OF SELWYN GRADUATES
From a sample taken in 1991

Clergy	40	
Schools	27	
Universities	22	
Other higher education	9	
Research – pre-doctoral	29	(a)
Research – post-doctoral	4	
Law	19	
Medicine	33	
Veterinary medicine	1	(b)
Business	38	
Banking	6	
Accountancy	7	
Industry/Engineering	17	
Science in industry	22	(c)
Public appointments – UK	18	(d)
Public appointments – foreign	6	
Armed services	4	
Politics	3	(e)
Social work	8	
Media – TV	3	
Media – Radio/cinema	9	
Media – Journalism	1	(f)
Authors	1	
Publishing	2	
Music	4	
Architects/Surveyors	2	

Notes
(a)   Includes twenty-six in residence at Selwyn.
(b)   Certainly an underestimate.
(c)   The majority in computer science.
(d)   Includes two ambassadors (E.J.E. Ratford, J.A. Shepherd).
(e)   MPs – J.S. Gummer (Minister of Agriculture and later Minster for the Environment), S.H.W. Hughes, R.P. Ground. Two members of the House of Lords (Lloyd of Kilgerran and Rayner) are not included.
(f)   Editor of the *Observer* (D.G. Trelford).

Finally, the imaginary visitor might observe a general air of prosperity around the College, and be told that Selwyn no longer laboured under the burden of poverty. The centenary appeal had been successful and Selwyn got a good income from conferences and summer schools, but even with these explanations the old member would be astounded if a glimpse of the College accounts revealed that Selwyn's investments were valued at over £15 million.[2]

So much for an overview of a notable decade; now for a closer look at personalities and events. Commander David Burge resigned as Bursar in September 1981 and was succeeded by another naval man, Vice-Admiral Sir Peter Berger, who had helped to make history in 1949 as navigator on HMS *Amethyst* when it ran the gauntlet of Chinese guns on the Yangtze. He had gone on to an outstanding career in the navy, including command of the nuclear submarine base at Faslane and then of the naval dockyard at Devonport. In 1979 he had been elected a Companion of the British Institute of Management in recognition of his 'eminent achievement in the practice of management' (a rare honour for a serving officer). The wonder to those who watched him at work in Selwyn was the ease and good humour with which he moved quickly from command of Britain's largest naval station to responsibility for the affairs of a small Cambridge college.

When the new Bursar took office, plans for a centenary appeal were well advanced. In 1976 it had been agreed to ask Hooker Craigmyle, a professional fund-raising firm, for a preliminary assessment, and in February 1977 its managing director told the Governing Body that £200,000 would be a realistic target. The comparatively low target figure was disappointing. Twenty inflation years earlier nearly £100,000 had been contributed by old members, and it seemed pessimistic to expect no more than £200,000 on such a unique occasion as the centenary, especially as the net would be cast widely to include business, industry, and charitable foundations. However, it was difficult to fly in the face of expert opinion, and the firm had a good track record. It was decided that it would be wise to aim low, hoping to get more. Accordingly in July 1977 it was agreed to use Hooker Craigmyle's services and launch the appeal early in 1982.

During the next four years the aims of the projected appeal were revised. In 1976 the most urgent need had been a new kitchen, but thanks to generous help from St John's College that was already completed by 1981. This left a large empty space under the Hall and it was decided to use that for an extension to the Junior Combination Room and a room for large meetings. In 1976 the emphasis had been on teaching needs but this shifted to research, and it was agreed to make the endowment of two research fellowships a major aim of the appeal. Other aims were a fund to assist students in need and a Bishop Selwyn memorial window in the Chapel. Finally, it was hoped that enough would be subscribed to form a capital reserve to pay for other needs as they arose.

Looking over these plans, Sir Peter Berger found them wanting. He thought that the charges by the fund-raising firm were high in view of the fact that much of the work would have to be done by Fellows and that they had underestimated what could be achieved (possibly to claim credit when more was raised). If the aims were intended to be realistic the target must be pitched higher. These arguments prevailed. It was decided to dispense with the professionals, rely on self-help, and raise the target to £1 million.

This decision was made easier because it was known that Mr John Chambers, formerly employed by Hooker Craigmyle but now a freelance appeal manager, was available and highly recommended. As executive secretary of the appeal he proved to be, in the strictest sense of the word, invaluable. An assistant secretary and typist was also engaged, and it was decided to appoint a director with long Selwyn connections and known to many old members. The choice fell upon the present writer. As the organization of the appeal may be of some interest, it is described in a note at the end of this chapter.[3]

Subscriptions from old members came in faster than anticipated. A preliminary approach to individual old members and Fellows, asking them to prime the pump before the public launch, produced almost half the target figure that the professional fund-raisers had predicted, and their whole figure was soon passed. Men who had matriculated between 1945 and 1965, at the peak of their careers in the 1980s, were particularly generous. Response from industry was less than had been hoped because the appeal coincided with a severe recession in which manufacturing was badly hit. Institutional and corporate donors included the Wolfson Foundation, Marks and Spencer, IBM (UK), all four English clearing banks, and a large number of smaller businesses. The Cripps Foundation gave a large sum but it had to be earmarked for repairs made necessary by faults in the flat roof of the Cripps buildings.

The pleasantest surprise in the whole campaign was generous help from two old and very distinguished colleges. It would have been understandable for St John's to rest on the generous contribution made toward the cost of the new kitchen, but instead it came forward with another very large donation. A wholly unexpected gift from Trinity endowed a research fellowship (named the Trevelyan Fellowship in memory of a former Master of Trinity and well-known historian who had lived at 23 West Road). A second research fellowship was endowed from general appeal funds.

The eventual outcome was much better than pessimists had predicted, though not quite so high as optimists had hoped. By the spring of 1983 the total given or promised under covenants stood at £640,000, the gift from Trinity College raised it to over £700,000, publicity given to the centenary celebrations jogged a few memories, and with the money earned on deposit the final figure was over £750,000.

All the aims of the appeal were achieved except the Selwyn memorial window, and that was not due to lack of money but to difficulty in finding a suitable artist and a feeling among some Fellows that more stained glass in the Chapel was undesirable. The conversion of the old kitchens was very successful. The JCR extension became a commodious College bar, and the new meeting room (the Chadwick room) is much used by College societies and is a very useful asset when negotiating with organizers of conferences and summer schools. Enough money remained to undertake one more major project, and the choice had to be made between a Library extension or a new organ in the Chapel. By a narrow margin the Library won the vote, but fortunately Lord Rayner came to the rescue with a large donation, in addition to what he had already given, and Selwyn got both its Library extension and a splendid organ.

The date chosen to celebrate the centenary was 9 June 1983. The Duke of Edinburgh, Chancellor of the University, spoke from a rostrum erected in the court. His address was brief but his words well chosen. Recalling that Bishop Selwyn had been both intellectually distinguished and physically extremely tough, he said, 'in some remarkable way, these qualities have been transferred to, or inherited by, Selwyn College'. The fact of survival for one hundred years was as good an excuse as any for a celebration, but that was not really the point.

> Selwyn College has not only survived, although considering that two other colleges founded at the same time failed this test, it is an achievement in itself. The important fact is that Selwyn has made a distinctive contribution to this University and, as I am sure many of its graduates and Fellows would acknowledge, it has had a significant influence on the lives and careers of many individuals.

The men who founded Selwyn and sustained it during its early years had had 'more than their share of difficulties' but their 'utter devotion and self-sacrifice' had overcome those. The recollection of past achievements was a spur to future effort, and 'on that score Selwyn College could look forward to a long a brilliant future'.

A week later the Archbishop of Canterbury, preaching at the Commemoration of Benefactors, also looked back to the men who had seen that 'education was not complete if learning was simply bulk and detail without shape or thrust'. To that end they had built the Chapel and placed it at the centre of their new College. The truth as they had seen it was no longer fashionable, but if Selwyn's next century was not to see 'a cultivated slide into meanness and mediocrity', the faith that begat energy must once again 'be seen as a vital ingredient in the make-up of a truly educated and civilized person'.

In proposing the health of Selwyn at the Commemoration dinner the Vice-Chancellor, Professor F.H. Hinsley, congratulated the College on adjusting 'to the demands set up by perpetual change, which, like those set up by advancing age, are not all welcome', and rising 'with ever-increasing confidence to the opportunities which change presents to those who retain the advantages of comparative youth'. As Vice-Chancellor he conveyed the good wishes of the whole University, but as the Master of Bishop Selwyn's own College, which was also the College of the present Master, he had 'a very special reason for bringing congratulation from St John's College'.

The centennial year was also marked by the election of five Honorary Fellows, four of them graduates of the College. Two outstanding businessmen who had also given much help during the appeal, Edwin Nixon (1943–4) (soon to be Sir Edwin) and Sir Derek Rayner (1949–41) (soon to be Lord Rayner), were honoured. The debt that the College owed to earlier generations was acknowledged by the election of Frank Woodward, graduate (1927), Fellow 1929–44, and benefactor. Gratitude to old members for their help was shown by the election of Sir John Paul (1936–9), a former colonial civil servant who had been Governor of the Gambia, Belize, and the Bahamas, and was closing his career as Governor-General of the Isle of Man. He was president of the Selwyn Association in the centenary year. Professor Fred Rimmer, Organ Scholar in 1946 and for many years Professor of Music at Glasgow, had set Selwyn music on the successful course that it had since followed. Finally, Selwyn's affiliation with the Church of England was recalled by the election of Lord Ramsey of Canterbury, the former archbishop and sometime member of the old Council.[4]

In retrospect it can be seen that the symbolism of the centenary conveyed another message. In the preceding chapters it has been remarked on several occasions that important steps in College development were taken in response to outward events. Government decisions over educational policy, student grants and university finance had prompted expansion and a change of direction. Indirectly pressure from the University had brought to an end denominational tests for Fellows and Scholars. It was largely pressure from outside that caused a rapid expansion of the Fellowship and with it erosion of the idea of the College as a family. The lowering of the voting age to 18 and nationwide student activism pressured the move towards their participation. The demand for more places for women at Cambridge and the example of other colleges prompted the decision to admit both sexes. The way in which Selwyn responded had decided the detail but the main thrust had come from outside.

Beginning around 1970 with the new admissions policy, Selwyn had begun to initiate rather than respond. No one ignored general shifts in attitudes and needs, but in the 1980s Selwyn took its own decisions in deciding what kind of College it should be. The use of the money raised by the appeal, the further expansion of the Fellowship, the admission of more graduate students, the adoption of policies designed to improve academic performance, and above all the new statutes resulted from internal discussion, not external prompting.

Owen Chadwick could have remained in office for three years after the centenary; but after twenty-seven years in the Lodge (one of the longest tenures in Cambridge annals) he thought it time to go. His powers were undiminished and he remained active in public life, serving a term as president of the British Academy, becoming chairman of the trustees of the National Portrait Gallery, and being elected Chancellor of the University of East Anglia. In addition to these public duties he continued to explore new fields in his research and added to his already long list of publications.

To the end of his Mastership he retained his unique gift for making people feel at ease, whether they were guests at High Table, undergraduates, or College servants. One lingering memory of his last year in office makes the point. He continued his normal practice of entertaining first-year undergraduates in the Lodge, and as ever the new arrivals were ill at ease and nervous of saying or doing the wrong thing. Each was welcomed as an individual worthy of respect, tension relaxed, and all settled down to enjoy a good party. How many others who had achieved such distinction and been so long

Alan Hugh Cook, 1983.

in office would have taken so much trouble with young men and women as they entered upon their university careers?

The Master had been awarded the KBE, but for him this was almost an empty honour as a clergyman of the Church of England cannot be addressed as 'Sir' nor his wife as 'Lady'. After his retirement Selwyn learned with delight that he had been awarded the Order of Merit, an honour more valued than any title.

The new Master, the first layman and the first scientist to occupy the Lodge, was Professor Alan Cook. He was a graduate of Corpus Christi and before returning to Cambridge had been

Professor of Geophysics at Edinburgh. At the time of his election he was a Fellow of King's, Jacksonian Professor of Natural Philosophy, head of the Cavendish Laboratory, a Fellow of the Royal Society, and a member of numerous academic and scientific committees. He was knighted soon after he became Master. He had strong links with the University of Trieste, and during his frequent visits to Italy he had acquired much knowledge about the art and architecture of that country. To those with long memories the fact that a scientist of this eminence accepted the Mastership was proof that Selwyn had come a long way since its Jubilee.

The outstanding features of Sir Alan Cook's ten years as Master were the expanding Fellowship, improved academic performance, the new Library extension, the new organ, and a very striking improvement in College finances. He had a special interest in a link with the University computer service that looked forward to the time when a Selwyn student, sitting in College, would call on to a computer screen the voluminous data stored in archives, libraries, and laboratories across the world. The Master also had wide cultural interests, especially in music, and was responsible for establishing the contacts that enabled the Chapel choir to make some very successful visits to European cities. Among many University duties he was chairman of the University Press Syndicate.

Any attempt to chronicle the doings of Fellows during this eventful decade would read like a potted biographical dictionary. Notes on some individuals will be found at the end of the chapter, but here there is space to record only those who held key positions in College administration.

Alistair MacFarlane came to Selwyn as a professorial Fellow in 1974, and quickly won the respect of the other Fellows. Six years later they departed from precedent by electing him Vice-Master (an office hitherto invariably occupied by long-serving Fellows). He presided over the first election of a Master under the 1955 statutes (the only time that its somewhat cumbersome procedure was used). In 1989 he left Selwyn to become Principal of Heriot-Watt University, but in the same year the Fellows showed their appreciation of his services by electing him to an Honorary Fellowship.

Dr E.H.R. Ford took over as Senior Tutor in 1979. After the innovations in the decade – student participation in College government, the shift to pre-A-level offers for admission, and the admission of women – it was time for consolidation rather than innovation. For this Edward Ford, with his urbane manner and measured response to events, was admirably suited. In 1988 he succeeded Alistair MacFarlane as Vice-Master but served in that office for only a short period as he reached the age of retirement in 1990.

When a layman was elected as Master the senior Fellow in Holy Orders became Dean of Chapel, and John Sweet held this office from 1983 to his retirement in 1994, with overall responsibility for religious activity in the College. In 1990 he succeeded Edward Ford as Vice-Master and had to organize and preside over the meetings to choose a successor to Sir Alan Cook. During the interregnum that followed Sir Alan's retirement, from October 1993 to April 1994, he was Acting Master. In carrying out those albeit temporary responsibilities he won much praise from his colleagues. An article about him in *The Church Times* described him as 'a don of the old school' and meant it as a compliment that was endorsed by all who knew him at Selwyn.

John Morrill, an Oxford graduate and historian, came to Selwyn in 1975 after a short period as a lecturer at Stirling. His forceful personality made an immediate impact and in 1982 he became Senior Tutor. He initiated a drive to improve tripos performance and to encourage the admission of graduates for research. His own growing reputation as a historian of England in the seventeenth century attracted a number of able young scholars to Selwyn. The ever-increasing volume of paperwork piled upon the Senior Tutor proved, after an eight-year tenure, to be incompatible with his academic commitments and ambitions, and in 1990 he handed over to Michael Tilby, who had been elected a Fellow in 1977 and appointed Admissions tutor when that office was first separated from the Senior Tutorship. In this capacity he had developed the open days and the visits to schools that attracted able students from a widened constituency.

Two other Fellows who played important parts in shaping College policy were J.R. Spencer and G. Johnson. John Spencer was a Selwyn graduate and lawyer who became a Fellow in 1970. On frequent occasions he has been called upon for legal advice, and he was mainly responsible for drafting the new statutes. At the same time he was building up first a national and then an international reputation as an academic lawyer and authority on criminal jurisprudence, the rules of evidence, and children as witnesses. Gordon Johnson was elected as a Fellow in 1974 after holding a Research Fellowship at Trinity. His principal work was in Indian history, but in the 1980s much of his time was devoted to University administration. He was elected to the Council of the Senate and served on numerous committees. In this way he came to assume in College affairs the place once occupied by W.J. Sartain with an unrivalled knowledge of the University and its relationship with the colleges. In 1993 he succeeded Sir Alan Cook as chairman of the University Press Syndicate and was also elected President of Wolfson College.

From 1983 to 1993 no fewer than fifty-two Fellows were elected. Sixteen were non-stipendiary Research Fellows with short tenure; and Keasbey, Trevelyan, and Centennial Research Fellows were elected for limited terms and then replaced. Twenty-three holders of College or University offices were elected. Two new Fellows were professors (Colin Humphreys, Professor of Materials Science, and David Ford, Regius Professor of Divinity) and two were chaplains. One Fellow in economics was supported jointly by Selwyn and a firm of financial consultants headed by J.F. Chown, an old Selwyn man. Another joint appointment was in law, in which Selwyn shared responsibility with a firm of London solicitors. This left seventeen new Fellows elected in the normal way to cover new fields or reinforce old ones.[5]

The diversity of subjects represented at High Table was remarkable. In addition to subjects long familiar, the Fellows and Research Fellows elected between 1979 and 1993 covered American literature, astro-physics, arctic ecology, Byzantine studies, Egyptology, international relations, linguistics, modern Greek, palaeontology, palaeobotany, social and political science, and veterinary medicine.

The decision to create a Council brought about a radical change in the way that the College was governed. The new statutes, incorporating this change, were not formally approved until 1989, but from 1985 an executive committee performed most of the duties assigned to the proposed Council.

The idea of a Council had been in the air for some years, but opinion had been divided. The former Master and several Fellows had been opposed on the ground that it would be divisive, would create tension, and would be no more efficient than the Governing Body, on which every Fellow had a voice. Others believed that the Governing Body had become too large for useful discussion and that business would be done more efficiently by a smaller body meeting more frequently. Whatever attraction collective wisdom had as an abstract proposition, the reality was that administration was already handled by a small group of Fellows who often found their work emasculated by ill-informed criticism in the Governing Body. The College could no longer be likened to a family; in modern times a more accurate comparison would be with a company having directors and share-holders.

By 1984 majority opinion had swung in favour of a Council. Deliberations in the Governing Body no longer inspired confidence. There were always a number of absentees, and if they appeared at the next meeting time was wasted in going over the issues again before a vote could be taken. As is inevitable in large bodies, there were always some who had not read the papers, which might not matter if they held their peace but was inconvenient if they held up business to raise irrelevant points. On the other hand, some Fellows resented the extent to which matters were settled by an in-group – but this feeling would be dissipated if the statutes laid down clearly who did what. The strongest case against the existing system was not so much its inefficiency as the irritation that it bred.

The proposed size of the Council ranged from twelve to twenty members, but sixteen was an acceptable mean. It must include the Master, Vice-Master, Bursar, and Senior Tutor *ex officio*. With surprising alacrity it was also agreed in principle that the students must be represented, but there was some hesitation over the number of places they should be given. The presidents of the Middle Combination Room and Junior Combination Room could hardly be denied *ex-officio* membership, but the JCR wanted two representatives and some Fellows thought that this was too many. After discussion it was agreed that in this situation two heads really were better than one, and the treasurer of the Junior Combination Room was given *ex-officio* membership. This left eight places to be filled by Fellows elected for four-year terms and retiring in rotation.

It had been accepted by the students that there would be reserved items for which they would not be present. These would include the election of Fellows, the assignment of duties to Fellows, and disciplinary matters. The Master has the right to declare that other items must be reserved, but this power is likely to be used sparingly. This apart, the statutory requirement for three *ex-officio* places gives students a firmer place in the administration than in most other colleges.

The proposal that the Council, without student members, should have the right to elect Fellows caused some concern. In most colleges this had always been done by the whole body of the Fellows and in Selwyn approval by two-thirds had been required. It was therefore to be expected that some would be reluctant to concede this right to the Master and twelve Fellows. Against this it was argued that election by the Governing Body, in which many members would know nothing about the candidate or the field of study, had become an empty formality. Indeed many Fellows had taken so little interest in the matter that on recent occasions it had been difficult to muster the required two-thirds, with consequent delays in electing persons who had been duly nominated and approved by those who knew what they were talking about. Even when there was no unreasonable delay the cumbersome procedure might let another college get in first when there was someone whom Selwyn particularly wanted to secure.

To achieve the main objective while making some concession to doubters, two methods were agreed: a slow and a fast track, with the Master to decide which was appropriate. When the slow track was used, the Governing Body would identify subject needs and decide priorities. The Council would seek out and elect persons who filled the bill, but if no member of the Council was familiar with the prescribed field the Director of Studies, or a Fellow familiar with the subject, should be co-opted. With the fast-track procedure the Council would take the initiative and proceed to elect without consulting the Governing Body. Under either procedure a prospective Fellow might be invited to lunch or dine, but this random exposure to Fellowship scrutiny would carry far less weight than in former times.

One argument against a Council had been that Fellows who already played little part in College business would be encouraged to devote even less time to it. This looked back to the time when the Fellowship was small and a member who did not take on his fair share of College administration was open to reproach. Under modern conditions and with large Fellowships it is better to recognize that it takes all sorts to make a successful college. Some must be ready to play their part in College administration, but others may heighten its reputation by the academic work to which they give most of their time. It is a muddled society if no one takes control, but a dull one if no one gives first priority to advancing the frontiers of knowledge. In practice some Fellows take an active part in College business while increasing their academic reputations, and others with major commitments to their subject are useful on College committees. Within limits the functions can be combined, but no one should be reproached if most of his or her time goes to the performance of one.

Although academic performance had steadily improved, it was not yet good enough. The baseline for the argument was that no one got in without a first-rate performance at A-level; if many people of this calibre did not rise above II.2 or III there was a presumption that they were not doing themselves full justice at Cambridge. If this were true it was up to the College to do some constructive self-criticism.

It was often possible to explain individual cases. Motivation might falter, emotional problems might develop, and there were always a few who made a conscious decision to devote the greater

Lunch in the Hall.

part of their time to politics, drama, or some other non-academic pursuit. However, the majority wanted to do well, and there was cause for concern if many were not doing well enough.

As Senior Tutor John Morrill suggested Selwyn might be the victim of its own virtues. Students were invited to enjoy a relaxed and friendly environment and might be left with the impression that the academic skills were easily acquired. The welcome could remain equally warm and, in the long run, be more appreciated if accompanied by positive guidance. There should be more than a simple admonition to work hard; there must be guidance on organizing work, on how to get value from lectures, and on what to expect from supervisions. There were also industrious students to be warned that the accumulation of knowledge might lead nowhere without reflection upon its implications. Others might be told that fresh air and reasonable exercise cleared the mind.

These issues were considered at length by a committee under the chairmanship of Professor MacFarlane, and student representative

In the Library.

were involved in all the discussions that ensued. Early briefing was endorsed, but the need to supervise supervisors was also stressed. Some old hands were suspected of being too casual and new people on the job did not always know what was expected of them. Tutors should insist on full terminal reports and early warning if there was cause for alarm. Directors of Studies might give fairly precise instructions to inexperienced supervisors. It was also recognized that a supervisor might be successful with some students and fail with others. If a student thought that he or she was getting nothing or getting the wrong thing, then a complaint was justified and must be considered seriously.

If reports on a student were adverse the College authorities must decide whether referral to the University Counselling Service or a summons to appear before a committee of Fellows was the right remedy. The latter procedure might affect more than the individual. If it became known that academic progress was being carefully monitored, the majority of students would accept it as evidence of concern for individual well-being, not an intrusion into privacy.

Whatever the arguments, the new emphasis was successful. In the early 1990s the tripos results were markedly better than they had been ten years earlier. There is no evidence that in innate ability the students of 1990 were superior to those of 1980, but it is possible that their motivation was stronger, and it was observed that some of the best came from Indian and South Asian families settled in Britain among whom parental pressure to achieve was strong. The continued policy of encouraging applications from maintained comprehensive schools may have gathered in students who would not otherwise have come to Cambridge. But the principal credit for improvement must go to the Tutors, Directors of Studies, and supervisors who worked so hard towards that end.

Selwyn entered the last decade of the century with much to be proud of and grateful for, but the achievement that gave most confidence for the future was the ascent from poverty. Compared with rich colleges such as Trinity and St John's, Selwyn was still poor, but it had moved ahead of several others. In 1963 the invested capital was valued at £151,890; ten years later it had risen to £666,049; and in 1978 it topped £1 million for the first time. The figures for 1980 to 1993 take up the story:

1980	1,651,217
1981	2,031914
1982	2,146,656
1983	3,236,131
1984	3,613,737
1985	4,709,797
1986	6,477,875
1987	8,902,478
1988	8,390,814
1989	10,062,444
1990	10,846,860
1991	11,574,867
1992	12,305,832
1993	15,377,272

The total income from all sources in 1992–3 was £2,648,901, and the surplus for the year was £442,078. When the income from endowments was taken in account the assessable income for reckoning the College contribution to the University was £868,775, and after allowable deductions Selwyn paid in £45,249. The boldest prophet of 1930 would not have dared to forecast such figures, and even the Fellows of 1970 could not have imagined them.

Selwyn's popularity as a conference centre was one explanation, and this was in part due to the building of Cripps Court and the new kitchens, and good use of the space under the Hall. An excellent investment committee, advised by Mr C.H.E. Tansley, a Selwyn graduate and partner in J.M. Finn & Co. (London stockbrokers), had acted boldly but wisely. Once a good start had been made, the high interest rates of the mid-1980s helped accumulation.

Sir Peter Berger's time as Bursar expired in 1991, but he left Selwyn's business in good hands. Mića Panić had been a Fellow in economics since 1984 and a University lecturer. Recognizing that managing College affairs was a full-time job, he resigned his University post when appointed as Bursar. His family was Serbian but he had spent all his working life in England and before coming to Cambridge had been on the research staff of the Bank of England.

Students knew little of this change in Selwyn's fortunes, but cheerfulness was in the air. Young men and women, brought together at a time of life when feelings are intense, cannot escape temptation or avoid frustration, but both College and University are much better prepared to deal with personal problems and crises than in the past. There are fewer breakdowns resulting from stress or emotional upsets in Selwyn than in most colleges, and this may be explained by the good relations that students have with each other and with those whose business it is to run the College. Selwyn has also been fortunate in its Chaplains, all men with strong though very different personalities, who have made important contributions to College life. Walking around the College, talking to students, taking a drink in the College bar, or dining

on a night when Hall is formal, the dominant impression is of
vitality and good humour. Student conventions and assumptions
are not those of earlier generations, but for most of them the
immediate focus of ambition is to get a good degree. Their casual
and sometimes noisy life-style is a counterweight to the seriousness
of life.[6]

Sir Alan Cook's tenure as Master closed in September 1993.
For the first time an advertisement in the national press invited
applications for the headship of house, and some extraordinary
speculations ensued in leading newspapers. One confidently identified the persons on the short list, but not a single name was
correct. Another predicted who would be chosen three days before
the matter was settled, but the person named had neither applied
nor been considered.

Lips are for the present sealed, but it is believed that the proceedings did not run smoothly. The names on the real short list
were distinguished, and any one of them might have secured a
majority but none could secure the necessary two-thirds. One who
was near success withdrew. Two Fellows of the College had strong
support but neither could break through the two-thirds barrier.

It was therefore with relief that it was learned that David
Harrison, ScD, Fellow in Engineering, Selwyn graduate and sometime Senior Tutor, Vice-Chancellor of Exeter and formerly of
Keele, chairman of the Committee of Vice-Chancellors and president of the Institute of Chemical Engineers, was willing to be
nominated. The required majority was quickly obtained although
the Master-elect could not be installed until April 1994 and
because of his age would not have long in office.

The elevation to the Mastership of a distinguished graduate is
a fitting point at which to close this narrative history of Selwyn
College. Some retrospective and prospective reflections are reserved
for a final chapter, but here it is enough to remark that the new
Master can truthfully repeat, for himself – and for so many others
who remember the past and look to the future – the words of
the Psalmist: 'The lot is fallen unto me in a fair ground: yea, I
have a goodly heritage.'

Notes and Comments

1. *Demolished buildings north of the C–F range*: No one objected to the removal of the unsightly bicycle sheds and handyman's workshop, but the latter – brick built with a curiously misshapen chimney – was the oldest building on the College site. It had been erected by the original contractors before the days of Portakabins.

2. *The old court and the garden*: To the visitor one sign of growing prosperity would be improvements in the old court. York paving stones had replaced tarmac along the east and south sides. In summer there was more colour in the court than heretofore – with hanging baskets, tubs full of flowers at the corner of the lawn, and a new arrangement of urns and plants in the space between the Lodge and the Chapel. The visitor might also learn that plans were afoot for developments in the garden with money to carry them out. In 1993 Dr Chivers, the Garden Steward, circulated with the *Calendar* an appeal for money for the garden, to which the proceeds from the sale of new aerial photographs of the College would be added. A modest response was anticipated but the result far exceeded expectations.

3. *The Centenary appeal*: The following were the principal stages in organizing the appeal.

   A. After the details had been settled a short list of old members who were thought to be well disposed and able to prime the pump was prepared. The Master wrote personally to them. Fellows were also asked to contribute ahead of the public launch as charitable foundations were usually more willing to help those who helped themselves.

   B. The main brochure was prepared. Although this cost money it was argued that a well-illustrated and, above all, an informative brochure would pay for itself.

   C. A card index of old members was prepared that included all available information. Fellows were asked to identify men to whom they were prepared to write personal letters.

   D. The brochure was sent to all old members and accompanied by a note from the director saying that the Fellows wished to call the fund to help students in need 'The Owen Chadwick Fund' in honour of the man who had led the College for more than a quarter of its life. Included in the brochure were instructions on how to subscribe, forms for making covenants and setting up bankers' orders, and an addressed envelope.

   E. Old members who had been active in the Selwyn Association were asked to do some local fund-raising. Personal visits or letters were the most effective method. A seven-year for £20 covenant yielded

£200 after recovery of tax (then at 30 per cent) and often was more financially effective than fund-raising events that it took much effort to organize. The emphasis on this did not preclude local meetings, and Fellows were ready to attend and speak if asked to do so.

F. Information was gathered about charitable foundations. If a Selwyn man, or someone who had contacts with the College, was identified among the trustees, his advice was sought in the hope that if an application went forward he would watch its progress.

G. Large companies that made charitable donations were identified. Selwyn was fortunate in being able to draw upon the advice of two Selwyn men who were prominent businessmen: Derek Rayner of Marks and Spencer and Edwin Nixon of IBM. Help was also given by Nigel Egerton, a merchant banker, and John Chown, a financial adviser. A London committee met several times. In a separate one-man operation, Lord Lloyd of Kilgerran gave active help by writing to many friends in high places.

H. After the appeal had been running for six months an interim report was prepared and circulated to all old members. This gave a list of those who had subscribed but not the amounts given. The list jogged memories, and enabled old members who had canvassed personally to identify those who had promised but not yet acted.

I. During the duration of the campaign there was a great deal of letter writing and investigation. The 'official' literature was essential but it was usually the personal approach that yielded results.

4. *Two Honorary Fellows in 1983*: Sir Edwin Nixon was at Selwyn for a year during the war (1943–4) and then returned to complete his degree (1947–50). He joined IBM in 1965 and rose to be chairman and managing director (UK) 1979–86 and chairman 1986–90. He was a director of several companies and deputy chairman of the National Westminster Bank. He was associated with many charitable and educational institutions (especially with Leicester University in his native city). He was awarded the CBE in 1974 and was knighted in 1984.

    Lord Rayner (Derek Rayner) read theology (1949–51). Soon after graduation he joined Marks and Spencer and rose to be chief executive 1983–8 and chairman 1984–91. From 1979 to 1983 he was a special adviser to the government on reorganization and efficiency in the central administration. He was knighted in 1973 and became a life peer in 1983.

5. *Two professorial Fellows*: Colin Humphreys, Professor of Materials Science, has the unusual distinction of holding degrees from three English universities: BSc (London), MA (Oxford), PhD (Cambridge). His international reputation brings frequent invitations to attend conferences

or give public lectures in different parts of the world and makes him the most travelled Selwyn Fellow (though closely followed by James Keeler (chemistry) and David Chivers (veterinary medicine).

David Ford, Regius Professor of Divinity, is a graduate of Trinity College, Dublin. He then came to St John's, Cambridge, as an affiliated student and continued in Cambridge to take a PhD on aspects of Karl Barth's theology. In 1976 he was appointed to a lectureship at Birmingham and in 1990, at an unusually early age, to the Regius chair at Cambridge.

6. *The Chaplains*: As the formal commitment to the Church has weakened, the importance of the Chaplains in College life has grown. Emotional strain is inevitable in a mixed community, and more than any other member of High Table the Chaplain is called upon to guide, counsel, and heal. It would be invidious to pick out the special qualities that each Chaplain has brought to the College, but one deserves notices as an unusual personality. Harry Potter (1984 to 1987) had worked in a large city parish and was deeply concerned with the problems of delinquent young people. It would give the wrong impression to say that this gave him special qualifications for appointment as College Chaplain, or that service in Selwyn was good training for his next appointment as chaplain at Wormwood Scrubs! But, in John Sweet's words, 'he was in touch with those furthest from formal religious commitment, and inspired activities with the under-privileged and anti-social'. After Wormwood Scrubs he decided to become a barrister and was called to the bar in 1993.

CHAPTER 16

Retrospect – Prospect

MELLOW RED BRICK, toned down by green shrubs and colourful climbers, the broad expanse of lawn, the glimpse of the garden beyond the fine railings, and the dignity of the Chapel give an impression of space, light, and admirable proportions. For those who know it well, the old court symbolizes their affection for Selwyn; for those who visit it by chance and have learned about Cambridge from guide books it comes as a revelation. The buildings, praised in early days, then spurned as mock-Tudor or Jacobean, are once more admired as architectural fashion discovers the merits of good Victorian and Edwardian buildings.

In its physical appearance this is the College of which the founders dreamed and which their successors strove to complete. What else remains of their intentions? They have been overtaken by events and worn down by time, and the answer may be 'Nothing but the name.' The struggling infant on to which they pinned their hopes has grown to flourishing maturity, but with progress has discarded almost everything that they regarded as essential.

There is nothing unusual in this. Most colleges respect their founders but no longer carry out their wishes. Everywhere customs once revered have been abandoned. Even endowments given for specific purposes have been converted to other uses more relevant to modern times. Once created, institutions acquire a life of their own and grow in the course of time into something that their original promoters would not recognize and might well dislike.

The history of Selwyn spans the great intellectual, technological, and social gulf that separates the nineteenth century from the coming twenty-first. Selwyn continued with the Charter in its original form for over seventy years and the one major change in the statutes in 1913 confirmed the original purpose. No one could have expected more. Beyond that the past could no longer legislate for the present and the living had to decide how the future should be shaped. 'There is a tide in the affairs of men, which, taken at the flood, leads on to fortune.' In the second half of the twentieth century Selwyn has taken the tide at the flood, sometimes hesitantly, sometimes eagerly, but with results that one need have no shame in recording.

Change has been the motif, continuity the theme. Since 1882 people have come and gone – undergraduates for a short three years, some Fellows for their working lives, but always with something passed on from year to year. The Second World War was a significant break but even then enough remained to form the nucleus of what was in many respects a new College. Continuity is always mysterious but none the less real.

Continuity means evolution. Much is conserved but always something is added or something discarded. The graduates of one year do not think about the College in exactly the same way as those of the year before. During a long tenure a Fellow may come to accept as normal what had previously been unthinkable, and a newly elected Fellow starts with a different perception of the College than the older generation. Academic institutions are notoriously slow to move but today's fixed positions may well prove to have been yesterday's novelties. From 1969 to 1974 the great issue was the admission of women. Twenty years on there were only five Fellows holding college offices who participated in that great debate, five were elected after the decision had been taken but before the first woman matriculated, two had known Selwyn as an all-male institution as undergraduates but not as Fellows, and thirty-six had never known the College without women. For a large majority of the Governing Body the radical move of 1974 had become part of the established order that no one would think of challenging.

The changes in national life are too familiar to require repetition, but the altered relationship between higher education and the State deserves examination. When Selwyn was founded no member of the University received a salary from public funds; all undergraduates were paid for by their parents or supported by

Selwyn from the Air.
The photograph (from the unit that J.K.S. St Joseph founded and for many
years directed, shows how the College has lost its geographical isolation. Beyond
the garden are the buildings for the Arts and Social Science Faculties. To the
left of the complex is the Music school and concert hall. A new Law building
will soon be added. In the middle distance are residential blocks for Caius and
Queens' (to which another building has been added since the photograph). To
the left and off the picture is the University Library. If the camera swung
round to face north-east it would show Cripps Court, the Corpus graduate
buildings at Leckhampton, Clare Hall, Robinson College, and in the distance
the Veterinery school and the Cavendish laboratory. To existing playing
fields will soon be added the new University sports centre.

College endowments; and every library, laboratory, and amenity was privately financed. Apart from occasional legislation (such as the University Tests Act), the University was independent, but being independent it could serve no more than a tiny fragment of the population.

Today public funds pay the salaries of most university teachers and the fees of most students, supply the capital for new university facilities, provide a major part of the cost of maintaining them, support many research projects, and pay for enormously expensive equipment. The universities have discretion to allocate money that has not been earmarked for specified purposes, but even then within parameters fixed by the government. The universities have become an arm of the State, but the sacrifice of freedom has enabled them to serve a much larger segment of the population.

Until 1970 the now defunct University Grants Committee was respected, successive governments endorsed expansion, and quality seemed to be assured by accepting 1:10 as the normal staff:student ratio. When economic stringency followed it was understood that funding would be less generous and scrutiny of expenditure more rigorous, but political inconsistency made hard times harder. As central control tightened long-term planning became impossible.

The recent history of national policy on student numbers makes the point. In 1992 ambitious targets for expansion were set. Cambridge was to take three thousand more undergraduates by the close of the century (an average increase of 120 in every college or ten new colleges the size of Selwyn) but with an injunction to cut the cost per student. In 1993 the target was dropped and contraction was ordered together with a further cut in unit cost. As the general secretary of the Association of University Teachers explained after an interview with the Minister for Higher Education, 'If their motto [in 1992] was "more and cheaper", it is now "fewer and cheaper still" '.

Under these circumstances a college in a residential university has acquired new functions. It continues to organize teaching and support research, provide accommodation and recreational facilities, and look after a growing number of graduate students. Now it must also provide shelter against the cold and unpredictable winds of official policy and use its resources to prevent the erosion of both material and intellectual standards.

The greater part of the salaries of most Fellows comes from the government, as do most fees paid by a majority of students, but a college receives no public money for upkeep of buildings and grounds or for the employment of secretarial and domestic staff. From its own resources or private gifts it must improve residential accommodation, beautify its chapel, extend and stock its library, maintain the kitchen, assist its sporting clubs, and make available such essential aids to modern study as computers and photo-copiers. It has also to provide administrative services that are handled elsewhere by central offices.

When the State assumed responsibility for financing higher education and deciding who should benefit from it, there was an expectation that private support had had its day; but higher education has always cost more than the State is prepared to give. There has been no public recognition that good amenities and comfortable accommodation improve the quality of academic life and create a suitable environment for intellectual effort. Cripps Court could not have been built without the Cripps Foundation. More recent improvement resulted from the centenary appeal, and if a new north court is built it must depend on private gifts and Selwyn's own resources.

Apart from the perennial challenge of finding the means to do what ought to be done, future planning is complicated by educational measures now being discussed nationally. One proposal is to divide universities between research and teaching institutions, but this finds little favour in Cambridge even though higher funding for its research might be a result. There are productive scholars who cannot teach, and there are excellent teachers who do no research; but for most Cambridge dons the activities are complementary. Original thinking is promoted by frequent calls to explain basic concepts and the most stimulating teachers are those who work on the frontiers of knowledge.

There is criticism of the three-term year and the three-year degree. Surely, it is argued, eight terms of ten weeks spread over two years would achieve as much as nine terms of eight weeks spread over three? That the idea attracts cost-conscious politicians is clear, but its rejection by most academics (except perhaps as an expedient for mature students) is predictable. The traditional method is not to cram the greatest amount of teaching into the shortest possible time, but to give young people the experience of living for an extended period in an environment where things of the mind take first place.

A plan that may be treated with more respect is to keep the three-year degree but to divide each year into two 21-week semesters, possibly running from September to January and from February to June with short breaks at Christmas and Easter. It has been argued that in one long semester it is possible to cover the broad outlines of a subject, introduce some study in depth, and avoid the intellectual scramble demanded by the weekly essay and lectures that never have time to go over the same ground twice. At the same time, if each course lasts for one semester and no more, it would be possible to achieve greater breadth in a degree curriculum.

The semester plan is often, though not necessarily, accompanied by arguments for a modular degree on the American plan. The qualification for a degree would be a stated number of credits awarded for separate courses, and a student moving from one university to another could count the credits already received at the first institution. Apart from encouraging student mobility, the advantage would lie in allowing universities to concentrate resources with the assurance that fields they did not cover could be studied elsewhere.

Arguments for extending the academic year are often accompanied by complaints that university buildings are empty and equipment unused during half the year. The reality is that most of them are in use the whole year round. Research is a full-time occupation, and except for the Christmas break there is never a time at Cambridge when the University Library and the Science Laboratories are not busy. Colleges depend much on the incomes from conferences and summer schools, but it is wrong-headed to see these merely as money-making exercises. The conferences are useful for their members, and many are made possible by the relative cheapness of college accommodation. Many of the summer schools are University enterprises and if their fees are welcome their cultural value is incalculable.

These are general influences and arguments that will affect College policy in the next fifty years, and it is predictable that others will arise. The question to be asked is whether Selwyn has made a good start in facing them. Have the changes and reforms achieved good results? Will more statute revision be necessary before the future can be faced with confidence? The following pages present a summary of answers to questions by Fellows who were closely concerned with College business between 1980 and 1993. There are a few direct quotations, but for the most part the answers are not given verbatim but convey consensus views.

Q. Has government by Council been a success?
A. Yes, with minor qualifications. It has tended to 'marginalize' some Fellows but they would probably have stood apart under any form of government. A Fellow who wants to be active in College affairs has ample opportunity. The Council has made possible informed discussion and speedy decision. Both are essential under modern conditions.

Q. Has too much power been taken from the Governing Body?
A. It is not so much a question of power as of the use of power, of interpreting rather than revising the statutes. It was intended that the Governing Body should be concerned with broad questions of general policy, but the Council has tended to become the policy-making body. The Governing Body approves or criticizes but does not initiate and often wastes time on the less important aspects of what has been decided.

Q. Has the election of Fellows by the Council rather than by the whole body of the Fellows been a success?
A. Here again, the format seemed to be right but it has not worked very well. The 'slow track' – with the Governing Body

deciding the priorities and the Council finding the persons – was intended to be normal, and the 'fast track' – with the Council acting without prior consultation – exceptional. In practice directives from the Governing Body have been too broad and inconclusive to be of much use, and the procedure tends to be 'fast track' even when nominally 'slow track'. But there can be no complaint about the quality of the Fellows elected.

Q. Have ex-officio *places for student representatives been a success?*
A. Yes. Too much cannot be expected from people who are here for only three years and members of the Council for only one, but on the day-to-day questions of College management their contributions as *ex-officio* members have been much more useful than when they were merely observers at Governing Body meetings. Any right can be abused but in Selwyn the experience has been that when people are entrusted with responsibility they act responsibly. Politically, student representation has been a great success and the two-way flow of information had taken the heat out of disputes that might have been acrimonious.

Q. Was it wise to lower the retiring age of the Master to 67?
A. In general, yes. If a Master holds a University post he must relinquish it at 67, and if he continues after that age his ability to represent the interests of the College in the University diminishes. It is better to make a clean break with both University and College responsibilities at the same time. An escape clause giving Fellows an option to continue a Master beyond the normal retiring age could lead to much friction and bitterness. One Fellow thought that a better course would be to give the electors power to fix the age of retirement when making an offer, taking into account the age and vigour of the nominee.

Q. Are there too many Fellows?
A. There are practical restraints: rooms, the size of High Table, and costs; but if these were overcome, there would be no point at which one could say with convincing logic 'thus far and no further'. There is not a single Fellow whose election was not

justified by performance or promise. Obviously in a large society some Fellows do not wish to take on College administration, but the College does not suffer as long as there is a sufficient number of Fellows who take a different view. It is better for some colleges to feel a little over-crowded than for a large number of University teachers and researchers to nourish resentment because no college wants them.

Q. Is the academic record satisfactory?
A. There is always room for 'could do better', but in general the College looks for good students and then lets them develop their talents without too much hot-house forcing for examinations or preoccupation with league tables. Recent experience shows that students appreciate this approach and often exceed expectations. There are good years and weak years but on the average the Selwyn performance compares well with other colleges.

Q. Is there a case for saying that the College would be healthier with more 'mixed ability' among its junior members?
A. If this is a plea for bending the rules in favour of good athletes it should be dismissed out of hand. Occasionally an applicant might be admitted whose examination record falls a little below the normal standard but who has unusual qualities or an interesting personality. This might apply especially to mature students but with discretion – many men and women in their 30s or 40s will not do well in a residential college where 21-year olds set the tone and tempo.

Q. Has Selwyn benefited from the admission of women?
A. Enormously; the community is better balanced. The presence of both sexes is intellectually and culturally stimulating. There have been 'no significant problems other than those that human nature takes with it everywhere'.

Q. What about graduate students?
A. Selwyn has made efforts to give the graduate students the accommodation and amenities that encourage them to develop a

sense of corporate existence; but more could be done. One Fellow wrote emphatically that they should not be regarded as 'money-raising cuckoos but an essential and increasingly demanding part of the whole, whose needs are still not yet fully addressed'. There is a special difficulty with graduate students here on one-year courses from other universities and a variety of countries. If the new north block is built it might be a good idea to fill it with Fellows and graduate students to make a college within the College.

These questions dealt with internal management. The College prospectus presents the external image that Selwyn wishes to present. It begins with a brief note on the origin of the College and of the man in whose memory it was founded. It states that 'its original aims were to extend university education to those unable to afford it, and to develop a Christian character in its students'. This marks a significant shift in historical interpretation, from 'principles of the Church of England' to 'Christian character'.

Since its foundation, the prospectus continues, Selwyn has 'grown and broadened out in scope and commitment'. There are no denominational tests and 'the College continues to look to the new needs of present day society'. The Chapel welcomes 'Christians and enquirers of all traditions and backgrounds', 'encourages discussion of all aspects of faith, ethics, and social concern', and is 'actively involved in a number of community programmes'. In this way the prospectus brings social concern to the fore, but with a hint that Selwyn is well abreast of such modern needs as engineering and computer science.

The prospectus points out that in Selwyn around 40 per cent of the students are women, and that it is one of the most genuinely mixed colleges in Cambridge. It says that the involvement of students in government and administration 'has succeeded to an extent unrivalled by most Colleges', and it is noted that the prospectus itself was prepared by two Fellows and two students.

Throughout the prospectus 'community' is a recurrent theme. The fact that everyone lives in the College or close by 'must help to foster the sense of community'. Junior members serve on several committees 'that administer the corporate life of the community'.

The Chapel is 'the focus of communal life'. The general statement of aims declares that 'whilst our main purpose is the pursuit of academic excellence in an intellectually challenging and exciting environment, we also view as important our long reputation as a friendly community'.

The prospectus refers only in general terms to the place of Fellows, and one must draw on other and more speculative sources to find how they understand their place in this community. Selwyn is fortunate, now as in the past, in having a core of Fellows who are closely concerned with College business and with the students for whom they are responsible. They are no longer substitute parents and students make their own moral decisions. The old apparatus of rules, designed – though inadequately – to protect adolescents from temptations of the flesh, has gone, and the admission of women has meant that the behavioural code that was once at the heart of collegiate life is irrelevant. For the Fellows active in College business the key to success is co-operation. As senior members they have a certain authority, but they employ it to help junior members make the best use of their talents. The College is a partnership between experience and youth.

Although paternalism has gone, there never has been a time when more people were ready to give more counsel. The Tutors are there to advise and occasionally to warn. Pastoral work that verges on social work occupies much of the Chaplain's time. The University Counselling Service and several voluntary agencies are there to help, and the College has appointed two senior members from other colleges as ombudspersons to whom appeal can be made if anyone suffers sexual harassment.

Apart from the small number engaged in day-to-day College business the Fellowship is no longer a close-knit body. For some, the primary allegiance is to their departments and their guiding light is the esteem of scholars in their chosen field. For them a college is a kind of club; affiliation is valued but mainly for the amenities that it provides. They do the teaching that is required of them (and probably do it well), but are quite content to leave college management in the hands of people who enjoy the work or have been persuaded to do it. People with nostalgic respect for a college as a family are inclined to reproach Fellows who stand apart from its mainstream, but it takes all sorts to make a modern college. Fellows on the periphery may well be at the centre of things in their academic fields, play a key part in research, and enhance the reputation of the college that has welcomed them as members.

However, the analogy of the college as a club is incomplete. Fellows are elected because they do certain jobs – teaching, research, or administration in College or University – and it is this that earns them their privileges. A college is a body of men and women organized to perform certain functions, and though its senior members are not formally assessed they must prove their worth. A Fellow who does not obtain a University post within six years of election may not have his or her Fellowship renewed – if continued, it will be because there is an essential College job to be done. This makes the Fellowship less like a club and more like a corporation with a board of directors (the Council) and with Fellows as executives at the head of its various divisions.

Not many will be happy with this corporate analogy, and much of the social life is designed to dispel the idea that the College is a commercial venture. There are matriculation and graduation dinners; Scholars and advanced students are entertained; Commemoration and Selwyn Association annual dinners perpetuate the idea that the College is not a mere business association lasting for three short years but a relationship that lasts for life.

What this relationship is or ought to be is difficult to explain and impossible to define. When Selwyn celebrated its Jubilee it was still possible to say, as the preamble to the Charter said, that its aim was to educate but also to train young men 'in simple and religious habits according to the principles of the Church of England'. Today the Fellowship includes Roman Catholics, members of other Christian denominations, at least one Jew and a Mohammedan, and others who might style themselves agnostic. The beliefs of some who are nominally Anglican would have been regarded as heretical in 1882. As no enquiry is made into the religious affiliation of students one can do no more than say that over a period of years all the major religions of the world will probably be represented. The Chapel continues to play a prominent part in College life but to keep that position it must be ecumenical in the widest sense of the word.

Must it therefore be said of the founders' intentions nothing remains but buildings and a name? Yes – but to perpetuate a memory is in itself an achievement. Bishop Selwyn was an eminent Victorian, but who save historians of the period would have heard of him today had there been no college bearing his name? As it is, the question will still be asked, 'Who was Selwyn?' And still an answer will be given.

In 1895 Archbishop Edward Benson preached at the dedication of the Chapel, and after referring to Selwyn's services to the Church said that it belonged also to:

> that wider area upon which the spirit and constitution of England, the wisdom and the policy and the tone of our country, have grown up inextricably intertwined with the spirit and growth of a Church which has nurtured and matured a State: each acting and reacting on the other; each mutually inspiring and supporting the other.

Today the Church of England can claim no monopoly but remains the strongest of the strands intertwined with the State's secular character.

The example of one towering personality who was greatly interested in the foundation of Selwyn College can be cited. William Ewart Gladstone's political opinions circled in the course of his long life from High Toryism to radicalism, but the pivot was always the ethical centre. No one changed more with the times or remained more firmly attached to moral standards. But the principles that he regarded as fixed and immutable in his youth shifted and changed with circumstances. This was not moral relativism but realization that the protection and props that one age regards as essential can be removed without destroying the inner temple.

Didactic moral instruction for people who have reached the age of discretion is no longer acceptable and that age has itself been lowered. The hope is that, by example, people who are older, who may be wiser, and who are certainly more knowledgeable will pass on to the rising generation the values of civilized society. On the one hand there is insistence on accuracy, industry, and the quest for truth; on the other emphasis on the College as a community, as a friendly society, as a place in which respect for others and concern about suffering is the normal way of life.

It is fitting to recall that the splendid gifts of George Augustus Selwyn were employed to bring faith and hope to peoples whom others regarded as savage and irredeemable. Few are called to missionary work on his scale, but in every part of life there is need to combat what Archbishop Runcie described in his centennial sermon as 'a cultivated slide into meanness and mediocrity'. One college cannot work miracles, but it can try. This is a duty that Selwyn has not neglected and will not shirk.

Appendix A
The Charter

VICTORIA, by the Grace of God, of the United Kingdom of Great Britain and Ireland, Queen, Defender of the Faith, To ALL TO WHOM these presents shall come, GREETING.

WHEREAS The Right Reverend Father in God, James Russell, Lord Bishop of Ely : The Very Reverend Edward Bickersteth, Dean of Lichfield, Doctor of Divinity : The Reverend Charles Old Goodford, Doctor of Divinity, Provost of Eton : The Reverend Brooke Foss Westcott, Regius Professor of Divinity in the University of Cambridge : The Reverend William Ince, Regius Professor of Divinity in the University of Oxford : The Right Honourable Edward James, Earl of Powis : The Right Honourable William, Lord Bagot : The Right Reverend Father in God, Joseph Barber, Lord Bishop of Durham : The Right Reverend Bishop Edmund Hobhouse : The Right Reverend Bishop Charles John Abraham : Sir Henry Wilmot, Baronet : Sir Walter Rockcliff Farquhar, Baronet : The Venerable Edward Balston, Archdeacon of Derby : The Reverend William Selwyn, Vicar of Bromfield, in the County of Salop: The Reverend Vincent Henry Stanton, Fellow of Trinity College, Cambridge: and William Ford, of 4, South Square, Gray's Inn, in the County of Middlesex, Esquire : HAVE presented their humble Petition to Us, setting forth that at a meeting held on the 21st day of April, 1878, of divers of Our humble Petitioners, with others of Our loving subjects, for the purpose of establishing a public and permanent Memorial of the long and devoted services of the Right Reverend George Augustus Selwyn, D.D., some time Lord Bishop of New Zealand, and late Lord Bishop of Lichfield, deceased, to the Church of

Christ, and in particular the Missionary development thereof, it was unanimously resolved "That the foundation of a College at Cambridge, to be called the 'Selwyn College,' should be submitted to the Church at large as a worthy object by which to perpetuate the noble name and labours of the late Lord Bishop of Lichfield, such College to include provision for the education of the sons of Clergymen and others to fill posts of Missionary work, whether at home or abroad." And that large sums of money had been contributed for carrying such resolution into effect, and for maintaining the College. And that by an Indenture, dated the 3rd day of November, 1879, and made between the Master or Keeper and Fellows of Corpus Christi College, in the University of Cambridge, of the one part, and our Petitioners, the said Edward Bickersteth, and Charles John Abraham, and the Rev. Frederick Thatcher, of the other part, a certain close or parcel of land, situate in the Parish of St. Giles, in the Borough of Cambridge, and in the same Indenture, and the map or plan drawn thereon, particularly described and delineated, with the appurtenances thereto, was granted and assured unto and to the use of the said Edward Bickersteth, Charles John Abraham, and Frederick Thatcher, and their heirs and assigns, in trust for the said proposed undertaking. And further setting forth that Our said Petitioners had been appointed a Council to manage the affairs of the said College ; and that they had elected and appointed the Honourable and Reverend Arthur Temple Lyttelton, M.A., of Trinity College, Cambridge, to be the first Master thereof ; and that Our said Petitioners desired that the said proposed College should be a permanent Memorial of the said George Augustus Selwyn, and should bear the impress of his self-denying character and convictions, and should aim at training young men in simple and religious habits according to the principles of the Church of England. And that Our said Petitioners were assured that the objects of the said undertaking would be more certainly and securely attained if it were protected by Our Royal sanction by means of Our Charter of Incorporation. Our said Petitioners therefore must humbly supplicated Us to grant to them, and to the said Arthur Temple Lyttelton, as the first or present Master and Council of the said

proposed College, and their successors, Our Royal Charter of
Incorporation, for the purpose of constituting them and their
successors a Corporation for the purpose of more effectually carrying
on and conducting the said undertaking, under such regulations and
restrictions, and with such powers as to Us might seem right and
expedient. Now KNOW YE that We, taking the premises into Our
Royal consideration, of Our especial grace, certain knowledge, and
mere motion have granted, constituted, and appointed, and by these
presents for Us, Our heirs, and successors, do grant, constitute,
and appoint as follows (that is to say) :–

1. That for the purpose of establishing, carrying on, and maintaining a College at Cambridge, to be called "Selwyn College,"
Our said Petitioners and the said Arthur Temple Lyttelton, and
their successors, Master and Council for the time being of the
said College, shall be, and they are hereby, constituted a body
politic and corporate by the name of "The Master and Council
of Selwyn College," and shall by that name, and for the purposes
herein mentioned, have perpetual succession and a Common Seal,
with the power to break, alter, and renew the same, at their
discretion, and shall by the same name sue and be sued, plead
and be impleaded, and answer and be answered in all Courts and
before all Justices, of Us Our heirs and successors.

2. That by the same name they shall be able and capable in
law to take, purchase, and hold to them and their successors any
goods, chattels, or personal property whatsoever, and shall also
be able and capable in law, notwithstanding the Statutes of Mortmain and Charitable Uses, and without any compliance with the
provisions of such Statutes as to enrolment or otherwise, to take,
purchase, and hold to them and their successors not only all such
lands, hereditaments, and possessions as are comprised in and
expressed to be assured by the hereinbefore-mentioned Indenture
of the 3rd day of November, 1879, with all buildings erected
thereon, and with such additions thereto as the Master and Council
for the time being may deem expedient, or such as may be from
time to time exclusively used and occupied for the immediate

purposes of the said College, but also any other lands, buildings, hereditaments, and possessions whatsoever, situated within Our United Kingdom of Great Britain and Ireland, not exceeding in the whole (exclusive of the hereditaments comprised in the said Indenture) the annual value of £5,000, such annual value to be calculated and ascertained at the period of taking, purchasing, or acquiring the same, and that they and their successors shall be able and capable in law to grant, demise, alien, exchange, mortgage, or otherwise deal with or dispose of all or any of the property, real or personal, belonging to the said College, upon such terms and in such manner as they shall think fit, and also to do all other matters incidental or appertaining to a body corporate. And We do hereby will, ordain, and declare that the said College is founded and constituted with the especial object and intent of providing persons desirous of academical education, and willing to live economically, with a College wherein sober living and high culture of the mind may be combined with Christian training, based upon the principles of the Church of England.

3. The Archbishop of Canterbury for the time being shall, by virtue of his office, be Visitor of the College, with power to visit and originate inquiry as often as to him shall seem meet.

4. The Master shall always be a Clerk in Holy Orders.

5. The appointment of the said Hon. and Rev. Arthur Temple Lyttelton as the first or present Master shall be and is hereby confirmed, and every future vacancy in the Office arising from any cause whatever shall be filled by such person as the Council shall elect and appoint.

6. The Master, except when prevented by illness or other urgent cause, or when his absence shall be authorised by the Council, shall reside in the College during the Academical terms.

7. Subject to the Statutes or Regulations (if any) for the time being in force, the Master shall have the entire charge of and

jurisdiction over the internal or domestic government of the College, and of its inmates, officers, and servants for the time being. The Bursar shall be subordinate to the Master of the College, but his appointment or removal shall rest with the Council, and to such appointment or removal the consent of the Master, if present, shall be necessary.

8. In case of the illness or absence of the Master, the Council may appoint a Vice-Master with such of the powers of the Master as they may think fit to vest in the Vice-Master.

9. The Master shall be removable from his office only by and at the discretion of the Visitor, and such discretion shall be exercised only under the circumstances hereinafter specified (that is to say) : If it shall appear to a majority consisting of not less than two-thirds in number of not less than seven Members present at a Meeting of the Council, specially convened to consider the propriety of such removal, that the Master is from any cause whatever unfit for the duties of his office, it shall be competent for them to apply in writing to the Visitor to remove the Master, and the Visitor shall have power at his absolute discretion either to act upon or to reject such application.

10. The council shall consist of not more than sixteen Members, and shall not (except as a matter of temporary necessity) be allowed to be reduced in number to less than ten.

11. The council shall consist of the said Earl of Powis, the said Lord Bagot, the said Lord Bishop of Durham, the said James Russell or other the Lord Bishop of Ely for the time being (*ex officio*), the said Edward Bickersteth or other the Dean of Lichfield for the time being (*ex officio*), the said Charles Old Goodford or other the Provost of Eton for the time being (*ex officio*), the said Brooke Foss Westcott or other the Regius Professor of Divinity, Cambridge, for the time being (*ex officio*), the said William Ince or other the Regius Professor of Divinity, Oxford, for the time being (*ex officio*), the said Edmund Hobhouse, the said Charles John Abraham, the said Sir Henry

Wilmot, the said Sir Walter Rockcliff Farquhar, the said Edward Balston, the said William Selwyn, the said Vincent Henry Stanton, and the said William Ford.

12. Each elected Member of Council shall continue to be a Member for his life, subject to the exceptions and provisions hereinafter contained ; but he may, at any time by notice, in writing, addressed to the Master, resign his office.

13. If any Member of Council shall, during the period of three consecutive years, attend no Meeting of the Council, he shall, upon the expiration of such period, cease to be a Member of Council, but he shall be eligible for re-election, either at once or upon the occurrence of any subsequent vacancy.

14. The Visitor, if required in writing by not less than ten Members of Council for the time being so to do, shall have power, if he think fit, by writing under his hand, to remove any elected Member of Council, and the vacancy caused by any such removal of a Member shall be supplied by the election of a new Member.

15. Every vacancy in the Council shall be supplied by the Council ; and the Master, upon receiving notice of a vacancy having occurred, shall, as soon as conveniently may be, convene a Special Meeting of Council for the purpose of electing some fit and able person to supply such vacancy. He shall give twenty-one days' notice of such election, and no election shall take place except in Term time. If such vacancy shall not be supplied before the expiration of six calendar months from the date of its occur-rence, it shall be lawful for the Visitor, if he think proper so to do, to supply the same within three calendar months next after the expiration of such period of six calendar months, or (upon the requisition in writing of a majority of the Members of Council for the time being) at any later period.

16. The Council shall meet for the dispatch of business at Cambridge or elsewhere once at least in every year, and on such

other occasions (if any) as circumstances may render a meeting necessary or desirable.

17. The consent of the Master, if present, shall be necessary to all acts of the Council other than those which relate to the appointment or removal of the Master, Vice-Master, or Members of the Council. He shall preside over the Meetings of the Council, and have the same power as any Member of the Council to propose subjects for consideration by the Council, and in case of there being an equality of votes, shall have a casting vote. If the Master shall be absent, or shall refuse to take the chair, the Chairman shall be such one of the Members present as a majority of such Members shall select, or in default of a selection then the Senior Member according to standing present, and willing to take the chair, shall be Chairman. And in case of equality of votes, such Chairman shall have a second or casting vote in addition to his own vote as a Member of Council.

18. No question shall be decided at any Meeting of the Council, nor shall any business be there transacted, unless at least five Members of Council, or four Members of the Council and the Master, shall be present, or if such business consist in the election of a Master, unless at least seven Members of Council shall be present, or if such business consist in the election of a Member of Council, unless at least seven Members of Council or six Members of Council and the Master shall be present.

19. In all cases, not herein otherwise provided for, the Master and Council shall have the entire management, direction, super-intendence, and control of and over the affairs, concerns, and property of the College, as well as receiving, issuing, investing, layout out, and disposing of all stock, effects, funds, moneys, and securities, as also in contracting for and purchasing messuages, lands, tenements, and hereditaments situated within Our United Kingdom of Great Britain and Ireland, and goods and chattels for the use of the College, and in selling, demising, aliening, mortgaging, exchanging, or otherwise disposing of or dealing with

any property whatever, real or personal, belonging thereto, also in the obtaining the incorporation of the College with the University of Cambridge, and of all gifts, bequests, exhibitions, and endowments which they may deem desirable for the purposes of the said College. Also, in regard to the appointment and removal, number and rank, powers and duties, stipend and emolument of the Bursar, Tutors, and Lecturers, and of the several persons employed in the College, the terms and conditions upon which Scholars and students shall be admitted, and also touching the mode and time of convening Meetings of the Council, and also touching the mode of conducting the business to be transacted at such Meetings respectively, also touching the qualifications as regards age and other circumstances, nomination, and admission of Scholars and Students, and all other matters relating thereto, and in general touching all other matters whatsoever relating to the said College.

20. All moneys belonging to the College shall from time to time be invested in the names or under the legal control of the Master and Council, in or upon some or one of the Public Stocks, or Funds, or Government Securities of our United Kingdom, or any securities, the interest on which is or shall be guaranteed by Parliament, or in Stock of the Bank of England, or of the Metropolitan Board of Works, or upon freehold, copyhold, or chattel real or leasehold securities in England or Wales (but not in Ireland), or in or upon the debentures or debenture stock of any railway company in Our United Kingdom, or the shares or stock of any such railway company, a fixed or minimum rate of dividend on which is guaranteed by the same or any other company, or secured by means of a fixed rental payable by any other company, or in or upon the debentures, debenture stock, shares, or securities, or the guaranteed or preference stock or shares of any insurance, dock, or canal, or other commercial company in Our United Kingdom which shall have paid a dividend of not less than £3 per centum per annum on their ordinary capital for at least three years prior to the date of the investment, or upon charges created under the Improvement of Land Act, 1864, or any mortgages thereof, or debentures issued under the Mortgage Debenture Act,

1865, or in or upon the bonds, debentures, or securities, of or issued by any public, municipal, or local body or authority, in Our United Kingdom, or on the security of rates or tolls made or levied by any such body or authority, or in any other mode of investment in Our United Kingdom, which shall for the time being be authorised as an investment for trustees by Statute or by the Chancery Division of the High Court of Justice, and such investments may, in the discretion of the said Master and Council, be from time to time varied or transposed into or for any others of any nature hereinbefore mentioned.

21. The Master and Council shall have full power from time to time, with the consent of the Visitor, to make and also to alter or vary any Statutes touching the government of the College, the stipend or emoluments of the Master, and also touching any of the matters and things over or in relation to which a general power of management and control is hereby given to the Master and Council, and all other matters relating thereto, and in general touching all other matters whatsoever relating to the College, so as such Statutes be not repugnant to the laws of Our realm, or the general design and spirit of this foundation. And all such Statutes, when reduced into writing, and after the Common Seal of the College hath been affixed thereto, shall be binding upon all persons members thereof.

22. It shall be lawful for the Master and Council for the time being, with the consent of the Visitor, to surrender this Charter, and to wind up the affairs of the Corporation, under and subject to such provisions and arrangements respecting the disposal of the property of the Corporation, and other matters, as the Master and Council shall deem expedient, and as the Visitor shall approve of, due regard being had to all then existing liabilities.

23. It shall be lawful for the Master and Council in all cases unprovided for by this Our Charter to act in such manner as shall appear to them best calculated to promote the welfare of the College.

24. And lastly, We do hereby for Us Our heirs and successors grant and declare that these Our Letters Patent, or the enrolment or exemplification thereof, shall be in all things valid and effectual in the Law according to the true intent and meaning of the same, and shall be construed and adjudged in the most favourable and beneficial sense for the best advantage of the said College, as well in all Our Courts as elsewhere, notwithstanding any recital, mis-recital, uncertainty, or imperfection in these Our Letters Patent. In Witness thereof We have caused these Our Letters to be made Patent. Witness Ourself at Our Palace at Westminster, the thir-teenth day of September, in the forty-sixth year of Our Reign.

By Her Majesty's Command.   (L.S.)   CARDEW.

Appendix B
The Present Statutes

The statutes in force in 1994 were approved by the Queen in Council on 7 February 1989. The principal statutes affecting the character and government of the College are printed below together with summaries in italics of those statutes and clauses that deal with minor, procedural, or technical matters.

STATUTES TO REVISE THE STATUTES OF SELWYN COLLEGE IN THE UNIVERSITY OF CAMBRIDGE, WHICH AMENDING STATUTES HAVING BEEN DULY MADE AT A MEETING OF THE GOVERNING BODY OF THE SAID COLLEGE, SPECIALLY SUMMONED FOR THE PURPOSE AND HELD ON THE THIRTY FIRST DAY OF MAY, 1988, AND PASSED AT SUCH MEETING BY THE VOTES OF NOT LESS THAN TWO-THIRDS OF THE NUMBER OF PERSONS PRESENT AND VOTING, AND NOTICE THEREOF HAVING BEEN GIVEN TO THE UNIVERSITY, ARE NOW SUBMITTED FOR THE APPROVAL OF HER MAJESTY IN COUNCIL.

We, the Governing Body of Selwyn College in the University of Cambridge, do hereby in pursuance of the power vested in us by section 7(2) of the Universities of Oxford and Cambridge Act, 1923, revise and amend the Statutes of the said College in the manner following, that is to say:–

PREAMBLE

Selwyn College was founded in 1882 in memory of George Augustus Selwyn, Bishop successively of New Zealand and of Lichfield, on land in the parish of St. Giles purchased from the Master, Fellows and Scholars of Corpus Christ College, with the object of providing a University education for young men in a College at Cambridge conducted in accordance with the principles of the Church of England.

It was incorporated by Royal Charter dated 13 September 1882 under the name of the Master and Council of Selwyn College. The Charter of Incorporation provided that the said Master and Council should have full power from time to time, with the consent of the Visitor of the College, to make and also to alter or vary statutes termed "Charter Statutes" touching all matters whatsoever relating to the College, so as such statutes should not be repugnant to the laws of the Realm, or the general design and spirit of the foundation of the said College. The Charter of Incorporation further provided that all such statutes, when reduced into writing, and after the Common Seal of the College should have been affixed thereto, should be binding upon all persons thereof. The Charter of Incorporation and the power of making charter Statutes thereunder were modified by statutes made by the University of Cambridge Commissioners dated 26 March 1926, under the provisions of the Universities of Oxford and Cambridge Act, 1923, which statutes were termed "Privy Council Statutes" and made subject to alteration from time to time in accordance with the eleventh of the said statutes.

Under the Universities of Oxford and Cambridge Act 1923, the Governing Body of a college has power to alter the statutes of a College. The Selwyn College Cambridge Act 1988, which was enacted on 15 March 1988, amends the Universities of Oxford and Cambridge Act 1923 so as to provide that the Governing Body of Selwyn College for the purposes of altering the statutes is the Head and all Fellows, not the Master and Council as originally provided for, and makes further provision for the government of the College.

The Charter of Incorporation and the Privy Council Statutes as heretofore altered have been further amended by these statues, which were approved by Her Majesty in Council on 7th February 1989 (hereinafter called the "date of operation").

STATUTE 1
Of the Name and Corporate Title of the College

The corporation created by the Royal Charter of Incorporation dated 13 September 1882 shall continue to be called Selwyn College Cambridge. Its corporate title shall henceforth be "The Head, Fellows and Scholars of Selwyn College".

STATUTE 2
Of the Visitor

The Visitor shall have final jurisdiction over the internal affairs of the College, including the interpretation, enforcement and application of the Charter, the Statutes and any Rules or Regulations made under them.

STATUTE 3
Of the Members of the College
The members of the College shall be the Head of House, the Fellows, the scholars, those students in residence who have been admitted under Statute 29, and such other persons as the College Council shall by Regulation determine.

STATUTE 4
Of the Governing Body
 1. Subject to Statute 33 on leave of absence, the Governing Body shall consist of the Head of House, all Fellows holding under any of the Titles A, B, C and D, and three junior members; except that for the transaction of reserved business as defined in Statute 35 of the Governing Body shall consist of the Head and Fellows holding under Titles A, B, C and D only.

 2. For the purpose of making and amending the statutes of the College the Governing Body shall be constituted as required by the Oxford and Cambridge Act 1923 (as amended by the Selwyn College Cambridge Act 1988), or such other legislation as is currently in force.

 3. The junior members referred to in section 1 shall be the President of the Middle Combination Room, and the President and Treasurer of the Junior Combination Room. The President of the Middle Combination Room shall be a resident student member of the College, and the President and Treasurer of the Junior Combination Room shall be resident student members of the College who are undergraduates.

 4. For the purpose of electing Junior Members of the Governing Body the Middle Combination Room shall consist of those resident student members of the College who have Ordinary or Honours Degrees or are affiliated students, excluding Fellows of the College, and the Junior Combination Room shall consist of all other resident student members. The election of Junior Members of the Governing Body shall take place according to a system approved by the Governing Body.

 5. The Head of House may invite any person to be present at any meeting of the Governing Body but without vote.

6. A meeting of the Governing Body shall be held at such intervals as the Governing Body shall by Regulation determine; provided

    (i) there shall always be at least one meeting in every Michaelmas Term for the election of the College Council,

    (ii) the Head of House shall summon a meeting whenever requested to do so by any six members of the Governing Body,

    (iii) the Head of House may summon a meeting whenever there is sufficient business.

7. Except where these statutes otherwise provide, the Governing Body shall be competent to transact its business if there are present at least ten members, but not otherwise.

8. The Governing Body shall elect one of its members to be Secretary. The Secretary shall serve for such period as is specified at the time of his or her election or re-election, but shall cease to hold office on ceasing to be a member of the Governing Body. The Secretary shall receive such emoluments as the College Council shall from time to time determine.

STATUTE 5
Of the College Council

1. The College Council shall consist of the Head of House, the Deputy, the Senior Tutor and the Bursar; eight senior members of the Governing Body elected by the senior members of the Governing Body in accordance with section 2 of this statute; and (except for the conduct of reserved business as defined in Statute 35) the three junior members referred to in Statute 4(3).

2. (*a*) Not later than the Division of the Michaelmas Term the Head of House shall invite senior members of the Governing Body to make nominations for the College Council.

    (*b*) A candidate may be nominated and seconded by other members of the Governing Body, provided he or she consents to stand. Alternatively, a member of the Governing Body may nominate himself or herself by notifying the Head of House that he or she wishes to be a candidate. To be valid a nomination must be received by the Head not later than seven days from the date on which the Head invited nominations. The Head shall notify all the senior members of the governing body of all nominations.

(c) If the number of nominations exceeds the number of vacancies the election shall take place according to a system laid down in Regulations by the Governing Body; provided that it shall always be by secret ballot, and no Fellow shall be entitled to cast more votes than any other.

(d) Members elected to the College Council shall take office on the first day of January following their election and shall hold office for four years, except where they are elected to fill a casual vacancy.

(e) The Governing Body shall have power by Regulation to fix the period (if any) which must elapse between the end of one period of service as an elected member of the College Council and the beginning of the next.

(f) If an elected member of the College Council shall
  (i) become an ex officio member; or
  (ii) cease to be a member of the Governing Body; or
  (iii) take leave of absence for more than a single University Term,
he or she shall cease to be an elected member of the College Council, and an election shall be held according to the procedure set out in paragraphs (b) and (c) of this Statute to fill any vacancy so occurring.

(g) When ex officio members of the College Council take leave of absence for one or more Terms, and when elected members take leave of absence for a single Term, the College Council shall replace them by temporarily co-opting other senior members of the Governing Body. Persons co-opted under this provision shall be in the same position as elected members for as long as they are co-opted.

(h) A member of the Governing Body shall be eligible for election to the Council notwithstanding that his or her Fellowship is due to expire within four years of the date upon which he or she would take office if elected.

(i) The first election to the College Council shall take place as soon as is practicable after these statutes come into force. Two of the members elected on this occasion shall serve for four years, two for three years, two for two years, and two for one year. After their election, the candidates shall draw lots among themselves to decide who shall serve for what period. Paragraph (e) above shall apply to all the members who are so elected to serve for two years or more, but not to those who are so elected to serve for one year only.

3. A meeting of the College Council shall be summoned by the Head of House whenever he or she considers that there is sufficient business, whenever any four members of the Council so request, or whenever any six members of the Governing Body so request under Statute 6(6); provided that there shall be at least three meetings each Term and not less than two in the Long Vacation.

4. Save as provided otherwise by these Statutes the College Council shall be competent to transact its business if there are present at least eight senior members, but not otherwise.

5. The College Council shall elect a Secretary who shall hold office for such period as it shall specify. The Secretary shall perform such duties and receive such emoluments as the Council shall from time to time determine. The Secretary may be, but need not be a member of the Council. If he or she is not a member of the Council the Secretary shall not have a vote.

6. Subject to Statute 35(8) (personal interest), any Fellow who is a member of the Governing Body shall have the right to attend meetings of the Council, but without the right to speak or vote.

7. The College Council may co-opt any member of the Governing Body for a particular purpose. That member shall have the right to speak, but not (except as provided by Statute 12(7) on the election of Fellows) to vote.

STATUTE 6

Of the powers and functions of the Governing Body and the College Council

1. The Governing Body may exercise any of the powers vested in the College by law, and shall have the control of the College as a place of religion, education, learning and research, except—

    (i) in so far as these Statutes grant powers and impose duties upon the College Council or upon other bodies or persons, and

(ii) in so far as the Governing Body shall delegate its powers and duties to the College Council.

2. The Governing Body may delegate to the College Council its powers and duties over general categories of business by making Regulations, when such powers and duties shall be exercisable by the Council and not by the Governing Body for as long as the Regulations remain in force. The Governing Body may also delegate specific items of business to the Council from time to time. Provided that the following matters shall not be delegated:

(i) making regulations for elections to the College Council (Statute 5);

(ii) removal of the Head of House (Statute 10);

(iii) election and removal of the Deputy Head of House (Statute 11);

(iv) removal of Fellows (Statute 13);

(v) election and removal of Honorary Fellows (Statute 17);

(vi) the changing and interpretation of Statutes (Statutes 36 and 37).

3. The College Council shall have such powers and duties as are conferred upon it by these Statutes, together with such of the powers and duties of the Governing Body as the Governing Body shall delegate it.

4. The Governing Body and the College Council shall have power to delegate any matter over which it has jurisdiction to a committee. In the case of the College Council, this power shall include the power to sub-delegate business delegated to it by the Governing Body. In either case, the committee may include persons who are not members of the parent body.

5. The Governing Body and the College Council shall have power to make Regulations for the purpose of ordering their own procedure and for the management of the College generally.

6. The Head of House shall call a special meeting of the Council if any six members of the Governing Body request this by written notice. Any six members of the Governing Body may require the Council to consider a specific item of business at such a meeting, or at an ordinary meeting, by giving written notice to the Head of House. Such rights shall not prejudice any other rights of members of the Governing Body to make representations to the Council which are conferred by these Statutes or by Regulations.

7. The Governing Body shall be entitled at any meeting

   (i) to pass resolutions criticising the College Council for its handling of any matter;

   (ii) to withdraw its delegation of any matter or class of matter of Governing Body business from the College Council;

   (iii) at a special meeting called under Statute 4(6)(ii) it shall in addition be entitled to remove from office the eight elected senior members of the Council.

8. If the eight elected senior members of the Council are so removed there shall be a fresh election. Statute ((2) shall govern the election, except that the election shall be held forthwith, and the Council members who were removed from office shall be eligible to stand for re-election, and those who are elected shall take office immediately and shall serve for periods laid down in Statute 5(2)(i).

9. If a special meeting of the Governing Body is called to discuss the College Council's handling of any particular matter, the College Council shall not proceed further in that matter until that meeting has been held; but no decision at such a meeting shall render invalid any decision which the College Council had validly made before that meeting was called.

10. The College Council shall not

   (i) sell any land,

   (ii) embark on any scheme of capital expenditure beyond any financial limit laid down from time to time in Regulations by the Governing Body,

   (iii) make any gift or grant in excess of any financial limit laid down from time to time in Regulations by the Governing Body,

without having given at least twenty-eight days' notice to the Governing Body; provided that no failure to observe this section of this Statute shall render any transaction invalid as against any person who does not know of it and who deals with the College Council in good faith.

STATUTE 7
Of the College Meeting

1. At a convenient date in each year the Head of House shall invite all Fellows to a College Meeting to receive the report of the Auditors of the plate and of the pictures and of such other property as the Governing

Body may have directed particular record to be kept, and to pass the Combination Room Accounts. The same Meeting shall nominate to the Governing Body two Auditors of the plate and common goods, and appoint a Secretary of the Combination Room, for the ensuing year.

2. The Head of House may, with the consent of the governing Body, summon the College Meeting at other times to discuss such amenities of the College as concern all Fellows.

3. No resolution shall be put at a College Meeting unless notice thereof has been given to the Fellows at least three days before the meeting.

4. Neither the Governing Body nor the College Council shall be bound to accept nominations or recommendations made by the College Meeting.

5. The Head may invite any College Officer who is not a Fellow to be present without vote at a College Meeting.

STATUTE 8
Of the Election of the Head of House

1. The Head of House shall be elected by the Fellows under Titles A, B, C and D, hereafter referred to as 'the electors'.

2. They shall elect that person whom they believe most suitable to exercise the functions of the Head of the College as a place of religion, education, learning and research, and who they believe will respect the Anglican tradition of the College.

3. The convenor of the electors shall be the Deputy Head of House, unless he or she is unable or unwilling, in which case it shall be the senior elector who is able and willing to act. The Deputy shall also be the chairman of the electors, unless he or she is unable or unwilling, or is or becomes a candidate for the office, in which case the electors shall choose one of their number who is not a candidate to act as chairman.

4. The quorum for a meeting of the electors shall be two-thirds of the electors.

Clauses 5 to 10 of Statute 8 deal with the procedure to be followed when electing a head of the house. Clause 11 gives the Visitor the right to appoint if the office has been vacant for more than twelve months. Clause 12 deals with obtaining the consent of the successful candidate to election, and with his or her admission by the Visitor or a deputy appointed by the Visitor.

Statute 8, Clause *13 requires the person elected to declare that he or she will 'respect the Anglican tradition of the College, and in all things endeavour to promote the honour and well-being of the College as a place of religion, education, learning and research'.*

STATUTE 9
Of the Head of House

1. If the Head of House is a man he shall be called the Master; if a woman she shall be called the Mistress.

2. It shall be the duty of the Head of House to protect and further the interests of the College in the University and elsewhere; to exercise a general superintendence over the affairs of the College; to see that these Statutes are duly observed; and in cases not provided for by these Statutes or by Regulations or by decisions of the Governing Body or the College Council, to make such provision for the good government of the College as he or she shall think fit.

3. The Head of House shall be entitled to such stipend and allowances in money, goods or services as the Electors shall determine at the time of his or her election. Thereafter both stipend and allowances may be varied by the College Council from time to time; provided that the stipend shall not be reduced during the Head's tenure of office without his or her consent given in writing.

4. The Head of House shall be entitled to the exclusive use of the Lodge free of rent and rates during tenure of the office if he or she chooses to reside there.

5. At the time of the election the Electors shall determine the distance from the College within which the Head of House shall ordinarily reside, and if he or she chooses not to make his or her home in the Lodge the Head shall reside within that distance. They shall also determine at the time of the election how long in each Term and each calendar year he or she must (unless on leave) reside within that distance. With the Head's consent, both the distance and the time may be varied thereafter by the Governing Body.

6. The Head of House shall not hold any other college office except, where he or she is a clerk in holy orders, that of Dean of Chapel. He or she may continue to hold such other offices, employments and public responsibilities (in the University or elsewhere) as the Electors may determine at the time of his or her election. Except when on leave, the

Head shall not acquire or hold any other time-consuming office, employment or public responsibility without the consent of the College Council, which shall not be unreasonably withheld.

7. The Head of House may at any time resign by giving notice to the Governing Body.

8. The Head of House shall vacate office at the end of the academical year in which he or she attains the age of sixty-seven.

9. A former Head of House may become a Fellow under Statute 15(1)(E)(iv), but not otherwise.

Statute 10 deals with the procedure for removing a head of house (a vote of two-thirds of the Fellows is required, and the head of the house has the right of appeal to the Visitor, whose decision will be final.

STATUTE II
Of the Deputy Head of House

1. The Governing Body shall elect a Fellow from among its members to be Deputy Head of House. If a man he shall be called the Vice-Master, if a woman she shall be called the Vice-Mistress.

Clauses 2 to 4 of Statute 11 deal with the tenure and duties of the Deputy Head of House.

STATUTE 12
Of the Election of Fellows

1. A fellow shall be elected by the College Council on the nomination of the Head of House.

2. Except where the expedited procedure for the election of a Fellow contained in Statute 12(8) is used, the Head of House shall not proceed to nominate a person for election to a Fellowship unless he or she has given eleven clear days' notice in writing to each senior member of the Governing Body of his intention to do so.

3. Subject to the provisions of Statute 12(8) that person shall be held elected as a Fellow who shall have received the votes of two-thirds at least of the members of the College Council present and voting (including co-opted members) provided that at least eight votes were recorded in his or her favour.

4. Every member of the College Council (including co-opted members) shall vote for that person whom he or she judges best qualified to promote the interests of the College as a place of religion, education, learning and research.

5. The Head of House shall, before nominating for election to a Fellowship, read aloud to the Council section 4 of this Statute.

6. When electing a Fellow, the Council shall declare the Title under which he or she is elected in accordance with the provisions of Statute 15(1), specify (subject to Statute 15(5) below) the tenure of the Fellowship, and name a date on which the election shall take effect.

7. Where the Head of House proposes to nominate a person for election as a teaching or research Fellow, the Council shall co-opt such members of the Governing Body as it shall declare to have special knowledge of the relevant area of scholarship. Such co-opted members shall be entitled to be present at the meeting of the Council while the relevant business is transacted and to speak and vote thereat. But no Fellow shall be so co-opted who will have ceased to be a Fellow before the person under consideration will have been admitted as a Fellow if he or she is elected.

8. As an alternative to the procedure in sections 2 and 3 of this Statute, the Council may adopt an expedited procedure for the election of Fellows. This procedure may only be used where the Governing Body has by resolution:
   (i) identified an area of scholarship in which the College has need of a Fellow and indicated that speed is required to make an election; and
   (ii) authorised the College Council to use the expedited procedure for such an election.

9. Where the expedited election procedure is used no notice of intention to nominate shall be required to be given to members of the Governing Body, but at least three days' notice in writing of intention to nominate shall be given by the Head of House to all Senior members of the Council (including members co-opted under section 7 of this Statute).

10. Election on the expedited procedure shall require the unanimous vote of all Council members present and voting, and at least eight votes recorded in favour of the nominee.

11. The provisions of sections 4, 5, and 6 of this Statute shall apply to elections on the expedited procedure.

12. Notwithstanding sections 2, 3, 4, 5, 6, 7, 8, 9 and 10 of this Statute the College Council may re-elect a person who already holds a Fellowship to a further period of tenure by a simple majority and without any special notice being given.

STATUTE 13
Of the removal of Fellows

1. If the Governing Body are satisfied that there is cause of sufficient gravity for so doing, it may by a resolution approved by two-thirds at least of the Governing Body deprive a Fellow of his or her Fellowship or suspend him or her therefrom.

2. Before voting to suspend a Fellow or to deprive him or her of his or her Fellowship the Governing Body shall first inform him or her of any matter against that Fellow and give him or her the opportunity to answer the case for removal from office, in person if he or she so desires. Provided that it shall not be necessary to inform that Fellow if his or her physical disability or any other irremovable cause makes it impossible to communicate with him or her.

3. A Fellow who has been suspended or deprived of his or her Fellowship shall be entitled within thirty days to appeal to the Visitor, who shall have power to confirm, vary or reverse the decision of the Governing Body, and whose decision shall be final.

STATUTE 14
Of the Admission of a Fellow-Elect

1. As soon after the election of a Fellow has taken effect as may be convenient he or she shall be admitted by the Head of House according to such procedure as may be determined from time to time by the Governing Body.

2. At the time of admission, the person elected shall first make and sign the following declaration, the Head and Fellows present bearing witness:

> "I A.B., solemnly declare that I will respect the Charter and observe the Statutes of the College, obey the Head of House in the exercise of his/her statutory powers, discharge to the best of my ability such business of the College as may be

entrusted to me, and endeavour at all times to promote the honour and usefulness of the College as a place of religion, education, learning and research."

3. Where immediately on the termination of his or her Fellowship a Fellow continues to be a Fellow under the same or another Title no re-admission shall be necessary; but it shall be necessary to admit a former Fellow where his or her Fellowship ceased before his or her election.

STATUTE 15
Of the Fellows

1. A Fellow shall hold his or her Fellowship under one or other of the following Titles, that is to say:

A. by holding one of the following offices in the College: Bursar, Assistant Bursar, Senior Tutor, Tutor, Chaplain, Lecturer; or by holding such other office as the Governing Body shall specify by Regulation;

B. by holding a University teaching or administrative office as defined by the Statutes and Ordinances of the University, the office being specified for the purpose of this Statute by the Governing Body at the time of election;

C. by election into a Fellowship on the grounds of academic or other distinction;

D. by election into a Research Fellowship in order to undertake or continue a course of research under such conditions as may be approved by the Governing Body;

E. by reason of any of the following:

   (i) having held a Fellowship under any of the foregoing titles for a period of twenty years and having ceased to hold it (otherwise than by removal under Statute 13);

   (ii) having held such a Fellowship for a period of five years and having ceased to hold it on attaining the age of sixty-seven;

   (iii) having held such a Fellowship for a period of ten years and having resigned in order to take premature retirement; provided in this case that the Governing Body resolves that he or she shall remain a Fellow;

   (iv) having retired or resigned from the office of Head of House.

2. A Fellow shall be entitled to such stipend, if any, as the College Council shall determine from time to time; provided that nothing in

this section shall authorise any person to be elected to a stipendiary Fellowship who holds a University office which by University Statute is not tenable with such a Fellowship.

3. The tenure of a Fellow holding under Title A, Title B, Title C, or Title D shall be determined by the College Council at the time of his or her election or re-election, provided that the period so determined shall not exceed five years, and that, in the case of a Fellow holding under Title D, the total tenure shall not exceed six years.

4. A person qualified for a Fellowship under Title E shall not need to be elected or admitted to his or her Fellowship. Subject to the provisions of Statute 13 (on expulsion) he or she shall be entitled to hold his or her Fellowship for life.

5. If a Fellow holding under Title B ceases to hold the office which qualifies him or her for such Fellowship, he or she shall cease to hold the Fellowship; but if he or she immediately assumes another office which qualifies him or her for a Fellowship under Title B the Governing Body may by resolution declare that he or she may continue to hold his or her Fellowship by virtue of the new office and accordingly Statute 12 (on election) shall not apply.

6. If a Fellow becomes Head of House he or she shall cease to be a Fellow unless and until he or she acquires a Fellowship by operation of section 1(E)(iv) of this Statute.

7. If a Fellow becomes Head or Fellow (other than an Honorary Fellow) of another College in Cambridge his or her Fellowship shall cease and he or she shall not become a Fellow under Title E.

8. If a Fellow under Title A, B, C or D becomes Head or a Fellow (other than an Honorary Fellow) at a College in the University of Oxford his or her Fellowship shall cease, and although otherwise qualified he or she shall not thereby become a Fellow under Title E unless the Governing Body so resolves.

9. If a Fellow under Title A, B, C or D takes up any full-time post outside the University of Cambridge his or her Fellowship shall cease, unless the Governing Body resolves that it shall continue. If it ceases, and he or she is otherwise qualified, he or she shall become a Fellow under Title E.

10. No Fellow shall hold under more than one Title at the same time.

11. A Fellow who has communicated his or her resignation of his or her Fellowship in writing to the Head of House and has not withdrawn it shall vacate the Fellowship when his or her resignation has been communicated to the College Council.

12. No-one shall be elected a Fellow under title A, B, C or D after he or she has attained the age of sixty-seven. A Fellow under Title A, B, C or D shall cease to hold such Fellowship at the end of the academic year in which he or she attains the age of sixty-seven.

13. Fellows shall rank in the following order of seniority:
   (i) former Heads of House, by date of office;
   (ii) the Deputy Head of House;
   (iii) other Fellows, by the date of their election.

In the case of a person who is re-elected when he or she already holds a Fellowship, his or her seniority shall date from the original election; in the case of a former Fellow who no longer holds a Fellowship at the time of election, seniority shall date from when he or she is elected being then a former Fellow, unless the College Council otherwise decides.

The College Council shall determine the seniority of Fellows who are elected on the same date, either at the date of their election, or as soon as possible thereafter.

STATUTE 16
Of the Rights and Privileges of the Fellows

Each Class of Fellows shall be entitled to such privileges, emoluments and allowances as the College Council shall determine. The College Council may add to the privileges of a Fellow holding under any Title, and vary or withdraw such privileges as have been granted.

Statute 17 deals with Honorary Fellows and Statue 18 with Visiting Fellows

STATUTE 19
Of the Scholars and Exhibitioners

1. The College Council may elect persons to scholarships and exhibitions. There shall be as many Scholars and Exhibitioners as the College Council shall from time to time determine.

2. The annual value of a Scholarship or an Exhibition or a prize or any other emoluments which may be paid to students shall be such as the College Council shall from time to time determine.

3. The College Council shall determine the tenure of a Scholarship or Exhibition at the time of election of a Scholar or Exhibitioner.

4. Every Scholar elect shall be admitted to his or her Scholarship by the Head of House according to the procedure laid down by the College Council.

5. The College Council may for sufficient reason suspend or terminate the tenure of a Scholarship or Exhibition. Before doing so the College Council shall inform the person concerned of the matter against him or her, and shall give him or her the opportunity to explain himself or herself, in person where practicable. He or she shall have the right to appeal within thirty days to the Governing Body, whose decision shall be final.

STATUTE 20
Of the Officers of the College

1. There shall be in the College a Bursar, a Senior Tutor, a Dean, a Praelector, a Librarian, a Chaplain, and as many Tutors and Lecturers and other Officers as the College Council may from time to time determine.

2. Any Officer to whom this Statute applies shall be appointed by the College Council on the nomination of the Head of House. The tenure of an Officer shall be fixed by the College Council at the time of appointment or reappointment, provided that the period so determined shall not exceed five years.

3. If the College Council is satisfied that there is cause of sufficient gravity for so doing, it may by a resolution approved by two-thirds at least of the College Council remove or suspend a College Officer from office. An Officer who has been suspended or deprived of Office shall be entitled to appeal within thirty days to the Visitor, who may confirm, vary, or reverse the decision of the College Council, and whose decision shall be final. Before voting to remove or suspend a College Officer the College Council shall first inform him or her of any matter against him or her and give him or her the opportunity to answer the case for his or her removal from office, in person where he or she so desires. Provided that it shall not be necessary to inform the officer if his or

her physical disability or any other irremovable cause makes it impossible to communicate with him or her.

4. Subject to what is expressly provided elsewhere in these statutes, the powers, duties, privileges and emoluments of College Officers appointed under this Statute shall be such as the College Council shall determine. They may be varied from time to time.

5. The College Council may by Regulation require any College Officer to live within a prescribed distance of the College.

6. A College Officer who has communicated his or her resignation from Office in writing to the Head of House and has not withdrawn it shall vacate Office when his or her resignation has been communicated to the College Council.

7. An Officer to whom this Statute applies shall cease to hold Office at the end of the academical year in which he or she attains the age of sixty-seven years.

8. If an Officer to whom this Statute applies is granted leave of absence, the College Council may appoint another person to act in his or her place. The person so appointed shall have all the powers of the Officer for whom he or she is acting.

Statute 21 deals with the superannuation scheme.

STATUTE 22
Of the Senior Tutor and Tutors

1. Every student member of the College shall be allocated as a pupil to a Tutor.

2. The allocation shall be made by the Head of House, or such other College Officer as he or she shall with the approval of the College Council appoint.

3. It shall be the duty of a Tutor to look after the welfare of his or her pupils, to advise them in respect of their studies, and to co-operate with the Dean in maintaining discipline among the students of the College.

4. In carrying out these duties, a Tutor shall have power to impose fines on his or her pupils within the limits laid down by Regulations,

and with the concurrence of the Head of House to order their temporary removal from College for a period which does not prevent them from keeping Term.

5. The Senior Tutor shall have such duties as the College Council shall from time to time determine.

STATUTE 23
Of the Dean

1. The Dean shall in conjunction with the Senior Tutor and Tutors be responsible to the Governing Body for maintaining good discipline and the observance of College Regulations on the part of students of the College.

Clauses 2, 3 and 4 of Statute 23 deal with powers of the Dean to fine and punish. Statute 24 deals with the Board of Discipline (normally Senior Tutor and three Tutors).

STATUTE 25
Of the College Chapel

1. There shall be a College Chapel.

2. Prayers according to the use of the Church of England, or such other order as the Dean of Chapel may allow, shall be said or sung each morning and evening in the College Chapel during Full Term and on such other days as the Dean of Chapel shall direct.

3. The Holy Communion according to the use of the Church of England, or such other order as the Visitor may approve, shall be celebrated on all Sundays and Holy Days in Full Term and on such other days as the Dean of Chapel shall direct, and there shall also be said in the Chapel such other services as the Dean of Chapel may think fit.

STATUTE 26
Of the Dean of Chapel

1. There shall be a Dean of Chapel. The Head of House, if a clerk in Anglican orders, shall be the Dean of Chapel; unless, at his or her request and with the approval of the Visitor, the Governing Body shall resolve that for the period of the Head's office another person shall be Dean of Chapel.

2. If the Head is not a clerk in Anglican orders, or if the Governing Body has passed a resolution under section 1 of this Statute, the Dean of Chapel shall be a Fellow who is a clerk in Anglican orders appointed by the College Council subject to the approval of the Visitor. He or she may be, but need not be, the Chaplain.

3. The Dean of Chapel shall have control over the services in the College Chapel; he or she shall be responsible for the Sacred Vessels, Ornaments and books in the College Chapel; his or her consent shall be necessary for any use of the Chapel for purposes other than those expressly authorised by these Statutes and any Regulations made under them; and he or she shall have such other duties and responsibilities as the College Council shall from time to time determine.

4. The Dean of Chapel may delegate the direction of the music in Chapel to a suitably qualified person.

5. Section (8) of Statute 20 (deputies during leave of absence) shall apply to the Dean of Chapel. The other provisions of Statute 20 shall apply to an elected Dean of Chapel except where they are inconsistent with the terms of this Statute.

STATUTE 27
Of the Chaplain

1. The College Council shall appoint a Chaplain to perform services in Chapel and to carry out such pastoral and other duties as the College Council shall from time to time determine.

STATUTE 28
Of the Bursar

1. The Bursar shall under the direction of the College Council have care of the property, income, and expenditure of the College, and shall be responsible for the proper keeping of its accounts ... and shall, with approval of the Head of House, appoint and dismiss servants of the College, agree their conditions of employment and regulate their work. *(Clause 2 gives the Council power to appoint a Steward or Assistant Bursar.)*

Statute 29 deals with the admission of students. They cannot be admitted unless they have satisfied the conditions laid down by the University, but subject to this rule the Council can determine who shall be admitted (normally delegating this power to named College officers) and on what conditions.

Statutes 30 to 34 deal with finance, audit, endowments, and use of the College seal.

Statute 35 deals with the conduct of meetings of the Council, Governing Body, and other committees. It defines the reserved business on which the student members have no vote and are present for discussion only if invited by the head of house. The reserved business includes matters affecting the employment of any individual (this includes the election of Fellows and appointment of College officers), discipline, and other matters at the discretion of the Chairman.

Statutes 36 to 39 deal with the power to change the statutes; in disputes over interpretation and contravention the decision of the Visitor is final if an appeal is lodged.

Statute 40 deals with the repeal of all former statutes but declares that 'the Charter of Incorporation of Selwyn College dated 13 September 1882 shall remain in force up to the words "within our United Kingdom of Great Britain and Northern Ireland" in Clause 2, and substituting for the words "Master and Council" in Clause 1 the words "Head, Fellows and Scholars of Selwyn College", and elsewhere the words "Governing Body" '.

Appendix C
The Masters and Fellows of
Selwyn 1913–94

Degrees other than DD, LittD, ScD, MD are not given.

Present (1994) holders are shown in bold type. Retired Fellows retaining their Fellowships (Class E) are marked (*).

Masters

1882–93	The Revd and Hon. Arthur Temple Lyttelton.
1893–98	The Right Revd John Richardson Selwyn – died in office.
1898–1907	The Very Revd Alexander Francis Kirkpatrick, DD.
1907–09	The Revd Richard Appleton – died in office.
1909–28	The Revd John Owen Farquhar Murray, DD.
1928–34	The Revd George Ernest Newsom – died in office.
1934–47	The Right Revd George Armitage Chase, MC.
1947–55	The Revd William Telfer, MC, DD.
1955–83	The Revd William Owen Chadwick, OM, KBE, DD, Hon Ltt.D, FBA, FRSE. (*)
1983–93	Sir Alan Cook Kt, FRS, FRSE, Sc.D. (*)
1994–	**David Harrison**, CBE, Sc.D, F.Eng.

* Now Fellows in Class E.

Fellows

Fellows are grouped by year of election in five-year periods.

Vice-Masters, Senior Tutors, and Bursars (but not other College offices) are noted.

No Fellow elected before 1934 is still living; Fellows and former Fellows who have died since that year are marked (d). Research Fellows are marked (R) unless elected on exspiry of their tenure to a Fellowship in another class.

Fellowships at other Cambridge Colleges, and in a few instances offices outside Cambridge, are given in italics.

1913–15

1913–35 Hammett Charles Knott – Mathematics – Bursar

1913–36 William Edward Jordan – History – Vice-Master

1913–46 Lancelot Alexander Borradaile – Zoology – Vice-Master. ScD.

1913–65 William Nalder Williams – Classics – Secretary of the Local Examinations Syndicate 1921–45.

1913–15 The Revd Spencer Cecil Carpenter – Theology – *Dean of Exeter, 1924.*

1915–20 The Revd Stanley Charles Phillips – Theology.

1924–4

1920–53 The Revd Fred Shipley Marsh – Lady Margaret's Professor of Divinity, 1935.

1920–61 George Burr Perrett – History – Bursar.

1923–90 Philip John Durrant – Chemistry – Senior Tutor, Vice-Master.

1923–7 The Revd John Raphael Peacey – Theology.

1925–9

1928–61 The Revd Arthur Cecil Blyth MC – Theology – Senior Tutor, Vice-Master.

1928–44 Frank Harrison Woodward – Economics, Honorary Fellow 1983–94.

1930–4

1933–46   Charles William Phillips – History – excavated Sutton Hoo ship burial, *Director Archaeological Survey, Ordnance Survey.*

1933–6   Kenneth Allan Caldwell Elliott – Biochemistry – *Montreal Institute of Neuroscience.*

1935–9

1935–40   John Cecil Walker – History.

1935–74   Wilfred James Sartain – Classics. Secretary-General of the Faculties – Vice-Master. (d)

1938–50   Leonard Wilson Forster – German – *Professor, University College, London 1950–61.* Re-elected 1961.

1939–94   John Kenneth Sinclair St Joseph – Geology – Vice-Master – Curator (later Professor) of Aerial Photographic Studies. CBE, LittD, FBA. (d)

1940–4

1944–54   George Douglas Hutton Bell – Agriculture. *Director, National Plant Breeding Institute.* Honorary Fellow 1967. CBE, FRS, Hon. Sc.D. (d)

1944–50   William Ernest Burcham – Physics – *Professor, Birmingham.* FRS.

1945–9

1945–82   Thomas George Perceval Spear – Bursar. OBE. (d)

1946–83   Hugh Bamford Cott – Zoology – ScD. (d)

1947–   **William Ranulf Brock** – History – *Professor, Glasgow 1967–81* – retained Fellowship (Class E). FBA. (*)

1948–9   The Revd John Stewart Lawton – Theology – Chaplain. Warden, St Deniol's, Hawarden.

1949–50   Alfred Augustus Caesar – Geography – *Fellow of St Catharine's College, Cambridge.*

1950–4

1950–62   Robert Auty – Slavonic languages – *Professor, London and Oxford.* FBA. (d)

1952–7   The Revd Edmund Lawrence Randall – Theology – Chaplain.

1952–65   James Winny – English. (d)

1954–61   The Revd Donald Peveril Hardy – Classics – Tutor, Bursar; *Rector of Coton.* (d)

1954–6   Arthur Frederick William Hughes – Zoology . ScD. (d)

1955–9

1955–76   Harry Helstrip Nicholson – Agriculture. Reader in Soil Science. MBE. (d)

1955–   **Donald Burkwood Welbourn** – Engineering – FEng. (*)

1955–65 Paul Clifton Melville, Deputy Registrary.

1957– **The Revd Jack Martin Plumley** – Professor of Egyptology.
(*)

1957–94 David Harrison – Chemical Engineering – Senior Tutor
1967–79. *Vice-Chancellor, Keele and later of Exeter* – retained-
Fellowship (Class E). Master 1994. CBE, ScD, FEng.

1957–60 Christopher Michael Paley Johnson – Physics, re-elected
1963.

1958– **The Revd John Philip McMurdo Sweet** – Theology –
Vice-Master 1990–4. Acting Master 1993–4. DD (Lambeth).
(*)

1958– **Edward Hugh Rawlinson Ford** – Medicine – Senior Tutor,
Vice-Master. MD (*)

1959–61 David William Barron – Physics – *Professor, Southampton.*

1960–4

1960–1 Clinton Lawrence Rossiter – Pitt Professor (visiting) of
American History. (d)

1960–71 Roger Paul Johnson – Engineering – *Professor, University of
Warwick.* FEng.

1960–7 Richard Mathias Griffiths – French. *Professor, Cardiff and
later at King's College, London.*

1960–72 Harry Culverwell Porter – History.

1961– **Leonard Wilson Forster** (Former Fellow, re-elected).
Schröeder Professor of German. LittD, FBA. (*)

1961–5 Richard John Watts-Tobin – Mathematics.

1961–5 The Revd Edward Robert Norman – History – *Fellow of
Jesus College, Cambridge, and then of Peterhouse; Dean of Christ-
church College, Canterbury.* DD.

1962– **Ian Douglas Muir** – Mineralogy. (*)

1962–70 The Revd Barry Sloan Mackay – Theology. (d)

1962–78 John Leslie Melville Trim – Linguistics. Hon. LittD.

1963–75 John Moffet Cuthbert Scott – Mathematics.(d)

1963–8 Alan William James – Classics.

1963–9 Christopher Michael Paley Johnson. (Former Fellow, re-
elected) – Bursar. *Senior Bursar of St John's College, Cambridge
1969–92.* **Honorary Fellow** 1990.

1963–5 Richard Kenneth Marlow – Music. *Fellow of Trinity College,
Cambridge.* FRCO. (R)

1964–74 Paul Brant Fairest – Law – *Professor, Hull.*

1964–8 John Wickham Steeds – Physics. *Professor, Bristol.* FRS.

1965–9

1965– **Robert David Jackson** – Engineering.

1965–72   Brian Thomas Rothwell – English. (d)
1965–72   The Revd Robert Maynard Hardy – Theology – Chaplain, *Bishop of Lincoln*. **Honorary Fellow** 1986.
1965–7   Michael Peter Ward – Economics. Re-elected 1970.
1966–70   Daryl John Daley – Physics. (R)
1967–9   Patrick McCarthy – Modern Languages. (R)
1967–9   Norman Hillas MacMillan – Metallurgy. (R) (d)
1967–77   Vivian Nutton – Classics, History of Medicine. *Professor, University College, London.*
1967–75   Ian Baxter – Chemistry.
1967–71   Sebastian Paul Brock – Oriental Languages. *Fellow, Wolfson College, Oxford.* FBA.
1968–   **John Wilbur Sanders** – English.
1968–70   Alan Gordon Armstrong – Economics. (R)
1968–73   James Derek Smith – Engineering. (R)
1968–72   Edward Royle – History.
1968–9   George Alan Neville Connell – Physics. (R)
1969–   **Alexis Peter Vlasto** – Slavonic Languages. (*)
1969–70   Rufus Muirhead Clarke – Medicine. (R)
1969–74   Jonathan Dwight Culler – French.
1969–70   Peter Michael Williams – Physics. (R)

1975–9

1970–4   Michael Peter Ward (former Fellow re-elected) – Economics.
1970–   **Harry David Burge** – Bursar, Commander RN. (*)
1970–   **John Rason Spencer** – Law. Reader.
1970–2   Adrian John Simmons – Mathematics. (R)
1970–3   John Alexander Guy – History – *Professor, St Andrew's.*
1971–   **William Wray Neale** – Physics. (*)
1971–   **Anthony Preston Hillier** – Physiology.
1971–3   Richard Geoffrey Haydon – Mathematics. (R)
1971–5   David Richard Sweatman Hedgeland – Engineering.
1972–   **Raymond Morgan O'Malley** – English. (*)
1972–4   Alastair Blair Worden – History – *Fellow, St Edmund Hall, Oxford.*
1972–4   Nicholas Routley – Music. (R)
1972–5   John Simms Whitehead – American History – first Keasbey Fellow. (R)
1972–7   The Revd David Christopher Garnett – Chaplain.
1972–6   Charles Benjamin Knights – English.
1974–89   Alistair George James MacFarlane – Professor of Electrical Engineering, Vice-Master 1977–88 – *Principal, Heriot-Watt University*. CBE, ScD, FRS, FEng. **Honorary Fellow** 1989.

1974–94 Gordon Johnson – History – *President, Wolfson College, Cambridge*. **Honorary Fellow** 1994.

1974–86 Peter Hutchinson – German – *Fellow, Trinity Hall, Cambridge*.

1974–85 Jonathan Edward Bounds Shephard – Byzantine History. *Fellow, Peterhouse, Cambridge*.

1974–5 Nicholas John Russell – Biochemistry. (R)

1974–8 Anthony Michael Judd – Engineering.

1974–6 Leslie James Hill – French. (R)

1975– **Kenneth Johnston Coutts** – Economics.

1975– **Robert Douglas Harding** – Mathematics.

1975– **John Stephen Morrill** – History – Senior Tutor, 1988-92; **Vice-Master**. Reader.

1975– **John Michael Young** – Pharmacology.

1975–6 Peter John Statham – Mineralogy and Petrology. (R)

1975–7 William Wynnewood Park – Law. *Professor, Boston University*. (R)

1976– **Andrew Vernon Jones** – Music.

1976– **Jeremy Keith Morris Sanders** – Chemistry. Reader.

1976– **David Edward Newland** – Professor of Civil Engineering. ScD (M.I.T.), F.Eng.

1976–8 William Andrew Laurie – Zoology. (R)

1977– **Jean Kathleen Chothia** – English – the first woman Fellow.

1977– **Michael John Tilby** – French – Senior Tutor.

1977–84 The Revd Richard William Hunt – Chaplain.

1977–8 Andrew Dennison Barker – Classics and Philosophy. (R)

1978– **Kenneth Michael Wallace** – Engineering.

1978– **Thomas Robert Hesketh** – Biochemistry.

1978–80 Christine Diana Gray – Law. (R)

1978–9 Andrew William Havard Bunch – Geophysics. (R)

1978–9 Keith Jones – Chemistry. (R)

1978–9 Mark Dementi Kaplanoff – American History. *Fellow, Pembroke College, Cambridge*. (R)

1979– **John David Ray** – Egyptology. Reader.

1979–81 John Stuart Foord – Materials Science. (R)

1980–4

1980–3 Graham Harold Gudgin – Economics

1980–3 Matthew Seccombe – American History. (R)

1980–3 Anne Elizabeth Keymer – Zoology. (R) (d)

1981– **Peter Egerton Capel Berger** – Bursar. Vice-Admiral. KCB, MVO, DSC. (*)

1981–7 Stephen Richard Tromans – Law.

1981–9 William Morton – Chemical Engineering.

1981–2 Stephen John Cowley – Mathematics – re-elected 1990. (R)

1982–	**David William Holton** – Modern Greek.
1982	Julian Hoppit – History. (R)
1982	David Anthony Kaner – Chemistry. (R)
1983–9	Max William Mill Saunders – English..
1983	Robert Philip Jones – English/Philosophy. (R)
1983–4	James Anthony Charles Bland – Physics – re-elected 1988. (R)
1983	Briony Jane Williams – Linguistics. (R)
1983–4	Christopher Frederic Clark – American History. (R)
1984–90	Anthony Norden Lasenby – Astrophysics. *Fellow, Queen's College, Cambridge.*
1984–	**Milovoje Panić – Economics – Bursar**.
1984–	**James Henry Keeler** – Chemistry.
1984	Ralph Anthony Cordey – Radio Astronomy. (R)
1984–6	Nicholas John Marston – Music. (R)
1984–7	David Roy Nicholls – Music. (R)
1984–7	The Revd Harry Drummond Potter – Chaplain.
1984–5	Robert Jefferson Norrell – American History. (R)

1985–9

1985–	**Ian Clark** – International Relations.
1985	Peter Lionel Spargo – Physic. (R)
1985	Hamish Ryder – Chemistry. (R)
1986–	**James Raistrick Matheson** – Engineering.
1986–	**Robert Henry Whitaker** – Medicine. MD, FRCS.
1986–93	Clive Buckland Lewis – Law.
1986–8	Edmund Martin Herzig – Economic History. (R)
1986–9	Catia Galatariotou – Byzantine Studies. (R)
1986–7	Leon Knopoff – Visiting Fellow – Geophysics.
1986	Katharine Laura Hibbert – Philology (German). (R)
1986	Paul Andrew Robertson – Engineering. (R)
1987–92	The Revd Martin Herbert Kelly – Chaplain.
1987–	**Michael Joseph Sewell** – History.
1987–8	Deborah Ann Kuterbach – Biology. (R)
1987–8	John Cavanagh – Chemistry. (R)
1987–8	Craig Mark Rose – History. (R)
1988–	**James Anthony Charles Bland** (former Fellow, re-elected) – Physics.
1988–	**April Mary Scott McMahon** – Linguistics.
1988–94	John Edwin Blake Walker – German.
1988–	**David Lawrence Smith** – History.
1988–9	Catharine Harmon Edwards – Classics. (R)
1988–9	Ray Gerard Gosine – Engineering. (R)
1989–	**Massimo Beber** – Economics.

1989–   **David John Chivers** – Veterinary Medicine.
1989–   **Colin John Humphreys** – Professor of Materials Science.
1989–   **Stephen Wayne Logan** – English.
1989–90   Dawn Rose Ann Bazely – Arctic Ecology. (R)
1989–   Akbar Ahmed – Islamic Studies – Visiting Fellow, Bye-Fellow 1990–4. Re-elected 1994.

1990–4

1990–   **Mark Richard Manning** – Computer officer.
1990–   **Katharine Jane Willis** – Palaeobotany. Royal Society Research Fellow. (R)
1990–   **Stephen John Cowley** - Mathematics (former Fellow re-elected).
1990–1   Guy Jonathan Reynolds – American Literature. (R)
1991–   **David Frank Ford** – Regius Professor of Divinity.
1991-   **Michael John Hounslow** – Chemical Engineering.
1991–3   Stephen Laurence Kenyon-Slade – Law.
1991–   **Frances Mary Ros Knight** – Ecclesiastical History. British Academy post-doctoral Fellow.
1992–   **The Revd Nicholas William Stewart Cranfield** – Chaplain.
1992–   **Nicholas James Butterfield** – Palaeontology. (R)
1992–   **Manuela-Maria Tecusan** – Classics/Philosophy. (R)
1992–   **Richard Martin Walsh** – American Literature. (R)
1992–   **Patrick Jacques Nicole Baert** – Political Science. (R)
1994-   **Akbar Ahmed** - Islamic Studies (former Fellow re-elected).
1994-   **Andrew Norman Chester** – Theology.
1994–   **William John Clegg** – Materials Science.
1994-   Peter Kendrew Fox – University Librarian.
1994-   **Janet Anne O'Sullivan** - Law.

THIS LIST DOES NOT INCLUDE FELLOWS ELECTED AFTER 30 SEPTEMBER 1994.

Honorary Fellows
in 1994

(including former Fellows listed above)

1965 Robert Kweku Alta Gardiner
1971 Sir Cyril Humphrey Cripps, Kt, Hon LL.D.
1978 Lionel Charles Knights.
1983 Sir John Warburton Paul, GCMG, OBE, MC.
1983 Frederick William Rimmer, CBE, FRCO.
1983 Sir Edwin Ronald Nixon, Kt, CBE.
1983 Lord Rayner.
1986 The Right Revd Robert Maynard Hardy.
1986 Sir David James Lumsden, Kt, FRCO.
1989 Alistair George James MacFarlane, CBE, ScD, FRS, FRSE, F.Eng.
1990 Christopher Michael Paley Johnson.
1992 David Kwok Po Li, OBE, Hon LL.D.
1994 Gordon Johnson.

Summary of Fellowship Elections

The first five Fellows were elected in 1913. The following table shows elections in each five-year period since 1915. Former Fellows re-elected are counted twice. Visitors elected for one year are included. Former Masters are not included.

Five-year period	Number elected	Short term research etc.	Left for other posts	Retired (Class E)
1915–9	1	–	1	
1920–4	4	–	1	–
1925–9	2	–	1	1
1930–4	4	–	1	1
1935–9	4	–	1	1
1940–4	–	–	1	1
1945–9	5	1	2	1
1950–5	5	–	3	–
1955–9	8	1	2	–
1960–4	13	2	3	1
1965–9	19	5	9 (1)	2
1970–4	20	7	9	3 (2)
1975–9	22	9	4 (1)	2 (2)
1980–4	23	14	1	3
1985–9	27	10 (3)	2	1
1990–4	18	7	3	2 (4)

Footnotes:
1. Includes one who retained Fellowship (Class E).
2. Includes one who died in office.
3. Includes two visiting Fellows.
4. Does not include Fellows elected after 30 September 1994.

Index

Fellows who retained Fellowships for life are described as 'Fellow'; all who resigned before reaching the age of retirement are described as 'former Fellow'. Former Fellows are not indexed unless mentioned in the text.

A

Abraham, Bishop Charles John, 17, 18, 22, 27–8, 54, 107, 115 115, 139; and Selwyn memorial committee 17–8, 57–9; on need to maintain intellectual standards 139

Academic Records of Selwyn undergraduates, (before 1914) 127, 152–3; (from 1920 to 1939) 164, 187; (in 1970s) 268–70; (since 1980) 280–1, 295–8

Admissions to Selwyn, prospectus 77, 149, 175–7, 313–4; schools and social background – before 1914 147–9, 154 note 4; in 1920s 160; in 1930s 174–9; 1946–50 205, 217; since 1950 238, 269, 273; pre-A level offers 269

Aldous, N. M., Selwyn's first rowing blue 164, 189

Ahmed, Akbar, Fellow 356

Amenities in college, complaints in 1883 86–7; before 1914 146–7; in the 1920s and 1930s 164, 182; since 1945 248–9; bar in the College 250–1

Appeals, (1878–82) 56–7, 65; (1901) 128; (1928–33); (1982–3) 272, 183–6, 301 note 3

Appleton, Revd Richard, Master, character and early career 141; as Master 141–2; and building the Hall 142; sudden death 142

Approved Foundation, Selwyn recognized as 163

Ashcombe, Lord, member of Council, Appendix A; donation by 128; gives Selwyn the advowson of Wonersh 140 note 8

Association Football Club, 151, 153, 164; wins cup competition 280

Athletics Club, 153, 181

Auty, Robert former Fellow, 222

Ayerst College, 68, 80 note 3

B

Bagot, Lord, 318

Balston, Ven. E., 318

Barber, Right Revd Joseph, 318

Baert, Patrick Jacques Nicole, Fellow 356

Baldwin, Rt. Hon Stanley, at Selwyn's Jubilee 168–9

Balfour, F. M., opposes recognition of Selwyn as public hostel 75

Barr, Lawrence Bend, Honorary Fellow, and new SCR 249

Beber, Massimo, Fellow, 355

Bell, George Douglas Hutton, former Fellow and Honorary Fellow, 213, 257 note 7

Benson, A. C., gift of panelling for the hall 144

Benson, Archbishop Edward, dedicates the Chapel 117; sermon 316

Berger, Vice-Admiral Sir Peter, Fellow and bursar, 283, 284, 354

Bickesteth, Very Revd Edward, 318, 319, 322

Bland, James Anthony Charles, Fellow, 355

Blomfield, Sir Arthur, architect, 59, 116, 232

Blore, Revd E. W., 68–9

Blyth, Revd A. C., Fellow, Senior Tutor, Vice-Master 160, 202; character and services to Selwyn 215–6

Boat Club formation, and early successes 88–9, 119; importance attached to 151, 184; outstanding years (1914) 153, (1926) 161, (1930, 1938) 184, during second war 218 in 1970s 270; Women's Boat Club 270, 281

Book Club 189

Borradaile, Lancelot Alexander, lecturer, Fellow, Senior Tutor, vice master, 118, 129, 162, 189; character and services to the College 133–6; later years 194–5, 197 note 9, 203

Breay, Revd John, 155 note 6

Brereton, Revd Joseph Lloyd, and Cavendish College 67–8

Bridges committee 343–4

Bright, Rt. Hon. John, 23, 24, 29, 35, 43

Brock, William Ranulf, Fellow, 214, 350

Brooke, Christopher, references to his *History of Cambridge University 1870–1990*, 86 note 5, 148, 152

Brown, Revd Algernon Leslie (and references to his *History of Selwyn College*) 61, 95, 137, 252

Browne, G. F., Bishop of Bristol, member of Council 130

Browning, Oscar, 72–4; opposition to recognition of Selwyn 74, 79, 92; correspondence with A. T. Lytteltons 94–5; letters to from Charles Copeman 104–7

Burcham, William Ernest, former Fellow, 214

Burge, Commander Harry David, Fellow, bursar, 271, 283

Burnaby, Revd John, member of Council, Honorary Fellow, 231

Burrows, James Herbert, undergraduate, College lecturer 107–8

Butterfield, Herbert, tribute to G. B. Perrett 159

Butterfield, Nicholas James, Fellow, 356

C

Caesar, A. A. L., former Fellow, 222

Cambridge Review, letters and articles in 39, 59, 66–7, 70 84, 116

Cambridge University, 43–4; regulations for undergraduates, 180–1

Cambridge University Act 1856, 32, 44

Carpenter, The Very Revd S. C., former Fellow, 137, 158; recollections of Selwyn 140 note 7

Cartwright, Rt. Revd David, 208 note 2

Cavendish College 67–8, 70

Cavendish, Lucy, aunt of A. T. Lyttelton, 26

Centenary Appeal, plans for 286–7; organization 301 note 3; outcome 285

Centenary celebrations and speeches 286–7; sermon by Archbishop Runcie 286

Chadwick, Revd William Owen, Master 1956–81, election 232, 240; views on future of College and the Fellowship 240, 243, 257 note 2; on finances of the college in 1970s 271–2; retirement 288–9; awards and honours 289; references to his *History of Selwyn* 14, 51 note 2, 117–8; tribute to Alec Vidler 170 note 2

Chambers, J. executive secretary of Centenary Appeal, 284

Chapel, building of 116–7; dedication 117; refurbishment of East End 232–3; stall canopies 232; organs 197 note 8, 285–6; compulsory attendance 90, 182, 194, 196 note 5; in 1989 statutes 346; place in contemporary college life 313-4

Charter (1882), Appendix A; principal provisions 53–5; means by which secured 53, 72, 77–8; and revision of statutes 382–9

Chase, Rt. Revd George Armitage, Master 1934–47, 186, 197, 200; appointment 173, 196 note 1; 'second founder of the College' 191, 193–4; gifts to the College 197 note 8

Chester, Andrew, Fellow, 356

Chivers David John, Fellow, 301 note 2, 355

Chothia, Jean, Fellow 273 note 3, 353

Chown, J. F. 302

Christian community, idea of Selwyn as 241–2, 274–5

Church of England, relationship with Selwyn College, Chapters 2 & 3 *passim* 146, 173, 223, 228, 236

Clark, Ian, Fellow, 355

Clark, Rev J. W., 10

Classical Society 185

Clegg, William John, Fellow, 356

Collins, William (Bishop of Gibraltar) 20, 101–4

Collister, Peter, 233 note 2, recollections 1946–9, 217

Commemoration Feast 120

Consultative committee see Student Representation

Controversialists Society 151

Cook, Sir Alan, Master 1983–93, earlier career 289–90; achievements during his Mastership 290

Cooke, Revd W., 118

Cooper, P H. M., 256 note 1

Copeman, Charles Edward Fraser, letters from and career 104–7

Corfield, W. G., member of Council 211, 230

Cott, Hugh Bamford, Fellow, scientist, artist 213–4

Cotton, William, clergyman in New Zealand 13

Council (under Charter of 1882), composition and powers 230–1, 322–7; Fellows elected to 191–3; abolition 224; reflections on services 230–1

Council (under 1989 statutes), 293–5, 331–5; opinions on 310–11

Coutts, Kenneth Johnston, Fellow, 354

Cowley, Stephen John, Fellow, 354

Cranfield, Revd Nicholas William Stewart, Fellow and chaplain, 355

Creighton, Rt. Revd Mandell, member of Council 102, 114–5

Cricket Club 153

Cripps Court, endowment and building 251-3

Cripps Feast 257 note 5

Cripps, Sir Humphrey, benefactor, Honorary Fellow 251–2, 257 note 5; speech at opening of Cripps Court 252

Cross Country Running 281

Crowe, Revd P. A. 256 note 1

Cunningham, Revd Canon B. K., offered Mastership 196 note 1

D

Davidson, Archbishop Randall, advises against a denominational test for scholars 149–50, 154 note 5

Dean, duties of 346

Dean of Chapel 346–7

Debating Society 153, 185

De Coetlogon, Revd C. E. G., 88

Denman, G., 115

Differential Calculus Society 151

Durrant, Philip John, Fellow, Senior Tutor, Vice-Master 160, 185, 202, 216; and completion of Chapel stalls 232; and new Senior combination Room 249–50

E

Easter, Revd F. C., first undergraduate enrolled 81

Edinburgh, Duke of, speech at centenary 286

Egerton, N. A. 256 note 1, 302

Elliot, Kenneth Allan Caldwell, former Fellow 188

Ellison, Douglas, complaints by in 1882–3, 86–7

Eton college 11, 12, 110

Examinations, see Academic Records

F

Fairest, Professor P. B., former Fellow, 257 note 3

Farquhar, Sir W. R., 318, 323

Fellowship, plan for suppressed (1902–4) 129–32, 139 note 4; established (1913) 144–6; first Fellows 146; state of in 1930s 188; from 1945 to 1960 206–7; case for and against expansion in 1960 242–4; increase of 1960–80 245, 271; character of in 1930s 187–90; since 1970, 246, 277, 279, 292, 311, 314–5, 338–43

Fisher, Archbishop Geoffrey, visitation by 226

Ford, David Frank, Professorial Fellow, Regius Professor of Divinity 303 note 5, 356

Ford, Edward Hugh Rawlinson, Fellow, Senior Tutor, Vice-Master 291

Ford, William, lawyer and Privy Council agent 72, 318

Forster, Leonard Wilson, Fellow 197 note 7, 202, 214, 351, 352; recollections by 217

Fox, Peter Kendrew, Fellow, University Librarian, 356

G

Gardiner, R. K-A Honorary Fellow 257 note 7

Garnett, Revd D. C. former Fellow and chaplain 262 note 5

Gladstone, Helen, principal of Newnham 117

Gladstone, Mary (daughter of W. E. G.), letters to and from A. T. Lyttelton 58, 78; extracts from her diary 57, 48–9

Gladstone, Rt. Hon. William Ewart 11, 20, 22, 23, 26, 34, 55, 61, 66, 96, 316; early friendship with G. A. Selwyn 11, 13, 16, 72; and Acts of Parliament affecting Universities 24, 36–50; endorses plan for a Selwyn memorial 16, 17, 57; supports foundations of the College 57; presents a chapel bell 117–8; visits Selwyn in 1887 98

Goodford, Charles, Provost of Eton, member of Council 1882, 53, 54, 318

Goodison, J. W., favourable verdict on chapel sculptures 233

Gore, Charles 116–7

Graduates from Selwyn, careers before 1906 148; from 1906 to 1914 148–9; in 1930s 179; since 1970 281–2, 239–40

Graduate students, in 1930s 178; increase in numbers 246, 279; in 1990s 312–3

Gummer, Rt. Hon. J. S. 256 note 1

H

Hall, building of 240–1; panelling 134

Hall E. M. ('Sam'), recollections 182–3, 196 note 4

Hall, H. E. 234 note 3

Harding, Robert Douglas, Fellow 354

Hardy, Right Revd Robert Maynard, former Fellow and chaplain, Honorary Fellow, 264, 276 note 5

Harries, Right Revd Richard 256 note 1

Harrison, David, Fellow and Master, as Senior Tutor 258, 269; promotes admission of women 266; election as Master 300

Head of House, duties 336–8; age of retirement 311

Hendrie, G. M. 218

Herringham, Revd W. W., gives living of Old Cleeve, 140 note 8

Hesketh, Thomas Robert, Fellow 354

Hillier, Anthony Preston, Fellow, 353

Hinsley, F. H., speech at centenary commemoration dinner 287

Hittites (society of doubtful purpose) 151

Hobhouse, Bishop Edmund, member of memorial committee 28–9, 60, 318; anonymous gift to the College 128, 139 note 2

Hockey Club 153, 281

Hodgson, Revd Leonard, member of Council, Honorary Fellow, 231

Holton, David William, Fellow 354

Hooker Craigmyle (appeal managers) 283–4

Hort, Fenton, 65; meets Gladstone in Selwyn 98

Hounslow, Michael John, Fellow 356

Hughes, Prebendary S. J., 139 note 1

Humphrey, A. P., bursar of Selwyn 94; letter (1885) on possible economies 99–100

Humphreys, Colin John, professorial Fellow 302 note 5, 355

Hunt, Revd R. W., former Fellow and Chaplain 262 note 5

I

Imber-Lloyd Awards 245

Ince, Professor W., member of Council 130

Irish Colleges Act 1845, 45

J

Jackson, Henry, opposes to recognition of Selwyn 75

Jackson, Robert David, Fellow 257 note 4, 352

Jebb, Sir Richard, member of Council 130

Johnson, Christopher Michael Paley, former Fellow and bursar, Honorary Fellow, 248–9

Johnson, Gordon, former Fellow, President of Wolfson College, Honorary Fellow 291–2

Johnson-Marshall, Stirrat, architect 250, 252

Jones, Andrew Vernon, Fellow 354

Jones, Professor J. R., 234 note 2

Jonzen, Karen, sculptress 233

Jordan, William Edward, Fellow, Vice-Master, 118, 162; services to College and legacy 137

Jory, Elizabeth, captain of Ladies Sailing Club 270

Jubilee celebrations 168–9, 172 note 8

Junior Combination Room, new building 250; bar in 250–1; president and treasurer members of Council 294

K

Keasbey Fellowship in American Studies 271

Keble College Oxford 37, 45, 49–50, 55, 66, 131

Keeler, James Henry, Fellow 234 note 2, 354

Kidson, Professor P., 234 note 2

Kingsley, Charles, 12

Kirkpatrick, Very Revd A. P., Master 125–6, 138–9 note 1

Knight, Frances Ros, Fellow 355

Knight, Revd Henry Joseph Corbett, Tutor 94–5, 116

Knight, Lionel Charles, graduate and Honorary Fellow 275 note 3, 357

Knott, Hammett Charles, Fellow and Bursar 133, 140 note 6, 154 note 8

L

Laurie, Hugh 270

Laurie, W.R. G. M. 184

Lay Readers, 145

Last, Harry, first secretary of the Boat Club 88

Liberals, divided views on Selwyn college 20, 21–2, 29, 39, 50–1, 62, 75–6

Liberation Society, speech at meeting by O. Browning 91–2

Library, building of, 168, 172 note 7; extension of, 285

Liddon H. P., 62–4

Lightfoot, Bishop Joseph Barber, 56

Lloyd, Gerran (Lord Lloyd of Kilgerran) Honorary Fellow, 245; and new Senior Combination Room 249; and Imber-Lloyd award 245

Logan, Stephen Wayne, Fellow 356

Logarithms Society 89, 185; explanation of name 89

Lumsden, Sir David, Honorary Fellow 218

Lyon, T. H., architect 168, 172 note 7

Lythe, Professor S. G., 196

Lyttelton family 25–6

Lytton, Hon. and Revd Arthur Temple, Master 1882–5, Chapter 5 passim; family and early career 25–6; appointed Master 57; correspondence with Oscar Browning 31, 55; defines character of Selwyn College 64–5; and the Charter 31–2, 55; resignation and later career 108

Lyttelton, Edward, Headmaster of Eton 23–4

Lyttelton, Kathleen, wife of A. T. Lyttelton 96–8

Lyttelton, Lady Sarah (grandmother of A. T. L.) 21

M

McEldowney, E. L., recollections of Selwyn in the 1920s 160; and Boat Club 160–1; history of the club 88, 161

MacFarlane, Alistair George James, former Fellow, Vice-Master, Honorary Fellow 290, 296–7

McIlwaine, G. A., rugger blue 154

McMahon, April Mary Scott, Fellow 355

Manning, Mark Richard, Fellow 356

Mansbridge, Albert, member of Council 230

Mark and Spencer plc, contribution to centenary appeal 285

Marsh, Revd Fred Shipley, Fellow, 'a useful and heavy forward' 151; election and services to the College 158–9; Lady Margaret's Professor of Divinity 158; contribution to revised English Bible 171 note 2

Martin, Sir William 17, 61, 113

Matheson, James Raistrick, Fellow 355

May Ball, first 221–2

Melanesia, Bishop Selwyn and 13–4, 111–2

Melwille, Paul, former Fellow 243

Miall, Edward, 35, 42

Middle combination Room 254, 260; president a member of Council 260, 294

Money, comparative value of 124, 210

Monks (College society) 151

Morley, John 11, 41

Morrill, John Stephen, Fellow, Senior Tutor and Vice-Master 291, 296, 353

Morrison, Fiona, rowing blue 267

Morrow, P. M., on clubs, societies and their ties 155 note 7

Muggeridge, Malcolm 170 note 2

Muir, Ian Douglas, Fellow 352

Murray, Revd J. O. F., Master 144–5, 154 note 3; the College during his Mastership 163–4

Murray, Mrs (wife of J. O. F. M.), influence on College 145; warns freshmen against women of the town 160

Music Society 151, 185–6, 218

N

Nation-Dixon, F., success in clay pigeon shooting 270

Neale, William Wray, Fellow 353

Netball Club 281

Newland, David Edward, graduate and professorial Fellow 354

Newsom, George Ernest, Master, 164–5; on College finances 166; and origin of Selwyn Association 166–7; and Jubilee 168; how he admitted a student 171 note 6; premature death 173

New Zealand, Bishop Selwyn's episcopate in 13–4

Nixon, Sir Edwin, Honorary Fellow 287, 302 note 4

O

Old Cleeve, Selwyn College given patronage of the living 140 note 8

Old Court, early appearance of 81–2, 95; last temporary buildings removed from 168; ceases to be a sunken court 255–6; present appearance of 301 note 2, 304

O'Malley, Raymond Morgan, Fellow 352

Orpen, Thomas Henry, Tutor, member of Council, 95, 126–7, 132; presents plan for a Fellowship 129–31; gifts to the college 116, 142

Oulds, E. A. L., architect of the hall 142, 144
Oxford University 37, 41
Oxford University Act 1854, 32, 37, 39–41, 43

P

Panić, Milivoje, Fellow and bursar 354
Patterson, John Coleridge 111–12; studentship in his memory 95–6
Pattison, Mark, 46, 80 note 7
Paul, Sir John, Honorary Fellow 257
Perrett, George Burr, Fellow and Bursar 155 note 6, 159, 189; anecdotes relating to 171 note 4
Perrior, T., distinction as an angler 270
Phillips, Charles William, former Fellow 171 note 5, 188, 197 note 6, 202; comments by cited 154 note 3, 164, 191
Phillips, Revd S. C., former Fellow 158
Pleydell-Bouverie, Edward M. P. 46
Plumley, Jack Martin, Fellow 351
Pollock, Revd C. A. E., 94
Porter, Professor A. T., 234 note 2
Potter, Revd Harry Drummond, former Fellow and chaplain 303 note 6
Powell, Sir Francis Bt. M. P., member of Council, opposes plan for a Fellowship 1904 131
Powis, Earl, member of Council 12, 17, 53, 57, 66, 78, 318, 322
Previous Examination (Little Go) 162–3, 176
Proctors and University discipline 180–1
Public Hostel, status explained 70–1, 75, 163

R

Ramsay, Archbishop Michael, member of Council, Visitor, Honorary Fellow, 231, 287
Raven, Revd Professor C. E., member of Council 211, 231
Ray, John David, Fellow 354
Rayner, Derek (Lord Rayner), Honorary Fellow 287, 302 note 4; gift for a new organ 285
Reeve, Rt Revd A. S., Honorary Fellow 189
Rendell, G. H., 66–7
Rich, Professor Edwin Edward, graduate and Honorary Fellow 161
Rimmer, Frederick William, graduate and Honorary Fellow 218, 287
Robbins report 237
Rose, Revd Edward, building at Selwyn in memory of, 80
Rossiter A. P., Fellow of Jesus 162
Rowley, Dr D., 208 note 1
Royle, Dr E., former Fellow 264
Rugby Football Club 153, 164, 270, 281
Runcie, Archbishop Edmund, centenary sermon, 286, 317
Russell, Lord John, 25, 29, 36, 37, 39, 42, 45–6

S

St John's College, Cambridge, gifts to Selwyn College 285; gift of Selwyn portrait 255
St John's College, Waimaite (later in Auckland) 13-4, 110
St Joseph, John Kenneth Sinclair, Fellow 202, 213, 351
Sanders, Jeremy Keith Morris, Fellow 354
Sampson, A. H., president of the Union 222

Sanders, John William, Fellow 353

Salisbury, Lord, 48, 57

Sams, Sir Hubert, bursar 1942–6, 202–3

Sartain, Wilfred James, Fellow and Vice-Master 193, 256

Science Society 151, 185

Searle, Revd Frederick Charles, Tutor 94

Selwyn, Annie, wife of John Richardson Selwyn, gifts by 142, 155 note 6; assists students in need 150

Selwyn college (major items and incidents):
foundation proposed and agreed 17–18, 25; purpose defined 19–20, 23, 25, 51, 61, 64, 272–5; site chosen 58–9; foundation stone laid 64–5; controversy over the proposal and recognition as a Public Hostel, 56, 69, 75
royal charter 31–2, 53, 72, Appendix A
status as an Approved Foundation, 163
requirement that Fellows and Scholars must be members of the Church of England dropped 223–30
recognition as a College of the University 229–30
arms (heraldic), 30 note 4; colours 88
fees charged (in 1930s), 176–7
regulations for undergraduates 90, 180–2
finance (1878–82) 56, 57, (1901–2) 128, (1919) 156–7, (1928) 166, (1946–7) 212–3, (1970s) 271–2, (since 1983) 283, 298–9
For buildings see Old Court, Chapel, Hall, Library, Senior Combination Room, Junior Combination Room, Cripps Court

See also Admissions, Academic records, Amenities, Appeals, Boat Club (and other entries for clubs and societies), Fellowship, Graduate students, Graduates from Selwyn.

Selwyn College (Dunedin) 56

Selwyn family 9–10; close relatives of George Augustus Selwyn – Sir Charles Jasper (brother) 10, John Richardson (son) Chapter 6 passim Laetitia Frances (nee Kynaston) (mother) 10, Laetitia Frances (sister) 59, 61, Sarah Harriet (wife) 60, Thomas Kynaston (brother) 10–11, William (brother) 10, William (son) 16, 54, 142, 318

Selwyn George Augustus, Chapter 1 passim, lineage and early life 9–12; as Bishop of New Zealand 13–14, 16, 112, 113; visit to Cambridge 14–5, 35; as Bishop of Lichfield 16; visit to America 16; portrait of given to College 255

Selwyn, John Richardson, Master 1895–8, Chapter 6 passim; early career 110–4; on need to maintain intellectual standards 139 note 3

Selwyn Memorial Committee 17, 18

Selwyn, Revd Stephen John, anonymous gift by 157, 170 note 1

Senior Combination Room (old), building of 140; customs and conventions in 120, 138, 188–9

Senior Combination Room (new) 249–50

Sewell, Michael Joseph, Fellow 355

Sidgwick, Henry, supports recognition of Selwyn as public hostel 75, 85

Simpson, Percy, graduate, Honorary Fellow 108, 223, 234 note 4

Sing, Revd George Herbert, first Tutor of Selwyn 87–9

Smith, David Lawrence, Fellow 355

Spear, Thomas George Perceval, Fellow and bursar, 211, 216–7, 218, 248

Spencer, John Rason, Fellow 291–2, 353

Sport, place of in college life 150–1, 184–5

Sports pavilion 255

Stanton, Revd V. H., member of Council 71, 130, 318; tribute to Appleton 141; gives money for the Hall 142

Statutes, Selwyn College, (1913) 145–6; revised (1956) 223–30; revised (1985–9) 279–80, Appendix B

Statutes, University of Cambridge 230

Sterling, James, plan for a new building rejected 246–8

Struckett, M., captain Sailing club 270

Student representation in college government 260–2; members of Council 260, 311

Sulley, A. L., rowing blue 169, 189

Sutton L. S., wrangler (1914) 155 note 8

Sweet, Revd John Philip McMurdo, Fellow, Vice-Master, Acting Master 1993–4, 291, 352

Tennis Club 281

Thatcher, Revd Frederick, 56, 318, 319

Tilby, Michael John, Fellow, Senior Tutor 291, 353

Trelford, D. G., editor of Observer 282

Trinity College, Cambridge, endows a research Fellowship at Selwyn 285

Trotter, Coutts 71; supports recognition of Selwyn 75

Tutors, duties of 190, 314, 345–6

U

Universities Act (1926) 162–3

Universities Test Act (1871) 32, 44, 47–9

University Lecturers, under 1926 Act, 162, 214; salaries of Selwyn Fellows (1926) 162

V

Van Hesselt, M., 234 note 2

Victoria, Queen, 21, 117

Vidler, Revd Alec, 170 note 2

Vlasto, Alexis Peter, Fellow 353

T

Talbot, Edward Stuart, brother-in-law of A. T. Lyttelton 25, 26, 57

Tansley, C. H. E., member of investments committee 299

Tecusan, Manuela-Maria, Fellow 356

Telfer, A. C., 157

Telfer, Revd W., Master 220–1; proposes to retain tests for Fellows and Scholars 220–7; and Roman Catholic undergraduates 225–6; note explaining the new statutes 234 note 6

W

Walker, John Cecil, former Fellow 202

Wallace, Kenneth Michael, Fellow 354

Walsh, Richard Martin, Fellow 356

War (first) Selwyn during 156–7; effects of 157–8

War (second) Selwyn during 198–204; effects of 204–7, 211, 217–8

Ward, Revd J. T., first lecturer in mathematics 77, 86

Warner, Revd Charles, and endowment of Patteson Studentship 95

Watson, Lt. Col. H. C., first bursar of Selwyn 86, 94

Weightman-Smith, G. C., athletics blue 164

Welbourn, Donald Burkewood, Fellow 222, 351; raises money to support Fellowships 244–5; heads committee recommending admission of women 264

Westcott, R. Revd Brooke Foss, 53, 54, 56, 318, 322

Wheatley-Balme, Edward, gifts to Selwyn College 79–80, 118

Whitaker, Robert Henry, Fellow 355

Williams, William Nalder, Fellow 132–3, 140 note 5, 189; references to his 'Social History of Selwyn College' 138, 145, 165; loses two bets and wins one 189

Willis, Katherine Jane, Fellow 356

Winny, J., former Fellow 222

Woollatt, Gordon, architect, and Cripps Building 252, 253

Wolfson Foundation, contribution to centenary appeal 285

Women, exclusion from male colleges prior to 1970, 263, 275 note 2; admission to Selwyn requested by undergraduates 261–2; recommended and rejected 264–5; again recommended and admitted 267, 312, 313

Women's Boat Club 267

Wonersh, Selwyn College given patronage of 140 note 8

Woods, Col. F. A., unflattering memory of Kirkpatrick 139 note 1

Woodward, F. H., former Fellow, Honorary Fellow, 160, 200–1, 287

Y

Young, John Michael, Fellow 354

Young, P. M. 179